U.S. MARINE CORPS
AVIATION
SINCE 1912

U.S. MARINE CORPS
AVIATION
SINCE 1912

Fourth Edition

PETER B. MERSKY

NAVAL INSTITUTE PRESS
Annapolis, Maryland

Naval Institute Press
291 Wood Road
Annapolis, Maryland 21402

Library of Congress Cataloging-in-Publication Data

Mersky, Peter B., 1945–

U.S. Marine Corps aviation since 1912 / Peter B. Mersky. — 4th ed.

    p. cm.

Includes bibliographical references and index.

ISBN 978-1-59114-516-5 (alk. paper)

1. United States. Marine Corps—Aviation—History. I. Title. II. Title: US Marine
Corps aviation since 1912.

  VG93.M48 2009

  359.9'6—dc22

                             2009027767

Printed in the United States of America

15 14 13 12 11 10 09   9 8 7 6 5 4 3 2
First printing

*Creative direction and book design: Chris Gamboa-Onrubia,
Fineline Graphics LLC, Maryland*

For Lt. Gen. Thomas H. Miller, USMC (Ret.),
who gave so much to Marine Corps aviation

Contents

Foreword by Senator John H. Glenn   ix
Preface for the Fourth Edition   xi
Acknowledgments   xiii

 1   The Beginning, 1912–1918   1
 2   Between Wars, 1919–1941   15
 3   World War II: On the Defensive   41
 4   Cactus in the Pacific: Guadalcanal   53
 5   Island Hopping   71
 6   Carrying the War to Japan   93
 7   Post-war Activities   111
 8   Another War in Asia: Korea   119
 9   Korean Stalemate   143
10   Post-Korean Developments   165
11   Vietnam: The Early Stages   191
12   The Communist Waiting Game Pays Off   235
13   Post-Vietnam Future   251
14   Fighting Terrorism in the 1980s   275
15   Taking the Measure of Saddam   281
16   Desert Storm   289
17   New Challenges for All   307
18   Fighting in the New World of Terrorism   319
19   Persian Gulf War II: Taking Saddam, Again!   329
20   Continuing the War That Was Finished   341
21   Dealing with the Present, Planning for the Future   363

Appendix A   First 100 Marine Corps Aviators   377
Appendix B   Directors, Deputy Chiefs of Staff, and Deputy   381
              Commandants for Marine Corps Aviation
List of Acronyms   383
Notes   387
Recommended Reading   393
Index   397

Two future leaders sit as squadron mates at El Centro, California, before leaving for the war zone in 1943. Tom Miller, second from left in the front row, rose to lieutenant general and was a record-setting aviator in the early 1960s. He also became Deputy Chief of Staff (Air). On his left is future astronaut and U.S. senator John Glenn. The two became fast friends and served together during their careers in war and peace.

Foreword by
Senator John H. Glenn

A CURRENT HISTORY OF U.S. MARINE CORPS AVIATION would be incomplete without including the special role played by the late Lt. Gen. Tom Miller, USMC.

Author Peter Mersky has very properly and thoughtfully dedicated this fourth edition to Tom's memory and in tribute to his outstanding contribution to Marine aviation.

Tom and I were the closest of friends, starting during flight training in the early days of World War II. We flew together in the Pacific and Korean Wars. By luck of assignments, we were stationed together for much of our Marine careers.

Also serving in Vietnam, Tom became a three-war Marine and was awarded numerous medals and honors for exceptional combat service. A recognized leader, he eventually became Deputy Chief of Staff for Aviation, directing all Marine aviation. During that period, his vision and concepts expanded and altered the role of Marine Corps aviation to make it even more effective as a part of the Marine Air-Ground Team.

He was the first American to fly the British Harrier fighter and attack aircraft—the so-called Jump-Jet. Its vertical takeoff capabilities enabled basing much nearer the combat zone with on-call, on-target times reduced to minutes instead of hours, vital support for Marines in ground combat. Tom's dedication to the concept and persistence led to the Harrier squadrons now part of the Marine Corps arsenal.

With similar farsightedness he saw the potential combat-enhancing role that could come from use of the MV-22 Osprey aircraft, which could take off vertically then convert to horizontal flight for higher speeds than are possible with helicopters. Very roughly, carrying a combat load of a platoon of Marines, it could fly twice as far, twice as fast, and with double the payload of most helicopters. Combat advantages and flexibility are obvious. That aircraft is now being procured for entry into Marine service.

Tom Miller's life was dedicated to the nation and the U.S. Marine Corps. He was a great Marine Corps fighter pilot, a visionary for the future of the Marine Corps, and an exemplary officer. I was proud to know him as a lifelong friend, and I am glad Peter Mersky has chosen to dedicate this book in his honor.

Preface for the
Fourth Edition

THE FOLLOWING THREE PARAGRAPHS were, in part, what I wrote for the first three editions of this book.

From its first tentative steps in 1912, as part of the Navy's flight training unit, to the tough, experienced, capable, and proud entity it is today, Marine aviation has always been unique among the world's flying services. It is the air arm of the United States Marines Corps, an organization of aviators, aircrews, and personnel within the larger framework of naval aviation. No other military service or air arm in the world includes such a dedicated group.

My first contact with Marine aviation came not with roaring jet engines and flashing wings, but with the deep, long-cultivated bellow of a Marine drill instructor (DI) at the Navy's Aviation Officer Candidate School at NAS Pensacola, Florida. On the damp, dark morning of February 9, 1968, barely able to move within the close confines of a supply closet, this close-shaven, immaculately dressed man thrust my first article of military clothing into my hands, a black plastic raincoat, and yelled at me to "Geddout, geddout, geddout!!" I never thought of it then, but during those strange, hellish weeks, these dedicated people were working hard, preparing me and the others in my class for the road ahead, whatever it might be. They have provided me with a wealth of experience, stories, and pride over the years and a bonding with others who went through the same educational process. Although the DI was not a pilot, he was as much a part of Marine aviation as the leather-jacketed, gold-winged aviators who followed him in the courses of instruction at Pensacola.

The Marines have had to constantly fight to justify their own air force, and there were times when it seemed that the Corps would lose its planes and pilots. But somehow Marine aviation has lasted.

A lot has happened since this book's third edition appeared in 1997. A lot for the world at large, for the U.S. military in general, and the Marine Corps specifically. Who could have guessed that the end point of the third edition, mainly the convoluted conflict in the Balkans, was nothing compared to what lay ahead in the dust and shattered metal and dreams of 9/11. As America and its allies prepared for a worldwide conflict, the like of which had not been seen for sixty years, Marine Corps aviation continued its programs of development and acquisition, all the while making do with aging aircraft and fighting political battles to win funding for those new programs amid changing generations and philosophies.

The World War II generation was fast leaving the scene. Marine aviators were passing, including several well-known aces. In 1998 Marion Carl was murdered in his own home in Oregon protecting his wife from a young punk bent on home invasion and robbery. This waste of a historic, dedicated human life accomplished what the cream of Japanese fighter pilots could not. Joe Foss followed, as did Ken Walsh, Bob Galer, John Bolt, and Jeff DeBlanc. Tough, gentleman warriors all, the stuff that America has always held close to its heart as defining the spirit and triumphant endeavor that have been hallmarks of this big, ambitious country for nearly 250 years.

We were also losing the men who fought in Korea and Vietnam, almost as if to make room in the heroes' pantheon for the Marines to follow from the War on Terror.

My life was changing, too. I retired from my civilian job at *Approach*, the naval aviation safety magazine published by the Naval Safety Center. After sixteen years in Norfolk, Virginia, I returned to the Washington, D.C., area. Always in the back of my mind was a fourth edition of this book, which had enjoyed the most success of all my writing activities.

But the gathering, processing, and writing of new information and photos was a daunting challenge, and I pushed the project farther back in favor of shorter endeavors. Finally, however, I realized that too much had occurred and the third edition was obsolete. So, here is the result: a new book, redesigned, refined, new information added to the existing publication, and new chapters to cover Marine Corps aviation of the early twenty-first century.

I always ended each preface with the observation that it is a great time to be a newly winged lieutenant of Marines, and those gold wings continue to go well with a well-blacked eagle, globe, and anchor. It still holds true, but there is less room and fewer cockpits because of finances, changes in technology, the disappearance of accepted forms of manned aircraft, and the uncertain future of civilization. We need our Marine Corps more than ever, and we sure need Marine aviators to do their job.

PETER B. MERSKY
Alexandria, Virginia

Acknowledgments

OVER THE YEARS, I have had help from many people in writing this book. In particular, I would like to thank Mr. Norman Polmar, a highly respected naval and military authority in his own right. Maj. John M. Elliott, USMCR (Ret.), is one of those gems one occasionally discovers during the course of a project. There is probably very little he does not know concerning Marine aviation (indeed, he participated in some of the events presented in this book), and whatever he does not know is most likely stashed away in his prodigious files. His four-volume set on Navy and Marine Corps aircraft markings, published by Monogram, is the standard on the subject. He extended every available assistance as well as reading the original manuscript.

Lt. Col. H. C. Brown, USMC, whose job included running the Marine aviation museum at Quantico in the early 1980s, regaled me with stories of his pre-Vietnam Shufly days and also provided some of his personal photography taken during his tours in Vietnam. Maj. Frank Batha, USMC (Ret.), of the Marine Corps History and Museums Division, was always a great source of help in projects of mine concerning the Marines.

There is, of course, the small group of people in the Washington Navy Yard forming the staff of the Naval Aviation History Office and *Naval Aviation News*, without whom a great deal of this book would have been impossible. To them goes a special word of appreciation.

Others who gave a lot of assistance were Capt. Charles H. Brown, USN (Ret.); Col. John E. Greenwood, USMC (Ret.), longtime editor of *The Marine Corps Gazette*; Cdr. Gary W. Riese, USNR (Ret.); Maj. Joseph Rice, USMCR; Capt. W. E. Wood, USMC; Maj. William Curtis, USMCR; Maj. David Fichtner, USMCR; Lt. Col. David Jones, USMC; Lt. Col. Terry Mattke, USMC; Col. Dave Seder, USMC; Maj. John T. Dyer Jr., USMC (Ret.); Maj. Fred C. Lash and Capt. Jay Farrar of the Division of Public Affairs, Headquarters, USMC; Lt. Col. (later Lt. Gen. and DCMC for Air) Fred McCorkle, USMC; Maj. Ron Faucher, USMC; Lt. Col. Earl Bufton, USMC; PHC Fred Gooding, USN; and IS2 Frank Rucker, USN.

Lt. Gen. Thomas H. Miller, USMC (Ret.); Maj. Gen. John P. Condon, USMC (Ret.); and Lt. Gen. Philip D. Shutler, USMC (Ret.), spent several hours discussing their careers and the policies that shaped Marine aviation in the post–World War II era.

Several representatives of various aircraft companies also came to my assistance: Harry Gann, McDonnell Douglas; Tommy L. Wilson and Monte D. Ditmer of Vought; Lois Lovisolo, Grumman Aerospace Corporation; Dick Tipton, Bell Helicopter; and Jeffrey P. Belmont, Sikorsky Aircraft.

Ann A. Ferrante and Regina Strother of the Museum Division, Clyde Gillespie, and Nicholas Williams, who has accumulated much material on the F4D Skyray, also contributed invaluable aid.

Walt Boyne, Robert Mikesh, and Tim Wooldridge, at one time all of the National Air and Space Museum, also lent that institution's resources when needed. Robert H. Baker also spent long hours copying many of the personal photographs lent by various contributors.

In addition to those Marines quoted in the narrative, I would like to thank the following people who helped gather information, experiences, and photos for this new edition. Military ranks given are from the time of their contribution. Mr. Benis Frank, Chief Historian, Marine Corps Historical Center; Ms. Catherine Kiley and Lt. Col. Henry Dewey of the Office of Aviation Manpower and Support, HQMC; Mr. W. H. Rever Jr., Bell Helicopter Textron; Col. J. P. Monroe, USMC (Ret.), Executive Director, Marine Corps Aviation Association; Col. Tim Hill, USMC, HQMC Safety Division; Maj. W. G. West, USMC, HQMC Safety Division; Lt. Col. John P. DeHart, USMCR, HMLA-773; Capt. Scott S. Creed, USMC, VMFA(AW)-332; Capt. E. A. Sweatt, USMC, Director, Joint Public Affairs Office, MCAS El Toro; CWO2 N. H. North, USMC Joint Public Affairs Office, MCAS New River; SSgt. Craig Larson, HQMC Public Affairs. Most especially, Col. Denis J. Kiely, USMC (Ret.), long-time friend and associate, and F-8 and F-4 driver.

I would also like to thank the Marine Corps Historical Foundation for its original support for this project.

Those people who helped and contributed to this fourth edition are many. In particular, Dan Crawford, Bob Aquilina, Lena Kaljot, Annette D. Amerman, and Maj. Fred Allison, USMCR (Ret.), of the History Division; Katie Shagman, Lon Nordeen, and John W. Hayn of Boeing; Jill Vacek of Insitu-Boeing; Hill Goodspeed of the National Naval Aviation Museum; Warren Thompson, Andrew Thomas, Tom Dolney, and Bob Leder of Bell Textron; Lt. Col. Tim Hogan and Maj. Eric Dent of USMC Headquarters; Harold Rubin and Cory Graff of the Museum of Flight in Seattle; and Joan Thomas and Vicki Stuart-Hill of the Marine Corps Art Collection.

Last, a special note of appreciation to my parents, Leonard and Muriel.

U.S. MARINE CORPS
AVIATION
SINCE 1912

1 The Beginning, 1912–1918

BY 1912, WHEN THE FIRST U.S. MARINE CORPS pilots were being trained, naval aviation had existed for nearly two years. On November 14, 1910, off Hampton Roads, Virginia, Eugene Ely, a persistent and resourceful test pilot for the Curtiss Airplane and Motor Company, took off from the deck of the USS *Birmingham* (CL-2) and flew to Willoughby Spit on the opposite shore. The military uses of aircraft, though immediately obvious to some, were somewhat limited by the imagination of the military leaders of the time and the performance of the little contraptions themselves. However, with time, the airplane gained in reliability and also made people think about military uses more seriously.

Soon after Ely's flight from the *Birmingham*, Glenn Curtiss offered to instruct a naval officer in flying at no charge to the government. The Navy sent Lt. T. G. Ellyson to San Diego, California, to take advantage of Curtiss' patriotic offer. Ellyson subsequently became Naval Aviator Number 1. The Navy was sufficiently impressed by the possibilities offered by the airplane to set up a small training camp, funded by a congressional appropriation of $25,000, at Annapolis, Maryland, across the Severn River from the Naval Academy. The service purchased three aircraft with the money, two Curtiss and one Wright. All three were hydroplanes, because in the early stages of aviation, the hydroplane offered the relative safety of a water landing should the somewhat unreliable engines quit in flight.

The companies trained an officer to pilot each aircraft, as well as an enlisted mechanic to take care of them. Lieutenants John Rodgers and John H. Towers reported to the camp, beginning a chain of pilot and mechanic trainees. To keep the operations going year-round, the camp moved to San Diego in December and then returned to Annapolis the following spring.

Something new was added, however, in the spring of 1912: a Marine officer. The Marines had been watching the Navy's progress in aviation with interest. They saw a use for their own aircraft operation as part of their Advance Base Force concept, then emerging after a long gestation period. With the apparent success of the Annapolis training camp, the Marine Corps' Commandant, Maj. Gen. William P. Biddle, concluded that training Marine Corps aviators might be a "great benefit" to the Marines. Two Marine first lieutenants were ordered to flight training in Annapolis.

[Opposite] 1st Lt. Alfred A. Cunningham, the first Marine officer to be designated a Naval Aviator, stands in front of a Curtiss "Jenny" trainer at NAS Pensacola in March 1914.

The first of these two officers to arrive was Alfred A. Cunningham, born in Atlanta, Georgia, in 1882 and an ardent aviation enthusiast. Assigned to the Marine Barracks in the Philadelphia Navy Yard, he reported on May 22, 1912, which has since become the official birthday of Marine Corps aviation.[1] However, almost as soon as he arrived, he was ordered away for expeditionary duty. When he returned in July, the disappointed Cunningham was told that there was no serviceable aircraft available and his training would be postponed again. Undaunted, he gained permission to travel to Marblehead, twenty miles north of Boston, where the Burgess Company was building Wright hydroplanes. There were instructors available there, and after only two and one-half hours of instruction, Cunningham soloed on August 20, 1912. He cited the reason for the brevity of his instructional period: "There being so few civilian flyers, the factory had to pay them a huge salary to teach us, and they were anxious to make it short and snappy. . . . I had only attempted to make two landings in rough weather, when one calm day they decided to risk the plane rather than continue to pay any instructors large salaries. I was asked if I was willing to try it alone and said I was."[2]

His first solo flight was uneventful, and he returned to the Annapolis camp to train other pilots, including the second Marine to report, 1st Lt. Bernard L. Smith of Richmond, Virginia. By the time Smith reported to the training camp on September 18, 1912, the three Navy aircraft had been repaired and were ready for operations.

At that time, Lieutenant Ellyson, who was designated as officer-in-charge of the camp, had an additional airplane available, bringing the total to four: one Curtiss A-1 and one Curtiss A-2, and one Wright B-1 and a Wright B-2. (He assigned an individual aircraft to a specific pilot, along with a specific mechanic.) The older Wright B-1 was assigned to Cunningham, while Lieutenant Smith received a Curtiss. In addition, the camp was divided, perhaps unintentionally, into the "Marine Camp," which included Cunningham and Sgt. James McGuire, the first enlisted man to go through pilot training (although McGuire reportedly did not stay with flying for very long), and the "Curtiss Camp," with Lieutenant Smith and Navy Lieutenant Towers.

Training was conducted throughout the remainder of the year and most of 1913, the fledgling aviators experimenting with flying and operational techniques. In January 1913, the aviation camp was ordered to join the annual fleet maneuvers off Guantánamo, Cuba. Having already developed some spotting and underwater-detection techniques, the Marine pilots were able to show themselves and their aircraft to the best advantage. During the exercises, the pilots tracked submerged submarines, scouted for enemy surface vessels, took photographs, and dropped aerial "missiles." In addition to their duties of supporting the fleet during the exercises, the Navy and Marine aviators also provided indoctrination rides for more than 150 Navy and Marine officers. These included one future Marine Corps Commandant and staunch aviation supporter, then–Lt. Col. John A. Lejeune.

This first operation by the Annapolis contingent was a success and alerted many skeptics that naval aviation was to be taken seriously. But Lieutenant Cunningham was not happy. He chafed at the limitations of his Wright B-1, a plane that had been wrecked and rebuilt more times than he cared to remember and whose every flight was suspect, even though he had made more than 400 flights with it. He pleaded for newer aircraft constantly, citing engine failure and structural problems as the reasons for his dissatisfaction.

The Curtiss C-3 on the catapult of the USS *North Carolina* in July 1916. The aircraft was assigned to the Marines for maneuvers in Puerto Rico.

By August 1913, Cunningham had one more problem common among aviators. He asked to be detached from flying duty as a result of his fiancée's fears for his flying safety. "My fiancée will not consent to marry me unless I give up flying," he wrote in requesting a transfer. Accordingly, and perhaps with some personal misgivings, he was assigned to ground duty at the Washington Navy Yard. But his heart and mind were still in the sky, and he remained a vocal and persistent advocate for Marine aviation. (He would eventually return to active flying.)

By the end of 1913, thirteen naval aviators had been trained at Annapolis, providing a cadre of pilots, in addition to the mechanic trainees, to train further personnel. Three of the pilots were Marines: Cunningham, Smith, and 2nd Lt. William M. McIlvain, who soloed in September 1913. The Commandant was sufficiently impressed with his Marines' progress that in October 1913, he recommended that a Marine flying camp be established at the Philadelphia Navy Yard along with the advance base regiment being formed there.

In August 1913, the General Board of the Navy, a senior advisory panel established in 1900, reporting directly to the Secretary of the Navy, called for the formal creation of a naval air service, with appropriate funding in the military budget for 1914. Accordingly, Secretary of the Navy Josephus Daniels created a seven-man board, headed by Navy Capt. W. I. Chambers, an early advocate of naval aviation. This panel, called the Chambers Board, which included 1st Lt. Alfred Cunningham, Marine Aviator Number 1, advised creation of a section of six aircraft as an advance group, shore based. The board also recommended that a Marine officer be appointed as a member of the staff of the new Director of Naval Aviation. Navy and Marine aviation was thus getting their share of attention in the military. But implementation of the board's recommendations was slow.

However, several notable events occurred in the next few months. The Annapolis training camp, along with its Marine contingent, was moved to the old Navy Yard at Pensacola, Florida, some fifty miles east of Mobile, Alabama, on the Florida panhandle. Meanwhile, Congress, in its biggest appropriation for military aviation so far, had voted a $1,000,000 budget for naval aviation. The money was to be spent under the eye of the Secretary of the Navy. Soon after, on January 5, 1914, a group of Marine pilots, enlisted mechanics, and equipment was detached from the main Annapolis group moving to Pensacola. Traveling north to Philadelphia, the group, with Lieutenants Smith and McIlvain among its members, embarked in the Navy transport *Hancock* and sailed for Puerto Rico to join the Advance Base Brigade in the annual Atlantic Fleet exercises. It was the first time an all-Marine aviation force was to operate as a special part of Marine ground forces.

For the next three weeks, using the Curtiss C-3—an F-model flying boat equipped with a pusher engine and a two-man crew—Smith and McIlvain demonstrated the capabilities of the aircraft in a variety of roles, including scouting and reconnaissance. By the time the exercises ended and the Marines departed for home on February 5, the two pilots had made fifty-two flights and spent nearly twenty hours in the air. The unit members were pleased with themselves, certain they had proved the value of Marine aviation. The members even recommended the expansion of the unit to five pilots and twenty mechanics with two aircraft. But it was not to be. Upon their arrival at Pensacola, the Marines found, to their dismay, that they had been disbanded as a separate unit and once more were simply part of the overall larger Navy establishment. There was, evidently, still much highly placed skepticism as to the value of aviation.

In 1914 the United States' long-simmering border dispute with Mexico, which was going through a long period of governmental instability, threatened to erupt into open warfare. Indeed, in April a small band of Marines was sent to participate in operations against the Mexican cities of Vera Cruz and Tampico. Although Lieutenant Smith was stationed with the fleet at Tampico, having been ordered from Pensacola along with several other Marines, he did not fly in support of the Marine brigade's activities. By January 1915, Lieutenant McIlvain was the sole remaining Marine pilot in the Marine Section of the Navy's flying school. (With the outbreak of World War I in August 1914, Lieutenant Smith had gone to France as an observer.) But Cunningham reappeared, reporting in April, evidently having relieved some of his wife's fears of his flying activities. In the summer, a fourth pilot, Lt. Francis T. Evans, arrived to begin flight training.

In August the Marines began training in land planes through an agreement with the Army's Signal Corps, McIlvain being one of the first aviators to receive Army pilot training. There was also more experimentation at Pensacola, particularly with launching aircraft from ships with catapults. Cunningham sustained a serious back injury on November 8, 1916, when, immediately after being shot from a catapult mount on the *North Carolina*, his AB-2 seaplane rolled inverted and crashed into the water.

The news from Europe had not been good during 1916. The war was expanding, and the Germans were on the offensive. Submarine attacks on supposedly neutral American shipping, spy fever in the United States itself, and sympathy for the hard-pressed Allies, gave notice that America could not remain neutral for much longer. Things were also becoming increasingly complicated by the possibility of war with Mexico.

With all these combative possibilities, in August 1916 Congress voted $3.5 million in appropriations for naval aircraft and equipment. A permanent Navy Flying Corps was created, with 150 officers and 350 enlisted men from both the Navy and Marine Corps. By the end of the year, sixty new aircraft, including thirty Curtiss N-9 floatplanes—variants of the famous "Jenny" training biplane—had been ordered, with twenty-five of the tractor-engined planes stationed at Pensacola by December.

The business of flying aircraft was still new, and there was much to be learned concerning the safe operation of these early aircraft. Several maneuvers that later generations take for granted could be terrifying, even fatal, for a hapless pilot. One of these maneuvers was the loop. A successful loop had been accomplished some years before, and by this time, a loop was a staple of every combat pilot's repertoire in the skies of Europe. However, no one had successfully looped a tractor-type seaplane in the United States. The heavy pontoons, the floats, upon which the aircraft maneuvered on the water, created drag problems, which could prove dangerous, even fatal, if a pilot tried to loop his ponderous craft.

On February 13, 1917, Evans did try to loop his N-9 from an altitude of 3,500 feet. His entry into the maneuver was not smooth, and the airplane went into a stall and then a spin. A spin was another terrifying, little-understood, gyration at the time, and it seemed that Lieutenant Evans was going to crash into Pensacola Bay. But, whether by design or instinct—even he was not sure—Evans pushed forward on the plane's control wheel and activated the rudder to slow the rapidly accelerating turn. The spin slowed, then stopped altogether, and Evans found himself in control of the airplane again.

Regaining his composure, he again tried to loop the plane and again fell into a spin. But he righted himself as before and tried another loop. Finally, he managed to complete the maneuver, repeating the entire show over the base to make sure he had witnesses. It was not long before his looping technique and life-saving spin recovery were incorporated into the syllabus at Pensacola, thereby solving a major safety problem and no doubt saving countless young aviators' lives. Evans was awarded the Distinguished Flying Cross nineteen years later, in 1936, for his efforts.

The First Combat Tests

On February 26, 1917, First Lieutenant Cunningham was directed to organize an Aviation Company at the Philadelphia Navy Yard to be associated with the Advance Base Force. The number of Marine pilots stood at five, with plans to double that number in the near future. With the Army taking most of the tactical side of aviation bombing—ground attack—for itself, and making clear that it did not want the Navy intruding into what it considered to be its territory, the Navy decided that its aviation units could serve best against

the German submarine menace. The extraordinarily ambitious program of building 1,700 seaplanes was adopted in October.

The Marines, eager to prove their proud claim of being "first to fight," immediately prepared a brigade to be sent to France. Anxious to take advantage of the rapid wartime expansion affecting all services, Cunningham, newly promoted to captain, strove to obtain more men and equipment, and, most important, to go to France and fight alongside the ground brigade. When the United States declared war against the Central Powers in April 1917, he would have that chance.

Renamed the Marine Aeronautic Company, the Philadelphia contingent absorbed men from Pensacola as well as from other Marine units. Its first duty was to fly anti-submarine patrols alongside the Navy. But there was also concern that the Marine aviators fly in support of their fellow Marines on the ground. Commandant Maj. Gen. George Barnett, therefore, was allowed to authorize formation of a second Marine aviation unit—this one with landplanes—to fly reconnaissance and artillery-spotting missions for the brigade of Marines bound for France.

Cunningham immediately began to fill the slots in the new second unit, personally addressing the incoming classes of officer candidates at Quantico and preaching the gospel of Marine aviation. He was not disappointed; the response was enthusiastic. The young college-age volunteers were naturally taken by the thrill and glamor of flying, and Cunningham was able to have his pick of qualified applicants, eventually choosing eighteen for the two aviation companies. Most of these pilot trainees were, by the nature of the wartime mobilization, civilians rather than career regulars and were commissioned in the Reserves. By October 1917, the 1st Marine Aeronautic Company had a total of 34 officers and 330 enlisted men, with two Curtiss R-6 floatplanes plus one French-built Farman landplane for flight training.

The 1st Marine Aeronautic Company, first of the two units ready for service and led by the newly promoted Captain Evans, took its Curtiss R-6s to the Naval Air Station at Cape May, New Jersey, to conduct further training and operational coastal patrols. The unit operated at Cape May from October 1917 to January 1918. On January 9 it left Philadelphia for the Azores, where it was to conduct anti-submarine patrols.

The company was beefed up with more aircraft, bringing the total to ten R-6s and two N-9s, both derivatives of the JN "Jenny" series of Curtiss biplanes. The N-9 had a second cockpit with a machine gun and a more powerful engine. A further increase brought six Curtiss HS-2L flying boats, which carried a pilot and a crewman at a speed of ninety miles per hour for a range of 400 miles. These single-engine aircraft represented a great improvement over the smaller floatplanes, and it was with great anticipation that the Marine aviators set up shop at Punta Delgada on the southwest coast of San Miguel Island.

Flying a seventy-mile arc from the island, the First Aeronautic Company had an idyllic setting to be at war, although one young pilot was moved to write directly to the Commandant, Major General Barnett, requesting more vigorous duty. The irate general fired back a letter that informed the anxious youth in no uncertain terms that it was his duty to accept his assignment and do his best. Also, the reply continued, although a new assignment had, in fact, been mailed to him, the Commandant was revoking the new orders.

Good weather and friendly inhabitants made the Marines' stay the best it could be. There were a few contacts; some submarines were sighted, and even attacked. But no real damage was done, and certainly no submarine was sunk.

The second unit of the Marine Aeronautic Company, the landplane section under Captain McIlvain, was to follow a more complicated path to the war. The plan originally called for the unit to receive basic training with Army instructors on Long Island, New York, and then proceed to Texas for further instruction. After that, the squadron—for it was now the First Aviation Squadron—would go to France.

At first everything went well. In October 1917, the squadron moved from Philadelphia to Mineola on Long Island and flew JN-4B Jennies with civilian instructors. While the 1st Aviation Squadron was in training, a third Marine aviation unit was formed, under Capt. Roy S. Geiger, the fifth Marine aviator, although this unit's mission was, as yet, undecided. Cunningham was running into a stone wall trying to find a mission for his landplane squadrons. The Army did not want anything to do with the Marine pilots and bluntly told them so. Typically, Cunningham tried to rethink the problem and come up with alternative solutions.

Eventually, he decided to concentrate on augmenting the Navy's anti-submarine effort. Apparently, the Navy had thought only in terms of attacking the German submarines while actually at sea. Cunningham came

up with a proposal to bomb the sub bases, thereby adding a second form of attack against the U-boat menace. The General Board of the Navy approved the formation of a so-called Northern Bombing Group in February 1918. By March 11, Cunningham had begun to set his plan in motion, combining Geiger's and McIlvain's units in Miami to form the 1st Marine Aviation Force.

The decision to create the Northern Bombing Group was much easier than the actual formation. The unit's mission was changed again and again. If the group was to be sent against the submarine bases, why couldn't they also fly fighters to escort the bombers? Or perhaps the Marines would be better employed on daylight bombing raids against other targets. The men and machines still had to get to the war.

While the debate evolved concerning the mission of the Northern Bombing Group to which it was assigned, McIlvain's Mineola-based group moved from the deep winter of Long Island, where temperatures had dipped to sixteen degrees below zero, with an accompanying halt in flight operations, to more hospitable southern climes. The Army's Gerstner Field in Louisiana was to host the Marines. There the Marines were also introduced to a new aircraft, the Standard E-1, a small, rotary-engine single-seater.

Captain Geiger's group in Philadelphia also moved to Miami, Florida, in February 1918. To forestall any complication arising from Army interference, Geiger appropriated the entire assets and grounds of the Curtiss Flying School, including the Jenny training planes. He promptly commissioned the civilian instructors as well. (Geiger had help in this unorthodox procedure from Cunningham, who also obtained additional trainers for Geiger.) Finally, McIlvain's squadron flew from Louisiana and joined Geiger's group in Miami, thereby bringing together the two main components of the 1st Marine Aviation Force.

However, Cunningham knew he needed more personnel to complete his grand plan for four squadrons in France, flying and fighting alongside the Navy. Subsequently, the intrepid captain boldly went to the Navy's main training bases at Pensacola and Key West and recruited eager young pilots, already designated as Naval Aviators, who were anxious to see action in France and did not care whether they saw it wearing a Navy or Marine uniform. Resigning from the Navy to be picked up by the Marines, these men completed Cunningham's requirement for 135 aviators who finally arrived in France. Seventy-eight of the 135 were these transferred pilots, most of them Naval Reserve officers.

As the time for departure for Europe drew near, the pace at the Miami Marine training facility quickened. Everything from seaplane training to aerobatics and gunnery was crammed into a few weeks. By June 16, 1918, Cunningham had reorganized the group into four squadrons, simply designated A, B, C, and D. Geiger, McIlvain, Capt. Douglas B. Roben, and 1st Lt. Russell A. Presley were the respective commanding officers. Three of the four skippers left for France to reconnoiter the situation (Presley and his Squadron D remained behind), and on July 10, the lst Marine Aviation Force received its marching orders, too. They left on the 13th by train for Philadelphia, which gave them a tremendous sendoff, thence to New York and the *De Kalb*, the Navy transport that was to take them to France.

The Marine Flying Field, which was the new name adopted by the Curtiss facility at Miami, was left to carry on continued training as well as complete the formation of Squadron D, which had been left behind to finish its training and then conduct patrols along the Florida coast. The wartime expansion of Marine aviation brought the strength up to 1,500 officers and 6,000 enlisted men. A new program of training enlisted pilots was established to help meet this manning requirement. (European nations, which had been at war for nearly four years, had come to depend on their nucleus of enlisted pilots and counted several former enlisted men, such as the French ace, Georges Guynemer, who began his flying career as a corporal, among their flying cadre.)

Initial Operations in France

The First Marine Aviation Force disembarked at Brest harbor on July 30, 1918. There were problems from the start. Captain Cunningham found himself without means of transporting his men and equipment to the base at Calais, some 400 miles away. Undaunted, the resourceful Cunningham obtained the use of a train for the two-day trip.

After reaching Calais, Cunningham found that now he had no aircraft! After the train trip and sorting out Marine motor-pool assets from a mix-up with the Army, this last problem was almost the last straw. Cunningham thought he had arranged the delivery of seventy-two DH-4 bombers, two-place, single-engine craft then being built under license in America. But the planes had arrived unassembled, and it would take a great deal of time to put them together, test them, and commence operations. Cunningham discovered that the De Havillands had somehow been shipped to England across the Channel.

He bargained with the British. It was agreed that, owing to the Americans' holding a fair number of Liberty engines, the power plant used by the DH-4, and the British having an equally large number of engineless DH-9A airframes, the DH-9A being a derivative of the DH-4, the British would deliver one complete DH-9A for every three Liberties supplied by the Americans. With the concurrence of the U.S. Navy, the deal was consummated, and, with the eventual delivery of some of the wayward DH-4s in September, the Marines had, by the November 11 armistice, thirty-six aircraft: one-half the planned complement.

But at the initial arrival, when there were *no* aircraft available for the Marines, how could they begin operations? The Royal Air Force once again supplied the answer. Because of a shortage of pilots, the RAF, which had been formed by combining the original Royal Flying Corps and the Royal Naval Air Service on April 1, 1918, had more aircraft than it could operate. The arrangement was made that each of the newly arrived Marines would fly three bombing missions with their British allies. RAF Squadrons 217 and 218 were only too glad to accommodate the Americans, who were equally pleased to gain experience with these combat-seasoned veterans.

It was not long before the Marines saw action and attained several notable milestones. While flying with 218 Squadron, on September 28, 1st Lt. E. S. Brewer and GySgt. H. B. Wersheiner scored the first aerial victory for the Marines when they were attacked by German fighters over Belgium, both crewmen sustaining wounds during the dogfight. A week later, on October 2 and October 3, again operating with 218 Squadron, Capt. Robert

A view of the Lewis gun on a Scarff ring mount in the rear cockpit of a DH-4 in France. Some aircraft carried two machine guns, as well as a forward-firing gun. Note the wind vane front sight, designed to lead a moving target.

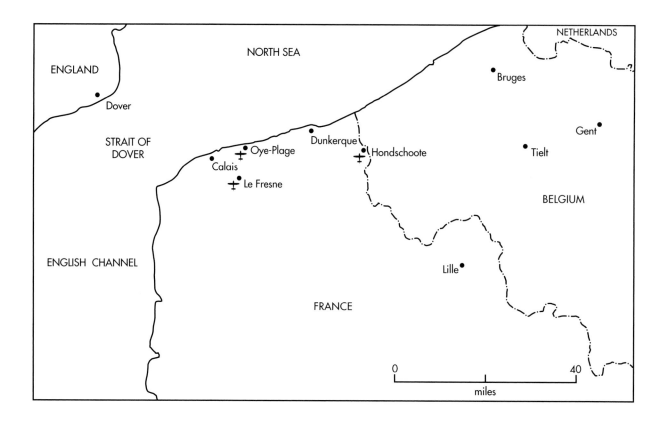

S. Lytle and GySgt. Amil Wiman, Capt. Francis P. Mulcahy and GySgt T. L. McCullough, and Lt. Frank Nelms and GySgt. Archie Paschal made the first aerial resupply drop in Marine aviation history. The three crews delivered 2,600 pounds of food and supplies to a surrounded French regiment. Lytle, Mulcahy, and Nelms were awarded the Distinguished Service Medal, while their enlisted crewmen received the Navy Cross. (At the time, the Navy Cross was a lesser medal, not the superior citation of today.)

By October Squadron D, originally left behind, had arrived with additional pilots and men. The 1st Marine Aviation Force's roster now stood at 149 officers and 842 enlisted personnel. The squadrons were renumbered, as 7, 8, 9, and 10. A change in the planned mission also occurred. Because the Germans had evacuated their submarine bases along the Channel coast, because of the pressure of the Allied offensives at the time, the original mission of attacking the German bases was unnecessary. Therefore, the Marine squadrons could operate alongside the RAF in support of the British and Belgian ground forces that were gathering steam for a final assault against the crumbling German army.

By mid-October, the Marines were ready to operate on their own. Having received enough DH-4s and DH-9As, through Cunningham's arrangement with the British, the Marines set out on October 14, 1918, to strike German-held rail yards at Tielt in occupied Belgium. Captain Lytle, now with Squadron 9, led a flight of five DH-4s and three DH-9As. The mission was to have double significance for the Corps, because as well as being the first time the Marines had flown a mission of their own, it was also to yield the first Medals of Honor won by Marines in aerial combat.

The flight to the rail yards and subsequent strike went without serious confrontation. However, on the return flight, the Marines were attacked by German fighters, a combination of Pfalz D-IIIs, highly maneuverable, though underpowered, fighters belonging to an earlier stage of the war, and Fokker D-VIIs, the top German fighters of the period, possessing speed and maneuverability, which made them distinctly dangerous opponents against the slower, less-agile Marine bombers.

The German fighters, which now numbered twelve, all seemed to converge on the machine piloted by 2nd Lt. Ralph Talbot, one of Cunningham's Naval Reserve "thefts" earlier in the year. His gunner, Cpl. Robert G. Robinson, shot down one of the Germans but was severely wounded by another pair of attackers who spattered the struggling DH with bullets. Although in great pain, and now with a jammed machine gun, Robinson worked to clear his weapon. He succeeded and began firing once more while Talbot maneuvered the aircraft, trying to throw off the Germans' aim. Hit twice more, in the hip and stomach, Robinson finally collapsed over his weapons, leaving Talbot to face the German onslaught alone.

The pilot turned his DH into the German attack and shot down a fighter with his own forward-firing guns. (Some DHs were equipped with a pair of guns firing forward as well as the normal pair mounted in the rear cockpit.) After this second victory, Talbot put his plane into a steep dive to escape the remainder of the German force and safely landed at Hondschoote airfield close to a hospital, where the wounded Robinson received medical attention. Talbot then took off to return to his home field at La Fresne. The intrepid pair of aviators would eventually receive the Medal of Honor for their actions that day.

Unfortunately, Lieutenant Talbot was killed eleven days later when, flying a post-maintenance check flight in the same, painstakingly repaired DH-4 in which he had so gallantly fended off the determined German fighters, his engine failed on takeoff. The De Havilland crashed into an embankment around an ammunition bunker, instantly killing Talbot. His gunner, 2nd Lt. Colgate W. Darden Jr., was not wearing his seat belt and was thrown 125 feet from the site. He was seriously injured but eventually recovered and became the governor of Virginia during World War II.

Captain Lytle and Gunnery Sergeant Wiman also had a harrowing experience when they tried to go to Talbot's and Robinson's aid. Turning his aircraft around when he saw his squadron mate under attack, Lytle's engine quit, leaving him to glide toward some Belgian troops he saw on the ground. He made a successful emergency landing. Later, he and Marine ground crews dismantled the aircraft and brought it back to their base. Captain Lytle and Gunnery Sergeant Wiman received the Distinguished Service Medal.

During the following week, the Marines continued to carry out raids against German positions, usually without benefit and comfort of fighter escort. On October 22, the Corps lost its first aircraft in action against the enemy. A DH-4, flown by Lts. H. G. Norman and C. C. Taylor, was shot down by German fighters during a raid.

By the time of the armistice on November 11, 1918, the 1st Marine Aviation Force had flown forty-three missions with the RAF, besides fourteen of their own, and had accounted for four confirmed German fighters, with claims for eight more. Four Marines had been killed in action. It had

[Opposite] Map 1. The airfields that hosted allied squadrons were clustered close together. The aerodrome at Oye was the base for A Squadron, under Capt. Roy S. Geiger, and B Squadron, led by Capt. William M. McIlvain. Le Fresne's field was the home of C Squadron, originally led by Capt. Douglas B. Roben, and D Squadron, under Capt. Russell A. Presley. Capt. Roben unfortunately became ill with flu and died in September. He was replaced by Capt. Robert S. Lytle.

A rare photo of a rare Marine fighter, ca. 1919, a Spad VII—one of the earliest production marks of the seminal French fighter—by this time most likely used simply for training and evaluation, not for combat. It was armed with one synchronized .303 machine gun. The later Spad XIII became the iconic fighter for initial American operations during the war, albeit with the Army's first fighter squadrons. (Courtesy Ed Szretjer via Warren Thompson)

been a short, but active beginning for Marine aviation, but Cunningham was now concerned with getting his men home before the onset of winter. Before returning to America in December 1918, he said, "I think we could accomplish much more at home, getting our Aviation service established under the new conditions of peace."[3] He was going to have his work cut out for him. Hard times lay ahead for Marine aviation.

2 Between Wars, 1919–1941

AS IN EVERY WAR, the period immediately following the cessation of hostilities was concerned with dismantling the war machine and bringing the men home. At the end of World War I, the 1st Marine Aviation Force had 282 officers and 2,180 enlisted men distributed among the three groups in the Azores, Marine Flying Field Miami, and Europe. In September 1919, however, the force disbanded, and its remaining assets were dispersed from Miami to Parris Island, South Carolina, and Quantico, Virginia.

Now a major, Cunningham began rebuilding his command, forming two squadrons, D and E, even as the Miami operation was shut down. Realizing that the very existence of its aviation section was hanging in the balance, the Marine Corps began lobbying Congress to maintain the force, at least at pre-war levels, as well as making Marine aviation a permanent force with its own bases.

Cunningham knew he also faced internal resistance. Many senior Marine officers remained skeptical, if not outright hostile, to Marine aviation. Many were angry that in Europe, the Aviation Force Marines—through no fault of their own—had not supported their brethren on the ground. Cunningham generally sympathized with their frustration, writing: "the only excuse for aviation in any service is its usefulness in assisting the troops on the ground to successfully carry out their operations."[1]

His persuasiveness paid off. After a year and a half of deliberation, Congress authorized the overall manning level for the entire Marine Corps as 20 percent of the Navy. This came out to 26,380 officers and men. In addition, Congress allowed 1,020 men for Marine aviation, as well as the establishment of permanent air stations at Quantico, San Diego, and Parris Island. But it was not for Major Cunningham to lead the Marines past 1920.

Even though he was the acknowledged spokesman for Marine aviation, a man more senior in rank took over in December. Lt. Col. Thomas C. Turner was, however, well qualified. Having entered the Corps in 1902, Turner, like Cunningham, was an avid aviation enthusiast and learned to fly at San Diego with the Army. During the war, he served at the Army's Ellington Field in Texas, gaining a designation as a Naval Aviator in March 1918.

Apparently jealous of Turner, Cunningham had sought to bar the senior officer from any participation in aviation matters. But, after a 1919 tour

in Haiti, where Turner was cited for bravery during a bandit attack, he prevailed on his friend, Maj. Gen. John A. Lejeune, now the Commandant, to order him to flying duty. Lejeune, who had flown with Lieutenant Evans in 1913 and was an early convert to aviation, recognized Turner's talents and placed him in charge of the Marine aviation department. Cunningham was given command of Marine aviation in the Dominican Republic.

Cunningham remained in Santo Domingo for a year and a half, then returned to ground duty in accordance with existing policy. A five-year tour in a flying status was followed by a non-flying billet. After all his dedication, work, and sacrifice, he would never fly again. In 1928 he asked to be returned to flight status but was turned down. He wrote the Commandant: "I was the first Marine officer to fly and spent the best years of my career working with enthusiasm to advance Marine Corps aviation. I did the unappreciated pioneer work and stuck by it during the time when no one considered it important enough to be desirable duty."[2]

But it was not enough. He was too old, he was told, to be returned to flight status. Embittered, he continued to serve in the Corps until he retired in 1935. He died four years later, at the age of fifty-seven, of a coronary thrombosis.

Turner became the driving force behind Marine aviation's struggle to survive during the 1920s. From 1920 to 1925, and again from 1929 until his death in 1931, Turner served as the chief of Marine aviation. Maj. E. G.

Brainard took over in March 1925, but after four years he resigned to go into private industry. Turner was recalled to his old post. With the sometime-triumverate of Cunningham, Turner, and Brainard lobbying in Washington, the programs began to solidify.

On October 30, 1920, Lejeune had approved a reorganization of the existing group to include groups of two-to-four squadrons, divided into flights. At the time, four squadrons of two flights were formed: Number 1 was based in the Dominican Republic, Numbers 2 and 3 at Quantico, and Number 4 was stationed at Port-au-Prince, Haiti, to support brigade operations in that Caribbean country. This organization was changed many times, and by 1926 there were also two aviation groups, one on either coast, to support respective expeditionary forces: the West Coast group based at San Diego, and the East Coast group at Quantico.

The 1920s

With a somewhat more stable organization established, attention could now be given to developing the physical aspect of Marine aviation. It was long overdue. The Marine aviators were still using the war surplus DH-4 for everything from ambulance to bomber to transport. Boeing in Seattle, Washington, one of the major American airplane companies to survive America's transition to peacetime, tried to modernize the DH-4 by rebuilding several with metal-frame fuselages. This model was designated the O2B-1 and was used for observation duties.

The American-designed and -built series of Thomas-Morse MB-3 Scouts were among the first aircraft to be procured especially for the Marines. Basically a World War I design, used as trainers in the States, these planes were barely adequate. The MB-3 was a redesign of the wartime S-4C, which used a rotary engine with resulting high torque levels. The MB-3, having used a stationary Hispano-Suiza inline, did not have such torque problems. Actually, only seven of eleven MB-3s were ever assembled, and these only flew four of the twenty-one months they were assigned to Quantico.

[Opposite] A Standard E-1 assigned to the Marines for training in 1918. These rotary-engine single-seaters were also flown by Marines training at the Army field at Gerstner, Louisiana.

[Bottom Right] A Boeing-manufactured O2B-1, an improved version of the DH-4, with a metal fuselage, shown at Quantico in 1926. Note the globe-and-anchor insignia below the rear cockpit.

With the war's end, the Germans had been required, by direct order in the Treaty of Versailles, to surrender some of their supreme fighters, the Fokker D-VIIs, and the few Marines who flew the handful of D-7s to be assembled were impressed with the German aircraft. It was about time, they thought, for some American-designed, American-manufactured equipment. Trying to answer this need, the fledgling Lewis and Vought Corporation came up with the VE-7 series. These biplanes were successful because of their reliability and relative agility in the air. They were also tractable, being used in two- and single-seat versions, as well as floatplanes. Vought also produced one of the mainstays of the Navy and Marine air arm during the 1920s and 1930s, the O2U Corsair two-seat dive bomber.

Not to be outdone, Curtiss initiated its enduring series of Navy "Hawk" fighters with the F6C-1, which was developed from the original Army XPW-8B/P-1 design of 1924. Built as one of the Navy's first carrier-based fighters, the first F6C-ls served only as proficiency trainers until they were transferred to the Marines in 1927. The Marines were never able to get enough of these nimble little biplane fighters but were enthusiastic about those they were able

to obtain. Apparently, 1931 was the year when the Corps had the greatest number of F6Cs on board—four of them in the East Coast Expeditionary Force at Quantico, serving with VF-8M and VO-6M (the "M" denoting, naturally, Marine). The other eight were with the West Coast unit at San Diego with VF-10M.

In July 1920, the Secretary of the Navy had established a formal designating system for both Navy aircraft and squadrons; the Marines were included. Aircraft were given three-character basic designators: the first letter indicating the basic mission of the plane, the numeral indicating the number design of the manufacturer, and the third letter signifying the manufacturer itself. Thus, "O2B" denoted the second observation design built by Boeing; "F6C" was the sixth fighter from Curtiss. (It was not until 1941 that the Navy Department also permitted official popular names to be included in an aircraft's designation.)

Navy squadrons were also designated according to their primary mission. The first letter, V, signified a unit using heavier-than-air equipment—

as opposed to airship squadrons, signified by a "Z"—and the following letter described the mission, that is, "F" for fighter or "O" for observation. Marine squadrons were designated by the simple method of adding an "M." Thus, VO-8M was Observation Squadron Eight (Marine). It was not until 1937 that the current method of designation—VMO—was created.

Boeing was also a competitor in fighter design, for both the Army and Navy during this period. The initial design, Model 15, first flew in September 1923 and continued to be developed by the Army as the XPW-9 series. The Navy was also interested in the design and ordered ten examples for the Marines as the FB. The Marines took these new fighters to China for a while in 1925.

The Boeing design continued to be developed and improved, the F2B and F3B models appearing in 1926 and 1928, respectively. But it was the definitive F4B model that became the symbol of military aviation—Army (as the P-12), Navy, and Marine Corps—in the late 1920s and mid-1930s.

The design refinement that followed the F3B was unusual in that it did not require the installation of a more powerful engine, normally the procedure to increase performance for a newer model of the same design. Enough aerodynamic refinement—such as the addition of an engine cowling (in the case of the -2 model) and different landing gear—gave a twenty-two-mile-per-hour increase in speed over the F3B. The XF4B-1 was also 400 pounds lighter than its predecessor. The F4B-2 was similar to the Army's P-12C and D fighters, while the final F4B-3 and -4 models followed the P-12E and F, respectively.

One of the prime operators of the little Boeing fighter was VF-9M, stationed at Quantico. Established on September 1, 1925, as VF-2M, with 1st Lt. Lawson H. M. Sanderson as its commanding officer, VF-9M went through a life of ups and downs, feasts and famines, that mirrored the fluctuating status of Marine aviation in general. Along with Sanderson, the unit eventually numbered several future Marine "greats" among its alumni, including 1st Lt. C. F. Schilt, who would receive the Medal of Honor in Nicaragua, and Aviation Cadet Gregory Boyington, who would also receive the Medal of Honor as well as become the Corps' top ace in World War II.

Initially equipped with Vought VE-7s, then-VF-2M obtained Boeing FB-1s in February 1926. It then immediately began to enter service competitions, including the 1926 National Air Races in Philadelphia, where the Boeings were also used in aerial displays. Competition entries were intended to keep Marine aviation in the public eye.

The squadron began to go through a succession of commanders when Sanderson departed in November to attend Company Officers School. He was replaced by 1st Lt. Jay Swartwout, who began training pilots as fast as he could. Several of the new naval aviators were Naval Aviation Pilots (NAPs)—enlisted men who retained their noncommissioned status even after getting their wings.

In December 1926, eight F6C-3s arrived for the rival squadron, VF-1M, and Swartwout wrote Major Brainard, now officer-in-charge of Marine aviation. Brainard promised that the next new batch of fighters would go to VF-2M. Swartwout turned over the squadron to Chief Marine Gunner Elmo Reagan—probably the only time a warrant officer has had command of a U.S. aviation squadron—on January 6, 1927. The "Gunner" was replaced in March, however, by Capt. W. T. Evans. One month later, true to his word, Major Brainard sent four new F6C-4s. By the following June, though, Evans had been relieved by 1st Lt. V. N. Guymon, who had only received his wings six months before!

[Opposite] The Martin MBT was used for training parachute jumpers, probably because of its stability in the air. These two views of parachutists in 1927 give a good idea of the size of the Martin bomber and the maze of struts and wires characteristic of most aircraft of the period.

[Right] Members of Quantico-based VF-2M in 1926 stand by a squadron FB-1. Lt. W. L. McKittrick, second from left, eventually commanded the squadron as VMF-1; Sgt. R. E. Fry, fourth from left, left the service to fly for the airlines and was the pilot of the Fokker airliner that crashed in 1931, killing all on board, including football great Knute Rockne. "Sandy" Sanderson, twice squadron CO, is second from right, talking with another member.

Problems developed with the new Curtiss fighters' landing gear, two aircraft suffering crashes because of structural failure, one aircraft coming to grief twice in one week. Guymon was obviously concerned and hoped that this apparent jinx on his first command would vanish when VF-2M was redesignated VF-9M on July 1, 1927. But the squadron continued to have problems. Aircraft A-7397, having returned from its second stay in the Brown Field repair shop, survived only long enough for 1st Lt. H. C. Busbey to put it into the Potomac River with a throttle stuck in the closed position. Thankfully, Guymon departed in October for what promised to be less hectic combat duty in Nicaragua. And so it went.

VF-9M seemed to be a training squadron for young COs, but on June 15, 1930, First Lieutenant Sanderson returned to Quantico to lead the squadron which had been re-redesignated VF-5M as of July 1, 1928. This change came as a result of a numbering reorganization. (This designation lasted until August 18, 1930, when it reverted to VF-9M.) With the aggressive, professional Sanderson back at the helm again, the squadron seemed to settle down finally into a routine. And Sanderson took his planes and pilots on tour whenever he could. The public had to be kept aware of its Marine aviators.

VF-9M continued flying Curtiss aircraft, the F6Cs having progressed to F7Cs in 1928. By 1932 the F7Cs were supposed to give way to Boeing F4B-4s, but in August the eight F7Cs still remained. As VF-9M was scheduled to appear at the Canadian Air Races in Montreal within three weeks, new aircraft were needed. The F7Cs had been prohibited from air show participation because of several crashes involving the type at public displays. The best that could be done was to borrow nine Curtiss O2C-1s from VO-6M. So, VF-9M operated yet another type of aircraft for a short period, painted with a distinctive arrowhead design on the O2Cs' cowlings and rudders.

[Opposite] A Boeing FB-1 of VF-1M in 1925. The circled "F" denoted a Marine fighter squadron instead of a Navy unit. The FB-1 was powered by a Curtiss D-12 engine and was developed from the Army's XPW-9.

[Top Right] The follow-on to the F6C was, naturally, the F7C of 1928. This example is from VF-5M, which was renumbered VF-9M and based at Quantico in 1930.

[Bottom Right] One of the most sought-after aircraft during the late 1920s was the Curtiss F6C-4. This example served with VF-10M at San Diego in the early 1930s.

By mid-September, however, the first three F4B-4s arrived by train, the entire squadron excitedly turning out to assemble the precious cargo. Within a week, on September 23, the engineering officer, Ed Pugh, had taken the first fighter for a test flight and, returning with a huge grin, proclaimed the thrill of flying a really modern aircraft. The end of the month saw VF-9M with six flyable F4Bs in operation.

Even with the influx of new modern equipment, manpower shortages remained a constant thorn in Sanderson's side, as it was for all Marine squadrons at the time. Air show commitments were always demanding a full complement of airplanes, but without the pilots to fly them, it didn't matter. Borrowing pilots from other squadrons sometimes provided relief.

In July 1933, VF-9M received an extra batch of F4Bs as VF-10M, a San Diego squadron, was redesignated a light-bombing squadron and its twelve Boeings reassigned to a hungry, happy VF-9M. Eighteen aircraft. Nine spares! It was a luxurious feeling, and Sanderson quickly prevailed on the Marines in California to ferry six of the new additions east. It was

[Left] A 1931 view of Brown Field, Quantico, showing the VF-9M flight line. The aircraft are Curtiss F7Cs.

[Opposite] Aircraft and crews of VF-9M in a squadron lineup in August 1932. VF-9M had to borrow the aircraft from VO-6M to meet its air show schedule. The squadron's own F7Cs were barred from participation because several of them had crashed.

up to Sanderson to get the remaining six himself, which he did, by ferrying two older multiplace aircraft out to North Island, near San Diego. Actually, by August Sanderson was in charge of a squadron of twenty-eight aircraft. Through an administrative oversight, the Bureau of Aeronautics had allotted six more airplanes in addition to the eighteen already on strength. A further letter authorized an increase in pilots to twenty-two. It was an incredible stroke of good luck and portended good times for the squadron.

Sanderson continued to be the main backer for public display. This, of course, is not to indicate that the Marine squadrons did not keep their primary military skills sharp. In between air shows, maneuvers and practice bombing drills were the order of the day. But these activities gave no chance for the public to watch their Marine aviators in action. Therefore, an active air show schedule was a must.

The October 1933 National Charity Air Pageant, held in New York, promised to be the biggest air show yet, and VF-9M and VO-7M, with nineteen Boeings and thirteen Curtiss Helldivers, respectively, were to participate. Roosevelt Field on Long Island was to be the host field, and the two Marine squadrons arrived en masse on October 7, after a three-and-one-half-hour flight from Quantico. The huge crowds were thrilled by the noisy, flashy demonstration of Marine air power, Sanderson having developed special aerobatic maneuvers for the event. The public response was so overwhelming that Rear Adm. Ernest J. King, Chief of the Bureau of Aeronautics, quickly revised the budget for Marine aviation.

Sanderson continued to lead VF-9M until July 1934, when he was relieved by Capt. Ford O. Rogers, a pilot who had flown in the war under Lt. William McIlvain in France. Handling an eighteen-plane squadron, both in the air and on the ground, was no mean trick, but Rogers was equal to the challenge and he quickly won the respect of his squadron. The years to come were typical, more air shows, maneuvers, and developmental exercises. VF-9M had established itself as the premier Marine fighter squadron. To have served in the Quantico unit was a source of great pride for officers and men alike.

VF-9M was even qualified aboard the carrier USS *Saratoga* (CV-3) in March 1937, off San Diego; the ship's skipper was Capt.—later Flt. Adm.—William Halsey. It was the first time most of the pilots had seen a carrier and although difficulties were encountered, the skill and natural ebullience of the Marines saw them through the rough spots.

Time was catching up with VF-9M, however. On July 1, 1937, another numbering reorganization redesignated it as VMF-1 (Marine Fighting Squadron 1). Another directive of the same date, ordered 65 percent of VF-9M's personnel to other duties, with replacements coming from newly designated pilots and Aviation Cadets.

The date July 1, 1937, was coming to have considerable significance for VMF-1. Ford Rogers, by now a major, was relieved by Capt. W. L. McKittrick. A longtime squadron member who had also commanded Quantico squadrons VO-6M and VO-7M, "Mac" had taken the squadron through the 1930s and the introduction of the tough new F3F series of fighters, manufactured by Grumman on Long Island, New York. Big, fast, and Grumman-tough, and with two relatively new features, an enclosed cockpit and retractable landing gear, these biplanes were the last such fighters to serve with the U.S. Navy or Marines; but they helped to establish Grumman as the main supplier of Navy aircraft.

McKittrick continued to follow the air show circuit established by his predecessors, but by July 1941, war seemed very close and a reorganization of Marine aviation was in order, with the establishment of two wings, rather than groups. VMF-1 was now renumbered VMF-111 and continued to serve as one of the leading Marine squadrons.

Combat Operations in the 1920s

The 1920s and 1930s were years of uncertain and erratic growth for Marine aviation. Many times, people involved were left to their own initiative and

resources to get things done and also keep the program going. Sometimes, the dedication and enthusiasm of these individuals were all that kept the program alive during the Depression years. These efforts provided America the tight nucleus of trained, experienced personnel who would sustain her through the dark days after Pearl Harbor.

Many of the senior Marine aviators in World War II gained their initial combat experience in action in Central America during the 1920s, especially in Nicaragua, Haiti, and the Dominican Republic. The situation was something like the situation in China at the same time, where a strong, centralized government was a near impossibility and local warlords, complete with their own armies, ruled their own specific areas.

Nicaragua had the traditional economic and political strife. From the late 1800s worried U.S. presidents sent the Marines into the country to protect American interests, beginning as early as 1853 at San Juan del Norte on the southeastern border with Costa Rica. Marines continued to go to Nicaragua periodically throughout the early 1900s as well, the political situation becoming more and more intolerable as dictators vied for overall control.

Problems also cropped up in the Dominican Republic and Haiti, the first Marine aircraft arriving in both countries in 1919 to support ground operations that had begun in 1916. Jenny trainers and Curtiss HS-2L flying boats, used for coastal patrols, flew in during February and March. It was during Marine operations in Haiti that development of the dive-bombing technique probably occurred, although it is difficult to pinpoint a specific event. Certainly, during World War I pilots of both sides used steep bomb

deliveries when the situation warranted. But the need to drop ordnance accurately through the dense jungle cover of the Caribbean countries gave men such as VO-9M's Lieutenant Sanderson—later of VF-9M and one of the premier Marine aviators of the period—the chance to develop the technique. This was not the steep, screaming, almost 90-degree dive of the German Stukas twenty years later, but rather a more gentle 45-degree dive. Still, for the aircraft of the day, it was a fairly steep angle.

The operations in Haiti and the Dominican Republic were mainly in support of men on the ground—reconnaissance, supply, and medical evacuation—with some primitive close air support. But it was in Nicaragua, eight years later, Marine aviation had its first real post–World War I test. The political situation in late 1926 erupted into a bloody civil war, and the United States sent in the Marines to protect U.S. citizens and property.

In January 1927 additional troops arrived at Bluefields, a town on the southeastern coast, near the Escondido River, and were followed in February by six DH-4s of VO-1M under forty-two-year-old Maj. Ross Rowell. The supplies and men poured in, but by late May, a diplomatic arrangement seemed to have been reached through the efforts of Henry L. Stimson, President Calvin Coolidge's personal representative. Bandit raids continued, however, and any hope for a lasting peace was dashed. All of this turmoil only paved the way for the appearance of Augusto C. Sandino, who aspired to become the "strong man" of Nicaragua. Afraid of American intervention, which could prohibit his rise to power, Sandino took his rebel forces into the hills and jungles. It was against the rebels that the Marines had their first taste of combat in Nicaragua; it was strangely suggestive of events half a world away and forty years, and even *eighty* years in the future.

On July 16, 1927, the Sandinistas, the popular name for Sandino's followers, attacked the northwest town of Ocotal, just over the border from neighboring Honduras. The position of the Marine garrison and loyalist defenders was precarious, and Marine air units were called in. A 10:30 AM attack by two aircraft kept the rebels' heads down, and by 2:35 PM, Major Rowell led a group of five DH-4s and Boeing O2Bs in a major bombing mission. Arriving over the besieged town, Rowell immediately struck the enemy positions, dropping bombs while the rear gunners fired curtains of machine-gun bullets. The devastating attack completely disrupted the

A rare 1932 view of a Pitcairn Autogyro of the type tested by the Marines in Nicaragua. Although the aircraft did well, it did not carry a useful payload and development was halted.

Sandinistas' operation, and they fled into the jungle. It taught Sandino the danger of a massed air strike, and he seldom let his forces be caught in such an open position again. Major Rowell became the first Marine aviator to receive the newly created Distinguished Flying Cross for his role in the attack.

Rowell had previously earned a bit of earlier fame when he posed for a popular recruiting poster by the well-known portraitist and illustrator Montgomery Flagg, probably best known for his depiction of a stern "Uncle Sam" pointing to the viewer, with the words "Uncle Sam Wants You" calling eager young recruits to service. In 1916 Rowell had been on temporary assignment with a recruiting office in New York City when Flagg selected him for his model. Wearing a field uniform with a blanket slung across his chest, Rowell posed with a raised pistol. With "First to Fight, Always Faithful" emblazoned across the portrait, it was an effective bit of recruiting propaganda.

Rowell came to aviation somewhat late, not beginning formal flight instruction until 1923 at the Army's Kelly Field at San Antonio, Texas. He had been flying as a self-taught aviator for two years, so he sailed through the Army's syllabus.

Operations continued on the ground through the summer months, with Marine transports—De Havillands and five big Fokker TA-1 trimotor transports—dropping into the rugged landing strips hacked out of the jungle. Skirmishes along Nicaragua's coastal area, however, did not do anything to reduce Sandino's immense popular support in the interior. As would be the case in Vietnam, the overwhelming technical and military superiority of U.S. forces meant nothing against an enemy who came and went at will, fading in and out of the jungle aided by the peasant populace.

The decision was made for a major offensive against the Sandinistas in December 1927. Heavy rains and the constant guerrilla action against the Marines and the Nicaraguan National Guard troops made the planned offensive not only more necessary, but also more difficult. Action at Quilali, a small village near the Coco River in the northwest border area with Honduras, highlighted both the power of the guerrillas and that of Marine aviation.

On December 30, 1927, the Sandinista forces ambushed a Marine ground force near the village, inflicting heavy casualties. Even with Marine air support, the situation became desperate; many men had been wounded and supplies were low. To make matters worse, the relief column, five miles away, was itself under attack. Eighteen Marines at Quilali needed immediate medical attention, and evacuation by air seemed to be their only hope.

The beleaguered troops called for help, and 1st Lt. C. F. Schilt, another stalwart of VF-9M, prepared to go in. After an emergency airstrip had been cleared and his Vought O2U-1 Corsair refitted with oversize wheels from a DH-4, Schilt took off on January 6, 1928, in the first attempt to evacuate the Marines at Quilali. Flying through low clouds and fire from the Sandinistas, Schilt dropped his aircraft into the short strip, while the troops on the ground ran forward to grab his plane and haul it to a stop because the Corsair's brakes didn't work. By the time Schilt had completed his tenth flight, on January 8, he had flown in 1,400 pounds of supplies and evacuated all of the eighteen seriously wounded personnel to Ocotal. It was an incredible display

of flying skill and Marine courage, for which Schilt received the third Medal of Honor awarded to a Marine aviator.

It was becoming painfully obvious that operations on the ground would have to take a back seat to continued air attacks; the guerrillas were just too powerful and slippery. Major Rowell, leading many air operations, was only too happy to oblige. In fact, he was later to write in an article in the September 1929 issue of the *Marine Corps Gazette*: "The primary objective in bush warfare is the enemy personnel. The secondary objectives are his supplies and animal transport. The primary objective is easier to destroy than the secondary ones."

On January 14, 1928, Rowell led a four-plane strike ahead of a major ground attack against San Albino, a rebel stronghold. Splitting his planes into two two-plane elements, Rowell attacked the enemy positions from two different directions. But the Sandinistas were ready. Experience with Marine air power had also taught them the advantages of anti-aircraft defenses, however primitive. Flying within range of rifle fire, Rowell's planes ran into heavy attack from the men on the ground. But the Marine crews still managed to drop their bombs and to heavily strafe the rebel positions.

The observers behind the pilots were able to drop fragmentation bombs and white phosphorus hand grenades. Writing in the same article, Rowell outlined the use of weapons against jungle-based guerrillas: "The principal weapon used is the fragmentation bomb, which should be about twenty-five pounds in size. This type of bomb is very satisfactory and can be effectively used in either diving or contour attacks. The fuze has sufficient delay action so that the bomb will penetrate inside buildings before detonating. No troops, guerrilla or otherwise, will stand in the face of a well-directed fragmentation bombing attack."

Throughout the middle of 1928, the Marines pushed the guerrillas back toward Honduras. The overall plan was to at least take away Sandino's military capabilities, and 1st Lt. Merrit A. Edson, who fifteen years later would be one of the Marines' most important commanders during the Guadalcanal campaign, led countless patrols and offensives, aided by

[Left] Shown on the day he received the Medal of Honor, 1st Lt. C. F. Schilt flew his Vought O2U into a small jungle landing strip in Nicaragua to transport wounded Marines to safety in January 1928. The mission called for the utmost bravery and skill.

[Right] An O2U of the type flown by Lieutenant Schilt takes off from a field in Managua, Nicaragua, in 1928. Two-seat Corsairs were active during the 1920s and 1930s.

A Ford Trimotor transport makes its approach for a supply drop in a clearing in Nicaragua in 1930. (USNI collection)

Rowell's air support. It was an effective, if bloody, combination. Sandino was beginning to feel the pressure by August, having dropped back to the Coco River and the nearby Honduras border.

With Sandino thus occupied, national elections could be held in a fairly open and hopeful atmosphere. However, Sandino's men still continued sporadic harassment of voting registration, and only the presence of protective Marines at each registration place made progress possible.

On November 4, 1928, the election was held and Jose Maria Moncada achieved a plurality, bringing his Liberal Party into power. But Sandino could not be held off forever, and the Marines' lines were being stretched thin. It was time for military action to resume. For the next two years, Marine aviation continued the supply and air support it had provided during its first years in

Nicaragua. On July 23, 1931, enlisted pilot SSgt. Gordon W. Heritage, on a support mission in the interior, was hit by enemy fire and forced to crash-land near rebel strongpoints. He and his observer, Cpl. Orville Simmons, managed to set fire to their airplane before beginning a forty-mile trek to relative safety at Puerto Cabezas.

The 1932 national election saw the same protection against the Sandinistas' marauding tactics supplied four years before. The election was held under heavy security because of Sandino's harassment, and a new president was elected. Juan B. Sacasa, an alternative candidate from Moncada for the badly disunited Liberal Party, was the victor. Sacasa was inaugurated in 1933, and a new leader of the National Guard, Anastasio Somoza, was installed. The Somoza family would have a long-lasting, if somewhat questionable, effect on this turbulent little country. But the Marine Corps' involvement had been a success; the Corps learned many valuable lessons during the protracted involvement in Nicaragua, lessons that were to be of inestimable value during the jungle campaigns in World War II.

Prelude to World War II

The decade of the 1930s did not start well for the Marine aviation section. The Depression was a drain on hoped-for programs. And Marine air lost one of its guiding pioneers, Lt. Col. Thomas C. Turner, Marine Aviator 73.

Turner was on his second tour as Director of Marine Aviation, having relieved Maj. Edward Brainard in May 1929. During an inspection trip to Haiti, Turner descended from his Sikorsky RS-1 amphibian. The big twin-engine craft's wheels had mired in the sand and Turner jumped from the plane to see the problem first hand. However, as he moved to the side of the plane, forgetting to allow for the still-swinging propeller, he was struck by the moving blades and severely injured. He died from his wounds two days later. Forty-nine years old, Turner was the highest ranking Marine aviator and was posthumously promoted to brigadier general.

Col. Thomas C. Turner, Marine Aviator 73 and the second director of Marine aviation. A dedicated and capable administrator, Turner was viewed as a competitor by Cunningham and only by intervention of the Commandant, a personal friend of Turner's, did Turner assume overall authority for Marine aviation. He was killed in October 1931 while on an inspection of Marine squadrons in Haiti. (USMC)

Turner's place was taken by Maj. Roy Geiger, Marine Aviator 5, and thus one of the most experienced pilots the Marines had. Geiger would guide the Marine aviation section through the early 1930s, ever vigilant of cost-cutting measures that affected his office, and he would eventually rise to command the Fleet Marine Force, Pacific, in 1945 as a lieutenant general. Geiger and his successor in 1935, Maj. Ross Rowell, who had gained much experience in Nicaragua, had their hands full. The Marines, interested in looking after themselves, set about looking for ways to cut costs. Squadrons

[Left] The Sikorsky RS-1 amphibian of Colonel Turner. Jumping out of this plane, which had become mired in mud, Turner was struck on the head by the still-turning propeller and eventually died of his injuries. The RS-1 carried a two-man crew and seven passengers.

[Top Right] An R4C-1 in California. Note the two nose-mounted landing lights. Between-the-war aircraft were immaculately maintained, as can be seen by the gleaming silver finish on this Condor, which was also a popular civilian airliner of the period featured in the 1934 Shirley Temple movie *Bright Eyes*.

[Bottom Right] A Boeing F4B-4 and Ford JR-3, two important aircraft of Marine aviation in the 1930s. The big trimotor transports did valuable work out of the primitive landing strips in Central America.

were either abolished or merged with sister units. Marine assets abroad were relocated back in the States. All the while, the Marines kept a watchful eye on new aircraft available to the Navy, and perhaps the Marines.

The debate over just what the Marines were to be used for was brought to a conclusion in 1933, with the creation of the Fleet Marine Force on December 8. The FMF, which dedicated the Marines to an amphibious warfare role, in cooperation with the Navy, also abolished the old East and West Coast Expeditionary Forces. Marine air was also incorporated into the FMF; the headquarters units were redesignated Aircraft One based at Quantico, and Aircraft Two at San Diego. The reorganization was another happy circumstance that afforded the Marines an important capability in the great conflict to come.

In 1935 an important treatise, the *Tentative Landing Operations Manual,* written by Marines, was published by the Navy Department. This manual detailed the necessary steps in conducting an amphibious assault, relationships, roles, and equipment placement and operations. Marine air's roles of reconnaissance, fighter escort, protection of the landing forces, artillery spotting, and close air support were formally established as the aviation units' responsibilities. In the same year, the Aviation Section of the Division of Operations and Training was placed directly under the Commandant, with now-Colonel Rowell as its first Director.

The General Board of the Navy, the senior advisory panel established in 1900, restated Marine air's mission in January 1939: to support the Fleet Marine Force in the amphibious landing operations and support the troops once they had passed the beachhead. Additionally, the Marine aviators were to provide backup squadrons for the Navy's regular carrier squadrons. This secondary carrier mission has always sparked controversy. But most Marine pilots overwhelmingly favor periodic carrier deployment of Marine squadrons, although in recent times, as before World War II, Marine aviators received only sporadic training for the exacting profession of carrier flying. This tended to give some carrier skippers more than the usual number of gray hairs as they watched the inexperienced Marines' operations. They were always game and enthusiastic but sometimes lacked the necessary finesse.

Aircraft in 1930–1941

Aircraft development in the 1930s was much different from the preceding period, as established designs gave way to experimentation and advancement. World War I had established the formula for most, though not all, successful military aircraft: a one- or two-place biplane with conventional landing gear (two large main wheels and a smaller tail wheel), radial engine, and two rifle-caliber forward-firing machine guns. It was a formula followed throughout the world, with few exceptions, well into the 1930s. However, by 1935 few aircraft designers would deny that the biplane had reached its peak of development and that the monoplane offered greater advantages in speed, design simplicity, and lightness.

In the early 1930s, the Marines flew a wide variety of biplanes. The Curtiss F6C/F7C series was still very much in use, as were the O2C/O3C two-seater dive bombers from the same manufacturer. Vought was also represented with its hardy O2U/O3U Corsair family of two-seaters, while Boeing F4B fighters and Curtiss R4C transports, military versions of the civilian Condor twin-engine airliner just entering service, continued to serve into the early 1940s.

By 1931 a new name had appeared: Grumman. Working out of Long Island, New York, this young company was eventually to become the mainstay of naval aircraft development and construction, its aircraft always representing the state of the art and establishing a reputation for tractability, endurance, and extraordinary toughness in combat. Grumman's initial effort was the FF-1, a two-seat biplane fighter with manually retracted landing

[Top] A Curtiss F8C-5. After serving with the regulars in the late 1920s and early 1930s, the remaining F8Cs went to the Reserves in mid-1931.

[Bottom] One of the classic fighters of all time, this Boeing F4B-3 of VB-4M is shown in October 1933. Note the telescopic gun sight protruding through the windscreen, and the curious bomb rack between the main landing gear struts. This arrangement was deleted on the later F4B-4, which used underwing bomb racks.

gear. The "Fifi," as the new plane was inevitably called, served mainly with Navy squadrons aboard the carriers *Lexington* (CV-2), *Saratoga* (CV-3), and *Ranger* (CV-4). The Marines operated a few FF-1s as "hacks" and several SF-1 scout models in their reserve squadrons. (The SF-1 differed from the FF-1 internally, while a later variant, the FF-2, had dual controls.)

A single-seat development of the FF-1 was the F2F, which had the same portly shape as its predecessor but offered increased performance. The Marines got only a few F2Fs, usually when the Navy was through with them. But it was not until the F3F came along that the Corps got its first real taste of a Grumman product. The last biplane fighter produced for either the Navy or Marines, the F3F served with VMF-1 at Quantico, and VMF-2 at San Diego, from 1937 to 1941.

By September 1937, a hot contest between Grumman and its Long Island rival, Brewster, had developed over new monoplane fighter designs. Responses to a 1935 Navy requirement, the two designs were immediately plunged into a race to see which would fly first. Brewster came up with a tubby, mid-fuselage monoplane with an enormous greenhouse canopy, while Grumman had originally redesigned its successful F3F series into the XF4F-1

[Top] VMF-2 flew the Grumman F3F-2. The F3F used the Wright Cyclone, which developed 200 more horsepower than the Wasp of the earlier F2F.

[Center] Vought SU-2s of VO-8M, 1933. The San Diego–based squadron had just taken delivery of these new aircraft. SU-2 scouts served throughout the remainder of the decade. (William T. Larkins)

[Bottom] Another Marine transport from Sikorsky, the JRS-1 is shown over North Island near San Diego in 1936. A squadron of ten aircraft was assigned to Pearl Harbor in 1940 and was present during the Japanese attack in 1941. They were armed with depth charges and bombs and sent out to find the fast-retreating Japanese fleet without success. (Courtesy Ed Szretjer via Warren Thompson)

[Left] The Grumman F4F Wildcat, in competition with the Brewster Buffalo, proved to be the only American fighter, Army or Navy, capable of fighting the Japanese Zero during the opening stages of the Pacific war. This aircraft is on maneuvers in 1941.

[Top Right] Curtiss SOC-3s of VMS-2 at San Diego, 1939. Although operated mainly by Navy squadrons, the SOC did serve with a few Marine units. The type could operate either as a land plane (as shown) or, more commonly, as a catapult floatplane, usually from cruisers. It served on several capital ships from 1938 to 1944. (William L. Swisher)

[Bottom Right] The big, tough Great Lakes BG-1 was used as a dive bomber during the mid-1930s. This "Bee Gee" of VMB-2 carries the "Winged Devil" insignia of VB-4M, the squadron's designation until July 1937. (William T. Larkins)

biplane. However, Grumman realized that the biplane was on the way out and made the fortuitous decision to change the design to a more advanced monoplane configuration, eventually ending up with the XF4F-2.

Even with a late start, the Grumman design flew in September 1937, before the problem-plagued Brewster XF2A-1, as the competitor aircraft had been designated; it did not fly until December.

From the beginning, the XF2A-1 displayed a disappointing performance, and it was never satisfactorily upgraded. And although a great deal of effort and publicity were expended and the plane was actually exported to several European countries, including Belgium, the Netherlands, Britain, and Finland, as well as seeing service with the U.S. Navy and Marines, it was only with the Finns that the fat little Brewster fighter achieved any success. (The Finns loved the Buffalo, as the aircraft was named, as much as the American pilots hated it, shooting down many Soviet aircraft during the 1940 war, and later as reluctant allies of the Germans in 1943.)

The Navy's VF-3 took the first delivery of the F2A in January 1939, operating for a time aboard the *Saratoga*. Only the Marines of VMF-221 took on the F2A-2, at their base at Ewa near Pearl Harbor.

The F4F, in contrast, was a success story. Although a contemporary of the unsuccessful F2A, the F4F Wildcat was an important fighter throughout all but the last year of the war, and certainly in the early days, to early 1943, it was the only U.S. fighter plane capable of meeting the Mitsubishi Zero on anything approaching equal terms. The Wildcat did not reach the Marines until May 1941, when VMF-111, VMF-121, and VMF-211 were formed.

Bombing aircraft were also changing in the late 1930s. The ubiquitous Curtiss and Vought biplanes began to give way to monoplane designs, although the Great Lakes Aircraft Corporation secured a production contract for sixty machines with their big BG-1, a two-seater biplane powered by a single 750-horsepower Pratt and Whitney radial. The "Bee-Gee," as the BG-1 was naturally called, remained in service until 1941, when it was replaced by one, then two, very different aircraft, both monoplanes. (It served with

VB-6M and VB-4M, later VMB-1 and VMB-2.) One other biplane scout/bomber put in some minor service with the Marines, the Curtiss SBC series, with the dash-4 version serving with several Marine Reserve squadrons, as well as "hack" aircraft with other units.

Two aircraft of the late 1930s represented the greatest jump in attack capability for the Marines: the Vought SB2U Vindicator and Douglas SBD Dauntless. Both were multi-seat, low-wing monoplanes, with retractable gear and a relatively new development in dive bombing—the bomb "displacing gear." This device, mounted along the centerline of the fuselage below the cockpit, held the large main bomb (lighter bombs could also be carried under the wings) and extended the bomb outside the propeller arc for release. This arrangement permitted a near-vertical, and thus more accurate, dive to be obtained, with the pilot literally aiming his aircraft at his target, on the sea or ground, and releasing the bomb at the opportune moment.

[Top Left] The last biplane bomber by Curtiss, the SBC-3 served with only a few Marine units, mainly Reserve squadrons. This well-proportioned dive bomber never saw combat, although the French were in the process of obtaining the type when they surrendered to the Germans in June 1940. (Rudy Arnold Photo Collection of the Smithsonian Institution)

[Bottom Left] Closeup of a Vought SB2U-3 of VMSB-131 based at Quantico in July 1941. This fabric-covered monoplane was to prove a great disappointment to both the Navy and Marines during its very few combat actions, notably at Midway in 1942. Note empty bomb crutch underneath cockpit. (Rudy Arnold Collection of the Smithsonian Institution)

[Top Right] A VMJ-1 Douglas R2D-1, military version of the civilian DC-2 airliner, seen at Boston in August 1939. The R2D was assigned to the Marines in 1935 as a paratroop trainer and a general transport.

[Center Right] An unusual member of VMF-1, this SB2U-1 Vindicator dive bomber was used for various pathfinder duties. It is shown in St. Thomas, Virgin Islands, 1939. It was equipped with a homing loop and extra radios. (Leroy M. McCallum)

[Bottom Right] Grumman J2Fs of VMS-3 over the Virgin Islands, August 1939. (Leroy M. McCallum)

A Grumman J2F-5, better known simply as a "Duck," in February 1940, still carrying the "neutrality" star markings, pre-war rudder striping and dark gray paint. This particular aircraft is serving with the American Aviation Mission to Central and South America. Col. V. E. Megee, left, served throughout the Pacific war, eventually taking charge of all Marine close air support in the Okinawa campaign. The J2F also served through the war, in several versions, mainly as a rescue aircraft.

The earlier Vought design resulted from a 1934 Navy Bureau of Aeronautics call for a new scout and dive bomber, Vought entering the competition along with the Brewster Company. The XSB2U-1 flew in January 1936 and was a low-wing, fabric-covered monoplane, powered by a 700-horsepower Pratt and Whitney radial. Although the prototype eventually crashed, killing its two crewmen, the Navy awarded Vought a production contract for fifty-four machines. The first SB2U-1s entered service with the Navy's VB-3 aboard the *Saratoga* in December 1937. Eventually, it was exported to France, where it served for a brief time during the German onslaught in June 1940. However, the Marines did not receive their first Vindicators until March 1941 with the deliveries of the SB2U-3 to VMS-2, a scouting squadron at San Diego. Poorly armed, even for a scout bomber, the Vindicator served without distinction, its only combat action in U.S. service being an abortive attack on Japanese ships during the Battle of Midway.

The 1930s and early 1940s held great promise—and disappointment—for the Marines. New aircraft were not always the best. Even though equipment was supposedly modern and up to world standards, only the F4F Wildcat and one other aircraft gave the Marines anything remotely resembling a modern airplane. Although somewhat forgotten in the initial hectic accounts of the war, that second aircraft, the Douglas SBD Dauntless, was subsequently recognized as one of the simplest, toughest, most capable, and most dependable of all naval aircraft. Designed by the now-legendary Ed Heinemann (1908–91), and actually the logical outgrowth of several abortive, yet profitable, designs, the Dauntless broke tradition by beginning operations with a Marine squadron rather than the Navy. Marine Air Group 2 at San Diego received its first SBD-1s in June 1940.

The approximately three decades of Marine aviation before December 1941 had seen a fledgling force of a few men and machines grow to two full wings of aircraft and personnel whose skill would be tested to the utmost in the dynamic years of World War II. There had been policy and administrative changes during those thirty years, some not always successful, or popular; but the Marines fortunately found themselves with a nucleus of seasoned, experienced dedicated airmen to fight the conflict suddenly thrust upon them.

3 World War II: *On the Defensive*

THE JAPANESE ATTACK ON PEARL HARBOR on December 7, 1941, caught most of the Marine Corps aircraft in Hawaii on the ground at Ewa. The only large groups of Marine planes to escape destruction were the F4F-3s (an early model of the Wildcat without folding wings) of VMF-211, which had flown aboard the carrier USS *Enterprise* (CV-6) on November 28 to be transported to the isolated U.S. base at Wake Island, and eighteen Vought SB2Us of VMSB-231 on the USS *Lexington*, also steaming for Wake.

Attention had been drawn to Wake for several weeks among the higher echelons of the U.S. defense establishment, as some sort of Japanese attack, somewhere, seemed probable. It seemed safe to assume that Wake would receive a workover, if not an outright invasion, and its military defenses needed bolstering.

Wake Island, which is really three small islands 2,000 miles southwest of Hawaii, had long been a minor U.S. outpost in the Pacific, serving primarily as a meteorological station and stopping-off point for the pioneering trans-Pacific flights of Pan American Airways. On October 15, 1941, Marine Maj. James P. Devereux arrived to assume command of the island's Marine garrison, which had arrived in August to beef up Wake's defenses. Throughout the next two months, Wake was reinforced with men, communications equipment, and aircraft, including the twelve F4F-3s of VMF-211, which flew off the *Enterprise* on December 4. Maj. Paul A. Putnam, the squadron's commanding officer, was also a veteran of combat in Nicaragua, where he had served alongside Major Devereux, although in the later stages. Putnam was a Michigan native who had joined the Marines in 1923 as a private and was eventually to rise to brigadier general.

The pilots of VMF-211 were unfamiliar with their new mounts, having traded in their F3Fs only a few weeks previously. There was also

One of America's first air heroes of the war was Capt. Henry T. Elrod, who fought in the skies above Wake Island before being killed on the ground by a Japanese Marine. Elrod received the Medal of Honor.

Grumman F4F Wildcats of VMF-211 immediately after the surrender of Wake. The all-gray fighters served the Marine aviators well during the hectic, hopeless battle.

little knowledge or experience amongst the enlisted ground crews, who were primarily ordnancemen drafted from a scout bomber squadron. There were mechanics at Ewa waiting to be flown to Wake, but the deteriorating situation precluded this course. The men on the island had to make do with what they had. The 5,000-foot runway at Wake was barely long enough, and its width of 200 feet permitted only one aircraft at a time to take off. Multiplane section takeoffs, normal operational practice in military squadrons, were impossible.

The Wildcats had to be fueled by hand, a time-consuming operation, and with no radar available, the Marines were forced to put up continuous patrols of F4Fs to scout for the Japanese fleet they knew was on the move. Action was not long in coming. Capt. Henry T. Elrod was leading a four-plane patrol at 12,000 feet over the north side of Wake at noontime on December 8, when he saw the first wave of Japanese bombers approaching from the south. The thirty-six twin-engine bombers had left Kwajalein Atoll, more than 600 miles away, and had made their approach undetected through rain.

The Japanese bombed and strafed the installations at Wake, destroying seven of the Wildcats on the ground, while an eighth was damaged and put out of service while the pilot was taxiing. In the early afternoon, the situation did not look good. VMF-211 had lost twenty men killed, including three pilots, with eleven more, among them four pilots, wounded.

On the 9th, the Wildcat patrol, all that was now left of the airborne defense, ran into a second Japanese attack at 11:45 AM, and this time two Marines, Lt. David S. Kliewer and TSgt. William Hamilton, each shot down a Japanese bomber, probably the first Marine aerial kills of the war. Ground fire accounted for another bomber, while damaging several more. The next day, December 10, Captain Elrod destroyed two more bombers. But it was rapidly becoming apparent that if reinforcements did not come soon, it was only a matter of time before the Japanese would assault and conquer Wake. There was just too little of everything.

Help seemed on the way. The *Saratoga* was steaming from Pearl with VMF-221, under Maj. Verne J. McCaul. The eighteen fighters in the squadron were the abhorred, obsolete Brewster Buffalos, good only for training duty in the States. There was also radar equipment, supplies, and ammunition. All of these would be welcomed, even the F2As. The *Lexington* had been tasked with flying patrols searching for the Japanese fleet, and its load of Vindicators would never reach Wake. Because of the horrible state of confusion and indecision in the aftermath of Pearl Harbor, "Sara" was held up from entering Pearl Harbor and did not actually depart until December 15. It was a fatal delay.

Things were rapidly deteriorating at Wake, where it was actually December 16 because of the placement of the International Date Line. The Japanese had, indeed, sent a force of destroyers and cruisers to pound the crumbling defenses on Wake's south coast, while transports prepared to launch their landing craft with invasion troops. As the shore guns were firing at the invaders, Major Putnam and three other pilots, including Captain Elrod, were airborne with small, 100-pound bombs carried on makeshift racks. The Japanese ships had been sufficiently damaged by shore fire that they were retreating from their close-in positions, and the four Marine

Wildcats found them. Putnam and his flight immediately began bombing and strafing the enemy ships, eventually hitting most of them.

The destroyer *Kisaragi*, which blew up at 8:15 AM, provided one of the continuing legends of the defense of Wake. In one of the first public propaganda releases, it was claimed that the 100-pound bombs and determined attacks of the outnumbered Marine pilots were totally responsible for the sinking of the destroyer. In the light of later examination, it seems more probable that, although severely damaged by the Wildcat attacks, the ship's fate was sealed when one of her own depth charges exploded from the fires started by the aerial attack.

The surviving aircraft of VMF-211 flew ten missions on the 16th and were involved in the sinking of two destroyers. But two F4Fs, piloted by Elrod and Capt. Herbert C. Freuler, were put out of commission as a result of Japanese anti-aircraft fire. The aerial defense of Wake now rested on only two F4Fs. And the Japanese air raids continued.

The sole contact the beleaguered defenders had with the outside world occurred on December 20, when a Navy PBY Catalina made it through, landing in the lagoon and bringing news of the relief force en route to Wake. But time was running out. The Japanese carriers *Soryu* and *Hiryu*, returning from the Pearl Harbor operation, had joined the fleet offshore, and their planes were intended to contribute to the continuing softening-up operation in preparation for the actual invasion.

December 22 saw the last of the Wildcats. Captain Freuler and Lt. Carl R. Davidson jumped a force of thirty-three bombers from the enemy carriers and were, themselves, immediately attacked by the Zero escort. Freuler tacked himself onto one of the Japanese fighters and shot it down. But the fragments of the dying Zero damaged his plane's controls, forcing Freuler to land. Looking around for his wingman, Lieutenant Davidson, he saw him once with another Zero on his tail, and that was all. Davidson was not seen again. Wounded by another Zero, Freuler crash-landed Wake's last Grumman. Now the Marine pilots on Wake became what all Marines are first considered, riflemen.

The situation was now bad enough that Vice Adm. William S. Pye, who was serving as Commander, Pacific Fleet, began to reconsider sending a relief force to Wake. The island's fall was now nearly a certainty. What good would sending more—but not enough—reinforcements do? After initially deciding to continue the rescue operation, even as Wake's aerial defense collapsed, Pye changed his mind and recalled Task Force 14, the relief force, at 8:11 AM Hawaiian time. To the anxious Marine pilots and sailors aboard *Saratoga*, the decision to leave Wake to its fate was both incomprehensible and shameful. But even as some cried and others railed against the decision makers, Sara was changing her course away from Wake. There was little the Marines aboard her could do.

The main Japanese attack began in the early hours of December 23, with landing barges disgorging Japanese troops. Bloody combat continued until 7:00 AM, when Cdr. Winfield S. Cunningham, the Navy commander of Wake, and Major Devereux bitterly concluded that further resistance was useless and would only result in needless loss of life. They had not only the lives of their own Marines and sailors to consider, but also those of the civilian workers who had joined in the fight alongside the Marines. And so Wake fell.

Among those killed during the Japanese assault was Capt. Hank Elrod, who had been involved in some of the siege's worst aerial action. Elrod was shot and killed by a Japanese playing possum. Elrod's performance, only learned after the war, earned him the Medal of Honor. Devereux and Major Putnam, along with the survivors—civilians, sailors, and Marines—were herded together by the victorious Japanese. Some would be held as prisoners of war in Japan, while some civilians were held at Wake to work the island's facilities. However, these unlucky personnel, after nearly two years of captivity, were executed in October 1943 by the commander of Wake at the time, in retaliation for American strikes on the Japanese-held base. (Rear Admiral Shigematsu Sakaibara was later tried as a war criminal and executed in 1947.)

The heroic, hopeless defense of Wake Island gave birth to the Marine Corps' modern perception of itself. Although 166 years of Marine Corps history had preceded it, Wake became a symbol to America and the Marines. A song, composed after Wake's fall, had a chorus that went:

> Wake Island, Wake Island.
> It's not even marked on the maps.
> But who would have thought a few crummy Marines
> Could stop the advance of the Japs.

Perhaps Major Putnam put the feeling a little more accurately and objectively when he filed a report that the visiting PBY took out two days before Wake surrendered. He wrote, in part, "All hands have behaved splendidly and held up in a manner of which the Marine Corps may well tell."

Prelude to Midway

The day of the attack on Pearl Harbor, another massive Japanese strike began against the Philippines. (Since the Philippines was on the other side of the International Date Line from Hawaii, this attack occurred on December 8.) Carrier-based dive bombers and fighters, as well as aircraft based on the island of Formosa (Taiwan), swept down on the island of Mindanao, and U.S. Army and Navy forces in the area, under Gen. Douglas MacArthur, were quickly overwhelmed. The big air base at Clark Field near Manila was particularly hard hit. By Christmas 1941, the Japanese had conquered most of the Philippines, as well as the British colony of Hong Kong on the Asian mainland to the north, and were heading toward the Netherlands East Indies—Java, Borneo, and Sumatra—in the south. The last-ditch stand by U.S. and Filipino forces on the Bataan Peninsula, near the harbor at Manila, made world headlines. But in mid-March 1942, President Franklin D. Roosevelt ordered MacArthur out, and the Philippines fell.

Japan ruled most of the southwestern Pacific. Smarting from the blow at Pearl Harbor and the unbroken string of Japanese successes, the United States sent a task force into Japanese home waters in a sneak attack of its own. Conceived by Lt. Col. Jimmy Doolittle, a well-known pre-war race pilot, with an engineering Ph.D. from the Massachusetts Institute of Technology, the plan called for sixteen B-25 Mitchell bombers to take off from the USS *Hornet* and attack the Japanese capital of Tokyo and several other important cities. Obviously, the value of such an attack would be more spiritual than physical: a strike against the enemy's homeland when he would least expect it.

Thus, on April 18, 1942, the twin-engine B-25s took off from the carrier's pitching deck. (An unfortunate encounter with a Japanese patrol boat had necessitated launching the planes 250 miles from the original launch point.) Doolittle led his men off, and the raiders were over Tokyo within four hours. Plans called for the aircraft to fly to China, but the severe weather caused many to stray off course, run out of fuel, and crash land. One came down in Soviet Siberia and the crew was interned. Others had the misfortune to land in Japanese-held territory, where their crews were executed. Most, including Doolittle, managed to make the Chinese coast, where their crews survived their landings.

The Japanese were not through, however, and they continued their drive southward, putting pressure on Australia. Early in May 1942, a Japanese task force headed for New Guinea met an American task force, with the USS *Yorktown* and USS *Lexington*, in the Coral Sea off Australia's northeast coast. On May 8, in an encounter that was the first naval battle in which the opponents' ships never saw each other, American and Japanese aircraft dive bombed and torpedoed the other's carriers, the Japanese sinking the *Lexington*—the first U.S. carrier lost in the war—in exchange for the light carrier *Shoho* and damage to other ships.

Although a tactical defeat for the United States, in terms of tonnage sunk, the Battle of the Coral Sea was the first strategic defeat of the war for the Japanese, whose steamroller advance had finally been halted. The Japanese realized more than ever that the American carriers had to be sunk or disabled, if a Japanese drive was to be sustained. The small mid-Pacific atoll of Midway looked like a good spot for a showdown.

Through mid-1942, the American military forces in the Pacific could be likened to a prize fighter gamely trying to fend off his opponent's blows as he staggers on his feet. He is resolved to remain standing while he looks for an opening and hopes for the bell that will end the round and give him some breathing space. Until June 1942, there were no campaigns, only specific battles such as Pearl Harbor, Wake, and Coral Sea, which the Japanese initiated, and with the exception of the Battle of the Coral Sea, easily won. These successes put a tremendous drain on the U.S. forward areas. But these early trials also gave American industry time to gather the steam that Admiral Isoroku Yamamoto, Commander-in-Chief of the Imperial Japanese Navy's Combined Fleet, feared would be the undoing of Japan's military ambitions, and of the island nation itself, if the war lasted more than six months after Pearl Harbor.

In the early days of 1942, though, the Japanese rolled unchecked across the Pacific. But the original intent of the attack on Pearl Harbor was not only to damage as much of the American Navy's Pacific Fleet as possible, but specifically also to destroy America's carriers. Fortunately for the United States, the carriers—*Lexington, Yorktown, Saratoga, Hornet,* and *Enterprise*—were either at sea or serving in the Atlantic and thus escaped the fury of the Japanese attack. Japan, therefore, saw the value of Midway Atoll, halfway between America and Japan, as a way-station for any further thrusts against Pearl and America's West Coast. She developed a plan to attack and occupy Midway, thus drawing the U.S. carriers into a battle with a refreshed Japanese battle fleet, which would stage from Midway. With four major carriers and a complete support fleet, the Japanese Navy felt itself invincible as it approached Midway from the northwest on the early morning of June 4, 1942.

Arrayed against the huge Imperial force, besides the carriers *Yorktown, Enterprise,* and *Hornet*—the *Lexington* having been sunk at Coral Sea one month before and the *Saratoga* laid up for repairs stateside—there were the land-based U.S. Army Air Force assets: four Martin B-26 Marauders and seventeen Boeing B-17 Flying Fortresses. There were also six brand-new Navy Grumman TBF Avenger torpedo bombers of VT-8. (The TBFs were actually on detachment from the main squadron aboard the *Hornet,* which was still flying antiquated Douglas TBD Devastators.)

Marine assets on that morning of June 4 included a total of sixty-four aircraft: nineteen Douglas SBD-2 Dauntlesses, seventeen obsolete Vought SB2U-3 Vindicators; twenty-one nearly useless Brewster F2A-3 Buffalos; and seven Grumman F4F-3 Wildcats. The mixed bag of fighters came from VMF-221, the same squadron that had sailed to relieve Wake on December 15, 1941, only to be turned back when all seemed lost at the isolated outpost. The seven F4Fs represented the only nearly modern fighter equipment available.

Additional manpower and aircraft had been pumped into Midway throughout the first five months of 1942 as Washington became rightly convinced of an impending Japanese attack. One of the more unusual visitors to Midway before the battle was an R4D-1 (the Navy version of the C-47 military derivative of the civilian DC-3) of VMJ-252, based at Ewa. The twin-engine aircraft, piloted by Capt. Albert S. Munsch, carried much-needed ammunition for the PBY and Buffalo aircraft already on Midway, as well as ten enlisted men to augment the Navy patrol squadrons, VP-23 and VP-44, whose Catalinas flew constant patrols from Midway. By exemplary overwater navigation, the transport reached Midway more than eight hours after taking off on June 2. It was a great demonstration of flying skill, but Lt. Col. Ira Kimes, commanding Marine Aircraft Group 22, could not afford to let the R4D crew rest. He greeted them and immediately sent them back to Hawaii with dispatches for Adm. Chester Nimitz.

In early March the Brewsters intercepted some marauding Japanese flying boats. Capt. James E. Neefus shot down one of two large Kawanishi Type 97 four-engine, parasol-winged boats, later code-named Mavis. These Japanese probes, along with other naval actions involving submarines and surface ships shelling Midway sporadically, only reinforced Admiral Nimitz's feeling that a major assault was coming. He visited Midway on May 2, and more anti-aircraft defenses, gasoline, and communications gear were delivered to the island soon afterward. By June Midway had 120 aircraft ready for action against the approaching Japanese. Although the three-day battle that developed on June 4 was primarily a Navy show, the Marines were very much in evidence, especially during the early stages of the action.

The Battle of Midway

As soon as the first PBY reports came in confirming the approach of the Japanese fleet, the Marines of MAG-22 sent off all available planes, both as a defensive measure, so that they would not be caught and destroyed on the ground, and also to be in a better position to attack when the time came. Circling at 8,500 feet, twenty miles east of Midway, was the combined SBD/

SB2U squadron, VMSB-241, under Maj. Lofton R. Henderson (in an SBD) and his Executive Officer, Maj. Ben Norris (flying an SB2U). The fighters of VMF-221, led by their skipper, Maj. Floyd B. Parks, numbered twenty-five Buffalos and Wildcats. Parks had just assumed command, the squadron's third CO in *seven* months, having relieved Captain Neefus, who had been reassigned in May. The fighters split into two sections of twelve and thirteen aircraft and orbited, waiting for word of the first attack. Within fifteen minutes of getting airborne, the Marines spotted a large force of Japanese bombers from the *Hiryu* and their Zero escorts, all heading for Midway.

At 6:16 in the morning, June 4, the section under Major Parks pushed over into screaming dives to meet the enemy 2,000 feet below them. Moments later, the second group, under Capt. Kirk Armistead, joined the fight. It was no contest. The courage of the Marine aviators, the majority of whom were inexperienced, could not offset the inadequacies of their fat old Buffalo fighters against the Zeros. And there were just not enough of the newer Wildcats. The faster, far more maneuverable Zeros, flown by seasoned combat veterans of the Japanese Navy—some of whom had seen much combat in China over the last five years—swarmed all over the struggling defending interceptors. There was little anyone could do.

It might be worth considering, in retrospect, that the Buffalo might not have been totally at fault for its reputation. After all, consider the Finns' sterling performance with the type. They, however, operated the lighter

F2A-1, while the Marines flew the -3, which, while incorporating extra fuel, with its accompanying 900 pounds of extra weight, still retained the -1's power plant. Added to this additional weight were extra armor protection, increased armament, and self-sealing fuel tanks. Of course, these additions were important and were derived from recent combat experience in Europe.

Nearly all Japanese aircraft lost in aerial combat at Midway went down before the guns of the Buffalos and Wildcats. Only seven of the latter were flown by Marine pilots at Midway, and three of these were lost in combat. Those and the remaining four could not have accounted for even a majority of the thirty-four Japanese planes destroyed in dogfights. The little F2As had to have had some hand in the action. Perhaps, the much-maligned Brewster deserves better from historians.

Twenty-two-year-old 2nd Lt. Charles Kunz was flying a Buffalo this day, side number MF-17. A native of Missouri, he was part of a four-plane

division at 21,000 feet, when Captain Armistead spotted a large formation of Japanese dive bombers and fighters headed for Midway below the Marines. Armistead led his division down, and Kunz quickly shot down two Vals, but was soon set upon by the Zero escort. With three Zeros on his tail, Kunz tried to make it back to Midway, flying twenty feet above the water. The Zeros broke off their attack, but the Marine's Buffalo was riddled with bullets, and he, himself, was bleeding from a scalp wound.

Reaching the beleaguered island, Kunz had to wait twenty minutes until an enemy strike force had cleared the area. Only six of the nineteen Buffalos that went out that morning returned. Kunz would eventually gain six more kills during the war and retire in 1967 a full colonel. He received the Navy Cross for his Midway mission. Kunz would fight again with VMF-224, this time over Guadalcanal in the coming September, sustaining another wound and shooting down three more Japanese aircraft, to become an ace.

He later commented on the F2A: "I did not like the 1200 h.p. Wright engine or the electrical prop control. But from personal experience, I do have to give an 'A' for ruggedness as numerous Jap 20-mm and 7.7 holes did not stop it from getting me back to Midway. . . . The F2A-3 was probably a few knots faster than the early Wildcat, but overall, the F4F was superior to the F2A in performance when compared to the Jap Zero. Neither the Buffalo or Wildcat was in its league . . . the enemy had the advantage of speed and maneuverability, a winning combination."[1]

Another young Marine Buffalo aviator, 2nd Lt. William V. Brooks, made it back to Midway with seventy-two holes in his fighter and one in his left leg. Unable to fully retract his landing gear after takeoff, he nonetheless joined the fight and engaged the Japanese, eventually being credited with two probables while flying Brewster's much-maligned fighter.

Although he might have been at odds with his fellow pilots, Brooks believed that with a more powerful engine and increased armament, specifically the battery of six .50-caliber machine guns that was becoming common in American fighters, the F2A "would have been a great fighter." Brooks retired as a lieutenant colonel and the last surviving American to have taken the Buffalo into combat.

[Opposite] Marines fuel an F2A-3, probably of VMF-212 at MCAS Ewa in May 1942. Note the large national insignia stars with red center, which was being painted out at this time to avoid confusion with the Japanese "meatball," and prominent red-and-white rudder stripes.

[Top Left] Capt. Charles Kunz, VMF-221 Buffalo pilot at Midway. He claimed two Aichi "Val" dive bombers in the battle. He is standing by a Corsair in 1943.

[Top Right] An unusual shot of Charles Kunz, now an ace with VMF-311, sitting in a captured Japanese "Tony" fighter, which he is about to fly to a rear-area base for intelligence analysis in 1944. One of only a few Japanese aircraft to use a liquid-cooled engine, the Tony was a formidable midwar Army fighter that served till war's end. (courtesy the Kunz family)

One young Marine Wildcat pilot who also survived, and even managed to shoot down a Zero (he has been sometimes incorrectly credited with two kills during the engagement) while flying an F4F at Midway, was Capt. Marion E. Carl. Having been promoted in May, Captain Carl, who was active throughout the early part of the war and eventually would rise to major general, found himself the target when two Zeros dove on him. As the Japanese bullets struck his plane, Carl chopped his throttle and skidded the Wildcat around, making the Zeros overshoot. Carl then ducked into a cloud. His pursuers gave up to seek other game.

Recomposing himself, the young aviator reentered the fight and lined up another Zero, only to find that the previous violent maneuvering had jammed his plane's four .50-caliber machine guns. He pulled at each of the four charging handles in the cockpit and eventually got three guns to fire. He soon dispatched his first victim, whose pilot apparently never knew he was being stalked, and returned to the smoking field at Midway. For his actions that day, he received the Navy Cross, one of two he would earn during his career.

VMF-221 was decimated. Of the twenty-five aircraft which took off at 6:00 AM, only thirteen returned, and only two of the returnees were fit to fly again. Major Parks was apparently shot down and did not return. Later reports described his having bailed out from his badly damaged Brewster, only to be strafed and killed in the water by Japanese fighters.

Noting that the squadron seemed to fall apart at this point, Marion Carl wrote in his diary, "Two fighters still in commission. Feeling better—ready for another fight. Zeros too fast for our planes."[2]

While the fighters of VMF-221 were doing their best to slow down the Japanese, the Army and Navy air contingents were also running into trouble. Four B-26s were sent out with torpedoes to find the Japanese fleet, but although the Army claimed that the hot new bombers had loosed all their torpedoes and had scored hits, that was not the case, and indeed, two of the four Marauders were shot down by Zeros or anti-aircraft fire.

The Grumman Avengers of the Navy fared little better. In a macabre emulation of their brethren aboard the *Hornet,* the VT-8 detachment lost five of the six new torpedo bombers. (VT-8 sent out fifteen TBDs, all of which were shot down; only one of the thirty crewmen survived.) The Zeros and anti-aircraft fire were a veritable wall between the Japanese ships and the U.S. bombers.

Things were not going well for the American defenders in the opening rounds of the battle. The Japanese did seem nearly invincible, too powerful, too experienced. The planes from the carrier *Hiryu,* which had punched through VMF-221's interceptors, although somewhat reduced in numbers, still managed to wreak havoc on Eastern and Sand islands, the two islands that compose Midway Atoll. Besides the human casualties, power facilities, fuel, and aircraft were destroyed in the Japanese bombing and strafing attacks.

Much has been written about the final outcome of the Battle of Midway, more than sixty-five years ago, concerning the record of the U.S. pilots and the problems of the Japanese commanders, especially Admiral Chuichi Nagumo, commanding the carrier task force. Basically, the tide of battle turned in favor of the Americans when Nagumo finally chose to rearm and

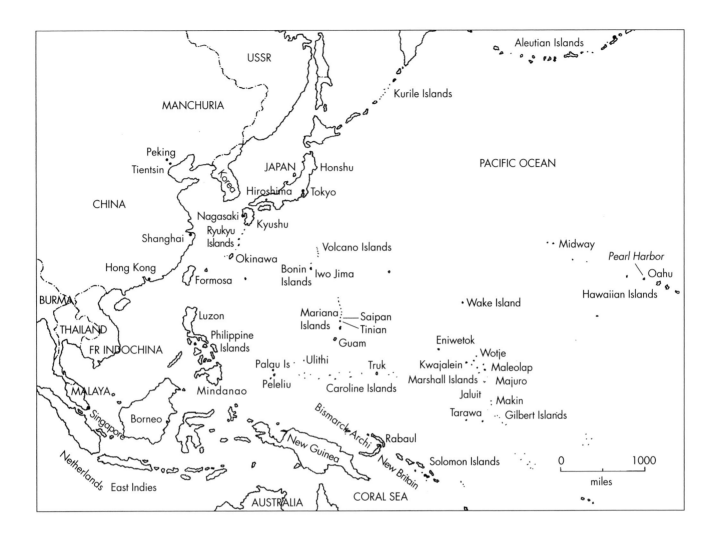

Map 2. The War in the Pacific, 1941–45

refuel his aircraft for another attack against Midway with bombs, instead of an attack against the U.S. carriers with torpedoes. He left his fleet without aerial defense. It was, indeed, a fatal error of judgment. By the time Nagumo received word that there were American carriers in the area and decided to change back to torpedoes, it was too late. Dauntlesses from the *Enterprise, Hornet,* and *Yorktown* caught the *Soryu,* then the *Kaga,* and finally the *Akagi* and sank them with devastating dive-bombing attacks.

Later in the day, the fourth Japanese carrier, the *Hiryu,* was hit after launching an attack on the *Yorktown.* The *Hiryu* sank the next day. The Japanese retreated with their first major carrier losses of the war. *Yorktown,* though mortally wounded, did not sink immediately and was finally finished off by a prowling Japanese submarine two days later. The losses and subsequent defeat were to have wide-ranging effect on the Japanese, because many of their most experienced aviators and crewmen, and nearly 400 aircraft, went down with their ships.

However, although the U.S. Navy's dive bombers won the day—land-based air power had very little effect on the fighting—the Marines were greatly involved, too. On the early morning of June 4, as Marine fighters tangled with Japanese raiders and the Army and Navy torpedo bombers thrust themselves through devastating anti-aircraft fire, to no avail, the

Dauntlesses and Vindicators of Majors Henderson and Norris were directed against the enemy task force 150 miles to the northwest.

Approaching the Japanese fleet, the bombers immediately encountered Zeros. Major Henderson was apparently the first loss, his group of SBDs reaching the target fifteen minutes before Norris' SB2Us. Eight of Henderson's sixteen SBDs were destroyed as they dove toward their targets. One pilot from Henderson's section, 1st Lt. Daniel Iverson, limped back to Midway with 259 holes in his aircraft and his throat mike shot away.

It is thought that relative inexperience and unfamiliarity with their new planes made the Marine pilots go into much shallower dives, almost glide-bombing deliveries, instead of the more direct and faster vertical technique that was the hallmark of the Douglas plane. This failure to use their aircraft correctly left the Marine crews open to deadly anti-aircraft fire and Zero interceptors.

The ancient SB2U Vindicators of Major Norris' section were little better off than the SBDs, losing three of the fabric-covered dive bombers to Zeros and flak. Capt. Richard E. Fleming's aircraft sustained 179 holes, and Fleming himself was wounded twice.

Regrouping at Midway, the Marines sent out another mission in the early evening. Eleven SBDs and SB2Us, led by Major Norris, who had taken over the squadron after Major Henderson's death that morning, sought a reportedly damaged Japanese carrier. Failing to locate the target, the bombers turned back toward Midway. However, forty miles out from the base, Major Norris was seen to go into a steep descending turn and disappear. Command of VMSB-241 turned over for the second time in twenty-four hours, this time to Capt. Marshall Tyler.

Tyler led his squadron on the first mission of the next day, taking off at 6:30 AM on June 5. The targets were Japanese battleships, 176 miles off to the west. Approaching the enemy ships, some of which had been damaged the day before and were leaking easily seen trails of oil, the twelve Marine bombers were staggered, with the Dauntlesses at 10,000 feet and the Vindicators at 4,000 feet.

Captain Fleming, who had survived murderous fire and being twice wounded the day before, was seen to run into more deadly flak, his SB2U bursting into flames as he dropped his bomb over the heavy cruiser *Mikuma*. Perhaps he was mortally wounded, or perhaps his plane could not climb; whatever the reason, Fleming and his burning aircraft fell onto the rear turret of the damaged Japanese vessel. Whether his destruction was the result of aircraft failure or the last desperate, courageous act of a brave man will never be known. Captain Fleming received a posthumous Medal of Honor.

The Battle of Midway continued through the 6th, with the Japanese finally retiring for safer waters. The Marines had suffered badly, along with the rest of the American forces. The fighter and bomber squadrons had each lost commanding officers. Enlisted ranks, with the loss of rear-seat gunners and ground crewmen, were also hard hit. The flight crews of MAG-22 had shot down seventeen enemy planes, including six VALs and ten Zeros. Ground fire had accounted for approximately ten more Japanese aircraft.[3]

4 Cactus in the Pacific: *Guadalcanal*

NOW THAT THE JAPANESE ADVANCE had been halted at Midway, the "breathing space" that decisive American victory afforded was put to good use. Plans were made for an American invasion of the Solomon Islands group, 1,300 miles northeast of Australia. The Solomons were chosen for the first Allied offensive in the Pacific because they were within the range capabilities of the limited U.S. carrier forces and also of the long-range Army and Navy reconnaissance aircraft based at Espíritu Santo. Tulagi Island was originally set to be the sole target, but when word came that the Japanese had begun building an airfield on nearby Guadalcanal, twenty miles across the Sealark Channel, the main target became Guadalcanal. Maj. Gen. A. A. Vandegrift, commander of the 1st Marine Division, had five weeks to set up his amphibious force, a monumental task. Operation Watchtower, as the invasion was named, was set for August 1, 1942, then postponed to August 7.

A lineup of Guadalcanal personalities: l. to r: Lt. Col. (later Lt. Gen.) Richard Mangrum, CO of VMSB-232; Maj. Robert Vampbell, CO of VMSB-233, recipient of two Navy Crosses; Maj. John L. Smith, CO of VMF-223, 19 kills, recipient of the Medal of Honor; and Capt. Joe Foss, VMF-121, 26 kills, recipient of the Medal of Honor.

The group of Marine pilots, men, and aircraft picked to provide the Corps' air contribution to the invasion was Marine Aircraft Group 23, composed of VMF-223 and VMF-224, VMSB-231, and VMSB-232, all manned by eager but inexperienced young men. The fighter squadrons had previously operated the hated Brewster Buffalo and were quickly reequipped with the more modern Grumman Wildcat, the newer F4F-4 model. The scout bombers upgraded their SBD-1 and -2 Dauntlesses to the newer SBD-3.

Capt. John L. Smith, CO of VMF-223, and Maj. Richard C. Mangrum, the skipper of VMSB-232, were highly experienced aviators and knew that they had only the barest of essentials to take into combat against an experienced and dangerous enemy. For Mangrum, this was his second tour as commanding officer, for he had led 232, then designated as VF-10M, for the month of September 1930, flying Curtiss F6C-4s. He would be nominated for the Medal of Honor for action on August 25, less than a week after he and his unit had arrived at Guadalcanal. Leading his squadron's SBDs against Japanese ships, his bomb did not drop on the first run, but Mangrum remained in the fight until he was able to drop his ordnance. He did not receive the prestigious award and even today, many of his friends believe it was well deserved. Numerous attempts to right what they believe was an injustice have met with failure. However, Mangrum enjoyed a full career and eventually rose to three-star rank.

Captain Smith made the quick decision to exchange twelve of his most junior pilots for a dozen more experienced aviators from VMF-212, based at Efate Island in the New Hebrides, near Espíritu Santo, under Maj. Harold W. Bauer. Major Mangrum flew the pants off his men, cramming in as much flight time and bombing practice as the month's lead time allowed.

The initial landings of August 7 went fairly well, and five days later General Vandegrift was able to report that the 2,600-foot airstrip, which had been partially completed by the Japanese, and finished by his Marines, was ready for operations. Named for Maj. Lofton R. Henderson, killed at Midway leading the Marine dive bombers of VMSB-241, the field received its first aircraft on August 12, when a Navy PBY landed there.

Under constant threat of aerial attacks from the Japanese squadrons based at their huge base at Rabaul, on the northeast tip of New Britain, the Marines on Guadalcanal began calling for their own air support. Transported to the vicinity of Guadalcanal by the escort carrier USS *Long Island* (CVE-1), VMF-223 and VMSB-232 took their nineteen Wildcats

and twelve Dauntlesses down the little carrier's catapults on the morning of August 20 and headed for Henderson Field. (VMF-224 and VMSB-231 remained behind at Espíritu Santo to complete training and would join their comrades soon.)

It was well that the Marine aircrews arrived on August 20, for early on the 21st, the Japanese attacked less than three miles from the air strip, and the newly arrived F4Fs and SBDs were quickly in action, bombing and strafing the 900-man enemy ground force. By noontime, the first aerial combat had taken place when Captain Smith led a four-plane section against six Zeros; the result was a trade-off. One Zero was shot down and two Wildcats barely made it back to Henderson, their pilots making dead-stick landings. TSgt. John Lindley was badly burned and blinded from oil when the tank blew up.

The next several days were taken up with bringing in supplies and preparing for future battle; American and Japanese forces both used the time to advantage. VMSB-232 was constantly in action, its SBDs harassing the Japanese wherever it found them—on the ground or at sea on transports preparing to come ashore. Major Mangrum and his crews were getting a great deal of experience.

The Japanese had a variety of aircraft in operation, from the big, twin-engine Mitsubishi land-based bomber—later code-named "Betty"—to scouting floatplanes such as the Kawanishi "Alf," a large, single-engine, three-seater. But, of course, above all, they had the Zero, ruler of the Pacific skies in the early war.

The Mitsubishi A6M fighter, popularly known as the Zero, resulted from a 1937 specification by the Imperial Japanese Navy for an "escort fighter with dogfight performance superior to that of its opponents . . . an interceptor capable of destroying enemy attacks."[1] The new fighter was the creation of Dr. Jiro Horikoshi, a young engineer with the Nagoya aircraft manufacturing plant of Mitsubishi Heavy Industries. The A6M was a trim, light, radial-engine pacesetter with an enclosed cockpit and retractable landing gear. New metal research, attention to weight saving, and other aerodynamic refinements gave the plane breathtaking maneuverability and incredible range. Both would be sorely needed in the vast reaches of the Pacific. Armed with two 20-mm cannon and two 7.7-mm machine guns, the A6M first flew in April 1939 and was operationally evaluated in China in 1940.

Combat results were beyond even the manufacturer's hopes and incredible to American and British intelligence gatherers. Although such forward observers as Claire Chennault and his Flying Tigers had much first hand experience with the Japanese fighter and tried to alert Allied military leaders to the dangers it posed, they were not believed. The United States went into the war firmly believing that the Japanese flew only copies of Western aircraft. (Even today, there are still adherents to the wartime theory that the Zero was "pirated" from such inadequate American designs as the Vultee P-66.)

For three years after its service introduction as the A6M1 in the summer of 1940, the Zero indeed ruled the Asian skies. No Allied fighter could match the quickness of turn and long legs that enabled the Zero to fight far from its base. (The name derived from the official designation of "Type 00" fighter. The "00," in turn, came from the custom of using the current year of the Japanese calendar, 1940 being 2600 by Japanese reckoning, hence, the shortened "0," or Zero, appellation, which the Japanese themselves liked and apparently used quite regularly.)

However, the seeds of the Zero's destruction lay in its very design. The fighter's high performance was at the expense of pilot and fuel-tank protection, the type being prone to blowing up in smoke and flames after a short burst of American .50-caliber machine-gun fire. Its dive capabilities were also pretty dismal, and any Allied pilot bounced by Zeros or caught in a turning fight with one, could usually disengage with a quick snap roll and dive. As soon as the U.S. pilots realized the Japanese fighter's weaknesses and how to exploit them, the Zero—or Zeke as it was eventually code-named—lost its superiority. Although improvements were made to the Zero throughout the war, including more powerful engines and armament, increased armorplate, and self-sealing fuel tanks, the newer American fighters to come, starting with the Grumman F6F Hellcat and Vought F4U Corsair, were too fast, too powerful, and too well supplied for the Zero.

As Allied experience and confidence grew, Japanese capability decreased. Midway had effectively wiped out a good proportion of the Japanese Navy's most experienced flight crews; Guadalcanal took more. By mid-1943, the Japanese were facing the other side of the coin. Although additional aircraft, many of excellent quality and high capability, continued to be produced, there were just not enough experienced pilots and crews to operate them successfully. The Zero was passé by 1944. And it all seemed to begin to end at Guadalcanal.

Cactus in the Pacific

"Cactus" was the Allied code name for Guadalcanal, and the Navy, Marine, and Army Air Force squadrons that fought in defense of the Allied invasion through the last months of 1942 were collectively known as the Cactus Air Force. It was a lonely, motley band of brother airmen who formed this group. At the core, however, were the Marines. It was their show. By August 30, the second group of MAG-23—VMF-224 and VMSB-231—had touched down at Henderson, bringing an additional nineteen Wildcats and twelve SBDs, giving the Marines a total of twenty-six F4Fs and thirty Dauntlesses.

Two important figures in the fighting in the Solomons. On the left, Maj. Gen. Roy S. Geiger, commanding the Cactus Air Force, and Capt. Joe Foss of VMF-121, who gained most of his 26 kills during the Guadalcanal campaign.

One further addition was fifty-seven-year-old Brig. Gen. Roy S. Geiger, Marine Aviator Number 5. Geiger, who had flown in World War I, now found himself in the thick of the most important battle the Marines had ever fought. He was in overall command of the Cactus Air Force. Arriving on September 3, Geiger began consolidating his resources. Action was constant and heavy, the SBDs and F4Fs losing many of their original crews, killed or wounded. The Japanese constantly harassed the troops at night with single-plane intruder flights and ground bombardment, which, if nothing else, prohibited sleep, an effective weapon in its own right. Tropical diseases, supply shortages, and maintenance problems made people grumble; their tempers were on short fuses. Undaunted, General Geiger ordered a Dauntless readied in the afternoon of September 22.

With a 1,000-pound bomb mounted on the belly rack, he took off and bombed the Japanese at Cape Esperance, some forty miles to the west. The general's mission gave a boost to the sagging morale on Guadalcanal.

More squadrons and aircraft began to trickle in: VMSB-141, under Maj. Gordon Bell, arrived on September 27, as well as flights of Grumman TBF Avengers, the new torpedo planes that had turned in such a poor showing at Midway but that were to prove to be one of the war's outstanding naval attack aircraft.

Several legends grew out of the constant combat at Guadalcanal, including the competition among the aces. Major Smith and Captain Carl were locked in an unofficial race for top score. Carl, of course, had fought at Midway, claiming one Zero on June 4. He shot down four more Japanese planes on August 24 over Guadalcanal to become the first Marine ace, with two more on the 26th. Smith shot down his first Zero on August 21 and had continued scoring steadily.

On September 9, with thirteen planes to his credit, Carl himself was shot down and listed as missing. "I was flying my thirteenth mission at Guadalcanal, in my old number thirteen Wildcat, and had just made my thirteenth kill. Next thing I knew I was sitting in a flying junk heap with a fire in the cockpit. Some crafty Zero pilot had hit me before I even knew he was there."[2] Bailing out of his burning Wildcat, Carl landed in the water. Rescued by natives who kept him hidden from patrolling Japanese, he eventually made it back to Henderson four days later. There he found Smith's score now stood at sixteen, three more than his own. For their efforts during the Guadalcanal campaign, the two aces received their country's highest medals. Carl gained his second Navy Cross, and Smith received the Medal of Honor, more for his overall performance than for any one action.

Smith was a tough, capable aviator from Oklahoma. After graduating from college in 1936, he had taken an Army commission in the artillery, but he swapped it for one in the Marine Corps. He always drove himself both in the air and on the ground. He could be difficult to work with and live with. He had a family and a strong wife in Louise Outland Smith, from Norfolk, Virginia. While her husband was at war, she kept the family together, as did countless thousands of other women. When he returned from the war zone, she always helped him as he adjusted to life away from the bullets and burning Zeros and Wildcats. But it was hard. Eventually, they separated, and Smith, whose career never went beyond his achieving the rank of colonel, to his great chagrin, took his own life in 1972.

Again, Marion Carl remembers:

> John L. Smith [was] an ambitious no-nonsense officer. It was peculiar how he was usually called by his full name, like J. Edgar Hoover, although some of us called him "Smitty." But whatever anyone called the CO, or whatever they thought about him, one thing became certain: John L. Smith may have had his faults, but combat leadership was not among them.
>
> War correspondent Richard Tregakis . . . described Smith as "a prairie type" [Smith was part Indian]; tanned face, wide cheekbones, erect head, a thick neck set on square shoulders and a big sinewy body. He has the steadiest eyes [I] have ever seen: brown and wideset.[3]

As another writer put it years later, "The true measure of John Smith's value . . . is found, not in heroism—of which he had much—but in tactical skill and leadership as a fighter squadron commander . . . He was a true professional and that was what it took to make fighter pilots out of a dozen boys in fifty days."[4]

By the time VMF-223 and MAG-23 rotated out of Guadalcanal in October, VMF-223 had accounted for eighty-three Japanese planes downed, two-thirds of the total achieved by the entire Cactus Air Force during the period August to October 1942. VMF-224, under Maj. Robert Galer, was not idle during this time. Arriving on August 30, the new pilots accompanied the aviators of VMF-223 for a few missions to gain their combat initiation. On September 2, their first contact with Japanese aircraft saw Major Galer

[Opposite] A Wildcat pilot positions his fighter for takeoff from Guadalcanal in February 1943. The dust and low-hanging clouds are characteristic of the weather and operating conditions.

[Below] Maj. Robert Galer leans against his Wildcat wearing his squadron ball cap. The CO of VMF-224 scored 13 kills in the Solomons, received the Medal of Honor and commanded an aircraft group in Korea before retiring as a brigadier general.

open his squadron's scorecard with two Zeros downed. He would eventually wind up with thirteen kills and the Medal of Honor. (Of the eleven Marine pilots who received the Medal of Honor in World War II, five received the award for action at Guadalcanal during 1942 and 1943.)

VMF-121's advance party arrived in late September, and the entire squadron arrived soon afterward with combat operations beginning October 11. The skipper of VMF-121 was an Annapolis Marine, Maj. Leonard Davis; his executive officer was a twenty-seven-year-old captain from South Dakota, Joseph J. Foss. Foss would become the Marines' second-ranking ace of the war, with twenty-six victories. Only "Pappy" Boyington, the hard-charging commander of VMF-214, would achieve a greater score of twenty-eight. VMF-121 flew throughout October, with Joe Foss gaining his first kill on the 13th, only to be nearly shot down himself, and making a hot, emergency landing back at Henderson.

The Japanese kept up the day and night bombardment of Guadalcanal. Sleep was a luxury seldom enjoyed. On the night of October 13, a particularly devastating shelling from two Japanese battleships had disabled most of the remaining operational SBDs. Only seven Dauntlesses were flyable. More than forty men had been killed, including the commanding officer, executive officer, and three pilots of VMSB-141. The makeshift operations building, nicknamed the Pagoda, was put out of commission and eventually torn down by order of General Geiger, who had long suspected the structure of being used as an aiming point by the offshore enemy. There were still Navy and Army fighters available, and these would be used to the utmost in the days to come.

On October 15 the Japanese began offloading men and supplies only ten miles away from Henderson, in preparation for an offensive to retake the air strip. Down to their last fuel supplies, the Marines of Cactus mounted what opposition they could against the enemy ships. The nightly bombardment continued and four more SBDs were destroyed. Two of the remaining three were written off in taxiing accidents, and the third, flown by Lt. Bob Patterson of VMSB-141, made a desultory solo attack against the transports anchored just offshore.

By this time, like a gift from the gods, a hidden two-day supply of fuel was found—it was probably cached by the Japanese in hopes of a possible return—and at least the Marine fighters were back in business. With no flyable SBDs, the offensive power of the Marine contingent was nil; the enemy transports continued to unload, unhindered, except for sporadic attention by Espíritu Santo–based B-17s and carrier-based Navy dive bombers. Even the fighters of VMF-121, led by Major Davis, made some strafing runs.

But the situation was desperate. The Japanese were coming, and the American resupply efforts that were under way would probably arrive too late to be of much help to the hard-pressed force. Thus, the effort of one Marine major on October 14 was very much appreciated. Jack R. Cram, aide and pilot to General Geiger, had been using Geiger's personal PBY, nicknamed the "Blue Goose," to bring in supplies from Espíritu Santo. On one run to Guadalcanal, he brought two torpedoes, filched from Navy Torpedo Squadron Eight, and he prevailed upon his boss to let him take a crack at the Japanese transports anchored so temptingly nearby. Reluctantly, General Geiger agreed, growling, "Don't get that plane shot up!"

With a jury-rigged bomb-release mechanism, Cram took off in the Catalina and headed for his targets at 6,000 feet, the PBY straining to climb to the altitude. A decoy flight of SBDs—twelve had been patched together by the miracle workers at Henderson—drew enemy fire away from the lumbering PBY as Cram began his run. Diving to 75 feet above the water, going at what he later said was 240 miles per hour, 90 mph faster than he should have, Cram dropped his two torpedoes while fierce anti-aircraft fire and waiting Zeros chased after him. Wringing the straining patrol bomber around, he headed back for Henderson, but not before he had the satisfaction of seeing one of the transports explode in a ball of flame, mortally wounded.

Arriving back over Henderson, Cram saw most of the Zeros depart in the face of concentrated American anti-aircraft fire, but one Japanese fighter grimly hung on, determined to scrub the audacious American raider.

Then a Wildcat, flown by 2nd Lt. Roger Haberman, entered the landing pattern, its wheels down in preparation for landing, its own engine smoking. Seeing the beleaguered Catalina's dilemma, and with his landing gear still down, Haberman hauled himself around and behind the pursuing Zero and dispatched it with a burst of machine-gun fire.

When he landed the PBY, Cram counted 175 bullet holes in the aircraft; fortunately, none of his crew was hurt. The general was advancing toward Cram, a scowl on his face, as he surveyed his aide and the remains of his personal plane. After reading Cram the riot act, threatening to court-martial him, Geiger could not keep up the charade and broke into a huge grin. He pumped Cram's hand and congratulated his pilot on the success of his courageous mission. On Geiger's recommendation, Cram was awarded the Navy Cross.

The press instantly labeled him "Mad Jack Cram." He later said, "I guess some people thought I was mad, or at least unbalanced!" (Cram went on to command VMB-612, a night bombing squadron, and rose to brigadier general before retiring in 1959.) Recalling his mission forty years later, Cram explained his reason for going: "At a time like that you don't think about anything but the situation. You have to remember that at any point there was some question whether we would be able to hold Guadalcanal. . . . It seemed like a reasonable solution to the problem."[5] Cram's raid gave a much-needed lift to the Cactus Air Force. Although subsequent attacks put a dent in the Japanese supply efforts, the threat of a massive attack continued. Indeed, Japanese surface ships cruised along the shore, pumping night-time fire into the lonely base at Henderson. By the morning of October 16, only nine F4Fs remained operational to confront a Japanese attack. Geiger put in a hurried call to Efate for Lt. Col. Harold W. Bauer's VMF-212, which arrived that afternoon with nineteen Wildcats and even seven fully crewed SBDs. The only problem was that VMF-212 arrived over Henderson during a Japanese bombing attack. Wasting no time, with his fuel nearly exhausted, Bauer pounced on the Aichi Type 99 "Val" dive bombers and quickly shot down four of the raiders in rapid succession and within plain view of the grateful witnesses on the field. This auspicious beginning to VMF-212's stay at Guadalcanal earned Bauer the Medal of Honor.

Things were changing in Marine air on Guadalcanal. People were rotating home for a much-deserved rest, while others came to take their places. John Smith and Marion Carl, and now–Lt. Col. Richard Mangrum, had left on October 11 and 12. MAG-23 was relieved on October 16 by MAG-14. During its tour on Guadalcanal from August 20 to October 16, the group had claimed 244 Japanese aircraft shot down, while losing twenty-two pilots serving with MAG-23 and another thirty-three who had put in tours of exchange duty with attached Navy and Army units.

The Battle of Santa Cruz

The months of October and November 1942 were to prove crucial in the Battle for Guadalcanal. The Japanese were preparing for a major offensive to throw the Americans off the island. On October 25, the attacks began, with raids on Henderson coming from air, sea, and land. Henderson and its

[Opposite] An exuberant Lt. Col. Harold Bauer demonstrates his Zero-killing technique for his admiring ground crew. Called "Indian Joe" or "Coach," Bauer was well liked and respected, and his loss in combat was keenly felt. Inspection of his flight suit fits reveals how thin he might have become since his football-playing days at Annapolis, indicating the less-than-acceptable conditions on the 'Canal.

adjacent fighter strip, nicknamed the "cow pasture" because of its propensity for turning into a quagmire during the torrential rains frequently seen in the area, were in for some very hard times.

A carrier battle developed on the 25th, involving two large opposing forces: two American task forces, 16 and 17, with the carriers *Enterprise* and *Hornet* as their respective centerpieces, and a large Japanese fleet with four carriers and major supporting vessels. Operating under its new commander, Adm. W. F. "Bull" Halsey, and after spending most of the previous day searching for the Japanese fleet, the American force drew first blood on the 26th. SBDs from the *Enterprise* found and heavily damaged the carrier *Zuiho*. The SBD Dauntlesses and TBF Avengers of the American task forces pounded the enemy fleet, while screening destroyers attempted to protect the carriers with intensive anti-aircraft fire.

The *Hornet*, however, was damaged around 9:00 AM on the 26th by a heavy and determined Japanese air attack that left the carrier gravely wounded and dead in the water. The battle raged back and forth between the carrier fleets, each side trading attack against counterattack, with several ships of all types sunk on both sides. The damaged *Hornet* was struck by a submarine-launched torpedo, and as the *Enterprise* recovered her own aircraft and those of her sister carrier, an afternoon aerial attack by Japanese planes sealed the *Hornet*'s fate. Still floating after attempts to sink her by gunfire had failed, the gallant ship—deliverer of America's first offensive operation, the April 18 Tokyo Raid by Jimmy Doolittle and his B-25s—was abandoned and left to the prowling Japanese who sunk her in the early morning of the 27th.

The Battle of Santa Cruz had cost the Japanese two carriers damaged, numerous support ships, and 100 aircraft; the Americans had lost the *Hornet* and 74 planes, as well as several surface vessels. But for the Americans, the major objective of the confrontation had been achieved: the Japanese had been denied entrance to the Sealark Channel, offshore of Henderson Field, and the Marines still held the "cow pasture."

In the hectic, pressure-filled months of late October and November 1942, there was only one fully operational U.S. carrier, the *Enterprise*. This situation caused the Navy to fly many of its aircraft to Henderson to operate alongside the Marines, as well as to take advantage of the maintenance facilities, such as they were, on Guadalcanal. This was one of the few times that Navy and Marine pilots flew and fought in the exact same aircraft; the Marines did not have different equipment from that of their Navy

[Opposite] Ground crews fight a small fire in a Wildcat started when Japanese raiders dropped bombs on target in December 1942. Every fighter was extremely valuable, and it was fortunate that this F4F was not badly damaged and was back in the air shortly after this photo was taken.

[Top Right] Marine SBDs fly to their target from Henderson Field in 1943. These aircraft carry a single 500-pound bomb on the main belly rack.

[Bottom Right] Grumman TBF Avenger torpedo bombers taxi on Henderson Field before a mission in 1943. The big TBF, nicknamed "Turkey" by its crews, served in several Marine, as well as Navy, squadrons as a torpedo bomber and, later at Okinawa, as a close-air-support aircraft.

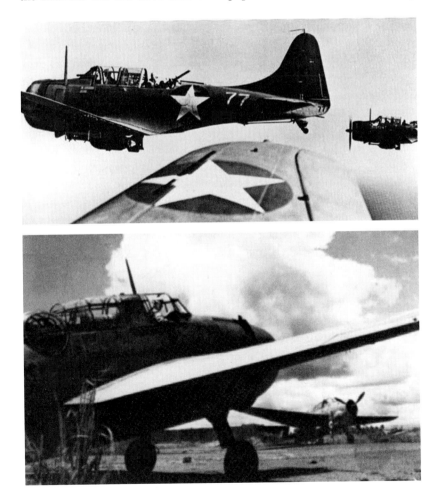

counterparts. Their Wildcats and Dauntlesses were the same. Thus, the Navy Department had two "carriers" operating at the "Canal": the mobile *Enterprise* and the "fixed, zero-speed" carrier at Henderson.

Even though no Japanese victory had been obtained, Admiral Isoroku Yamomoto, Commander-in-Chief of the Imperial Navy's Combined Fleet, was not through. He had masterminded the Pearl Harbor attack, and now he had supplies and more than 14,000 troops in transports headed for Guadalcanal, protected by battleships and cruisers. Target date for a landing was November 13.

The Americans themselves were bringing in new men and aircraft to fortify Cactus Base and Henderson Field. A new air group, MAG-11, arrived on November 1, the SBDs of VMSB-132 arriving first, with VMF-112 landing the next day. Also, a major personnel change occurred on November 7, when Major General Geiger, the quintessential Air Marine, was relieved by newly promoted Brig. Gen. Lou Woods. Geiger's departure was tinged with bitterness on his part, because he felt he was being unjustly relieved just when the most crucial battles were coming. But the strain on Geiger was there for all to see. He had been there since the beginning and had no apologies to make for the way he ran things. A younger, fresher man in the slot was perhaps the best thing.

Soon after Geiger's departure, MAG-11 was put to its first combat test when seven SBDs of VMSB-132 were sent out to attack a large destroyer fleet trying to land troops. Covered by twelve P-39s of the veteran 67th Pursuit Squadron, longtime denizens of Henderson, the Dauntlesses pressed their attacks. They were met by ten Rufe fighters, floatplane adaptations of the Zero built by Nakajima. VMF-112, led by Maj. Paul Fontana, with seven F4Fs, shot down six Rufes, their pilots successfully bailing out. Then, as if by signal, all six Japanese fliers unbuckled their parachute harnesses to drop to their deaths in the water below.

VMF-121 was along, too. Captain Foss shot down a float biplane, probably from one of the destroyers below, and then turned to meet another Japanese aircraft. The crew of the second floatplane was more cunning, and the pilot cut power to make Foss overshoot and give the rear gunner a good target. Hit in the cowling and cockpit canopy, Foss swung his Wildcat around and finally dispatched the enemy aircraft with a burst. Foss shot down another two-seat scout, for a total of three kills that afternoon, and suddenly found himself very much alone in the sky.

Disoriented, his fuel low, and his aircraft's engine running rough, he was forced to ditch offshore of little Malaita Island, where some natives sheltered him for the night. The next day, Jack Cram flew up to transport Foss home to Henderson. Foss was also to receive the Medal of Honor for his overall contribution during his time at Guadalcanal, rather than for a specific action, similar to John Smith's award.

The Battle for Guadalcanal

On the night of November 12–13, American ships fought a classic naval battle against a larger Japanese force in what has been called the First Battle of Guadalcanal. Steaming south toward Florida Island, the Japanese delivered

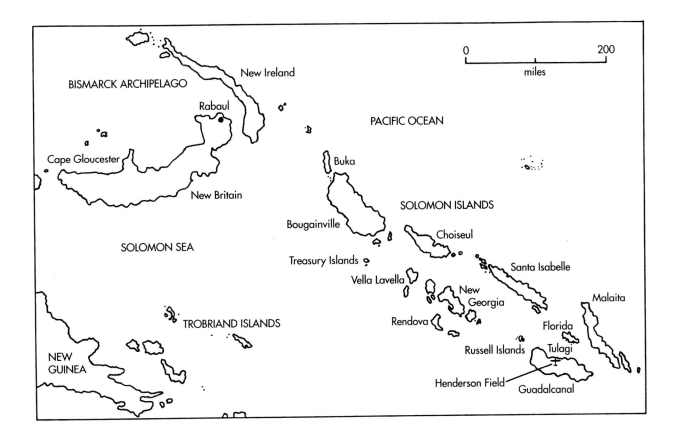

BISMARCK ARCHIPELAGO

New Ireland

Rabaul

Cape Gloucester

New Britain

PACIFIC OCEAN

Buka

SOLOMON ISLANDS

SOLOMON SEA

Bougainville

Choiseul

Treasury Islands

Santa Isabelle

Vella Lavella

Malaita

New
Georgia

TROBRIAND ISLANDS

Rendova

Florida

Russell Islands

Tulagi

NEW
GUINEA

Henderson Field

Guadalcanal

0   200
miles

Map 3: The Southwest Pacific
Campaign, 1942–44

a tactical defeat to the American fleet, sinking a cruiser and four destroyers and damaging several other ships. During the battle, two American rear admirals were killed, Daniel Callaghan on the bridge of his flagship USS *San Francisco* (CA-38), and Norman Scott, on the bridge of the cruiser USS *Atlanta* (CLAA-51). These men, their commands, and the sacrifice, albeit unintentional, of their ships, kept the attention of the Japanese away from their objective, Henderson.

On November 14–15, the Second Battle of Guadalcanal was fought, some of it in daylight. The Japanese were sending a huge reinforcement group down The Slot, the channel between the northern shores of New Georgia and Guadalcanal, and the southern coasts of the islands of Choiseul and Santa Isabel. This looked like it could be the battle. Planes from the *Enterprise* made continuous attacks, along with land-based raiders from Cactus, starting at 8:30 AM, right until sunset. Even B-17s from Espíritu Santo flew some missions. Six transports—one-half the transport fleet—were sunk. However, by midnight another night engagement had developed as a second Japanese force, coming from the north, had been discovered by a small American fleet of two battleships and four destroyers. When it was over, the Japanese had lost two battleships, a cruiser, three destroyers, and ten transports, as well as 4,000 troops and their equipment.

Henderson continued to suffer nightly bombardment. The Army Air Force's resources had been augmented by the arrival of eight Lockheed P-38s on November 12, and the twin-engine, twin-tailed fighters were welcome additions to the always hard-pressed P-39 squadron, the 67th.

SBDs from VMSB-142 attacked the old battleship *Hiei,* one Marine Dauntless planting a 1,000-pound bomb squarely amidships. Joe Foss led six Wildcats as escorts for a second attack by VMSB-131, and also to try their luck at strafing the struggling *Hiei,* which had suffered more than eighty-five hits and had lost steering control. TBF torpedo planes bracketed the *Hiei* for good measure. The Japanese ended up scuttling the ship.

Strikes on the 14th were on a shuttle schedule, with Marine and Navy dive and torpedo bombers taking off for runs on the advancing Japanese, meeting with varying degrees of success and opposition. However, a major loss was that of Lt. Col. "Indian Joe" Bauer, who *was* part Indian, commanding officer of VMF-212, who had put in such a spectacular opening performance upon his arrival. Flying escort for the last attacks on November 14, Bauer and his F4Fs were jumped by Zeros, one of which Bauer shot down. He was then apparently hit by anti-aircraft fire from the ships below and had to ditch his fighter. The last Joe Foss and another pilot saw of Bauer, he was swimming away from his sinking airplane, seemingly okay. Although search missions were launched, no trace of Bauer was found. In a few brief weeks, he had shot down eleven Japanese aircraft and gained the respect and admiration of all who flew and fought with him.

The Second Battle of Guadalcanal permanently denied the Japanese any major landing on the island and a chance to retake their airfield. Admiral Halsey wrote later: "Now, nearly five years later, I can face the alternative frankly. If our ships and planes had been routed in this battle, if we had lost it, our troops on Guadalcanal would have been trapped as were our troops on Bataan . . . the enemy would have driven south."[6] This is in the clear light of historical perspective. At the time, however, the Japanese had a few thoughts yet on Guadalcanal, but their supplies had now to be floated in on the tide.

New blood was being supplied to the Marines, too. For the combat-weary mud-Marines of the 1st Marine Division, the Army sent in its 25th Infantry Division. Brigadier General Woods was relieved as COMAIRCACTUS, a somewhat unofficial title, by Brig. Gen. Francis P. Mulcahy, Marine Aviator Number 64, another old hand. The first units of the Allies' air resources made their appearance on November 26 when a Royal New Zealand Air Force squadron of Lockheed Hudsons—twin-engine, land-based patrol bombers—landed at Henderson.

[Opposite] A squadron of Nakajima A6M2-N Rufe floatplanes at their base somewhere in the Solomons, 1943. The Rufe was a version of the Mitsubishi Zero, which was produced by the rival Nakajima firm. Despite the heavy, drag-producing floats, the Rufe retained much of the legendary maneuverability of the landplane Zero. (Courtesy Robert Mikesh)

[Right] Another Medal of Honor recipient from Guadalcanal, Jefferson DeBlanc shot down five Japanese fighters while he was escorting a strike group on January 31, 1943.

December saw aerial action continue, though at a somewhat reduced pace from the earlier hectic months. On December 1, Maj. Joe Sailer Jr., tireless commander of VMSB-132, was shot down by an enemy floatplane after making an attack on Japanese destroyers. Sailer radioed that his dive brakes would not retract, which meant he would have to ditch his now-disabled Dauntless. It was at this vulnerable moment that he was hit by the "Pete" biplane, which was often a dangerous opponent, enjoying good maneuverability and when flown by a competent crew able to give a good account of itself. Sailer had flown twenty-five missions in five weeks and had scored six hits on enemy ships. His loss was that of a future leader and highly skilled dive bomber pilot, and he received a posthumous Navy Cross for his work.

By Christmas 1942 the Japanese position was really untenable. Their troops remaining on Guadalcanal were sick and short of food, medicine, and ammunition, and the American base at Henderson was searching out and destroying the enemy everywhere. January brought an increase in Japanese strength and activity, but it was not the same as the early summer and fall days of the past year.

The Marine units, VMF-112, VMF-121, VMSB-144, and VMSB-234, were active. And on January 31, 1943, Lt. Jeff DeBlanc earned the Medal of Honor when he escorted a strike over Vella Lavella, near Bougainville, a main Japanese staging area. Leading six Wildcats, DeBlanc, flying at 14,000 feet, sighted a number of Zeros and Rufe floatplanes heading for his charges. The Louisiana native immediately dove to break off the Japanese attack, shooting down three Rufes and two Zeros that had joined the fight. His skill and bravery enabled the bombers to complete their mission, although DeBlanc and another pilot, SSgt. James A. Feliton, had to abandon their Wildcats over Kolombangara Island to the west. They were cared for by a coast watcher on Kolombangara until a plane could be sent up from Guadalcanal to get them.

By early February 1943, it was all but over. Japanese ships began evacuation on the 7th, continuing until the next day. Japan had been handed its first major land defeat after six months of the bloodiest fighting in the history of warfare. Because of the intensity of the fighting, as well as lack of record keeping during and immediately after the battle, the cost for both sides is open to conjecture. Estimates of Japanese aircraft lost during the campaign range from 36 fighters and bombers to 263, including 75 various types, such as floatplanes and transports. The American estimates of the Cactus Air Force's losses are put at 101 aircraft, a ratio of 1.3:1 or 2.6:1.

Ninety-four American pilots were killed at Guadalcanal. However, as Brig. Gen. Samuel B. Griffith II, who, as a lieutenant colonel, commanded the much-feared and admired Marine Raiders on Guadalcanal during some of the fiercest fighting on the island, later wrote, "In the cold perspective of history, the relative importance of a military campaign is not judged by statistics . . . it is the ultimate effect which the battle . . . exerts on the conduct and result of the war that should be considered."[7] As satisfying and deserving a victory as Guadalcanal was for the Americans, it is also important to note that the Japanese seemed to have the momentum knocked out of them. The vital force that had carried the island nation from China to Pearl Harbor and the Philippines was lost, along with Guadalcanal. As the search for reasons began in Tokyo, many accusing fingers were pointed. But, one who would not be there, and one who would have certainly come in for his share of criticism, was Admiral Isoroku Yamamoto.

This brilliant tactician was shot down and killed in his transport on April 18, 1943, while on an inspection trip in the Solomons area. In a beautifully executed mission, Army Air Force P-38s caught the two Betty transports and their Zero escorts in a surprise strike and shot down the two bombers, killing Yamamoto. (The wreck of his plane still survives in the jungle.) The Japanese were denied the mind and leadership of this professional soldier at a time when they could not afford such a loss.

An interesting sidelight to the Yamamoto mission was that it was a Marine who actually plotted the intercept course for the Army fighters. Maj. John P. Condon was the Fighter Command Operations officer for ComAirSols, and he duly laid out a route that would take the eighteen P-38s in through the back door at Kahili, fifty feet above the water, to avoid Japanese radar detection. Because the Japanese code had been broken, Yamamoto's itinerary was known, down to the last detail—takeoff times, route, and number of escorting Zeros.

The P-38s were divided into two sections, escorts and "shooters, those Lightnings that would actually go after the admiral's transport." As they drifted out of communications range on the morning of the 18th, there was little anyone on the ground could do but wait. Finally, the excited voices of the Army pilots began to come in, telling of their success. As the fighters approached their home field, Capt. Thomas G. Lanphier and his wingman, Lt. Rex T. Barber, swung into victory rolls. Lanphier radioed Major Condon that "that S.O.B. would never dictate anything in the White House—or anywhere!" It was a proud moment for everyone concerned. The Japanese were understandably furious, because that night they pounded the Americans from sunset to sunrise. It was a sure thing, as far as U.S. servicemen were concerned, that Yamamoto was indeed dead.

5 Island Hopping

THE CAMPAIGN FOR GUADALCANAL gave proponents of Marine aviation ammunition in making their case for a beefed-up air arm. Outgoing Marine Corps Commandant, Gen. Thomas Holcomb, had named Gen. Alexander Vandegrift as his successor, but Vandegrift had to take temporary command of I Marine Amphibious Corps (I MAC). He later turned over this important job to Maj. Gen. Roy Geiger.

After Guadalcanal, the drive through the Solomons to gain the bases needed to support a strategic bombing campaign against the Japanese home islands—hopefully with the powerful new B-29 Superfortresses that were beginning to roll off various Boeing assembly lines—began to take shape. New aircraft had also begun to arrive in Marine fighter squadrons to replace the dependable, but obsolescent, F4F Wildcat. The first of these new fighters was the big Chance Vought F4U Corsair. Known variously as "Hose Nose," "Hog," "Bent-wing Bird," or just plain "U," the Corsair was one of the greatest naval aircraft of the war.

A Corsair production line in 1942. The massive 2,000-hp Pratt & Whitney engine and various "plumbing" behind the engine are well shown. (Vought Photo)

The prototype XF4U-1 first flew in May 1940, with an inverted gull wing enabling the 2,000-horsepower Pratt and Whitney radial to swing a thirteen-foot-diameter propeller without correspondingly long landing gear. The huge fighter was an obvious world beater, but the massive nose and resulting limited visibility gave rise to fears that carrier landings could present dangerous problems. Reluctant to accept the new fighter for carrier operations, the Navy handed it over to the Marines. By June 1942, Corsair production was in full swing and September brought the first carrier qualification tests.

Fears about the plane's handling around the ship were borne out, the F4U developing a stall and resulting loss of control during the close-in, slower-speed phase of the landing approach. Modifications were instituted, but in the meantime, the plane was desperately needed in the Pacific, and it was determined that it would operate from land bases, with both Navy and Marine units.

Accordingly, VMF-124, under Maj. William E. Gise, flew its new F4U-1s to Guadalcanal in February 1943. The new fighters began combat operations in company with Army P-38s and P-40s, acting as escorts for an attack by Navy PB4Y-1s, the Navy models of the B-24 Liberator four-engine bomber, against Kahili, a big Japanese airfield on Bougainville. The combat debut of the Corsair was hardly auspicious. More than fifty defending Zeros met the attack head on, shooting down ten American aircraft, including two of the new F4Us, for the loss of only four of their own.

Shaken, the Marines of VMF-124 determined to use their new mount's superior speed and firepower to combat the lighter, more maneuverable Zero. By September 1943, all eight Marine fighter squadrons in the Pacific had transitioned to the Corsair. Indeed, as far as the public at home was concerned, the F4U was the only aircraft flown by the Marines. The average American could hardly be blamed for thinking so, with names like Walsh, Hanson, and Boyington—all recipients of the Medal of Honor for action in the Corsairs—constantly in the headlines and movie newsreels.

Once its pilots learned its idiosyncrasies and adjusted for the lack of view forward, the F4U did everything: bombing, strafing, rocket delivery, photo reconnaissance, and, of course, aerial combat. The Corsair accounted for 2,140 enemy aircraft in the Pacific, with a loss of 189 F4Us (this total includes both Navy and Marine victories), second only to the Grumman Hellcat in total kills for a single type. The Corsair was to continue in production until January 1953, when the last of 12,571 "Us" rolled off the line.

Bougainville and the Solomons

After Guadalcanal, Navy carrier resources in the Pacific were at an all-time low. Only the *Enterprise* and *Saratoga* were operational, and it would be mid-summer before any new flattops joined the fleet. The Marines would have to shoulder much of the burden for the Navy's air contribution to the war effort. In February 1943 Rear Adm. Charles P. Mason was chosen to head the newly established post of Commander, Aircraft, Solomons (ComAirSols). This new organization had control of all land-based naval air assets, excluding search and rescue, which accounted for thirty-two fighter

1st. Lt. Ken Walsh connects his earphones in the cockpit of his VMF-124 Corsair in August 1943. He is flying a "bird cage" F4U-1, an early model with a distinctive canopy. Also note the white tape just below the windscreen, which was used to prevent fuel leaks. Walsh received the Medal of Honor when he tangled with 50 Japanese airplanes. A former enlisted pilot, Walsh ended the war with 21 kills.

and bomber squadrons, including six Marine units. AirSols was composed of Army, Navy, Marine, and New Zealand officers, and the post of commander rotated among them with fair regularity.

After their humiliating defeat at Guadalcanal, the Japanese organized a massive punitive sweep against Guadalcanal and New Guinea, called the "I Operation." To begin the offensive, fifty-eight Zeros attempted to raid Guadalcanal on April 1, 1943. They met a force of American fighter pilots, including the eager young Marines of VMF-124, anxious to rack up some kills with their new Corsairs. Among the Marines of VMF-124 was 1st Lt. Ken Walsh, a former enlisted Naval Aviation Pilot (NAP), who had been commissioned after Pearl Harbor and posted to the squadron. Walsh had nearly been killed a few months before when he had to ditch his F4U after the engine quit. The heavy aircraft sank like a stone, taking its pilot down with it, but, keeping his cool, Walsh quickly unstrapped underwater and bobbed to the surface.

On April 1 Walsh had ample opportunity to test the Corsair's reliability and combat prowess, shooting down two Zeros. A second ditching, however, followed a few days later, but did not lessen his enthusiasm. On May 13, he became the first Corsair ace when he destroyed three more Zeros. By mid-August, he had doubled his score to ten. On August 30, Walsh fought an incredible battle against fifty Japanese aircraft, which he originally mistook for the bombers he was tasked with escorting.

He shot down four enemy fighters in the melee before another Zero tacked itself onto his tail and proceeded to shoot holes in his airplane, mortally wounding the struggling Corsair. With his engine crippled, Walsh prepared for his third water landing in six months! But the Zero kept hammering him from behind until another Corsair and an Army P-40 arrived to scare off the Japanese pilot, leaving Walsh to ditch in peace. Rescued, Walsh was returned to the United States, where President Franklin D. Roosevelt awarded him the Medal of Honor for his exploits. He finished the war with twenty-one kills to his credit, most of which were obtained during the intense period of combat in mid-1943.

On April 7, another big Japanese attack found seventy-six Army, Navy, and Marine defenders waiting. The American pilots piled into the Japanese formations, and 1st Lt. James E. Swett, flying an F4F, shot down seven Val

dive bombers, the greatest number of kills on a single mission scored to that time. Swett, too, was forced to ditch his battered fighter and await rescue. He also received the Medal of Honor.

The I Operation was not a very successful venture for the Japanese, and after two large attacks on New Guinea, the operation was recalled by Admiral Yamamoto. This was his last official act as commander of the Japanese fleet resources.

Marine fighter squadrons, with an increasing number of Corsairs, were in action continually. VMF-213 was especially active. Its pilots had some incredible experiences, including Lt. Gil Percy's 2,000-foot fall with a streaming parachute on June 7 (he lived to talk about it) and SSgt. William Coffeen's odyssey by raft after being shot down on April 13 near Munda. With his survival equipment lost when his raft capsized, Coffeen paddled to a deserted island, rested for two days, and then struck out for another island. Existing on whatever food he found, he was rescued in a state of delirium by a native who looked after him until a PBY came for him. Coffeen had been missing for seventy-three days.

Lt. Sheldon Hall, also of VMF-213, was shot down on July 18. After the enemy pilot strafed him in his raft, Hall paddled to an island, which turned out to be held by the Japanese. He spent the next four days hiding out, eventually finding a native village whose inhabitants proved helpful—it was not always that way—and fed him. They finally took him to a coast watcher, who called a PBY to rescue Hall and a TBF crew the coast watcher had been guarding. The Pacific theater was full of escape, evasion, and rescue stories like these.

"Pappy" Boyington

The assault on Bougainville, largest of the Solomon Islands, began on November 1, 1943, catching the Japanese off guard, but they counterattacked

on the 7th. The battle continued through the interminable rain, mud, and jungle heat that taxed attacker and defender alike. The storming of Bougainville received generous air support. ComAirSols was now Maj. Gen. Ralph J. Mitchell, who had been Director of Marine Corps Aviation from 1939 to 1943. He had fifty-two squadrons at his command, including fourteen Marine units, and 728 aircraft. Army fighters and bombers—B-24s, B-25s, and P-40s—pounded the Japanese daily, while Marine squadrons, all now converted to the Corsair, participated in fighter sweeps, the main practitioner of which was a twenty-nine-year-old major named Gregory R. Boyington from Idaho. His squadron, VMF-214, called him "Grandpappy," or "Gramps," because of his "advanced" age for a fighter pilot; the newspapers shortened it to "Pappy." His older associates referred to him by his pre-war moniker of "Rats," while what some of his superiors may have called him is best left unsaid.

Boyington was one of a kind, the archetypical fighter pilot: cool, self-confident almost to abrasiveness, sure of eye, and always ready for a fight, in the air or on the ground; the opponent made no difference. He had been an aviation cadet with VF-9M, flying Boeing F4Bs, and was usually in some sort of light-hearted trouble. As a first lieutenant, he resigned his commission in 1941 to join the Flying Tigers, or American Volunteer Group (AVG), as Claire Chennault's band was actually known. (The Flying Tiger sobriquet was attributed to the high-spirited remarks of Chiang Kai-shek's wife, a patron of the AVG.) Boyington claimed six—not all officially substantiated—kills in China, making him one of the first American aces, albeit not under American colors, before the U.S. entry into World War II.

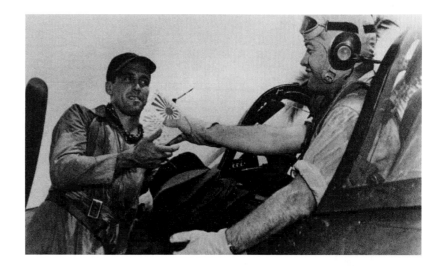

Ultimately returning to the States after Pearl Harbor, Boyington was shocked and angered to find that he was labeled a traitor and malcontent who had left his country in time of crisis. Even though he was an experienced fighter pilot, an ace, he was told that his services were not needed. While he parked cars, Boyington fumed, sent off a letter to the Assistant Secretary of the Navy, and eventually received orders to active duty and a commission as a major.

Shipping overseas to Guadalcanal in May 1943, Boyington found himself a squadron. He later wrote: "I finally thought my break had arrived . . . for Elmer Brackett was able to get me into his squadron as an executive officer. . . . We had no more than arrived when Elmer was promoted out of the squadron and I was assigned as commanding officer."[1] He was with VMF-122, flying intensive patrols in the Solomons, but he had no kills to show for it. After several weeks alternating between different squadrons, Boyington prevailed on an old acquaintance, now-Col. "Sandy" Sanderson, a friend from Boyington's VF-9M days, to get him into a real combat squadron. Boyington was given command of VMF-214, which was, at that, even a loaner, the original VMF-214 having just completed a cruise. VMF-214's crew has been described as an outfit of misfits, brawlers, and washouts nobody else wanted. It certainly seemed that way, as Boyington tried to form them into a cohesive unit with himself, an aging fighter pilot, as the skipper.

They needed a nickname. "Boyington's Bastards" was alliterative, but the newspapers would never have printed it, and they settled on "Black Sheep," with an appropriate insignia. The squadron was equipped with the F4U, which Boyington called "a sweet flying baby if ever I flew one," and went into action in the Solomons late in 1943.

On December 17, 1943, he led the first fighter sweep over Rabaul, hurling goading challenges over the radio to the Japanese below to come up and fight. By the end of the year, he had tied the existing score of Foss' twenty-six kills and found himself the object of much publicity. Some of the attention was a little too much for his pugnacious nature, and Boyington did not take his newfound fame too easily. But time was running out for Pappy.

He led a Black Sheep flight over Rabaul on January 3, 1944, from their strip at Vella Lavella. Japanese fighters were waiting, and though he brought down two more Zeros to bring his score to twenty-eight, his wingman was

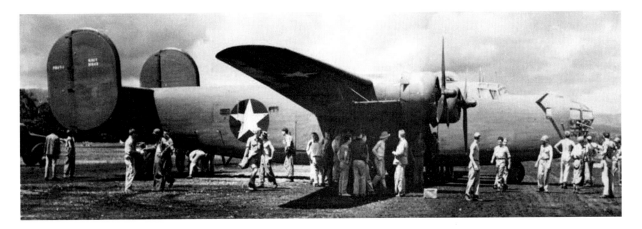

shot down, and Boyington himself finally had to jump from his burning Corsair. Wounded, he floated in the water until he was taken prisoner by the crew of a Japanese submarine. Sent to a prison camp in Japan, Boyington waited out the last twenty months of the war. Listed as missing in action, the fact that he was alive was learned only when his name was painted in huge letters on the roof of one of the camp huts for pilots of American aircraft to see when they dropped supplies to the prisoners of war after the Japanese surrender in August 1945.

Returning home, Boyington found he had been awarded the Medal of Honor. Somewhat belatedly, the Marines gave him the Navy Cross and sent him on a Victory Bond tour. As tough and realistic a man as he was, Boyington took the awards with a touch of cynicism and anger, but his war record remains one of the most colorful of all American combat pilots. The top Marine ace, he later wrote a book, which has become a minor classic of wartime autobiography, *Baa Baa Black Sheep*, published in 1958.

Capt. John M. Foster, a Corsair pilot with VMF-222, a neighbor fighter squadron to Boyington's VMF-214, was one of the "other" aviators who flew, although sporadically, with Boyington. He knew the Marine ace from a distance, and his own book *Hell in the Heavens*, published in 1961, throws some interesting light on how the other pilots viewed Boyington, his reputation, and his flying skill.

Foster first saw Boyington as the VMF-214 commander was reporting a score of four kills to intelligence officers, and later recounts one of the various stories that involved Boyington. The tale concerns a hectic combat during which his squadron mates inquired over the radio as to the ace's whereabouts. He replied that he was occupied.

"I've got five Zeros surrounded."

"Where are they?"

"Outside this cloud they've got me in!"

Foster denied being struck by any hero worship or awe:

I was only interested in Boyington for what information I could learn from him about fighting. . . .

When you're actually associating with such men . . . you do not look upon them with awe. They are just other pilots who sit across the table and eat with you, whom you shower with, get bombed with, and sometimes fight with.[2]

When Boyington was reported missing, Foster admits, the loss was taken pretty hard by everyone, but especially, quite naturally, by the men of VMF-214. "That evening, his heartsick friends went out in the face of a storm to search for Boyington, but they found nothing, not even a trace of wreckage. . . . Every time I saw Boyington I always seemed to think of a bulldog. Perhaps it was the set of his jaw. Perhaps it was the legend he had built around himself."[3]

Retired Lt. Col. John F. Bolt offered several comments about Boyington. As a first lieutenant flying with the Black Sheep, Bolt gained six kills over Japanese Zeros and would go on to become the Corps' first and only jet ace in Korea. "Boyington was a cautious pilot when there was nothing to be gained by being bold or adventurous. He wasn't a good navigator. He usually flew to the closest island he could see, then to the next island. . . . He changed, though. He drank heavily starting pretty much with the second tour. By the time he was lost, he had a real alcohol problem, which caused him to deteriorate in all respects—administration, concern for the other pilots. We were losing a lot of pilots at that point, too. We started going up to Rabaul at the middle of the second tour and Boyington's alcohol problem got the best of him several times."[4]

Bolt commented that "Boyington was a better aviator than most of the COs. He had flown in China with the AVG. . . . A lot of the COs weren't good pilots, didn't know the fine points, and couldn't give the level of leadership that Boyington could—to analyze and anticipate. By the time Boyington had us up in combat for a tour, he had taught us a lot. Our level of expertise was climbing while his deteriorated."

Several veteran Marine fighter squadrons returned to their old Pacific haunts during this time, among them VMF-223, now led by the redoubtable Maj. Marion Carl, veteran of Midway and Guadalcanal. VMF-223 left its base at El Toro, south of Los Angeles, in July and slowly made its way west, through Alameda, Ewa, and Midway. While working up at Midway, the squadron lost four Corsairs and one pilot, largely to engine malfunctions, and was airlifted back to Hawaii to reequip, subsequently being reassigned to MAG-23.

After getting new aircraft, VMF-223 sailed for Espíritu Santo, arriving on November 11, and by the end of the month, it was firmly ensconced at Vella Lavella, alongside other F4U squadrons, including 214 and 222. VMF-223's first combat action of the new tour occurred on December 23, four kills being registered by Bulldog pilots. But the pickings were slim. Early February saw Carl reassigned to a staff job in MAG-12.

While the aircrews were fighting their way up from Guadalcanal, the Japanese abandoned Bougainville by early 1944 and attention could now be directed toward Rabaul. The decision was made to land an amphibious force at Cape Gloucester on the west end of New Britain; Rabaul was on the northeast tip, directly across the island. Guarded by a natural barrier of five volcanoes, Rabaul Harbor had been a natural place for the Japanese to set up their huge staging base in January 1942, after taking it from a small Australian garrison. It had been a thorn in Adm. Halsey's side, and he was determined to remove it.

It was during this campaign, which was quickly dubbed "Ring Around Rabaul," that pilots like Boyington and 1st Lt. Robert Hanson were especially active. Hanson probably was one of Boyington's closest competitors. The son of missionaries, Hanson called the small town of Newtonville, Massachusetts, ten miles west of Boston, his home, although he spent most of his early life following his parents from India to Vienna. Enlisting in the Marines in May 1942, he was designated a Naval Aviator in early 1943 and joined VMF-215 at Vella Lavella, flying the Corsair. Although a friendly, outgoing sort on the ground, the burly Hanson disdained in-flight discipline, so necessary in combat involving large groups of aircraft. He preferred to lead rather than follow as a wingman and would frequently find excuses to break formation and go after a kill on his own, although he was not a glory seeker in any sense.

Hanson's first kills came while he and his squadron were covering the landings at Bougainville on November 1, 1943. The twenty-three-year-old pilot shot down a Val that was

attempting to bomb the Navy ships during the landing. The next several days saw Hanson bringing down Japanese planes at an almost unbelievable rate, three, four, and five at a time. The newspapers picked up his story and labeled him "The One-Man Air Force," and "Butcher Bob." His squadron mates took it in stride, but as his score approached the magic twenty-six, Hanson became all too aware of the constant publicity. (The American World War I ace, Captain Eddie Rickenbacker, obtained twenty-six kills in 1918 and the number had become the goal of all U.S. fighter pilots.)

On January 30, 1944, Hanson shot down four Zeros, part of the intercepting fighter force against a large raid. His score now stood at twenty-five; he had been in continuous combat for nearly three months.

One day before his twenty-fourth birthday, on February 3, Hanson participated in a sweep over Rabaul, but the Marines found the target obscured by clouds and returned to their base. On the return flight, Hanson asked permission to strafe a lighthouse that had proved troublesome as a Japanese flak tower and observation post. Capt. Harold Spears, the flight leader, consented, and Hanson broke away to begin his run. The next thing his horrified friends saw was Hanson's aircraft shudder from flak hits, its wing disintegrating. Hanson apparently tried to ditch but lost control of the cartwheeling Corsair and crashed into the ocean, leaving only scattered debris.

Captain Foster knew Hanson and wrote in his book, "He had flirted with death so often he could laugh at her, but this, the third day of February

An F4U-1—note the early "bird cage" canopy—on a takeoff roll at the Marine base at Munda in the Solomons, August 1943. The aircraft possibly belongs to VMF-214. Humidity aaccounts for the visible vapor describing the propeller arc.

1944, she decided to embrace him, and nothing remained behind, only some debris and an oil slick and a record."[5] Robert Hanson received a posthumous Medal of Honor on August 1, 1944, for his performance during his three months of intensive combat in the Solomons: twenty-five kills during that period, twenty in only seventeen days. He became the third-ranking Marine fighter ace of World War II.

The landing at Cape Gloucester took place on December 26, 1943, the veteran 1st Marine Division storming ashore and meeting very little initial resistance. But by afternoon, the Japanese launched a large air raid, much of which was dispersed by Army P-38s. One little-known Marine operation, which took place for the first time, was the use of small Piper Cubs designated for artillery spotting. Flown by officers and enlisted men, the ten little single-engine craft did valuable work during the later stages of the landings.

Army, Navy, and Marine air power continuously pounded the Japanese. VMTB-232, newly redesignated and reequipped VMSB-232 of Guadalcanal fame, flew its TBFs on daily raids against enemy shipping in Simpson Harbor. The squadron had arrived in New Caledonia in August and then went to Espíritu Santo in September, operating in the vicinity of Bougainville, assigned to MAG-24.

By mid-February, under constant attack, the Japanese had had enough and began pulling out, even as American Navy and Marine squadrons took over recently captured airstrips. The Japanese had, by some estimates, lost

400–700 aircraft during the Bougainville/Rabaul operation, 393 of which were claimed by Marine aircrews. The real numbers, because of the huge free-for-all aerial battles of December 1943 and January 1944, will never be known.

Charles A. Lindbergh's Combat Tour

A world-famous personality appeared in the Pacific in the spring of 1944. At forty-one, he might have been considered pretty old to be flying combat missions in a Corsair; what made the situation even more unusual was the pilot's civilian status. But Charles A. Lindbergh was no stranger to unusual situations. And as far as his "advanced" age was concerned, he had been flying before many of his future wingmen had even been born.

His 1927 New York–to–Paris flight had established his life and fortune. As highly acclaimed as he was in the 1930s, the pendulum swung in the opposite direction later in the decade as Lindbergh was reviled for his stand in favor of American isolationism and his professed admiration for Nazi Germany. (Some speculated that he was really involved in spying for American interests during his contacts with the Germans.) But when war came in 1941, he immediately offered his services to the military. After his 1927 flight, he had been elevated to colonel in the Army Reserve. His senior rank, a gift though it might have been for his youthful achievement (after all, he was only twenty-five at the time of his New York–to–Paris flight), had become an embarrassment to the American military.

Charles A. Lindbergh walks with two of the Marines' leading aces, Joe Foss (with mustache) and Marion Carl (center). Lindbergh made a whirlwind tour of the various fighter units in the Pacific, Marine and Army. He brought new operating techniques for the Corsair and P-38. He also shot down a Japanese Sonia scout plane but was never officially credited because he was a civilian.

The War Department did not know exactly what to do with so famous a personage. He had originally been rebuffed by President Franklin D. Roosevelt, payment to a degree for Lindbergh's pro-Nazi stand. Finally, he was made a consultant with United Aircraft, of which Chance Vought was a part. By January 1944 he was heavily involved with Corsair development and had checked out in the F4U. He flew to various stateside Marine installations to discuss his theories with senior Marine aviators. After going through several weeks of combat training with the Corsair, Lindbergh flew out to the Pacific in April 1944 and spent several days with Marine units working-up with his aircraft in Hawaii and Midway.

May found him at Espíritu Santo, and on May 22 he flew his first combat mission—still in a civilian status—with VMF-222. It was a strafing run over islands near Rabaul. He eventually flew with most of the active

Corsair units, VMF-218, VMF-223, and VMF-212 of MAG-24, VMF-224 and VMF-311 of MAG-31. In all, it is estimated that Lindbergh flew more than fifty missions with the Marines, and later with the Army Air Force's P-38-equipped 475th Fighter Group. (With the latter organization, the trans-Atlantic pioneer shot down a Sonia observation plane.)

Lindbergh was convinced that the powerful Corsair could carry much more ordnance than it had been. On September 8, he flew an aircraft with a specially modified belly rack, carrying a 2,000-pound bomb. Taking off from Roi Island, he flew out to Wotje Island, which had been the recipient of recent Marine attention, and dropped the weapon on a Japanese installation. Subsequent missions with increased payload proved Lindbergh's contention, although some difficulties were experienced in releasing the big bombs in dives. He was still not satisfied that the Corsair had reached its limit.

Accordingly, on September 13, 1944, Lindbergh had his plane, an F4U-1D, loaded with one 2,000-pound bomb and two 1,000-pounders. Using up almost every foot of runway, he managed to pull the shuddering plane into the air and proceed to Wotje, where he dropped the heaviest load carried by a single fighter up to that time. Lindbergh described his dive in his wartime diary.

I flew upwind over my target . . . at 8,000 feet, rolled over and started my dive. I was pointed downward at an angle of about 65 degrees, the steepest I have used with a heavy bombload. . . . There was just time. I tripped the bomb releases and pulled up steeply.

When the period of grayout was over, I looked back to see the black column of debris rising above the main naval-gun installation in that area of the island. . . . I could not have selected a better target area even if it had been intentional, with plenty of time to consider. My bombs had completely wiped out the southern portion of the gun position and probably dislocated the gun itself.[6]

The Night Fighters

During this intense year of action, the Marines were in the forefront of a new area of combat for Americans, night fighting. Aerial combat at night was not new, of course. World War I had seen night bombing attacks by both British and German squadrons, which drew the appropriate development from the opposing sides: the night fighter. At that time, this defensive aircraft was usually a single-seater such as the Sopwith Camel, modified to fly and fight in the dark. Normally, these modifications were limited to cockpit lighting and flame dampeners for engine exhausts or machine-gun muzzles. A good pair of eyes also helped.

However, the German aerial blitz on London in 1941 encouraged the British to develop their new weapon of radar to be carried by the larger, twin-engine aircraft in service, such as Bristol's Blenheim bomber and Beaufighter multi-seat fighter. An unsuccessful single-engine day fighter, the Boulton-Paul Defiant, armed solely with a four-gun turret behind the pilot, was also equipped with radar and saw brief service during the Blitz.

The British also had taken to bombing at night, and, naturally, the Germans countered with their own stable of night fighters, usually Bf-110s and Ju 88s, twin-engined products of the Messerschmitt and Junkers concerns, respectively. But single-engine fighters such as the Bf-109 and Focke-Wulf 190, and lesser aircraft like the Dornier 217, and a later night fighter, the Heinkel 219, were also used and were, unfortunately for the British, very successful.

While the development of aerial combat at night was proceeding in the European theater, the Pacific saw little of it, until the introduction of Marine squadron VMF(N)-531 on January 1, 1943. Night-time intruder raids at Guadalcanal, by one or two Japanese planes, were accomplishing their objectives: harassment of American troops, loss of sleep, resulting in reduced combat effectiveness and morale. A way of dealing with these marauders had to be found. But it was not until March that the initial contingent of VMF(N)-531 arrived in the Pacific.

On April 1, Marine Night Fighting Group 53, MAG(N)-53, was formed, splitting VMF(N)-531 into two squadrons, VMF(N)-531 and VMF(N)-532. VMF(N)-531 had been operating the Lockheed Vega PV-1 Ventura, a development of the pre-war Lodestar transport. The Marines were not happy with their mount's capabilities, especially its low operating ceiling of 15,000 feet. However, the PV-1s went into service and on December 6, 1943, the executive officer of VMF(N)-531, Maj. John D. Harshberger, scored the first kill, destroying a Japanese floatplane near Bougainville. In close radio contact with the GCI (ground control intercept) site on Vella Lavella, the night-fighter crews were vectored toward their quarry with directional-bearing information until visual contact could be made.

On February 9, 1944, Major Harshberger was up over Rabaul and was quickly vectored toward two Japanese bombers. The enemy crews were alert, however, and raked the Ventura with 20-mm cannon fire, one shell entering the cockpit just behind Harshberger's head. With most of his forward-firing guns knocked out, Harshberger closed in on the Bettys, allowing his turret gunner, SSgt. Walter Tiedman, a good shot. One Mitsubishi eventually burst into flames and went down; the other escaped in the night. Coming back to Bougainville, jittery "friendly" anti-aircraft gun crews almost finished the job the Japanese bombers started.

The other night-fighter squadron of MAG(N)-53, VMF(N)-532, was much better equipped than its sister unit, and was one of only three squadrons to use the F4U-2 model of the Corsair, the other two squadrons being the Navy's VF(N)-75 and VF(N)-10. The F4U-2 was a dedicated night fighter, incorporating wing-mounted scanner radar enclosed in a nacelle on the right wing tip. The radar was manufactured by Sperry and operated in the X-band range, 5.2 to 10.9 megacycles.

After much testing and development, the first F4U-2, converted from an existing dash 1 with the familiar "birdcage" canopy, flew in January 1943 at the Naval Air Station, Quonset Point, Rhode Island, across from Newport. Exhaust-flame dampeners, IFF/transponder beacon, VHF radio, and a radar altimeter were installed in the night fighter. An oddity was the deletion of one .50-caliber machine gun in the right wing, presumably to accommodate the radar unit, leaving the aircraft armed with five guns instead of the normal six, still lethal enough. The aircraft was also left in the normal day-fighter scheme of three-tone blue, there being no provision for a regular night-fighter paint scheme. Thirty-two F4U-1s were converted to dash 2s. Twelve of them went to VMF(N)-532, commanded by Maj. Everette H. Vaughn, once an airline pilot for TWA.

By December 1943, the twenty-one pilots of VMF(N)-532 had completed training and had shipped out to the Pacific, arriving in Hawaii on Christmas Day aboard a transport ship. Another ship carried them to the Gilbert Islands, arriving there on January 14, 1944, at Tarawa Atoll. Tarawa welcomed the newcomers, having been the recent subject of attentions from Japanese intruders.

The Navy's ground radar was in desperate need of repair but was finally fixed to some extent, and functioned sporadically for the next several nights, the pilots of VMF(N)-532 trying their best to make do with the situation. Finally, a detachment of eight aircraft was sent down to Kwajalein in the Marshall Islands. Major Vaughn led the Corsairs to Roi, where they stayed for the next three months, having little initial success until the night of April 13–14, 1944.

In their first successful interception, VMF(N)-532 pilots shot down two Bettys and scared off the remaining ten. One pilot apparently got lost in the dark and was listed as missing in action.

Two definite kills and one probable were gained that night, although Lt. Joel Bonner was forced to parachute from his plane after taking hits from a Betty. Bonner spent the night in his raft and was rescued by a destroyer escort the next afternoon.

In May, Vice Adm. Marc Mitscher paid a visit to the Marine night-fighter detachment and was so impressed with them that he later took two of the Corsairs, having them flown out to his task force for inspection, promising to deliver two brand-new replacements. He was as good as his word; however, the new F4Us were day fighters and had to be modified for night operations.

July saw the entire squadron loaded aboard the USS *Windham Bay* (CVE-92) and landed on Saipan, where they were tasked with conducting night-time patrols as well as predawn bombing raids on Japanese positions. This last type of operation did not sit too well with Major Vaughn, who knew how much training was involved in making a good night-fighter pilot, only to have that hard work thrown away simply to deliver bombs. Eventually, VMF(N)-532 was returned to the States to work-up on Grumman F7Fs. The squadron record was not impressive at first sight; however, because they had accomplished their objective of denying the night-time skies to the enemy during important operations, the pilots and crews of VMF(N)-532 had accomplished their task.

The War Continues

The relentless march northward toward Japan began to gather steam with invasions of the Gilbert Islands, the Marshalls, and the Marianas. Names like Tarawa, Kwajalein, and Peleliu were etched into the public consciousness by the blood used to buy each of these island groups. For the Marines who were in the van of almost every invasion, it was the ultimate test of combat for the 160-year-old Corps. At Tarawa, the tough and bloody battle for the airfield runways on Betio Island from November 20 to 24, 1943, cost 3,318 American casualties with 1,085 deaths, of which 984 were Marines. The battle for Kwajalein began on January 31, 1944, and by February 5 the island group was declared secure. Some 8,400 Japanese died, and 500 American GIs, Army and Marine, were killed. Marine aviation had taken a back seat to these frantic amphibious operations. The "mud-Marines" had to take these islands themselves.

Something interesting, and perhaps unfortunate for the Marines on the ground, had transpired during the island invasions. Marine aviation resources—aircraft, crews, pilots, and support—had become so tied to the more traditional roles of land-based air power that the purpose for which Marine aviation had been developed had been subordinated, if not completely forgotten: providing close air support for the men on the ground.

The Marines, perhaps, were partly to blame for this turn of events. The gusto with which their fighter pilots and bomber crews went after the Zeros or bombed Japanese shipping served to push close-air-support functions into the background. The Navy, always the watchful and jealous big brother, was only too glad to let the Marines take care of things from land bases, leaving Navy air to its rightful dominion: carrier-based operations. Of course, the Marines could also operate from carriers. Adding fuel to the controversy was the Army's jealousy of a Marine air arm and the Corps' expansion into

what the Army viewed as its own territory: land warfare. Lt. Gen. Holland Smith, ever the vocal advocate for the Marines, proposed a combined Army-Marine amphibious organization under his command with Maj. Gen. Roy Geiger's III Amphibious Corps as its nucleus.

Not surprisingly, Adm. Chester Nimitz, with Commandant Vandegrift's approval, rejected Smith's proposal but did authorize creation of a consolidated logistical and administrative group under Smith, known as Fleet Marine Force, Pacific. Included in FMFPac was Aircraft/Fleet Marine Force, Pacific, which covered the supply and administrative aspects of Marine aviation in the area. Nimitz wanted the operational control of Marine air to remain with the Navy, under Commander, Air Force, Pacific Fleet.

But the vast distances involved in some Pacific island operations, especially those in the Gilberts and Marianas, forced the Navy's hand. The Marines were brought aboard some of the escort carriers now beginning to populate the various task forces. With fifty-four flattops, the Navy seemed to have enough ships, and with 10,000 pilots and 126 squadrons, the Marines certainly had enough manpower and resources to fly from them. Their new job was not welcomed by Maj. Gen. Ross Rowell, the senior Marine air commander in the Pacific. Rowell became so negative that he was relieved by

[Opposite] Marine ground crews work on a Corsair between missions. Note the large open bay containing a fuel tank immediately forward of the cockpit. The tank occasionally leaked, requiring what became a characteristic "marking" of a pattern of white tape on the upper forward fuselage of many F4Us.

[Right] Lt. Donald Balch smiles as he considers his good luck by the shot-up tail of his Corsair. The Corsair is down on its rear fuselage—indicating no tail wheel—and its elevators have been badly damaged. There are bullet or flak holes in the rudder as well. This photo was probably taken in early 1943 indicated by the "bird cage" canopy and the star-in-a-circle national marking, which had been modified with bars by late summer 1943. Balch eventually became an ace, with five kills.

Vandegrift on September 16, 1944, and sent to Lima, Peru, as the chief of the Naval Air Mission there, certainly a sorry end to a dedicated man's career. Maj. Gen. Francis P. Mulcahy took Rowell's place in the Pacific.

Marine Carrier Groups, Aircraft, Fleet Marine Force, Pacific, was born on October 21, 1944, and had its headquarters at MCAS Santa Barbara, California, Col. Albert D. Cooley commanding. This organization was composed of two air groups, each group containing a complete set of two squadrons for each of four carriers: an eighteen-plane fighter squadron and a twelve-plane torpedo squadron. By summer, the order to carrier-train Marine pilots had been given and the Marines finally brought the battle-tested F4U home. With several improvements added since its initial carrier approach in September 1942, the Corsair had become more docile around the ship, but it still retained its reputation as fairly unforgiving of lackadaisical treatment. Although most of the pilots were thrilled about carrier flying, the impression their little escort carriers—CVEs—gave was less enthusiastic. A song composed during the Korean War went:

> The *Midway* has 1,000-foot runways.
> The *Leyte*, 810.
> But we still wouldn't have much of a carrier
> If we laid two of ours end to end.

In actuality, the Marine carrier program did not really get going until January 1945, but by the middle of the month, the carrier Marines were in the thick of Pacific combat. On January 12, Marine fighter pilots aboard the USS *Essex* (CV-9) claimed their first kills off Okinawa. There were other areas of combat with names that would become all-too-familiar to another generation of Marine aviators twenty years later. Names like Saigon, Bien Hoa, Than Son Nhut, the South China Sea, and Hanoi, all in what was then French Indochina.

The flight crew of a PBJ looks at a 65-foot scroll bearing the names of 35,000 Oklahoma City school children who contributed to the purchase of the bomber. The scroll was dropped over Japanese positions, as requested by the young contributors. The PBJ was the Marine version of the Army's B-25 Mitchell, a highly successful, heavily armed medium bomber that served in every theater of the war.

Aircraft and Missions

As the hierarchy wrestled with the weighty problems of organization and deployment, the war went on. By mid-1943, the Marine Corps had been the beneficiary of American over-production. Too many North American B-25 Mitchells had been turned out, and the Army could not find enough work for the twin-engine, twin-tail bombers. Ever anxious for more planes, the Marines grabbed surplus B-25s, which were designated PBJs, and quickly established eight squadrons by mid-October to operate them. Only seven of

the squadrons actually saw combat. The eighth, VMB-614, was in the last stages of moving out to the war zone when the Japanese surrendered in mid-August 1945. The three main types of Mitchells used by the Marines were PBJ-1D, -1H and -1J, which corresponded to the Army's B-25D, H, and J models, with a few PBJ-1Cs serving with a training unit, OTS-8.

VMB-413, under Lt. Col. Andrew Galatian Jr., arrived at Espíritu Santo in January 1944 with their PBJ-IDs, and by March the Flying Nightmares were bombing Japanese installations at Rabaul, Kavieng, and on Bougainville, losing five aircraft and thirty-two crewmen by May in combat action.

One of the more unusual PBJ outfits was VMB-612, in the central Pacific, skippered by Jack Cram, now a lieutenant colonel. The PBJ-IHs (B-25Hs) and PBJ-1Js (B-25Js) of Cram's squadron were specially fitted with zero-length rocket launchers under the wings, radar bomb sights, and other electronics gear; the mission of VMB-612 was to harass Japanese shipping at night. The squadron arrived at Saipan in November 1944, and before beginning operations, the Mitchells were again modified by having the dorsal turret removed, as well as other components that were not essential to flying or navigation. Range and endurance were all important; the night missions promised to be long. It took a lot of patient training to get the green crews combat ready, but by April, with Iwo Jima secured and ready for American flight operations, VMB-612 began flying against Japanese harbors. Between

April 10 and July 28, the squadron flew 251 sorties, with claims for fifty-three ships damaged and five sunk.

Two aircraft that began to appear in Marine squadrons, although in limited numbers and roles, were the Grumman Hellcat and Curtiss Helldiver. Of the two, the former was much more successful. Derived from operational experience gained from the F4F Wildcat, the Hellcat was a big flying barrel of a fighter, supported by huge broadchord wings (the distance from the wing's leading edge to the trailing edge) that carried the heavy single-seater without correspondingly high wingloading factors; the wings and the relatively low wing loading gave the big Grumman the agility to meet the still-dangerous Zero on near-equal terms, although the Mitsubishi still held the edge in maneuverability.

The Zero's combat superiority had begun to wane by early 1943 with the introduction of the Corsair and disappeared with the advent of the Hellcat. However, in the hands of the few experienced Japanese aces still alive in 1944, the Zero could still be a formidable opponent and was to be treated with respect by Allied fighter pilots.

[Top] Lt. Col. Jack Cram (right), skipper of VMB-612, prepares to take off on a mission. He flew a heroic raid against Japanese shipping at Guadalcanal and received the Navy Cross. He later led this squadron of specially modified PBJs.

[Bottom] An excellent view of a VMB-612 Mitchell, painted dull black. Note this bomber's painted-over nose windows and the huge radar blister immediately in front of the cockpit. VMB-612's PBJs probably flew the last Marine mission of the war.

Powered by the big 2,000-horsepower Pratt and Whitney radial engine, the F6F-3 went to the Navy's VF-9 aboard the *Essex*, and VF-5 in the new *Yorktown* (CV-10). The two squadrons took the Hellcat into action on August 31, 1943, and the aircraft immediately established itself as the Zero's nemesis. The Marines operated three versions of the Hellcat: the basic F6F-3/5 fighter, which flew from land bases and sporadically from carriers; the F6F-5P, photo reconnaissance, and the F6F-3/5(N) for night fighting.

Interest in night-fighting techniques was still high in mid-1944, and VMF(N)-541 was detailed to the Philippines to combat the Japanese Hayabusa (code-named Oscar), a fighter many mistook for the Zero because of its similar appearance, great maneuverability, and light construction. The Nakajima-built Army fighter (the Zero flew only with Imperial Navy units) had been used as a nuisance raider, proving too fast for the U.S. Army Air Force's P-61 Black Widow night fighters.

VMF(N)-541 arrived at Tacloban on San Pedro Bay on the northeastern coast of Leyte Island in December, led by Col. Peter Lambrecht. After some initial problems stemming from the inexperienced Army radar operators, Lt. Rodney E. Montgomery scored the first kill on December 5, shooting down an Oscar while he was covering a four-ship convoy. (One of VMF(N)-541's collateral duties was providing night combat air patrols [CAPs], something that did not sit well with the pilots.) Two more Oscars were downed on the 6th, but these were the squadron's last night kills because it was put on regularly scheduled day patrols and convoy protection. However, seventeen more kills were scored through the remainder of December, the early-morning mission of the 12th resulting in eleven Japanese planes downed in a single mission.

Seven Bateye Hellcats were airborne at 6:50 in the morning and covering a convoy when the ground radar detected a large enemy force approaching. Arranged in three- and four-plane divisions, the Marine fighters pounced on the Japanese bombers, numbering thirty-three aircraft, and during three passes, destroyed one-third of the attacking planes, with no losses themselves.

Other night-fighter units, VMF(N)-533, -542, and -543, flew during operations in the Philippines, and during the operations around Okinawa beginning in April 1945; these squadrons were flying the new F6F-5N Hellcat. VMF(N)-533 ended up with the high score among Marine night-fighter squadrons with thirty-five confirmed kills, achieved during the Okinawa campaign. The squadron's Capt. Robert Baird became the *only* all-night Marine night-fighter ace with six kills (which were all gained at night whereas other Marine night aces counted at least one or two day kills in their overall totals), the last of which was obtained on July 14 using the new mixed armament of 20-mm cannon and four .50-caliber machine guns.

Marine Hellcats also flew from USS *Block Island* (CVE-106), VMF-511 operating a mixed bag of Corsairs and Hellcat reconnaissance and fighter aircraft. Operating in conjunction with a British task force, the *Block Island* was supporting operations off Okinawa using its planes against small watercraft. VMF-511 lost its skipper, Maj. Robert Maze, when his Corsair was hit by flak and crashed into the sea.

The Curtiss SB2C Helldiver was this company's last operational design. There were other products, but the Curtiss company finally closed its doors in 1947 after a forty-year period of supplying military and civilian aircraft to the world. The SB2C was a problem right from the beginning, for both the Navy and Curtiss. Loaded down with constraints and requirements, Curtiss had trouble meeting the Navy's demands. Derived from a 1938 design requirement, the XSB2C-1 did not fly until December 18, 1940. Its development and contractual problems plagued the Helldiver, to the extent

[Opposite Left] F4U-2s of VMF(N)-532 aboard USS *Windham Bay* (CVE-92) in July 1944 on their way to Saipan. One of the few photographs of this squadron's night-fighter Corsairs, it gives a good view of the radar fairing on the right wing, the early cockpit canopy, and the difficult view over the long nose, which made approaches in the Corsair very demanding.

[Opposite Right] An F6F-5N of VMF(N)-533 from USS *Block Island* on patrol in 1945. The war was very close to Japan by this time, and the Marine fighters aboard the CVEs were called upon to fly missions during the day as well as at night. VMF(N)-533 was the top-scoring Marine night-fighter squadron, with 35 confirmed kills.

[Bottom] "The Beast." A view of a Marine SB2C-4 Helldiver in April 1945. The big Curtiss dive bomber was an underpowered brute that never satisfactorily replaced the SBD Dauntless, at least as far as the Marines were concerned. Note the rear gunner's deployed weapons and the huge vertical tail, hallmark of the type.

that the first production aircraft did not reach VB-17 aboard the *Yorktown* until late 1942. The Navy squadron did not take its new dive bombers aboard the carrier until July 1943 and into combat until that November. Intended to replace the obsolescent SBD Dauntless, the SB2C never lived up to expectations, being unforgiving to fly and vastly underpowered in view of its burgeoning operational weight and ordnance loads. Development proceeded with the -2 and -3 models.

The Marines first made the SB2C's acquaintance in a typically off-handed manner. The Army gained several hundred aircraft, designating them A-25As (the SBD had been used in New Guinea in 1942 as the A-24), deleting the Navy's wing-folding mechanism; but the Army quickly became unhappy with its new dive bombers and hurriedly gave them to the Marines as SB2C-1As. The Marines took the almost 400 new aircraft and used them in the States as trainers in several VMSB squadrons; the -1 never flew in combat with the Corps.

Like their Navy counterparts, the Marines never developed the respect and affection they had for the SBD for the big-tailed Curtiss, which many pilots called derisively "the Beast." By May 1945, however, many VMSBs had given up their trusty Dauntlesses for the Helldiver. VMSB-244 and VMSB-245 were probably typical of the 1945 version of the Marine Scout/Bombing unit, and were active during the invasion of the Philippines. May 19, 1945, saw VMSB-244 trade its SBDs for SB2C-4s and use them in support of ground units, toting bombs and 5-inch rockets.

6 Carrying the War to Japan

BY MID-1944, HAVING SECURED the Gilberts, Marshalls, and Marianas, Allied commanders could now see ultimate victory in the Pacific was in sight. The battles on Saipan and Guam, especially Saipan, presented some of the bloodiest fighting yet encountered, as Japanese troops entrenched themselves in caves, waiting to rain mortars and machine-gun fire on the advancing Marine landing parties that stormed ashore in June and July 1944. In time, the new island bases for the oncoming B-29 offensive were secured, however, and it was time to allow Gen. Douglas MacArthur to make good on his promise to "return" to the Philippines.

Intelligence reports told of weak Japanese air power in the Philippines area. According to Far East Air Force (FEAF) intelligence, there were sixty-five known operational Japanese airstrips throughout the islands with 692 aircraft, 340 of which could be expected to be operational. But considering the low experience level and manning shortages of the Japanese units, it was estimated that only 130 of these planes could be fielded at any one time; hence, the threat to a U. S. invasion was minimal. MacArthur was given the green light. October was the target month and the initial invasion would be on Leyte Island in the central Philippines. After securing Leyte, the Allies would head north toward Luzon and the capital city of Manila.

Lt. Gen. George C. Kenney, in charge of MacArthur's air operations, told Marine Maj. Gen. Ralph J. Mitchell, ComAirNorSols (Commander, Air, Northern Solomons) to get his 1st Marine Aircraft Wing (MAW) ready to support the Leyte operation, which would be spearheaded by Army troops. Kenney had seen Marine dive bombers at work in the Solomons and greatly admired their skills; he wanted them for his operation. Mitchell ordered MAG-24 and MAG-32 to stand by.

Although the invasion on October 20, 1944, went off well, the Japanese response was to send its Combined Fleet into action. This turned out to be the last time this once-invincible armada would come out in force, and its sortie resulted in the climactic battle for Leyte Gulf, October 23–26, which would include the first planned use of kamikaze suicide aircraft by the desperate Japanese.

The first air strip opened for U.S. operations was at Tacloban, taken from the Japanese during the initial landings on October 20. Three major typhoons in late October and early November, however, brought operations down to a minimum as the strips turned into oceans of mud. It was not until late November that the first Marine air elements arrived to begin working up to operational strength and capability. In addition to the previously mentioned Hellcats of VMF(N)-541, Corsairs of MAG 12—VMFs -115, -211, -218, and -313—were in action by December 7, 1944, flying against Japanese shipping and providing CAP for U.S. convoys. (These units were actually operating FG-1s, Corsairs built by Goodyear, which deleted the wing-folding mechanism.)

On December 7, twenty-one FG-1s of the four fighter squadrons struck a seven-ship convoy, sinking four freighters and one troop transport in a deluge of 1,000-pound bombs. Two Corsairs made mast-level attacks on the accompanying destroyers, seriously damaging two. It was a hectic battle for the Japanese, accomplished without a single American loss.

All of the Corsair squadrons were kept busy covering the U.S. convoys or attacking the enemy. The orders were to get past the protecting Japanese air cover and concentrate on the ships below. Naturally, however, there were times when the Zeros could not be safely ignored. Aerial combat took place particularly during Japanese attacks on Allied convoys, the covering FG pilots usually having their hands full.

On December 11, four VMF-313 aircraft engaged sixteen bomb-laden Zeros headed for ships at only 2,500-foot altitude under the cover of a rain squall. Radar had not detected the approaching enemy formation hidden behind the highly reflective water-laden clouds. It was not until the Japanese were little more than a mile from their targets that they were spotted by a screening destroyer, which gave a frantic call for the CAP aircraft. The four Corsairs plunged into the Zeros, flaming five on the first pass; the survivors dropped their bombs and fled. Every Marine pilot shot down at least one Zero, while 2nd Lt. Clyde R. Jarrett scored twice.

With all the aerial action evidently occurring over water instead of land, there was very little close support for the ground troops, one of the main reasons for bringing Marine air power to the Philippines in support of what was largely an Army show. Marine Corsairs, when they were involved in action against ground targets during the early stages of the action, seemed to be used against selected targets, as opposed to ground liaison–directed attacks against Japanese troops or fortifications immediately impeding an advance. In other words, the Marines were given their targets before leaving the ground, never receiving any instructions that would characterize a direct close-air-support mission.

On December 17 thirty-two "Corsairmen," as one Marine writer called them, carried 1,000-pound bombs with instantaneous fuses to a road intersection, causing a lot of smoke but little ascertainable damage to enemy installations. VMF-211 aircraft did apparently hit a local warehouse, and VMF-115 planes demolished a building, but the actual benefits of such a massive strike were negligible.

However, the Marines were learning their trade for the invasion of Luzon. The "training" had not been without cost, for while MAG 12 fighters had flown 264 missions of all types—CAP, strikes, and ground support— nine pilots and thirty-four aircraft had been lost. On the other side of the ledger, more than forty Japanese planes had been destroyed in the air and on the ground, and twenty-two ships, from destroyers to transports, had been sunk, with eleven others damaged.

December 25, 1944, with the capture of Palompon on Leyte's west coast, saw the remaining Japanese sealed off with no hope of rescue or reinforcement, and the island was effectively secured the next day. There were, of course, many mopping-up operations, lasting well into 1945, but attention could now be directed northward for the January invasion of Luzon.

Even as the Hellcats of VMF(N)-541 continued to deal with the Japanese at night through the first weeks of the new year, destroying twenty-two enemy aircraft in the air, preparations had begun for the invasion of Luzon, the next step in the liberation of the Philippines. The Sixth Army landed at Lingayen on January 9, 1945, under the sheltering support of MAG-12 and MAG-14, while the trusty SBDs of MAG-24 and MAG-32 flew into an airstrip hacked out of the rice paddies by the ground crews of the 1st MAW. By the end of the month, seven Dauntless squadrons were in the country flying support for the Army.

The men and pilots of the Marine squadrons did not mind flying support for the Army instead of their own Marines. Here, at last, was an opportunity to prove their theories on close air support. With visionaries like Lt. Col. Keith B. McCutcheon, one of the driving forces of future marine aviation developments, right through the Vietnam War, the Marines were anxious for any chance to prove themselves. McCutcheon was the operations officer for MAG 24, which included VMSBs -133, -236, -241, and -341. MAG 32 was newly formed from MAG-12's VMSB-142 and VMSB-243, and MAG-14's VMSB-244. McCutcheon saw close air support as a "tool," an "additional weapon," which was only effective if it were used by the ground commander on the scene, or close to it, to be tasked, directed, and coordinated as he saw fit. There was no need for inflexible preflight briefings which left no room for the inevitable changes of a major battle, and therefore rendered ineffective those missions that had been called close air support.

The Marines in the cockpits were in total sympathy with the concept as put forth by McCutcheon; before he is a pilot, a Marine aviator is, of course, a Marine, a rifleman, a "grunt." Whether from actual combat or at least from rigorous training before he ever sees an airplane, a Marine pilot has gone through ground soldier training, and he knows what it means to advance on an enemy machine-gun nest or other fortification, or engage in hand-to-hand combat. Therefore, most Marine aviators felt that if there was any way they could better serve their compatriots on the ground, so much the better. With men like Lieutenant Colonel McCutcheon, the way seemed clear.

The first missions were flown on January 27 with a 9:00 AM strike against San Fernando, which served as a fuel dump and bivouac area for the Japanese. Eighteen SBDs of VMSB-241, under escort of four Army P-47s, obliterated the target area. In the afternoon, VMSB-133 sent eighteen aircraft against targets north of Manila. The other squadrons got into action in the following days, dive bombing enemy airfields and positions. In one week, five squadrons flew seventeen missions and dropped 207,800 pounds of ordnance, ranging up to 150 miles from the airstrip at Mangaladan.

The Marines were still not involved in true close air support; the communications facilities, supposedly provided by the Army, were not in place in mobile jeeps. The Army was perhaps still afraid to allow Marine crews to go in so close to its troops. Thus, the initial missions had to come down from Sixth Army Headquarters itself, rather than from the field commands. But proof of the Marines' expertise was soon to come. In the meantime, the Dauntlesses bombed and strafed far ahead of the Army squads on the ground.

Veteran VMF-223 was also in action in the Philippines, having arrived on January 12. The Bulldog Corsairs ranged throughout the region on combat sweeps. During one of these missions, on January 23, 2nd Lt. Kenneth G. Pomasl became lost and, running low on fuel, he made a controlled ditching off Cebu. Hustling over the side of the cockpit, he saw a trio of native canoes coming toward him. The natives were friendly and pulled the Marine pilot into one of their canoes, just as fire from Japanese watching from shore began. Startled, everyone dove back into the water. Suddenly, Pomasl found himself very much alone and under fire. However, he paddled to shore and hid from the Japanese for almost two days. He was found by more natives on the 25th and cared for until they brought him to a contact point to be finally rescued by Americans.

True Marine close air support finally arrived during the February drive to the Philippine capital, Manila, on the central west coast of Luzon. Preliminary meetings between Sixth Army commanders and their Marine counterparts provided for equipping jeeps with radios and operator/drivers. Together with a group of support personnel, these jeeps would accompany the 1st Cavalry Division as it moved through the field, relaying messages and requirements back to MAG headquarters, where Lieutenant Colonel McCutcheon was running operations.

On February 1, 1945, at a minute after midnight, the Army units moved out along with the Marine radio jeeps from MAG-24 and MAG-32. These Marines rode with the 1st CavDiv as it thrust toward Manila and beyond. During the initial drive, February 1–3, the Dauntlesses were directed twenty to thirty miles ahead of or behind the Army columns, looking for enemy troops and reporting instantaneously to the radio jeeps. These aerial scouting missions also enabled the Army to know the best ways to proceed toward any given objective, allowing for natural obstacles such as rivers, bridges, and blocked trails.

On February 2, forty-five aircraft of VMSBs -133, -142, and -241 were diverted from a prearranged strike. The aircraft were already airborne when they got the call to change their target to the town of San Isidro, which lay directly ahead of the advancing Army troops. The SBDs achieved great accuracy and left the town in smoking ruins, clearing the way for the men on the ground and proving the effectiveness of radio-jeep/airborne liaison. The same day, Army units ran up against a well-entrenched Japanese battalion. The patrolling SBDs were called down by the company commander. Because of the proximity of American forces, the Dauntless crews made several runs on the enemy positions without firing. This so unnerved and distracted the Japanese that the U.S. soldiers were able to overcome the enemy with very little resistance.

By the time the 1st CavDiv entered Manila on February 4, the Army was sold on Marine close air support. The division commander, Maj. Gen. Verne D. Mudge, said, "The Marine dive-bomber pilots on Luzon are well-qualified for the job they are doing, and I have the greatest confidence in their

[Top] Open-air maintenance in the Philippines, 1945. Ground crew tend to the SBDs of VMSB-341 during the campaign to retake the island nation. Although the Dauntless had left frontline service in the Navy, the Marines still clung to their trusted dive bomber, putting it to good use in close air support. (via Jerry Coleman)

[Bottom] Torrid Turtle Dauntlesses wait to be bombed up, Luzon, PI, 1945. (via Jerry Coleman)

ability. On our drive to Manila, I depended solely on the Marines to protect my left flank from the air against possible Japanese counterattack. The job they turned in speaks for itself. We are here. . . . I cannot say enough in praise of these dive-bomber pilots and their gunners and I am commending them through proper channels for the job they have done."[1]

Throughout the following week, the Army consolidated its position in Manila, the Marine SBD squadrons supporting the progress with pin-point bomb deliveries directly ahead of the American troops.

While Manila was being secured, operations in the southern Philippines began to heat up. MAG-32 was ordered to pack and head south to support the Eighth Army at Mindanao and Zamboanga; MAG-24 would remain on Luzon to continue supporting the Sixth Army, at least for a time. VMB-611 was also ordered to bring its PBJs from the Solomons; MAG-12 would bring its Corsairs as well. Meanwhile, operations around Manila continued through early February, MAGSDAGUPAN (Marine Aircraft Groups,

Dagupan) crews launching a forty-eight-plane strike against enemy ships still in Manila harbor on February 19.

Naturally, there were developments in the way the close-air-support missions were flown. Radio-jeep communications had developed to the point where the single VHF channel could not carry all the traffic and the Marines switched to medium-frequency channels. Napalm was one of the most successful weapons in the Philippines, causing the Japanese the greatest discomfort, as can well be imagined. The jellied gasoline mixture stuck to anything it touched and spilled and flowed into even the safest of entrenchments, bursting into almost unquenchable flame.

Although landings were accomplished on March 10 at Zamboanga, MAG-32 with its four SBD squadrons (VMSB-224 had been transferred from MAG-24) remained on Luzon until an air strip was ready at their new base. This suited the Sixth Army just fine, because it gave the Army troops more use of the Marine dive bombers. Finally, however, on March 23 word came for the first echelons of MAG-32 to depart for the south. By March 26 the group was in place after a fifty-six-day campaign on Luzon. MAG-24 continued to fly in the north until late April, when it completed the move behind MAG-32.

During the Luzon operation, the Marines of both MAGs flew 8,556 individual sorties. An indicator of how active the SBDs were is the fact that, although the Dauntlesses composed only 13 percent of Luzon-based U.S. aircraft—a total of 1,294 aircraft, including much of the Fifth Army Air Force—they flew nearly 50 percent of the total individual sorties during the campaign.

The Southern Philippines

Col. Clayton C. Jerome, commanding MAG-32, was put in overall charge of the four MAGs in the southern Philippines by Gen. William Mitchell. It was a good choice, because the seasoned Jerome was "a man full of ideas," as one fellow officer called him later. MAG-14—VMFs -115, -222, -223, and -251—was to provide close air support from its base on Samar, northeast of Leyte, because it was known that the group was going to Okinawa only a few months later. Aircraft of MAG-12, in company with 13th Army Air Force bombers, strafed the beaches on Zamboanga on March 10, but the 41st Infantry Division encountered little opposition even as it moved inland. The only notice the Japanese appeared to take was to drop mortar fire sporadically on the invasion force.

As the Army troops kept moving, it would have been good to move the MAG to a bigger, finished airstrip like the nearby airfield at San Rogue, but Colonel Jerome kept the fighters at the temporary airstrip at Dipalog until the larger field could be secured. Finally, VMF-115 brought its planes into San Rogue, closely followed by the other squadrons. By March 15 the first missions had been flown from the new strip, renamed Moret Field in honor of Lt. Col. Paul Moret, who died in a crash at New Caledonia in 1943. The Marine groups under Colonel Jerome were also lumped together under the improbable title MAGSZAM (Marine Aircraft Groups, Zamboanga). The number of planes eventually totaled 293, including F4Us, PBJs, SB2Cs, various single types, and, of course, the trusty SBDs.

The collective name for the Southern Philippines operations was Victor. Throughout the Victor invasions, Corsairs of MAG-12 and MAG-14 were active in every type of mission, from convoy CAP to strafing and close air support for the Filipino guerrillas, which greatly enhanced the U.S. Army's capabilities on the ground. The Corsairs had the ability to carry bombs and rockets as well as their normal fixed armament of six .50-caliber machine guns. They were naturally much faster than the SBDs and also had the luxury of both VHF and MHF radios, which enabled them to be quickly integrated into the air-ground liaison teams. The Corsairs could also take care of themselves after delivering their ordnance, and thus could also escort the less agile Dauntlesses.

By this time, there was no need to sell the Army on the value of close air support, and links between the various field commands and the Marine squadrons were close. Frequently, Marine pilots would travel up to the front to observe the situation first hand and discuss points of interest with their Army counterparts. There were also the rare situations when the Army returned the visits, such as on March 27. Guerrillas had run up against a Japanese troop concentration near Dipalog and word was received by VMF-115 that an air strike might dislodge the enemy.

However, without photos, maps, or proper communications gear, it was going to be nearly impossible to point out the target to the Marine pilots. Undaunted, Army Maj. Donald Wills climbed into a VMF-115 aircraft! First Lieutenant Winfield Sharpe followed and, sitting on Wills' lap, Sharpe took off, leading three other squadron planes. With the Army officer providing direct liaison, the four-plane division strafed the Japanese positions, dispersing the threat.

Late March and early April saw MAG-24 participating in a growing number of close-air-support missions, working closely with coordinators in 13th Air Force B-24s. The big bombers would lead the fighters toward the target and point out special objectives. Even bad weather in April failed to put a dent in operations. Each group of aircraft put in the unusually high average of nine hours in the air every day, for a monthly total of 5,800 hours. Replacement aircraft were doled out sparingly; when a squadron was short an airplane—though not a pilot—it was not uncommon for a neighboring commanding officer to lend an aircraft, but only if one of his pilots flew it. MAG-14 continued to fly until mid-May when orders were received to begin packing for Okinawa. On June 1, 1945, VMF-251 was disestablished and its pilots were absorbed by the remaining squadrons of the group. On June 7, MAG-14 said good-bye to the Philippines and headed for Japan. The operational record for the group for its four-month tour on Samar included 7,396 individual sorties, totaling 22,671 combat hours.

Victors I and II (operations against the islands of Panay and Cebu) had been successfully concluded. Victor III, against the island of Palawan, westernmost of the Philippine archipelago, had been conducted on February 28, while Victor IV against Zamboanga had been a big success. Victor IV continued through most of April with additional action on Jolo and Sanga Sanga islands, the Sulu Archipelago. MAG-32 SBDs and MAG-12 Corsairs flew close air support for the men of the 41st Infantry Division once again. Only Victor V, the invasion of Mindanao, remained.

Landings on Mindanao were scheduled for April 17, and for two weeks before that date, MAGSZAM crews went over the area with Filipino guerrillas until the Marines were thoroughly briefed on the region. The invasion went off as scheduled, SBDs and PBJs dropping 500-pound bombs on the Japanese while Corsairs flew CAP over the beaches. MAG-24 had finally arrived from Luzon on April 20 and had set up shop at Malabang, 150 miles across the Moro Gulf, east of Zamboanga.

The operation on Mindanao saw the use of airborne coordinators increase as the last remnants of Japanese resistance were dive bombed. Whole wooded areas were literally blown away, as SBDs and SB2Cs blasted them with bombs and napalm. By June 30, operations on Mindanao had ended and the Philippines were almost entirely secure. July 16 was an important day for the men of MAG-24. It was the day their beloved SBDs were finally retired in favor of what many felt was a much-less-capable successor, the SB2C Helldiver. This left the four squadrons of MAG-32 to continue flying the Dauntless until the end of the war itself. On August 1, MAG-32 stood down.

The Philippines had been liberated, in no small part because of the efforts of the Marines. The main beneficiaries of the Marines' work, the men of the 41st Infantry Division, gave MAGSZAM a six-by-four-foot plaque, decorated with a Japanese machine gun and various captured Japanese flags. On the huge trophy, the simple words "In Appreciation—41st Infantry Division" were inscribed. Maj. Gen. Jens A. Doe, commanding the 41st, gave an address during the presentation ceremonies. He expressed the entire division's gratitude to the assembled Marines. "The readiness of the Marine Air [sic] Groups to engage in any mission requested of them, their skill and courage as airmen, and their splendid spirit of cooperation in aiding ground troops has given the division the most effective air support yet received in any of its operations."[2]

Years later, the commanding general of the Eighth Army, Gen. Robert L. Eichelberger, wrote, "Nothing comforts a soldier, ankle-deep in mud, faced by a roadblock or fortified strong-holds, as much as the sight of bombs wreaking havoc on stubborn enemy positions. It puts heart into him."[3] General Eichelberger was writing in praise of the MAGSZAM Marines.

Return to Carriers

The last six months of the Pacific War, February to August 1945, were like a final examination for Marine aviation; all the skills learned in the preceding three years of tough combat were to be tested in two major confrontations: Iwo Jima and Okinawa. In between these two important battles, carrier-based Marine air was further refined.

Marine airplanes aboard carriers had always been an option the Navy was reluctant to consider. However, by 1943 the march across the Pacific toward Japan showed the need for more carrier support. The ships were there, but there were not enough squadrons to adequately man them. This situation proved especially true during the late fall of 1944, when the Japanese unleashed their terrifying new weapon, the kamikaze. The call for more fighters aboard the carriers to protect the fleet against this effective new threat was answered by placing two Marine fighter squadrons aboard the *Essex*. VMF-124 and VMF-213 joined the men and ships of Task Force 38 as it made its way through the South China Sea.

These Marine squadrons were in the midst of carrier strikes against Indochina in mid-January 1945. Weather played a major role in the loss of thirteen aircraft and seven pilots in navigational and deck-landing accidents. The Marines said that overwater navigation and carrier approaches could not be learned in a week or two, which was certainly an accurate statement, but they pressed on with the fast carriers.

VMF-124 and VMF-213 claimed ten to twelve Japanese planes destroyed on the ground during the January 12 raid on Saigon. In an unusual circumstance, the *Essex* air wing was skippered by a Marine officer after Navy Cdr. Otto Klinsman was shot down by flak. Lt. Col. William A. Millington, commanding VMF-124, then took over command of the wing.

As the task force ran northward along the China coast and then turned east toward the Philippines, the Marines proved particularly adept at shooting down snooper aircraft, mostly Japanese multi-engine bombers that were tasked with suicide missions against the fleet. On January 20 the Marine CAP destroyed eight out of fifteen aircraft shot down, Lt. William McGill accounting for three in as many minutes.

By early February, three other carriers—the *Bennington* (CV-20), *Wasp* (CV-18), and *Bunker Hill* (CV-17)—had joined the *Essex* as part of Task Force 58. The *Bennington* had VMF-112 and VMF-123 on board; the *Wasp* had VMF-216 and VMF-217; the *Bunker Hill* carried VMF-221 and VMF-451. There were now eight Marine Corsair squadrons aboard four carriers. The task force left the big staging area at Ulithi Atoll on February 10, bound for Tokyo, with a later stop at Iwo Jima to support the big invasion there on the 19th.

On February 16 the carriers all launched a massive strike against Tokyo and Yokosuka, aimed at several airfields that could be used as staging areas for Japanese aircraft defending Iwo Jima against the American invasion. The strike in the early hours of the 16th was moderately effective. Tokyo was covered by weather, but enough damage was done on the ground and in the air to make the effort worthwhile.

The next day the weather worsened, and only a few missions were flown. VMF-112 sent eight F4Us over Tokyo, followed by other squadrons. All types of enemy aircraft were encountered, from Bettys to Zeros. For the two-day offensive, the carrier Marines claimed twenty-one aerial kills and sixty planes destroyed on the ground before the operation was canceled and the task force turned toward Iwo Jima, 800 miles to the south.

Iwo Jima

The Battle for Iwo Jima needs little introduction. Most people have heard of this bloody, hand-to-hand struggle between the Marines and Japanese defenders that lasted thirty-six days. One of the war's most famous photographs—that of the raising of the American flag on Mount Suribachi—has come to symbolize the very essence of the Marine Corps to the outside world and to the Marines themselves. Although Iwo Jima was largely a

Marine operation, the aerial support delivered before and during the battle came, for the most part, from Army and Navy air power. Marine aviation was only available through the eight squadrons aboard the carriers of Task Force 58 and an unusual but abortive experiment with LST-borne Consolidated OY liaison/spotter planes.

The latter consisted of aircraft from VMO-4 and VMO-5, which sailed with the LSTs. The little planes were launched from the LSTs by a contraption named after its inventor, Army 1st Lt. James H. Brodie. This so-called Brodie Gear consisted of upright beams and cables from which the planes hung, slid along, and launched themselves into the air. It took great skill and courage to go through a takeoff, and the OYs, although they gave great service during the invasion, usually ended up as the targets for mortars as they landed on makeshift landing strips on Iwo. These little Grasshoppers, as they were called by the troops, conducted nearly 600 spotter missions in nineteen days.

On the early morning of D-Day, February 19, Colonel Millington led forty-eight Navy and Marine fighters on a strike at the beach areas, just before the actual invasion. This softening up had been going on for three days, and the Marines who actually stormed ashore did so with very little opposition. By 10:00 AM, all seven battalions were on the beach and moving inland. That afternoon *Bunker Hill* aircraft made more strikes, and the *Bennington* sent her air group in on the 20th, along with Marine Corsairs from the *Wasp*. February 22 saw other missions, but by noontime the weather had closed down operations and effectively ended Marine air's contribution to the three-week battle on Iwo Jima. The task force was not through, however.

Turning back toward Japan on February 25, the carriers launched a big strike in concert with a B-29 raid against Tokyo, which was still protected by weather. The Marines scored aerial victories; Colonel Millington shot down a George, one of the newest of the Imperial Navy's fighters, and a very dangerous opponent, even for the maneuverable Hellcat and powerful Corsair. Turning back to Ulithi, the task force made a pass at Okinawa, obtaining photographic coverage of the island in anticipation of the invasion to come.

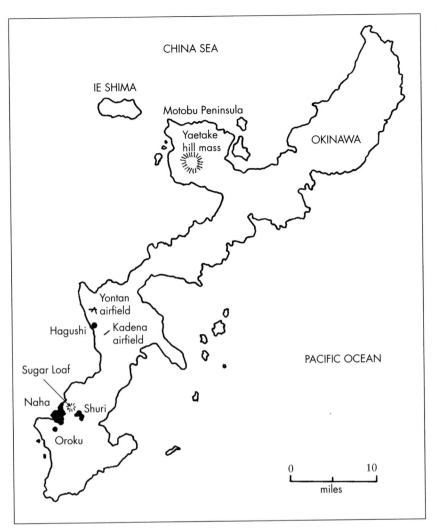

[Opposite] This little Consolidated OY-1 was the first aircraft to land on captured Iwo Jima. Tiny "Grass-hoppers" did valuable work in the later part of the war, flying artillery-spotting and ambulance rescue missions right under the guns of the enemy. A Marine rifleman sits on the wing strut to guide the pilot to a protected area.

Map 4. The Campaign for Okinawa, April–June 1945

Within the map:

CHINA SEA

IE SHIMA

Motobu Peninsula

Yaetake hill mass

OKINAWA

Yontan airfield

Hagushi

Kadena airfield

Sugar Loaf

PACIFIC OCEAN

Naha   Shuri

Oroku

0   10
miles

When TF 58 returned to Ulithi on March 10, the *Wasp* gave up its Air Group 81, including VMF-216 and VMF-217. Many of the non-pilot maintenance personnel of the Marine squadrons elected to remain on board the carriers to assist the Navy Corsair squadrons now beginning to make their appearance. Four days later, the task force departed again for the war zone, with the new carrier, the USS *Franklin* (CV-13), carrying VMF-214 and VMF-452. (VMF-214, of course, was the famous "Black Sheep" squadron of Pappy Boyington's Bougainville crowd. The Marine ace was cooling his heels in a Japanese prison camp and was no doubt witness to many of the raids over the Japanese homeland at this time.)

The task force made hit-and-run raids against the island of Kyushu, many of the 102 kills claimed by the flight crews going to Marine aviators. There was a reason for these quick thrusts against the airfields on the island: it was reckoned that these fields would be the staging areas for many suicide missions during the coming Okinawa operation. Perhaps, when the big battle did begin, the kamikazes were delayed because of these preemptive strikes.

However, luck was not with CV-13. Shortly after 7:00 AM on March 19, a single Japanese plane snuck up on the carrier and dropped two bombs, which burst among aircraft on the flight deck preparing for a mission. The

inferno that resulted created a living hell for all aboard the *Franklin*. For four hours the big carrier lay dead in the water, only fifty-five miles off the coast, while her men fought the flames. The cruiser USS *Pittsburgh* was finally able to take the carrier in tow back to Ulithi.

The casualty figures were high. Of the 772 dead, 65 Marines died in the blaze, all from the two fighter squadrons. VMF-214 and VMF-452 were out of the war with only two days of combat operations to show for their troubles.

Only four Marine squadrons were left on two carriers. Both the *Bennington* and *Bunker Hill* launched strikes even as their sister carrier fought for her life. Corsairs from VMF-451 in the *Bunker Hill* escorted Avengers and Helldivers against the remnants of the imperial fleet, hitting three carriers as they sat at the piers. In a prelude to the Okinawa landings, the *Bennington*'s VMF-112 and VMF-123 contributed to a strike against the island on March 23 and again on the 29th.

The Battle of Okinawa

The Battle of Okinawa drew upon every facet of Marine aviation, from fighter escort and CAP to torpedo and dive bombing, as well as defense against the hordes of kamikaze aircraft, and even ground suicide squads. It was the finale for Japan, and she grimly cast everything she had left into the combat arena. Okinawa was the most horrible battle, lasting two and a half months; it drained invader and defender alike.

Adm. Raymond A. Spruance, who had led the American carriers at Midway, had charge of the fast carriers offshore, while Lt. Gen. Simon Bolivar Buckner Jr. commanded the 10th Army and related expeditionary forces, including Maj. Gen. Roy Geiger's III Amphibious Corps. (General Buckner was well qualified to lead this momentous invasion. He had been in command of American ground and air forces during the yearlong battle in the Alaskan Aleutians. This drawn-out battle—the only fighting on anything that could be called U.S. soil—saw the Americans and Japanese trading punches in some of the most inhospitable weather and ended in a Japanese withdrawal in mid-1943.)

More than 182,000 troops were under Buckner, of which 81,000 were Marines. The initial landings hit the beaches at 8:30 AM, April 1, 1945, Easter Sunday. To their surprise and relief, the beaches were undefended and nothing of consequence was heard from the Japanese until April 4, when the enemy counterattacked.

During the initial phases of the Okinawa landings, the carrier Marines flew several support missions along the beaches, as well as meeting Japanese aircraft in the sky. But April 6 and 7 brought more than 300 kamikaze attacks against the task force offshore. TF 58 aircraft and ship air defenses claimed 300 Japanese aircraft shot down. It was April 6 when the giant battleship *Yamato* made her long-awaited sortie from Tokuyama to attack the American fleet. Her crew considered themselves already dead men and therefore this was another suicide mission; they were right.

As she cleared the southernmost point of Kyushu after noontime, the world's biggest battleship was set upon like a bear by a swarm of bees. Navy and Marine fighters and torpedo bombers made run after run on the *Yamato* until she blew up and sank at nearly 2:30 PM under the weight of ten torpedoes, including nine on the port side, and six direct bomb hits. More than 3,000 of her crew members died with her, including the captain. This action was probably mainly a psychological victory for the U.S. aviators, because the huge battleship could have done little to disrupt the Okinawa operation, either at sea or by bombarding the beaches.

The kamikazes kept coming in droves, hurling themselves through the flak and CAP fighters. It was one of the oldest Japanese ploys: strength through numbers. For every ten aircraft shot down, perhaps one would break through to its target. The desperation of the Japanese at this time can be seen in the battle slogan of the 32nd Army on Okinawa: "One plane for one warship. One boat for one ship. One man for ten enemy. One man for one tank."[4] It was a brutally honest approach to war, and one that bore terrible fruit. The slaughter at Okinawa was all the more terrible because of these unrelenting suicide attacks. The carriers *Enterprise* and *Intrepid* (CV-11), with several exchange Marine pilots serving with Corsair squadrons, as well as other ships, were damaged by kamikazes. The *Bennington* and *Bunker Hill*, however, plowed right through these harrowing experiences without a scratch.

On May 11 the *Bunker Hill*'s luck ran out. A lone Zero, followed by a Judy dive bomber, crashed themselves on the carrier's flight deck. Through the late afternoon, the crew fought to save their ship. The fires were brought under control, but the *Bunker Hill* was out of action, as was her air group, including VMF-221 and VMF-451. Only the *Bennington*'s Marines remained. But help was coming.

[Opposite] VMF-323 Corsairs fly in formation on a rocket strike against Japanese positions south of the front-lines on Okinawa in June 1945. The squadron CO is Maj. (later Lt. Gen.) George C. Axtell, who shot down five kamikazes on April 22, 1945. (Cpl. Beall)

Besides additional land-based squadrons, two escort carriers—the *Block Island* (CVE-106) and *Gilbert Islands* (CVE-107)—were on the way, the former arriving in the war zone on May 10 with an all-Marine air group. On board was a mixed squadron, VMF-511, of Corsairs and night-fighter Hellcats, and a twelve-plane torpedo squadron, VMTB-233, equipped with Avengers. The *Gilbert Islands* arrived a week later with VMF-512 and VMTB-143.

Other squadrons flying toward Okinawa included Jack Cram's VMB-612, with their specially modified PBJ Mitchells, and VMOs -2, -3, -6 and -7, with Consolidated OYs for spotter duties and general hack work. VMTB-232 and VMTB-231 also arrived with their Avengers, originally for anti-submarine duties, but these squadrons found themselves employed against land-based targets in the thick of the fighting.

All of these units and more, including four MAGs, were under the command of Maj. Gen. Francis P. Mulcahy, as commanding officer of the 10th Army's Tactical Air Force (TAF), which was directly subordinate to General Buckner. TAF included fifteen day- and night-fighter squadrons, operating 700 aircraft, 450 of which were to be used in actual combat.

The first TAF aircraft, OYs of VMO-2, landed on April 2, flying from the carriers offshore. The other spotter squadrons followed later. Marine aircraft flew from other carriers that had transported them to their objectives. MAG-31 (VMFs -224, -311, -441, and VMF(N)-542) launched from the USS *Sitkoh Bay* (CVE-86) and USS *Breton* (CVE-23), and landed on Yontan, one of the first operational fields on Okinawa. The new cannon-armed F4U-1C Corsairs of VMF-311 had had to contend with a single bomber's kamikaze attack on their carrier, but the enemy plane was dispatched fifty yards from the little *Sitkoh Bay*.

VMF-311, which had spent most of the war attached to MAG-31 in Samoa, far behind the frontlines, had seen only sporadic combat, flying strike and escort missions in the Marshalls. In March the word came to bring their new cannon Corsairs aboard the CVE, which would transport them to Okinawa. The first aerial engagement for the squadron resulted in the destruction of the kamikaze, credit going to Capt. Ralph G. McCormick and 1st Lt. John J. Doherty. Landing at Yontan, VMF-311 operated as part of TAF through April and May, scoring 71 aerial kills by the end of the war, second only to VMF-323, which tallied 124 victories.

Another squadron that was new to combat was VMF-312, operating Goodyear-built FG-1s, as part of MAG-33, 2nd MAW. On their first mission, VMF-312 aviators accounted for eight Zeros with only four Corsairs, the rudders of which were painted with a distinctive checkerboard pattern that became the squadron motif.

VMF-312's 1st Lt. Robert R. Klingman figured in one of the more bizarre combat victories of the late Pacific war. Together with Capt. Ken Reusser, Klingman spotted a high-flying Japanese reconnaissance plane somewhere around 38,000 feet, 13,000 feet above the American patrol. After laboriously climbing to get above the enemy plane, Klingman and Reusser attacked, firing off most of their ammunition, obtaining some hits. In frustration, Klingman pursued the fleeing Japanese and proceeded to saw off the tail of the enemy plane with his own plane's propeller. The Japanese aircraft went down after Klingman's third pass. The two Marines

turned quickly for the safety of Kadena airfield, where Klingman made an emergency landing.

Kadena and Yontan had been the primary objectives of the April 1 landings, and the two airfields were finally, though tentatively, declared secure on April 7. MAG-33 began operating from Kadena with VMFs -312, -322, -323, and VMF(N)-543. All squadrons were kept very busy intercepting the constant kamikaze raids, which had sunk fourteen American ships by April 16.

May 11 brought another big suicide attack as Buckner's 10th Army seemed to slow down, and the ships standing offshore to support the ground action became tempting targets for the kamikazes. Night-fighter Marines shot down nineteen Japanese, but two other enemy planes plowed through and headed toward the lonely little picket destroyers. Two Kadena Corsairs, probably of VMF-323, closed on a large enemy formation around 0830 on the 11th. The two Marines shot down four Japanese planes apiece in the midst of heavy fire from the ships that were the intended targets. The fighter director on board the USS *Hadley* said, in reporting this particular action, "The highest award for flying skill and courage is not too much for this pilot. His wingman stayed at masthead height in the flak and assisted in driving the planes away from the ship."[5]

May 11 was a costly day for American ground forces. General Buckner's offensive against the so-called Shuri line, extending across the width of Okinawa's southern tip, failed. The fiercely defended enemy line was not overcome until May 28. By this time, 20,000 Americans had been killed or wounded, and 63,000 Japanese had died on Okinawa, most at the Shuri line action. Unfortunately, one of the later American casualties was General Buckner himself. Buckner went up to observe frontline action on June 18, and while at a forward observation post, he was struck by shell fragments and killed. His death was, naturally, a heavy blow for the U.S. forces fighting desperately but successfully on the island.

A Corsair drops napalm on Japanese positions. Note that the pilot has not retracted his landing gear because of the proximity of the enemy to the landing field.

Close air support during the Okinawa campaign, although far from minimal, was not all it could have been, or was originally intended, because of the preoccupation with the kamikaze threat. On April 13 TAF aircraft flew the first regular close-air-support missions against Japanese artillery, but for the next three weeks only 20 percent of the total sorties flown by Marines were in the close-air-support role. The terrain was partly to blame for the lack of support missions. The close proximity of the opposing sides on the tiny island, the great amount of artillery fire, which made controlling operations dangerous and sometimes impossible, and the very nature of the Japanese defense, again the network of caves and warrens, which required methodical and extremely dangerous hand-to-hand treatment, precluded the freewheeling type of close air support actively used in the Philippines. Nonetheless, TAF provided as much support as it could under the circumstances.

As previously related, two CVEs had arrived by mid-May with all-Marine air groups. The *Block Island* with MCVG-1 (VMTB-233 and VMF-511) began operations on May 10 with a small close-air-support mission by four TBMs (General Motors-manufactured TBFs). The *Gilbert Islands* arrived on May 17 with MCVG-2 (VMTB-143 and VMF-512) and four days later began operations in company with the *Block Island*. Two other CVEs with all-Marine air groups barely made the war zone before the war ended. The USS *Cape Gloucester* (CVE-109) with MCVG-4 left Okinawan waters for a protracted sortie along the China coast, while the USS *Vella Gulf* (CVE-111) and MCVG-3 arrived off Okinawa on August 9. (The CVEs were going to play big support roles in Operation Olympic, the planned invasion of Kyushu, but the atomic bombs on Hiroshima and Nagasaki made their use in such a role unnecessary.)

As the fighting on Okinawa progressed through May, developing into a war of attrition for the hard-pressed Japanese defenders, more airfields were taken and reopened by U.S. forces. More fields meant more airplanes; the flood was overwhelming. MAG-22 arrived at Ie Shima on May 6, with VMFs -113, -314, and -422, while VMF(N)-533 and VMTB-131 arrived sometime later. Together with aircraft from the Army Air Force, these Marines brought the total number on Ie Shima to more than 200. VMF(B)-533's arrival was especially welcome because of the large number

of night-time nuisance flights by the Japanese. With a ring of radar sites set up on the little islands around Okinawa, ground control intercept (GCI) facilities were perhaps the best in the war. VMF(N)-533 was in the process of converting to the brand-new Grumman F7F-3N Tigercat, the Navy's first specially designed night fighter, but only a handful of the twin-engine aircraft arrived before the cessation of hostilities.

A large kamikaze attack of 165 planes occurred on May 25. U.S. interceptors shot down 75 of

the raiders, Marines scoring 39 kills. VMFs -312, -422, -322, and -323 all shared in the action. Two days later, another big raid of 150 aircraft struck U.S. ships in a day-long procession. Bad weather, however, hampered the performance of Marine air's primary mission on Okinawa. Carrier and land-based aircraft flew more than 14,200 specific sorties in support of the ground forces from April 1 to June 21, when Okinawa was officially declared secure. Landing Force Air Support Control Units (LFASCUs) were shipboard controlling authorities under Col. Vernon E. Megee. Some ground units, however, which knew of the great coordination possibilities, chafed at having to go through a larger, more distant authority instead of having aircraft in direct communication with the field commands.

In fairness to those on the ships, there were times when several air strikes were going on together, and to have had each strike individually controlled by different commands would have probably resulted in tremendous confusion and very little positive gain. As it was, the proximity of the opposing forces led to several instances where U.S. troops were in the line of fire, with resulting casualties. There were shining examples however. On May 20 four TBMs of VMTB-232, along with Navy Avengers, flew runs in support of Army infantry. The big Grummans flew over American troops at only fifteen feet altitude, seemingly diving below the crests of hills hiding Japanese. Corsairs joined in the strike with strafing runs. In a fantastic display of flying skill and coordination, all the bombs and bullets fell in the target area, and all the planes returned safely.

General Mulcahy was relieved as head of TAF on June 11 by Maj. Gen. Louis E. Woods. On the 18th, General Geiger was named as interim commander of the 10th Army when General Buckner was killed. This was probably the only time a Marine was in command of a U.S. Army unit. On June 23 Geiger was, in turn, relieved by Gen. Joseph "Vinegar Joe" Stilwell—the old "China hand"—when Okinawa was declared secure on

June 21. It was a fitting finale for the Pacific war, the largest amphibious operation in history. At a terrible cost in men and materiel, the last link in the island chain of the Pacific had been won and Japan lay naked across the East China Sea.

Victory

With Okinawa firmly in American hands, plans were solidified for the final massive invasion of the home islands. Victory in Europe in May had released armies and resources that would crush the Japanese. The outcome, however bloody it might be, was not in doubt. Japan was doomed. With their work basically done, the Marines of TAF stood by waiting and watching as Army B-25s, A-26s, and B-24s descended on Okinawa. B-29s were also to operate from the captured island as part of the rejuvenated Eighth Air Force, fabled victor in the daylight bombing campaigns against Germany.

Japan itself was gathering its remaining resources for a last-ditch defense, spearheaded by thousands of kamikazes. There were estimated to be 11,000 aircraft of all types remaining in Japan, with more than enough pilots to man them. But by the time the last Marine aerial kill was scored early on the morning of August 8, by Lt. William E. Jennings in a Hellcat, all but the most fanatical diehards in the islands realized the war was over. The overwhelming strength and technology of the United States—as witnessed by the August 6 and August 9 atomic bombings—were undeniable.

The last Marine air combat missions were probably flown by VMB-612, Jack Cram's PBJs only recently arrived from Iwo Jima. From August 1 to August 15, the squadron flew thirty-one sorties around the Sea of Japan. With the formal surrender aboard the USS *Missouri* on September 2, 1945, World War II was, indeed, officially over. And, as Brig. Gen. E. H. Simmons wrote, "Standing little-noticed on a deck filled with U.S. and foreign dignitaries was one solitary senior Marine, Lieutenant General Roy Geiger, who had succeeded Holland Smith as commanding general, Fleet Marine Force, Pacific."[6]

In 1939 there were but two aircraft groups, with a total of nine squadrons, representing the whole of Marine aviation. By September 1944 there were 5 wings, including 31 Marine Aircraft Groups and 145 squadrons. Even at war's end, the 5 wings included 29 MAGs and 132 squadrons. From a 1939 total of 232 designated pilots—officer and enlisted—the number had grown by January 1945 to 10,412. There had been eleven Medals of Honor won by Marine pilots. Marine crews had shot down 2,355 enemy aircraft, while 367 Marine aviators had died in combat; 198 were listed as missing in action.

The ground Marines had developed into the world's foremost amphibious force, and Marine air had closely allied itself as the most experienced practitioner of close air support. However, the sobering fact was, as Allan R. Millett wrote, the Marines flew in support of the general naval campaign rather than in support of amphibious operations. Even when Marine squadrons went to sea aboard carriers in the war's closing stages, they flew proportionately few close support sorties. After the Philippines experience, there was no question that Marine pilots could deliver close air support with unmatched effectiveness.[7]

7 Post-war Activities

WITH THE ARMY TAKING DIRECT CHARGE, both administratively and physically, of the occupation of Japan, the Marine Corps deflated. There were many retirees in the senior ranks; others chose to revert to a lower rank to remain on active duty. Pilots were ordered to serve tours of duty with ground units, unless they wanted to resign. The occupation of Japan, approached with apprehensive caution by all the services, turned out to be a smooth-running, dignified operation, because the Japanese kept their own national dignity and grace even in defeat. While the Marine Corps air squadrons still on active alert contributed low-keyed security patrols, their brethren on the ground tended to rather mundane activities, gathering war materiel and releasing Allied prisoners of war.

However, things were not going all that smoothly or peacefully across the water in China. Although the troops loyal to Chiang Kai-shek and those under Mao Tse-tung had fought together against the Japanese, the civil conflict flared anew once the Japanese had surrendered and withdrawn from China. American attempts to arrange a lasting truce were to no avail, and the Marines were sent into the troubled areas in September 1945, arriving at Tientsin, fifty miles southeast of Peking on October 1. The 1st Marine Aircraft Wing, under Maj. Gen. Claude E. Larkins, arrived on the 6th, with components of MAGs -12, -24, -25, -31, and -32.

The planes were largely for security patrols to let the U.S. presence be seen by both sides. F7Fs and OYs flew over the rocky terrain, keeping watch on the situation, but rarely did anything else. Attempts were made to get the Communists and Nationalists to the conference table, but there was really very little movement toward a peaceful solution.

In February 1946, it was decided to return most Marine ground and air units to the United States. By March VMF(N)-541, VMTB-134, and part of MAG-12 had left. VMF(N)-533 and VMF-115, as well as VMO-6, left for Hawaii later in the year. VMO-6 had reached Tsingtao on the coast, 300 miles southeast of Peking, by October 1945. The squadron was reassigned to MAG-32, 1st MAW, and began flying reconnaissance and rescue missions with its OYs. By mid-1946, VMO-6 was preparing to return to the United States but was ordered to remain in China because of increased Communist activities. It was reassigned to MAG-25, under the operational control of the 3rd Marine Brigade.

VMO-6 stayed in China throughout 1946, serving in various liaison roles with distinction. The missions were hazardous because of occasionally intense Communist ground fire. But on January 3, 1947, VMO-6 finally left the embattled Chinese to return home. The Communists, watchful and resentful of U.S. aid to the Nationalists, bided their time. By December 1948, the fall of Chiang's government was all but assured, and evacuation of U.S. personnel became essential. VMF-211's Corsairs were to cover the evacuation. In April the Communist drive to Nanking, the Nationalists' capital, was accomplished and the Communists were in control of China. There was not much a few thousand Marines could do about it, except provide security for U.S. citizens and interests. There would be plenty of time and opportunity for the Chinese and Marines to fight in Korea, in little more than a year's time.

New Developments

Meanwhile, Marine aviation was experiencing two major developments that would shape its future course: the advent of the jet aircraft and the helicopter. Of course, the jet-propelled aircraft had seen combat in the closing stages of World War II in Europe. Germany had the greatest success, while England used its few operational jets to combat the V-1 buzz bomb menace. Even the Japanese had been experimenting with a jet fighter of their own and a rocket-propelled interceptor, virtually a copy of the frightening German Komet.

The United States had built its first jet aircraft, the Bell YP-59A Airacomet, in 1943 and by war's end had several worthy designs on the boards as well as under construction. The most notable of these early jets was the Army's Lockheed P-80. However, the Navy had a jet design of its own, the McDonnell XFD-1 Phantom, later redesignated the FH-1. Powered by two small Westinghouse turbojets, the aircraft flew in early 1945, with initial carrier-qualification testing being conducted in July 1946.

Maj. Marion Carl, one of the top aces to remain on active duty after the war, first flew the FH-1 in March 1947. Carl was not new to jets, though.

He had been responsible for testing the new P-80 to determine its suitability for carrier operations in November 1946 and was probably the first Marine to make an arrested landing in a jet aboard a carrier. He was promoted to lieutenant colonel and given command of VMF-122, the first Marine jet squadron.

In August 1947, Carl set a world's speed record of 650.6 miles per hour in the scarlet-painted Douglas D-558-1 Skystreak, for which he was awarded his fourth Distinguished Flying Cross (DFC). While with VMF-122, Carl formed the world's first jet aerobatic team from members of his squadron, with the inevitable name of "The Marine Phantoms."

The second Marine jet squadron, and the first on the West Coast (VMF-122 was stationed at MCAS Cherry Point, North Carolina), was to be VMF-311 at MCAS El Toro, California, recently returned from duty as part of the occupation forces in Japan. However, it was not until mid-June 1948, after nearly a year's training and preparation, that VMF-311, under Lt. Col. John P. Condon, received two Lockheed TO-1s, similar to Air Force F-80Cs. By August a full complement of twelve of the single-seat Shooting Stars had arrived, and initiation flights and training began in earnest, several enlisted Marine pilots receiving their initial TO-1 indoctrination at MCAS El Toro in the fall of 1948.

There had been a growing problem in retaining young, eager Marine pilots who saw their fortunate Air Force counterparts getting racy new jet aircraft, while the Marines were forced to make do with outdated Corsairs. Colonel Condon finally prevailed upon the Marines to obtain fifty of the Air Force's F-80C Shooting Star fighters for a cost of $13.5 million. Although his plan ran up against initial opposition from the Bureau of Aeronautics, when Vice Adm. J. D. Price took over as Deputy Chief of Naval Operations Air (CNO Air), the plan was immediately approved. Price directed the stubborn BuAer to stop dragging its feet and obtain the jets. Fifteen of the

TO-1s actually went to the Marines, twenty-five went to the Navy at North Island, and the remaining ten were scattered around the country at various development centers.

These first jets gave valuable service as training tools. During an interview before his death, General Condon referred to these first days of Marine jet aviation as a "turning of the corner," indoctrinating Marine pilots, ground crews, and record keepers into the new world. There were different maintenance considerations. For instance, an engine change or periodic inspection normally took the airplane out of service for several days. However, while he was CO of VMF-311, Colonel Condon instituted the procedure of always having a spare engine ready to go, and when an aircraft's engine came up for a change, the standby was merely inserted in the airframe in a matter of hours, and the plane remained in service. VMF-311 gave many ground crewmen their first jet instruction and thereby laid the groundwork for generations to come.

Colonel Condon and Col. Paul J. Fontana, a Guadalcanal veteran and ace, had been in friendly competition for command of a jet squadron. The two men being equal, it was decided to flip a coin. Colonel Condon won and assumed command in April 1948. Colonel Fontana relieved him in July 1949. Up to this time, VMF-311 had independent status as a training squadron, apart from any group association. But on October 1, 1949, the squadron was reassigned to MAG-12 and soon afterward, in February 1950, was given its first real Navy jet fighter, the F9F-2 Panther.

The F9F series was Grumman's first jet venture, the XF9F-1 being an abortive twin-engine, two-seat night fighter that was never built. The XF9F-2 was a complete redesign, a single-engine, single-seat day fighter, characteristically Grumman-tubby and strong. The -2 flew for the first time in November 1947 and was first issued to Navy fighter squadron VF-41, and then to the Marines' VMFs -311, -115, and -451. The type was to be a major workhorse during the next several years, especially in Korea.

Two lesser designs, although their association with the Marines was to prove surprisingly long lived, were the McDonnell F2H Banshee and Douglas F3D Skyknight. Originally the XF2D-1, the Banshee, was an obvious development of the early Phantom and first flew in January 1947. It was to fly primarily from Navy carriers (providing the basis for James Michener's realistic novella *The Bridges at Toko-ri*), but it also found employment with the Marines as a reconnaissance aircraft in the F2H-2P version.

The Douglas Skyknight was a big, twin-engine, multi-seat fighter, which flew in March 1948 but was found to be vastly underpowered. The F3D-2 incorporated larger engines and weight-saving measures. The -2 was issued to the Marines in 1950, although they had been using the -1 as a trainer. The F3D-2 was to be used as a night fighter, and as such was to score the first successful night-fighter kill by a U.S. jet.

The Helicopter Arrives

Post-war developments arose concerning the role of Marine troops, especially their traditional role in amphibious operations with air support. Nuclear warfare presented a clear and present danger to the long, involved

amphibious invasion, where incoming troops were exposed for long, dangerous periods to enemy defense fire. The Communists, both the Chinese and their Soviet patrons, posed a large and distinct threat, and traditional service rivalries made the Fleet Marine Force's (FMF's) development, indeed existence, tenuous at best. To make matters worse and more involved, the Army was lobbying for control of all land-based air assets, leaving the Navy to pursue its traditional role of protection of the sea-lanes.

The development of the helicopter by the Marines as an expansion of their amphibious-invasion role had the greatest overall impact on them. They had experimented with rotary-winged aircraft as far back as 1932, under actual combat conditions in Nicaragua. The aircraft involved was the Pitcairn Autogyro, which used a normally mounted radial engine to pull the craft to operating speeds at which it could drive the vertically mounted rotor blades to pull it up more or less vertically after a short takeoff run. The Autogyro worked, but it could carry virtually no useful payload, and then–Lt. Col. Roy Geiger recommended that its development by the Marines be curtailed.

It was only when Igor I. Sikorsky, who had made a name for himself in his native Russia for building large conventional aircraft, flew his VS-300 in 1939 that a practical helicopter appeared. Under an Army contract, Sikorsky developed several refinements of his basic design, and the Army actually used these aircraft for rescue and observation in the Pacific during late 1944 and 1945. Other developers of helicopters soon appeared, Bell and Piasecki being the most noteworthy.

It was Frank Piasecki who designed the first experimental helicopter for the Navy, the XHRP, a tandem-rotor (a Piasecki hallmark), banana-shaped airplane that could carry 900 pounds of useful payload, although it would not be delivered to the Navy for two years. Sikorsky had in the meantime designed an aircraft that would serve well into the 1950s, the HO3S-1, the shape of which would come to mean "helicopter" for the public.

With the infant helicopter industry growing by leaps and bounds, the Marine Corps, under Gen. A. A. Vandegrift, the eighteenth Commandant, were quick to profess interest in the new form of aerial transportation. Lieutenant General Geiger, who had seen early A-bomb tests, was very concerned that one of these horrible weapons could quickly obliterate a Marine invasion force. He urged Vandegrift to seek alternatives to the traditional amphibious landing. (This was probably one of the last of Geiger's major official inputs to Marine policy, because he died in January 1947, one week short of his retirement, at age sixty-one. A Congressional bill elevated him to four-star rank, the only Marine aviator to attain such a position, albeit posthumously, up to that time.)

The helicopter seemed to hold great promise, and the seeds of modern vertical assault were sown at this time. A special board under Maj. Gen. R. C. Shepherd, later the Corps' twentieth Commandant, drew up the Marines' specifications for a practical helicopter, sort of a "wish list." Basically, the board envisioned a craft that could carry 5,000 pounds of payload for 200 miles to 300 miles at 100 knots, at altitudes from 4,000 feet to 15,000 feet. It was a very optimistic set of demands, but Sikorsky and Piasecki said they could build such an aircraft.

The Shepherd Board issued its report in early December 1946, recommending two paths of research: the helicopter, and a large transport seaplane, which could also act in concert with any envisioned helicopter invasion operation. The paper also called for the establishment of a Marine helicopter squadron for training and indoctrination. The Commandant quickly endorsed the report and forwarded it up to the Chief of Naval Operations. After a lengthy period of correspondence and refinement of the original proposals, the CNO finally decided that, because of post-war budgetary constraints, a separate Marine helicopter program was impractical; however, a section of the overall 1949 Navy budget could be set aside with approval for the Piasecki-designed HRP. Development of a separate Marine heavy transport helicopter was thus restricted to some desultory research efforts.

However, approval was given to create HMX-1, the Marine Corps helicopter development squadron, with Col. Edward C. Dyer as the commanding officer. Dyer chose Quantico as the site for his squadron because of its relative proximity to the Sikorsky and Piasecki plants in Connecticut, and to the Marine Corps' Schools from which he planned to draw most of his unit. HMX-1 was established in January 1948, with HO3Ss and HRPs, with a first test of its capabilities coming in May.

Five aircraft transported sixty-six troops from the carrier USS *Palau* (CVE-122) to Camp Lejeune, North Carolina, during a school exercise. The five HO3Ss could only carry three troops apiece, so it was necessary to make thirty-five flights to carry all the Marines to the landing zone. But the operation, which was called Packard II, clearly indicated the possibilities of the helicopter. Packard II was the first chance the Marines had to try out the new doctrine of vertical assault, which was being assembled in a publication titled *Amphibious Operations-Employment of the Helicopter (Tentative)*, but known colloquially as *Phib-31*.

The helicopter, stated the report, "possesses certain distinctive characteristics which, if exploited, can enhance greatly the speed and flexibility of the amphibious assault, while at the same time permitting a desirable increase in the dispersion of the attacking Naval forces. . . . [Its] ability to circumvent powerful beach defenses, and to land assault forces accurately . . . endow helicopter operations with many of the desirable characteristics of the conventional airborne attack while avoiding undesirable dispersal of forces which accompany such operations. . . . [The] evolution of a set of principles governing the helicopter employment cannot await the perfection of the craft itself."[1]

By 1949 HMX-1 was heavily involved in spreading the helicopter gospel, participating in additional demonstrations of rapid troop insertion and deployment, including Packard III in May 1949. Overflying the choppy seas, which swamped several landing craft, the HRPs quickly deposited their troops, 230 in all, as well as 14,000 pounds of cargo. It was a tremendous success for HMX-1, the Marine Corps, and the helicopter itself.

Colonel Dyer turned over command to Lt. Col. John Carey in June, but by the end of the year, the HRPs had to be grounded because of mechanical problems, leaving the HO3Ss to carry the load until the following April. In June 1950, all the aircraft were back in operation and they provided a flyby for ceremonies accompanying the change of command of the Marine Corps schools. The ceremonies were attended by many senior military and civilian dignitaries, including President Harry S. Truman. As outgoing Lieutenant General Shepherd relinquished command, thirteen helicopters of HMX-1 chopped their way across the field in front of the reviewing stand.

The relative success of the helicopter, at least in basic terms, and seen with the help of some imagination for the future of the machine, had been the bright spot in an otherwise dim post-war economic picture for the Marines. It would seem that during the immediate pre-Korean years, the fixed-wing community was suffering, to some extent, at the expense of the new helicopter visionaries. With zealous government-sponsored budget cuts affecting everything from manpower to equipment supply—even, at times, the very existence of the Marine Corps itself—Marine aviation in general had very few things to cheer about.

Contained within just two MAWs, the Marines flew outdated, though not totally obsolescent, Corsairs, whose usefulness and modernity had been rendered questionable almost overnight by the jet airplane. The Marines were, of course, having some opportunity to try the new jets, but the aircraft and support were slow to come into squadron use.

The Marine Corps had decided to make as strong a case for the development of the helicopter as possible, as a new and necessary tool for the FMF itself, and as the wave of the future. Successes like Packard II and III helped the cause, but there were a few basic problems that still had to be addressed. The big problem was, of course, the budget, followed by the lack of a satisfactory aircraft, one which could carry a meaningful payload, and then the provision for required helicopter squadrons and training facilities had to be considered.

Colonel Dyer, the commanding officer of HMX-1, suggested that the joint Navy/Air Force program responsible for the Piasecki XH-16 be considered for the Marine Corps as well. Until the XH-16 was ready, Dyer further advised, an additional program aimed at a smaller aircraft capable of carrying a 3,000-pound payload, or fifteen troops for 100 miles, should also be considered. A negative reply to Dyer's detailed letter was almost a certainty, given the economic conditions for the Marines in 1949, but when the reply came, although it did refute Dyer's suggestions, it did suggest a conference to determine the Marines' position and requirements for a future helicopter program.

A study group had been formed to consider various points of contention and formulate a list of requirements for a helicopter to be procured in 1952–53. The final list included a 3,000-pound to 3,500-pound payload carried for 250 nautical miles, or a thirteen-to-fifteen combat-troop capability, in addition to a two-man crew. The aircraft was also to be carried and stowed aboard the CVEs. The last point was important, as the board also stated that the big Piasecki XH-16 would not fit aboard a little escort carrier. Additional requirements included provision in the 1953–54 budget for two Marine assault transport helicopter squadrons, and that HMX-1 would develop an organizational structure for such squadrons.

The joint conference—called the Marine Corps Board—recommended by Colonel Dyer and Lieutenant Colonel Carey, convened in March 1950, with fourteen members from CNO and Marine agencies. The board members basically desired further development of a specific Marine aircraft with an uprated capacity of twenty troops. The helicopter was also to be multi-engine and still operated from CVEs. (This new helicopter proposal would result in the Sikorsky XHR2S-1 of 1956.)

Attempts by the Marines to upgrade the priority of the proposals met with some success, with a two-section program being developed. This program gave attention to canceling participation in the faltering XH-16 program, marshalling support for the XHR2S, and finding an interim helicopter.

Thus, as Korea erupted in June 1950 and the Marine Corps and the United States found themselves once again involved in a major war on the Asian mainland, the Corps had also come to several developmental forks in the road. Immediately after World War II, the Marines had been in distinct danger of being disbanded, lost in the tidal wave of post-war budgetary cuts. But war in Korea provided them with more than enough ammunition for their case, and Marine aviation, both fixed wing and rotary wing, was to play a big part in the operation.

8 Another War in Asia: *Korea*

THE COMMUNIST TAKEOVER IN CHINA in 1949 made it clear that civil strife on the Asian mainland was far from over; Korea promised to be next, and soon. Russian troops had invaded the Korean Peninsula on August 12, 1945. The Soviets had declared war on the already-prostate Japanese corpse on the 8th to make sure of getting a share of the post-war spoils in Asia. As the Japanese were surrendering, Russian troops swept into Korea, bolstered by Korean and Chinese Communist sympathizers, and installed a puppet government at Pyongyang, above the 38th parallel. The American forces arrived in the South on September 8, only to find the situation fairly well set regarding Russian position and influence. Korea was thus permanently divided at the 38th parallel, creating North Korea and South Korea.

Kim Il-sung, the North Korean prime minister and dictator, immediately focused his country's attention on the perceived struggle with the South, which was bound to come soon. Border raids by Northern troops made matters worse, and it was only a matter of time before hostilities began.

On Sunday afternoon, June 25, 1950, North Korean troops and armored units poured across the dividing line into South Korea, spearheaded by sporadic strafing attacks by Russian-built Yakovlov prop fighters, seconded to the North. The objective of the drive was Seoul, capital of South Korea.

Like a replay of a tired old movie, the United States and its Republic of Korea allies were ill prepared to meet the onslaught. The task of repelling, or at least stalling, the invasion fell to the U.S. Army. The veteran 24th Infantry Division provided the only reasonably effective ground opposition, holding as best it could until reinforcements were sent. The U.S. forces were far-flung throughout the Far East. Air Force fighter units in Japan and the Philippines totaled more than 550 aircraft, 365 of which were F-80C jet fighter-bombers. Navy forces included units of TF 77 in Japan and at sea, with the carrier USS *Valley Forge* (CV-45) being the only flattop available when the North Koreans invaded. With Carrier Air Group 5 aboard, the carrier had 86 aircraft embarked, including F9F Panthers, F4U-4B Corsairs, and AD-4 Skyraiders. The *Valley Forge* replenished in the Philippines and by June 27 was headed north into combat, joined by a British carrier, HMS *Triumph*, on July 1.

On July 3, the two carriers arrived seventy-five miles off the Korean coast and launched the first carrier strikes of the war, at 5:45 and 6:00 AM. The *Valley Forge* aircraft rocketed Pyongyang, while the *Triumph*'s planes— Fairey Fireflies (two-seat, single-engine prop fighters) and Supermarine Seafires (shipboard versions of the famous Spitfire)—went after airfield and rail targets at Haeju, just above the 38th parallel, to the south. The enemy was completely surprised by the devastating attacks. More strikes were launched in the afternoon, and for the next two days, the North Koreans were given a convincing demonstration of carrier air power.

As the small carrier task force pounded the North Koreans, the decision was being made in the United States to send the Marines. The 1st Provisional Marine Brigade, consisting of the 5th Marines and MAG-33 (VMF-214, VMF-323, VMF(N)-513, and VMO-6) left San Diego on July 12. MAG-33 rode on two transports and the escort carrier USS *Badoeng Strait* (CVE-116). In total the brigade had 6,534 officers and men, pilots, and ground-support personnel. (VMO-6 would have the honor of being the first U.S. helicopter squadron in the fighting with their four HO3S-1s.) The 1st Provisional Marine Brigade's formation and departure had been a marvel of logistical coordination, involving activation of Reserve components and creation of new ground units almost overnight.

The brigade landed at Pusan on Korea's extreme southeast coast on August 2, 1950. The F4Us of VMF-323 aboard the *Badoeng Strait* and another group of the gull-wing World War II fighters with VMF-214 from

[Opposite] An F4U-4B of VMF-214 ready to launch from USS *Sicily* in September 1950 before the Inchon landings. Carrier-based air power pounded the Communist positions before the landings. Note the pilot has his canopy slid back to facilitate an exit from the aircraft if needed.

[Right] A VMO-6 HO3S-1 takes off with a wounded passenger. (Note the litter projecting from the cabin window.) The HO3S's payload was limited. This aircraft is equipped with a headlight for night operations and a rescue winch, mounted immediately above the cabin in the stowed position.

the carrier USS *Sicily* (CVE-118), which had arrived from Guam, began flight operations immediately upon arrival. They began flying close-air-support missions for U. S. and Republic of Korea (ROK) soldiers near Pusan. On August 3, Maj. Robert P. Keller, the Black Sheep's executive officer, led eight Corsairs from the *Sicily* on the first Marine air strike of the war. With the arrival of the *Valley Forge, Philippine Sea* (CV-47), and *Triumph,* the number of carriers off Korea was five, with 250 aircraft.

Fighting along Korea's southern coast from Pusan westward to Masan and Chinju intensified, and the 1st Provisional Marine Brigade was thrown right into battle on August 7, with VMF-323 and VMF-214 Corsairs flying constant close-air-support strikes ahead of the Marines and Army troops on the ground. During one mission, four VMF-214 aircraft delivered their bombs at the end of a canyon, climbing up over the cliff above. The target was a concentration of enemy troops, and the Corsairs made repeated rocket and strafing runs only to have the North Koreans dart into half-concealed caves at the end of the canyon. The strike leader, Maj. Ken Reusser, received permission to fly right into the canyon and drop his napalm tank, where another airplane could set the weapon afire with machine-gun fire. The routine worked, and the enemy troops were wiped out.

Corsairs, rockets, and napalm were an effective combination during these early operations. In fact, the prop-driven Corsairs were probably the most valuable aircraft in the Marine inventory at the time. The short-legged jets could not loiter above the battlefield, and airfields in-country were not

[Below] A Bell HTL-4 of VMO-6 waits as a wounded Marine is strapped to one of its outrigger stations for transportation to a hospital ship. (Thanks to the success of the television show M*A*S*H, these little bubble-topped helicopters are among the best-known aircraft of the Korean War.)

[Opposite] An OY-1 of VMO-6 flies over the rugged Korean terrain during a spotting mission. OYs flew dangerous low-level missions throughout the war. Their pilots, several of whom were enlisted NAPs, were exposed to some of the most intense concentrations of flak and small-arms fire.

yet available. The carriers from which the fighters operated allowed more fuel and more on-station time, as well. So, it fell to the veteran Corsairs—both Navy and Marine—to carry the war at this time.

Having just arrived on August 2 amid the heavy fighting in the so-called Pusan Perimeter, VMO-6's helicopters were very active, too. Brig. Gen. Edward A. Craig, commanding general of the 1st Provisional Marine Brigade, said, "Marine helicopters have proven invaluable. . . . They have been used for every conceivable type of mission."

One of the first helicopter rescues by Marine crews occurred on August 10, 1950, when an HO3S-1 flown by Lt. Gustave F. Lueddeke picked up Capt. Vivian M. Moses of VMF-323. Moses' Corsair had been hit by enemy ground fire, lost oil pressure, and he had to ditch. (In a sad twist, Captain Moses volunteered for another mission the following day, only to be shot down again. After being thrown from his aircraft on crashing in a rice paddy, he drowned: the MAG's first combat death.)

Lt. Leuddeke continued rescuing downed pilots, sometimes behind enemy lines. On one mission, he carried General Craig along. Craig had wanted to see the helicopter operation for himself. The pilot hovered over 2nd Lt. Doyle H. Cole also of VMF-323 and pulled the young pilot to safety. As Cole entered the cabin, he slapped what he thought was an enlisted man on the back and said, "Thanks, Mac." He was somewhat chagrined to find he was addressing the brigade commander.

VMO-6 also operated several OYs, artillery-spotting aircraft, grasshoppers, as they had been called in World War II. Although these little planes were usually unarmed, their line of work was highly dangerous, and after taking ground fire, several spotter pilots retaliated. Capt. Francis A.

McCaleb took to carrying hand grenades, tossing them out over any small group of enemy troops that fired on him. But VMO-6's immediate claim to fame were the helos. The success of the "pinwheels," as the aircraft were called at the time, led General Craig to recommend the formation and deployment of a new transport helicopter squadron with Sikorsky S-55s, HRS-1s as they were designated in Navy service.

The Marines had become quickly interested in the larger HRS, with its unique front-mounted Pratt and Whitney engine, which made maintenance much easier. Official support gathered momentum, taking in along the way provision for observation helicopters like the Sikorsky HO5S-1, and the little bug-like Bell HTL-4, which was to go to VMO-6 until the larger HO5S arrived.

As the action pushed the Communists back, the two squadrons of MAG-33 aboard the carriers (VMF-214 and VMF-323) and the shore-based night fighters of VMF(N)-513, flying Grumman F7F Tigercats (about which more later), contributed morale-building and strategically important close-air-support missions. From August 3 to September 14, 1950, the three squadrons flew 1,511 support missions, of which 995 were close air support. VMO-6, of course, was in a class by itself, pioneering new tactics and procedures on a daily basis. For its continued record during the opening conflict, the 1st Provisional Marine Brigade received the first Presidential Unit Citation for action in Korea.

The action at Pusan pushed the North Koreans back from their lightning gains of the summer. The Marines, however, were suddenly ordered to disengage and hurry to another battle shaping up, where they met Communist T-34 tanks for the first time. On August 17 MAG-33 Corsairs, in conjunction with the Marines' M-26 tanks, helped destroy five of the World War II tanks.

The Inchon Operation

Plans were being rapidly developed for a Marine landing at Inchon, on the west Korean coast, which served as the port facility for Seoul, now under Communist domination. A joint task force of U.S., British, and ROK assets began assembling for the invasion, while the 1st Marine Aircraft Wing, under Maj. Gen. Field Harris, left MCAS El Toro on September 1, with MAG-12 (VMFs -212 and -312, and VMF[N]-542).

There was a great deal of planning for Inchon. The great tides moving on the harbor, with differences of as much as thirty-five feet, were of prime consideration; in fact, the tides actually set the invasion date of September 15, when the flood tide would be highest. There were differences between Army and Navy and Marine planners as well. But Gen. Douglas MacArthur, overall commander of forces in the Pacific, wanted the invasion, which had been dubbed Operation Chromite, and so planning went ahead on schedule.

Marine aviation support initially came from carrier-based squadrons aboard the *Badoeng Strait* and *Sicily.* In company with regular Navy carrier planes, elements of MAG-33 would be under tactical air control (TAC), with VMF-212 and VMF-312, and VMF(N)-542 waiting to come ashore to the airfield at Kimpo, which would be the main target objective of the initial landing. So, as the invasion date approached, 230 ships assembled off the coast, including six carriers. There were five U.S. flattops: the *Philippine Sea, Valley Forge, Boxer* (which had just arrived from the West Coast with sixty-four Corsairs, sixteen ADs, and fourteen other aircraft), and the two workhorse CVEs *Badoeng Strait* and *Sicily.* The sixth carrier was the veteran British *Triumph.* This mighty armada of ships, aircraft, and men from America, the UK, New Zealand, Korea, Japan, and France was designated Joint Task Force 7, with Task Force 77 actually numbering the U.S. carriers within its complement.

Carrier strikes softened up the Inchon-Seoul area before the actual landings. The initial target was the little island of Wolmi-do, connected to Inchon by a causeway. VMF-323 and VMF-214 Corsairs made early morning strikes on September 10 with napalm to clear away trees that were shielding North Korean artillery. Attacks kept coming throughout the morning as the CVEs concentrated on Wolmi-do. The Corsairs also served as naval gunfire spotters for the Navy ships' offshore bombardment. This softening up continued through the evening of September 14, as the invasion force prepared for action the following morning.

Finally at 6:33 AM, September 15, 1950, the Marines hit Green Beach on the northwestern tip of Wolmi-do under a covering umbrella of close air support, the Corsairs hosing enemy positions not fifty yards ahead of the assault columns with machine-gun fire. Men and tanks poured ashore, but resistance was surprisingly light or poorly coordinated. The North Koreans had badly underestimated the U.S. capability to mount such a massive invasion so soon after World War II. They had also guessed wrong concerning the American commanders' resolve to gamble with the dangerous tides and currents of the Inchon shore.

The action shifted to the mainland area and met with stiffer, though not insurmountable, resistance. At 7:00 AM on September 16, North Korean tanks were moving through a village on the outskirts of the city. Eight Corsairs of VMF-214 swept in and inundated the T-34s in napalm, in full view of cheering Marines on the ground. The enthusiasm was somewhat dampened when one of the F4Us crashed, the pilot apparently failing to pull out of his dive soon enough. Additional anti-tank strikes effectively neutralized enemy armored threats with rockets and bombs. The invasion force fought northeastward, battling toward the major objective of Kimpo Airfield.

In the meantime, a second front had been opened in the South at Pusan by American and South Korean units. The North Koreans were caught in a vise, and their resolve and resources were rapidly dissolving. Action on September 17 and 18 secured the airfield, and on September 18, at 10:00 in the morning, a VMO-6 HO3S-1, with Lt. Gen. L. C. Shepherd Jr., Commanding General FMFPAC, touched down to find several North Korean aircraft scattered about, mainly Russian-built Yak fighters and Ilyushin Il-10 ground attack aircraft. That evening MAG-33 was ordered to occupy Kimpo.

There was some initial confusion, as MAG-33 and MAG-12 apparently switched squadrons. Major General Harris, perhaps, wanted veterans VMF-214 and VMF-323 to remain on the carriers doing the job they were doing so well, and thus allow relative newcomers VMF-212, VMF-312, and VMF(N)-542 to come to Kimpo and start operations almost immediately. Close air support was becoming more and more important as North Korean units began to dig in and hit back. On the 18th and 19th alone, nearly fifty CAS missions were flown even before the fighter squadrons had arrived at Kimpo.

The first squadron to arrive at Kimpo was VMF(N)-542, led by Lt. Col. Max J. Volcansek Jr. Six twin-engine F7F-3Ns landed in the early evening, coming from their base at Itami, Japan. At 7:35 the next morning, VMF(N)-542 flew the first combat missions from Kimpo, as four Tigercats shot up enemy railroad traffic. Sometime later, Colonel Volcansek had a harrowing experience. Just before beginning an attack, he tried to blow away his underwing fuel tank, only to have the tank jam between the fuselage and right engine nacelle. The airplane became uncontrollable, and at only 1,000 feet Volcansek tried to leave the airplane but was forced back by the slipstream. In desperation, he kicked the control stick with his foot, sending the F7F into a steep dive, and forcing himself free. His chute opened at only 500 feet, but he landed safely and was picked up by the intrepid Lieutenant Leuddeke in a helicopter.

VMF-212 and VMF-312 also landed at Kimpo on the 19th and went into action on the 20th, right behind VMF(N)-542. The commanding officer of VMF-212, Lt. Col. Richard W. Wyczawski, also had a narrow escape when his Corsair developed an oil leak on takeoff, and as Wyczawski turned back to the field, the plane burst into flame. The pilot crash-landed and jumped out of the burning plane but collapsed only a few feet away. With the flames coming closer to the napalm and rockets, there did not seem to be much time for a rescue, but Navy Hospital Corpsman 3rd Class Charles B. Stalcup rushed into the inferno and pulled the unconscious pilot out of danger seconds before the napalm exploded.

With Kimpo secured and operations begun, the liberation of Seoul was a matter of time, although the 1st Marine Division was finding the going rough, encountering the stiffest resistance of the operation in house-to-house fighting in the capital city itself. But, backed up by solid close air support, both from shore- and carrier-based aircraft, the 1st and 5th Marine Regiments marched into Seoul on September 24th, and by the 27th the city was declared secure.

Thus, the Inchon Operation was a complete success; it proved that the Marine amphibious operation was alive and well, and, most important, it routed the Communists from the South Korean capital. Operation Chromite also upheld the hard-won doctrine of Marine close air support, the Marine Corsair squadrons especially coming in for high praise from Army and Marine commanders.

The action figures speak for themselves. In a thirty-three-day period, September 7 to October 9, the four F4U squadrons—VMF-214 and VMF-323 aboard the carriers and VMF-212 and VMF-313 at Kimpo—flew 2,163 individual sorties, while VMF(N)-542, basically a night-fighter squadron, flew 573, for a grand total of 2,736 missions. Eleven aircraft had been lost to enemy ground fire, with six pilots killed in action. VMO-6 came in for its own special commendation, for many of the 139 seriously wounded men were evacuated to hospitals by helicopters of this pioneer unit. The operation had been a success, but difficult times were coming in subsequent action at Wonsan and Chosin.

Wonsan and the Chosin Reservoir Breakout

After succeeding at Inchon, General MacArthur's attention turned north-eastward to the harbor at Wonsan, on the east coast of the Korean Peninsula, some eighty miles above the 38th parallel. It was all part of the drive to regain lost territory. Indeed, MacArthur had strong thoughts of crossing the Yalu River and attacking Red China. By September plans were laid for the Wonsan operation. The harbor had been heavily mined by the Communists, and while Navy PBM Mariner flying boats and surface mine sweepers conducted neutralizing operations, MAG-12 moved from Kimpo (which was later designated K-14) to the airfield at Wonsan, VMF-312 and VMF(N)-513 arriving on October 14, 1950.

The invasion took place on October 26, with VMF-312 providing close air support. The action worked its way north toward the crucial Chosin Reservoir. Unexpectedly stiff resistance from fresh troops of the Red Chinese Army, who fought with guerrilla tactics, had slowed the Marine advance. But the 1st, 5th, and 7th Marine Regiments finally defeated the Chinese and North Korean forces after five days of heavy combat.

By mid-November, the Korean winter, with its horrible cold, had begun to descend, creating a new danger for friend and foe alike. The Marines faced a huge enemy force of ten Chinese divisions, totaling 100,000 men. Names such as Hagaru-ri and Koto-ri have been etched into Marine Corps history, for it was in these little villages and towns that Marine fortitude, dedication, and skill were tested to the utmost in the bitter cold. Outnumbered, fighting against the unexpected Chinese offensive, the Marines began to withdraw against heavy Chinese attack from Chosin—"frozen Chosin," as it was called. It was an epic story of survival and courage.

The main force fell back to Hagaru-ri to regroup and be resupplied, then to go south to Koto-ri. This withdrawal was accomplished under heavy enemy attack, as well as the immobilizing cold. The MAG-33 squadrons did their best to hamper the enemy, VMF-312 accumulating nearly 2,000 flight hours, while losing four aircraft and one pilot, even while moving to Yonpo airfield near Hamhung on December 1. By November 28, the situation was becoming quite desperate, as Chinese troops harassed positions at Hagaru-ri, where a 2,900-foot airstrip had become crucial to the resupply effort. On December 6 the 7th Marines led the so-called Chosin Breakout, making for Koto-ri in the south.

Essential to the final outcome of the breakout was the air supply operation mounted by Marine transports. Twin-boomed Marine R4Q-1s, the designation for the Air Force's Fairchild C-119 Flying Boxcar twin-engined transport, of the 1st Air Delivery Platoon made most of the supply drops to Marines at Hagaru-ri and Koto-ri, delivering some 800,000 pounds at Hagaru-ri and 1 million pounds at Koto-ri, including a nineteen-ton bridge in eight sections.

During the breakout, Corsairs from all the Marine squadrons participated in day-long strikes; VMF-212 and VMF-312, VMF(N)-513, and VMF(N)-542 from Wonsan and Yonpo, and the carrier-based VMF-214 and VMF-323 lifted off even with the sky still completely black, to be over the battlefields at daybreak, helping Marine and Army troops battle their way south. VMO-6 OYs flew artillery-spotting missions, while squadron helicopters performed their usual, but no less valuable, medevac and rescue duties, sometimes behind enemy lines.

VMF-212 was very active on November 28, when ten strikes controlled by forward air controllers (FAC) were made in the morning and afternoon around the Reservoir area against Chinese positions, the Corsairs running in with rockets and napalm, as well as making strafing runs with machine guns perilously close to the overhanging ridges that ringed the area. The next day, the 29th, after a six-inch snowfall had covered the airfields at Wonsan and hindered early-morning operations at sea, the Corsairs struck Chinese troops again, on sixty-one separate occasions, VMF-212 and VMF-312 moving up and down the line between Hagaru-ri and Koto-ri in search of targets. The crowded air above the Allied lines was filled both with cargo planes, dropping much-needed supplies, and the Corsairs diving and wheeling over enemy positions; the FACs were obviously very busy.

The value of the Chance Vought F4U Corsair cannot be overestimated. Rugged and powerful, the dependable Corsair was in constant action, from sea and land bases. It was viewed with real affection by the men on the ground. One of the innumerable songs of the period paid tribute to the Corsair and its role in the Chosin campaign.

Up in Korea midst rocks, ice, and snow,
The poor Chinese Commie is feeling so low,
As our Corsairs roar by overhead,
He knows that his buddies will all soon be dead.

Lin Pao went way up to cold Koto-ri,
His prize Chinese Army in action to see,
He said that his soldiers no battle could lose,
But all that he found was their hats and their shoes.

Of course, the chauvinism might be understood and forgiven by less interested parties, but the verses do convey the feeling.

It was a tired lot of Marines that left Hungnam in December 1950, aboard Navy transport ships; others had gone by airlift. The Chosin campaign had been one of the bloodiest, yet proudest stories in the Corps' history. There were 4,400 casualties, with 730 killed, in exchange for estimated Chinese losses of 25,000 dead. But the initial steam of the surprise Chinese offensive had been destroyed.

Of course, a large part of the story was the contribution of Marine aviation. Close air support—Marine style—under forward air control had become an accepted tool during the campaign. Both Army and Marine commanders praised the skill of the Corsair pilots, who operated in much less than ideal conditions, where a shoot down, even though the pilot was not initially wounded, could eventually prove fatal. The bitter cold of either the inhospitable land or the icy China Sea made survival as much a skill as flying. Two VMF-212 pilots almost took a dip in the water after attacking Chinese positions. Capt. Irving Barney and Tech. Sgt. Charles Radford encountered icing conditions off the coast. With their gyros inoperative, their pitot tubes frozen—which made flying on instruments difficult—and their fuel down to nothing, the pair found the carrier *Badoeng Strait* and landed, Radford actually running out of gas just before he touched down.

The weather hampered flight operations at sea, as well as on land; sixty-eight-knot winds, ice, and snow periodically blew across the carrier decks, closing down all flight operations. The land bases at Kimpo and Wonsan were also subject to the effects of weather, and Marines and their Air Force neighbors (the Air Force conducted its own effective operation, usually from the same airfields as the Marines, though with its own distinctive rules) would combine to clear the snow from the runways and aircraft.

Airlift missions were generally considered greatly responsible for the successful withdrawal down to the coast, naturally under the protection of Marine Corsairs, and again VMO-6 rang up an impressive tally, making reconnaissance and rescue missions under the most trying of conditions. There were times when the tireless pilots of the little OYs and helos were the only link between units that had become separated under fire.

As 1950 drew to a close, and no matter how great the success and relief at the conclusion of the Chosin operation, it was obvious that the "home for Christmas" hopes of the men of the task forces and ground divisions would not become fact. There was still a lot of fighting left to do.

The Marines at this time were flying some fifteen different types of aircraft in Korea, including Bell and Sikorsky helicopters, Douglas and Fairchild transports, the workhorse F4U Corsair, the unsung OY grasshopper, the Douglas AD Skyraider, and even the occasional Grumman TBM, used for liaison and hack work.

The new Grumman F9F Panthers of VMF-311 had appeared during the closing days of the Chosin campaign as well. But there was also a plane whose record has been largely overlooked, perhaps because it was active for only a relatively short period of time and was eclipsed by its better-known contemporary, the Corsair, and the newer, more glamorous jets. This lonely performer was the Grumman F7F Tigercat.

The Grumman Tigercat descended from the company's XF5F-1/XP-50 designs of early 1940. The Navy issued further authorization for the progressive development of the XF7F-1 in 1941, with the prototype's first flight occurring on December 2, 1943. A graceful, well-proportioned two-seater, the twin-engine Tigercat boasted a top speed in excess of 400 miles per hour, but was considered too hot a plane to operate from aircraft carriers. The Navy, therefore, decided to give the entire production run to the Marines to fly from land bases. Twelve squadrons were planned and some of the aircraft were actually en route to the Pacific when the war ended in August 1945, a few F7Fs getting to Okinawa with VMF(N)-533, a mere day before the August 15 cease-fire.

The F7F found a place in post-war Marine squadrons, especially as a night fighter in the -3N model, which incorporated nose-mounted radar and a taller vertical tail. (The F7F-3 was a single-seat model used primarily as a fast ground-attack aircraft.) When the Korean War broke

out, VMF(N)-542 brought its Tigercats to Japan and then to Korea itself to be used as night fighters, although the pace of action dictated their use during the day as well.

Starting usually around sunset and continuing well into the night and predawn hours, the two-man crews took off in search of Communist truck traffic wandering down from Manchuria and China, delivering supplies under the cover of darkness, much like the infamous Ho Chi Minh Trail of Laos and Vietnam two decades later. (Sometimes the parallels between Asian wars are so striking that one wonders if the people involved have not discovered the secret of immortality!) The F7Fs were usually under forward air control—usually FACs of the Air Force as in Vietnam—and would be called down on targets from rail traffic to troop concentrations. It was dangerous work. Sometimes the Communists would string cables across known flight paths to entangle unwary fighters. Capt. Don Derryberry of VMF(N)-513 was out one night making strafing runs when he hit a cable, 200 feet of which wrapped around both engines, necessitating one powerplant being shut down. Derryberry struggled with the staggering plane, fighting to maintain control with his windshield shattered, and eventually brought the Tigercat back to an emergency field.

[Opposite] K-1 at Pusan, 1951. Corsairs and TBMs line the field perimeters, while a tent city, typical of Marine forward-area bases, populates the background.

[Right] The Tigercats and Corsairs took a terrible beating flying their low-level missions. This F7F's black finish shows considerable wear and tear on the lead edge of its wings and nose. The Grumman twin was a very graceful, well-proportioned design whose lines were somewhat marred by the two large engine nacelles. Nonetheless, the plane's look bespoke menacing power.

The F7F scored two air-to-air kills at night, although against somewhat unworthy game. On July 1, 1951, VMF(N)-513's Capt. Edwin B. Long and his radar operator, WO Robert C. Buckingham, spotted an ancient North Korean PO-2 biplane engaged on an intruder mission. The F7F pilot made three passes before downing the slow old craft north of Kimpo. VMF(N)-542's Maj. Eugene A. Van Grumby and MSgt. Thomas H. Ullom shot down another PO-2 on September 23. These were the only aerial kills scored by the Tigercat, but the type was a valuable member of the Marine close-air-support team during the Wonsan/Chosin operation, bombing and strafing Communist positions around the clock, if needed.

During March 1951, VMF(N)-513 set a record of 2,010 night-combat flight hours, during which time its F7Fs and F4Us destroyed nearly 400 Communist trucks and damaged 193 more. (When VMF(N)-542 was rotated back to the States, its Tigercats were given to VMF(N)-513, which accounts for the two types in one squadron.) The Tigercat was also used as a photo reconnaissance aircraft in its -3P model.

However, by the time Maj. Gen. Christian Schilt, who received the Medal of Honor during the Nicaraguan campaign and was now commanding general of the 1st Marine Aircraft Wing, flew his F7F-3 Tigercat over the combat lines on November 10, 1951, to celebrate the 176th birthday of the Marine Corps, the F7F was well on its way to retirement. It had been finally overtaken by jet aircraft now operating from land bases. (As commanding general of the 1st MAW, Schilt had exclusive use of an AirPac day fighter, which was maintained in spit-and-polish condition by the troops at K-3. The general would often climb into the Tigercat in the early evening and put on a show for the men on the ground, zoom-climbing to 3,000 feet before rolling over in a split-S. The troops loved it.) The twin-engine Grumman had fared somewhat better than its company stablemate, the lithe little F8F Bearcat, which saw little U.S. Navy service, and then not during combat operations. The Tigercat was available when it was needed during the hectic first eighteen months of combat in Korea, and it did its demanding, somewhat tedious, job well.

The Jet Squadron: VMF-311

By early 1951, the two CVEs *Badoeng Strait* and *Sicily* (whose skipper was Capt. John S. Thach, famous Navy World War II fighter ace and tactician) had returned to the States, having been in action almost from the beginning. *Sicily* had sometimes been known as the "Black Sheep Jeep," because it was the home of the Corsairs of VMF-214, Pappy Boyington's old outfit. F4Us from the carrier had flown more than 8,100 combat hours between July 4, 1950, and January 4, 1951, against every type of target the North Koreans and Communist Chinese had, including locomotives and camel-drawn convoys.

The new year of 1951 saw the intensified use of jets from land bases. VMF-311 had arrived at Yonpo near Chosin by December 10, 1950, and that afternoon two F9F-2 Panthers flew the first Marine jet combat missions. With the successful withdrawal from Chosin, VMF-311 was ordered south to Pusan East (Airfield K-9), where it flew missions all over Korea, usually under forward air control, or even airborne air controllers in T-6 "Mosquito" aircraft. Although the squadron accumulated more than 400 hours of combat flying in December alone, by January 16 all of its aircraft were grounded because of difficulties with the Pratt and Whitney engines. The unit was ordered back to Japan to take care of the problems.

In February VMF-311 was reassigned from MAG-12 to MAG-33 and relocated to Pohang's Yongil-man Airfield (K-3), fifty miles north of Pusan, originally built by the Japanese as a Zero fighter base. By February 19 the "Panther Pack," as the squadron called itself, was back in combat, flying close air support and armed reconnaissance. In March 1951 MAG-33 consisted of VMF-212 and VMF-311, while MAG-12, which had moved to Bradshaw airfield, Pusan West (K-1), had VMFs -214, -312, -323, and VMF(N)-513. Only VMF-311 had jets, however. During March and April, the F9Fs evolved the practice of maintaining ten-minute standby alerts with four ready aircraft, the pilots in the cockpits. This arrangement allowed the unit to respond to unforeseen scrambles and calls for close air support from the Tactical Air Control Center (TACC). However, a better system allowed four aircraft to be already airborne, where they could be briefed and arrive over the target ready to go.

On May 9, 1951, VMF-311 put up twenty Panthers as part of the largest U.S. raid on North Korea to that time. Three hundred aircraft, including seventy-five Corsairs and Panthers from the lst MAW, attacked airfields at Sinuiju, on the southern Yalu shore. There were some MiG sightings, but the Russian-built and often Russian-flown fighters kept their distance. The Marine pilots were hungry for air-to-air combat and were anxious to chalk up a score next to the Navy's first MiG kill, and the second U.S. jet kill—one day behind an Air Force score—by VF-111's skipper, Lt. Cdr. William T. Amen, on November 9, 1950. But aerial encounters by Marine-piloted planes were somewhat rare, and most—*though not all*—MiG kills by Marines were registered while flying exchange duty with the Air Force. (Recent reconsideration and discovery of information from declassified Soviet records now indicate that the USAF kill was not correct, the MiG pilot having returned to his base. Thus, the Navy score would *appear* to be the first jet-to-jet victory.)

Until February 1952, VMF-311 was the sole Marine jet squadron in Korea, and the Panthers did yeoman service up and down the length of Korea, wherever close air support was needed. VMF-115 arrived that month with F9Fs, and in March Marine Photographic Squadron 1 (VMJ-1) brought its McDonnell F2H-2P Banshees for reconnaissance work. By the time Korean action ceased on July 27, 1953, VMF-311 pilots had racked up 18,851 combat sorties in two and one-half years, and even after the cease-fire, the squadron remained on station, overseeing the repatriation of prisoners.

VMO-6 and HMR-161

VMO-6 continued its unique record of rescues during this period. On Friday, April 13, 1951, Capt. Valdemar Schmidt Jr. and Cpl. Robert Sarvia were called in to rescue a downed Air Force F-51 pilot north of Kwachon Reservoir. With a combined group of Air Force Mustangs and Marine Corsairs flying escort, the Marine Sikorsky crew flew out to the downed pilot. But enemy ground fire struck the helicopter and it crashed near the waiting pilot. The Air Force pilot and the two Marines huddled in some nearby bushes as the Chinese combed the area.

Capt. Frank E. Wilson flew another chopper out at dusk with four VMF-214 Corsairs, which attacked the Chinese positions, thereby allowing the helicopter to hover over the Americans. In a slow, arduous process, the first helo's enlisted crewman pulled himself into the trembling chopper. Wilson found a clearing where he was able to land, allowing the remaining two pilots to scramble inside. All was not over yet.

With five men, the HO3S became nose heavy, and without hesitating, Captain Schmidt, pilot of the first helicopter, leaped out so that Captain Wilson could regain control and shift sandbags around to retrim the aircraft. With everything set, Schmidt got back into the helicopter. All of this action took place at night under heavy enemy fire.

First Lieutenant Robert E. Mathewson was flying a Bell HTL-4 when he was shot down, crash-landing among a group of mud-Marines. Without a helicopter, Mathewson quickly became an infantryman when his brethren handed him an M-1 rifle. For most of the day, he fought alongside the others, fighting his way out of a Communist Chinese trap.

VMO-6 helicopters set a record of seventy-seven casualties evacuated in one day in April 1951. Flying their bubble-topped Bells, squadron pilots shuttled in and out of the rugged mountains of the Kwachon Reservoir, which had become the scene of the Chinese spring counteroffensive. The area, which included a big valley ringed with ridgelines, was nicknamed the "Punchbowl." First Lieutenant Joseph C. Gardiner Jr. brought seventeen wounded Marines out during this period.

VMO-6 logged a record 2,626 combat hours in May 1952, which saw the second phase of the Chinese offensive, the squadron operating three types of helicopters—Sikorsky HO3Ss and larger HO5S observation aircraft, and Bell HTLs—as well as Cessna OE-1s, the high-wing tail-draggers later known as Birddogs, which the squadron had begun to receive in May. The normal amount of flight time was between 1,500 and 1,750 hours a month. This action usually included artillery-spotting missions by the OEs, equipped with wing-mounted flares to mark targets, as well as the rescue missions usually flown by the helicopters whenever required. The OEs were engaged in highly dangerous work. MSgt. John R. Stone's aircraft was hit by 85-mm shell fragments that blew out one of his main tires.

All of these actions and more were accomplished under primitive living conditions in what amounted to a tent city, 100 yards from the flight line. The runway was only 1,100 feet of hard-pressed gravel. Rescue operations were accomplished day and night.

The HRS-1 Arrives with HMR-161

Although the gallant Bell and Sikorsky helicopters of VMO-6 were doing a tremendous job in Korea, a larger, more capable aircraft was needed. By September 1951, HMR-161, equipped with the larger HRS-1, had arrived in Korea. The time had come to combat test the developing doctrine of vertical envelopment: the moving of Marine combat troops and their equipment to the battlefield, and the continuing supply of these men for as long as necessary, all by helicopter.

Established on January 15, 1951, Marine Helicopter Transport Squadron 161, equipped with the latest helicopter the Navy could offer, was the result of the Marine Corps' stated requirement for an offshoot of HMX-1. The HRS-1, Sikorsky's model S-55, was a revolutionary aircraft, with its engine mounted in the nose, below and in front of the cockpit, behind two clamshell doors. With a top speed of ninety knots, it could carry 1,500 pounds of cargo with a crew of two. Still a long way from the dream of a 3,000-pound payload, but the best available. Working up, the squadron got its first HRS in April 1951 and was alerted for overseas duty in July. Traveling to Korea on board the carrier *Sitkoh Bay*, which was also ferrying Air Force F-86s across, the fifteen Sikorskys and 270 squadron personnel left the United States on August 16, arriving at Pusan on September 2. HMR-161 was quickly attached to the 1st MAW and stationed first at K-18, near Kang Nung, and then relocated to auxiliary field X-83, where VMO-6 operated.

Within two weeks, the unit flew its first resupply mission, the first such helicopter mission of the war, on September 13. September 19 saw another successful resupply mission, and it was decided to use the HRS-1s on a tactical airlift on September 21. In Operation Summit, an effort to relieve an embattled Republic of Korea unit, HMR-161 helos carried 224 troops and 17,772 pounds of cargo to a hill overlooking the action. In addition to inserting troops, the HRSs also carried telephone wire to connect reconnaissance teams with the command post. The operation was a total success. The Marine Corps Commandant, Gen. Lemuel C. Shepherd Jr., was lavish in his praise of the highly publicized event.

From these early efforts, including airlifts at night on September 28, HMR-161, under Lt. Col. George W. Herring, and then-Col. Keith B. McCutcheon, helped establish the helicopter as a major tactical weapon. October 11, 1951, saw Operation Bumblebee, wherein reinforcements were helicoptered in, with only one pilot per aircraft. Twelve HRS-1s made 156 round trips with 958 troops. Squadron aircraft also took care of the men in the field by airlifting such niceties as Marine Corps birthday cakes (on November 10th) and Thanksgiving turkey dinners to the frontlines.

The HRSs also took up the challenge of combat rescue. A May 1952 rescue involved HMR-161 aircraft trying to reach a stranded Navy pilot who had bailed out of his Corsair after it was hit by anti-aircraft fire. Initial rescue attempts by Navy helos were unsuccessful, and the larger aircraft of HMR-161 were called out to the carrier *Valley Forge* for briefings and another assault. Escorted by Corsairs, two HRS-1s made their way on May 28 to the plateau where the Navy pilot was supposedly waiting. Communist troops were around, and high winds made flying very treacherous. Approaching the rescue site, the first helo was stopped cold by a downdraft and dashed to the ground, fortunately without injuries among the crew. Rain then moved in and the rescue mission was halted for two days.

With the clouds still obscuring much of the area, a second Marine helicopter took off for the windy plateau. Rather than attempt a landing, the helo crew dropped a forty-foot rope ladder. One Marine on the ground grabbed the ladder and climbed into the HRS. The second had trouble, being weakened by his ordeal of the last few days, and had to be assisted into the aircraft by the third man, the helicopter pilot. The tragic part of the story was that the Navy pilot was nowhere to be seen, and under enemy fire, the helicopter had to turn for home or risk being shot down itself.

A similar mission occurred in February 1952, when a Navy pilot and crew of a Marine helicopter were down forty miles behind Communist lines. A second chopper had been driven away by intense ground fire. A third HRS-1 and eight escort aircraft flew out and found the ridges overlooking the rescue site jammed with enemy troops. The fighters were called in to strafe the Chinese positions, while the rescue helo snuck in from another direction. However, the rescue crew could not see any signs of life from the Americans on the ground and reluctantly flew back to base.

In February 1952, the squadron aircraft were grounded after a series of accidents involving tail-rotor drive shafts. A design modification in March returned the helicopters to service status. In April HMR-161 moved to Army field A-17 on the western front and began to supply Marines of the 1st Division. The next several months involved a series of operations to move various Marine groups in and out of the battle areas.

The Skyraiders and MAG-12

It was used by only three Marine squadrons in Korea—VMA-121, VMA-251, and VMC-1—but the extent of its use, its great success in other military services, and its incredible longevity, made the Douglas AD (later A-1) Skyraider unique among the world's combat aircraft. Created by Douglas' master designer Ed Heinemann (1908–1991) during the closing days of World War II, and originally designated XBT2D-1, the AD flew some of the first attack missions of the Korean War from the deck of the carrier *Valley Forge*, with VA-55, on July 3, 1950. The Skyraider served

throughout the Korean conflict as a vital part of the Navy's carrier wings and right through the early part of the Vietnam War in the mid-1960s. And even when the Navy finally retired its A-1s in 1968 for the new A-7 Corsair II, the Air Force continued using it as a rescue coordinator through the early 1970s. It was an impressive record of service for any military combat aircraft. The Marines' only combat use of the type, however, came in Korea.

The Wolf Raiders were originally based at Naval Air Station, Glenview, Illinois, flying Corsairs and F8F Bearcats. In mid-1951 the unit received mobilization orders and moved west to El Toro, where it transitioned to AD-2s and was redesignated VMA-121. After arriving in Japan, -121 traveled to Korea, arriving on October 19, 1951. K-3 airfield at Pohang was the only strip that had cement runways with the strength necessary to support the heavily loaded ADs, which could carry more than 5,000 pounds of ordnance in addition to the airplane's two wing-mounted 20-mm cannon.

Assigned to MAG-33, the squadron's first mission came on October 27, 1951, and before the Wolf Raiders left Korea, they had flown thousands of sorties against airfields, supply dumps, rail yards, and bridges. In June 1953 sixteen aircraft of VMA-121 set a record for a single day's ordnance delivery: 156 tons. (It should be noted that several squadrons had been redesignated by June 1952 from fighter to attack. Thus, VMF-323 became VMA-323 and VMF-312 became VMA-312.)

VMA-121 pilot 2nd Lt. Ted Uhlemeyer Jr. had a narrow escape in the summer of 1952 when his Skyraider was hit by flak, which tore a tremendous hole in his wing, flipping the plane upside down. With his controls severely damaged and his landing gear jammed in the up position, Uhlemeyer wrapped both arms and a leg around the control stick, and after dropping his two 1,000-pound bombs on the enemy positions, he flew his battered AD home to K-6, Pyongtaek, which had become the home of MAG-12 on April 20, 1952.

As mentioned, there were two other Marine Skyraider units in Korea. VMC-1, Composite Squadron One, used AD-2Qs, which carried two-man crews for radar countermeasures duties. VMA-251, which relieved VMA-323, arrived at the very end of the war, in July 1953. VMC-1 was commissioned on September 15, 1952, with Lt. Col. Lawrence F. Fox as the CO. It was the culmination of two years of experimentation in airborne early warning and electronic countermeasures. The 2nd MAW at MCAS Cherry Point had used three AD-3Ws and two TBM-3Qs to develop equipment and tactics in the new arena of electronic warfare.

When the Korean War started, reports began filtering in about North Korean use of radar-controlled anti-aircraft guns. Efforts to jam these weapons proved unreliable at best, and a more intense program began, which eventually developed into a dedicated section of the 1st MAW's Headquarters Squadron 1, using two AD-2Qs at K-3. These Skyraiders served as a start, but this early phase of electronic countermeasures (ECM) went without a host as the section struggled to find a home. SSgt—later Maj.—Daniel C. Georgia wrote, "Aircrew training in those days was quick and informal. [The NCOIC took] me to one of the AD-2Qs and showed me how to turn on the equipment, followed by local training flights on

March 30 and April 2, 1952. My first combat mission came on April 3. Since there was only room for one aircrew in the ECM compartment, there was no inflight instruction by a qualified [instructor] in the AD-2Q."[1] Initial missions for the section were passive ECM during the day, in clear weather, flying straight and level at 10,000 feet. More people were assigned to the unit, and by its commissioning, VMC-1 had seventeen officers and forty-six enlisted members. All the ECM operators, with the exception of one newly promoted second lieutenant, were enlisted, and there was one enlisted pilot.

For the several months after its commissioning, VMC-1 flew several variants of the multiplace AD-2: AD-2Q, AD-3N, AD-4N, AD-4NL, and AD-4W. The different models featured equipment changes and updates, and in the case of the AD-4NL, the addition of another enlisted operator in the rear-fuselage compartment behind and below the pilot.

Dan Georgia, who had now gained considerable experience, was tasked with overseeing the equipment of an AD-4NL with more electronics. After a test flight on November 17, 1952, Georgia and his crew took the prototype, assigned as RM 1, on its first combat mission over Wonsan Harbor. The Skyraider, which had been borrowed from the Navy, was of some concern with all its modifications. The Navy also stipulated its return in its original configuration.

However, RM 1 was lost on March 1, 1953, when its engine blew a cylinder, and the crew—Capt. Gordon Keller Jr. (pilot) and MSgt. Donald

[Opposite] Map 5. The network of "K" fields was an Air Force development, but the Marines availed themselves of these strategically placed bases. The "K" meant actually nothing more than "Korea." While the Marines and the Air Force shared the airfields with relative good will, there were occasions when the operational pace could get tight, and there were instances where the two organizations found their aircraft on the same bit of taxiway or runway at the same time, sometimes going in the opposite direction!

Smith (ECM operator)—made a wheels-up landing on the beach of Chodo Island (K-54 strip). Although there were high cliffs on either end of the strip, Captain Keller cleared the obstructions, but the aircraft was a write-off, with a broken back and engine mounts. The squadron sent a team to salvage what parts they could and then to destroy the AD.

The Skyraider was proving to be a rugged, reliable aircraft, but keeping the crew warm could be a problem, as Major Georgia wrote:

Our main problems were with the engine, and they consisted of ignition-system problems and manifold absolute-pressure regulator failures. Engine-oil consumption was fairly high, but that was normal for the Wright R3350-26WA. During the cold weather months, the 20-mm wing guns had a high stoppage rate, which we attributed to lack of a good low-temperature lubricant.

Operator-compartment heat was a source of annoyance in all models of the AD. The compartment heat in the Q and NL came from gasoline combustion heaters, which when working provided more than enough warmth. When they failed, winter flights up north could be downright frigid. The rear-compartment heat for the W model was from waste heat from cooling the APS-20A modulator, and I could never detect any useful heat coming into the rear compartment from this source. The pilot's heat came from a muff heater on the exhaust manifold, and they always had plenty of heat.[2]

VMC-1 Skyraiders were active on both coasts of the Korean Peninsula, although they never flew across to another coast on a single mission, which could last up to 4.5 hours with a 150-gallon fuel tank on the centerline station. Flights approaching North Korea could be met by MiG interceptors, especially if the route took the Marine crews close to the Yalu River.

When it became evident that the enemy had realized that a new aircraft type had entered the war, they began shutting down their radars, making it hard to track their positions. A suggestion to follow the hard-pressed Air Force B-29s into the target, when the North Koreans had to turn on their radars, was briefly considered but rejected. Ultimately, Douglas F3D-2 Skyknights were offered as the solution to the B-29s' problems.

In the spring of 1953, North Korea began sending night hecklers over Seoul and Inchon to harass the cities with bombs or single mortar shells. Although these intruder missions were of little strategic importance, they did keep the population on edge. The small PO-2 biplanes flew too slowly—around 100 knots—to be intercepted by jets such as the F3D or the Air Force's Lockheed F-94. The small wooden slow-flying PO-2s proved hard to track on radar, and the ADs got the job.

The AD-4NL carried the more powerful APS-31 search radar, and with the -4NL's four wing-mounted 20-mm cannon, the Marines hoped to stop the North Koreans. VMC-1 sent a detachment of two AD-4NLs to K-14 at Kimpo, later moving to K-13 at Seoul. With the Air Force maintaining an alert with its F-86s during the day, the Marines took over the watch after sundown. Several scrambles against the little biplanes were unsuccessful, and the Marine crew found they had to fly their big, unwieldy ADs close to stall speed, which often raised the threat of overheating the engine. Over-

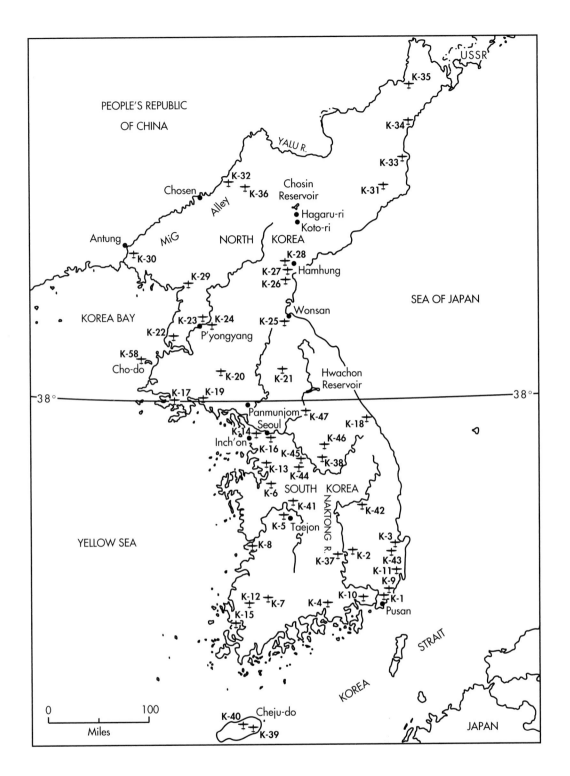

zealous flak crews on the ground also made things difficult. Two kills were eventually claimed. One was confirmed on June 15, 1953, by Maj. George H. Linnemeier and Chief WO Vernon Kramer; the other was listed as a possible. With Warrant Officer Kramer working the radar, Major Linnemeier tracked the contact for twenty miles before he could confirm its identity. He fired a burst, and the cannon shells ripped the wing off the little enemy biplane. It was the last kill for Marine night fighters in Korea.

From this meager beginning came today's ECM program, exemplified by the four VMCJ squadrons with their highly prized EA-6B Prowlers.

These squadrons were part of MAG-12. VMA-121 was reassigned by the time the group moved to K-6. MAG-12 was commanded by World War II ace, Guadalcanal veteran, and Medal of Honor holder Col. Robert F. Galer. The group actually came under the control of the Fifth Air Force, which determined when and where the VMAs would go, except for the sorties of VMA-312, which was stationed offshore aboard the carrier *Bataan*.

VMA-323 had brought a new, and as it turned out, the final, variant of the veteran Corsair to Korea, the AU-1, a model made especially for ground attack, with more armor and a more powerful engine. Only 110 AU-1s were produced, although several comparable F4U-7s were produced for the French through January 1953, bringing the total production of the fabulous U-bird to 12,571.

Colonel Galer, who had shot down thirteen Japanese airplanes, went on missions several times a week and was shot down for the fifth time in his career in August 1952. As Galer pulled out from his bomb run, his Corsair was hit by Communist flak in its wings and engine. The power plant quit soon afterward, and Galer bailed out. However, his foot caught in a strap in the cockpit and the Corsair went into a steep dive, dragging the struggling pilot with it. Galer finally managed to free himself, but as he fell from the plane, he struck its tail. Opening his chute only 150 feet above the ground, he landed by the wreck of his plane, and under fire from nearby Communist troops. Galer was rescued but required hospitalization and rotation back to the States. He was awarded the Legion of Merit for his performance in leading MAG-12; Col. John P. Condon, another experienced Pacific veteran, succeeded Galer as MAG-12 commander. (Galer retired in July 1957 as a brigadier general.)

Colonel Condon had had MAG-33 for several months, and when Galer was wounded, there was a dilemma as to who would replace him as leader of MAG-12; there were not enough experienced aviators to go around. Fortunately, Condon had been sufficiently impressed with his new executive officer, Col. Herbert Williamson, to recommend to Maj. Gen. Clayton C. Jerome, commanding the 1st MAW, that Williamson take over MAG-33 and that he, Condon, replace Galer at MAG-12. Jerome was initially skeptical but eventually agreed to the suggestion. Colonel Condon became one of perhaps only two Marines to command both MAGs.

VMA-312 pilot Maj. David Cleeland figured in an unusual rescue on February 23, 1953. On a strike against some bridges, Cleeland's F4U-4B was shot up by ground fire, and he made a successful crash landing on the frozen Annyong Reservoir. As he climbed out of his plane, his three squadron mates circled overhead for protection. Suddenly, a unit of Mongolian cavalry appeared and plunged toward the surprised pilot, who started to run. The Marine pilots overhead immediately dove to the rescue and bombed and strafed the Communists, dumping the horsemen in the icy water of the reservoir as the ice broke under the barrage of bombs and bullets. This gave time for a helicopter to move in, rescue Cleeland, and return him to the *Bataan*.

9 Korean Stalemate

AIR-TO-AIR COMBAT FOR THE MARINES in Korea was not the free-wheeling affair it had been in World War II. As previously mentioned, the high degree to which Marine fighters were used for aerial combat in the Pacific actually worked against the Corps, because the aircraft were not involved in close air support, their raison d'être. In the last year of the war and afterward, there were many senior officers who questioned the need for a Marine air arm. Therefore, in Korea great pains were taken to keep aerial combat to a minimum, although certainly if the opportunity arose, it was proper for a Marine aviator to engage the enemy. For the most part, however, aerial combat was left to the Air Force, and, to a lesser extent, the carrier Navy, while the Marine planes supported the men on the ground. Very few chances arose for Marines to fight in the air, and those who did score against Russian-built Yaks or MiGs were usually, though not always, on exchange duty with the Air Force.

The first aerial victory for the naval service involving an enemy jet aircraft in Korea came on November 9, 1950, when Lt. Cdr. William T. Amen, commanding officer of VF-111 aboard the USS *Philippine Sea*, shot down a MiG-15 with his F9F Panther. The kill came one day after the Air Force had the honor of scoring the first U.S. kill over a jet with another jet; Lt. Russell Brown shot down a MiG-15 while flying a Lockheed F-80. (Recent research into newly available Soviet records suggests that Russell's target was simply diving away and safely recovered at its base. Thus, it would seem that credit for the milestone *world's* first jet-to-jet kill should also go to Lieutenant Commander Amen.)

Aerial combat was sporadic at least from the Navy's standpoint, most of the action in Korea occurring with the Air Force's F-86 squadrons operating from Kimpo and Suwon. In the early months of the war, the enemy was reluctant to commit its modern MiG-15 fighters to combat, preferring instead to use up its World War II vintage Yakovlev prop fighters, usually Yak-9s, in hit-and-run raids against U.S. positions. (Actually, the Yak-9 was one of the best, if not the best, Russian fighter of the last war, but of course it had been rendered obsolete nearly overnight by the advent of the jet.) It was almost inevitable that the Yaks should tangle with Marine fighters.

Capt. Phillip C. DeLong and 1st Lt. Harold Daigh, flying from the USS *Bataan*, were jumped by four North Korean Yaks. Daigh quickly shot down one of the enemy planes, and DeLong, a World War II ace with eleven kills, disposed of two more in rapid succession. Daigh damaged the fourth plane, which fled. When UN troops discovered a Yak fighter and the body of its Communist Chinese pilot a week later in shallow water offshore, Daigh's probable claim was changed to confirmed.

VMF-312 scored again on September 10, 1952, when Capt. Jesse G. Folmar shot down a MiG-15, quite an achievement, since Folmar was flying a prop-driven F4U. Flying from the USS *Sicily*, Folmar and his wingman, Lt.

W. L. Daniels, were jumped by four MiGs, which probably considered the Marine aircraft easy prey. Folmar later described the action for the magazine *Naval Aviation News:* "They attacked in pairs. The second section had just passed and was in a climbing left turn. I turned inside them and gave the nearest one a five-second burst of 20-mm. The MiG belched black smoke and the pilot flew into the air from his ejection seat. His chute opened but it was already on fire."[1]

VMF-312 had exchanged its F4U-4s with machine guns for VMF-323's cannon-armed F4U-4Bs in March because of logistics problems with maintaining adequate ammunition supplies aboard ship. Folmar did not have much time to celebrate his kill, as the MiG's wingman came around and poured cannon fire into the Corsair, forcing Folmar to bail out. He was rescued shortly afterward by an Air Force Albatross amphibian. (There

It took two wars, but 1st Lt. John W. Andre made ace in Korea by shooting down a North Korean Yak in June 1952, flying with VMF(N)-513 at night. Seated in a Nightmare Corsair, he wears a gold flight helmet current during this period. (Sgt. Frank S. Johnson)

were other instances of prop aircraft destroying MiGs; the Air Force's F-51 Mustangs claimed several, and even the Royal Navy scored a kill with a powerful Hawker Sea Fury.)

The Corsair was not the only Marine prop fighter to score aerial kills in Korea. As previously mentioned, Grumman F7F Tigercats of VMF(N)-513 shot down two PO-2 biplanes at night. Another VMF(N)-513 pilot, 1st Lt. John Andre, a Marine aviator in World War II, shot down a Yak-9 on June 7, 1952, flying an F4U-5N. This kill was Andre's fifth, making him an ace. During World War II, he had shot down four Japanese aircraft in the Philippines. Spotting the North Korean aircraft while he was on an interdiction mission, Andre swung his Corsair onto the Yak's tail and shot it down.

The Marines were anxious to score against the MiG-15, hottest operational fighter in the world at that time. To some extent, the high-tailed MiG-15 had established a mystique comparable to the Japanese Zero of the last war. It was an unknown quantity, and its introduction and tremendous performance capabilities came from an unexpected source, the Soviet Union.

Russian aircraft designers were thought to be stodgy old bureaucrats incapable of creating anything that could compete with Western designs. They even had to borrow a British Rolls-Royce Nene jet engine to get started. But the MiG-15 (the term "MiG" is an acronym derived from the last names of the two men—Mikoyan and Gurevich—who founded the design bureau), which flew in July 1947, was a world-beater, fast and heavily armed.

The only Western aircraft capable of meeting it with a good chance of winning was the U.S. Air Force's North American F-86 Sabre. Even then, many thought that the Sabre's edge was not the plane itself, but the level of experience and training of its pilots, many of whom had flown during World War II. It was the F-86 that provided the Marines with most of their MiG-15 kills, for, of the twenty-seven Russian jets shot down by Marine crews (twenty-six MiGs and one Yak-15), all except six were downed by

[Top] MiG-15s in Korea. Recent release of classified Soviet archives confirmed what most U.S. pilots knew: the men in the MiGs—especially the high-scoring aces—were Russian. Although there were Chinese and North Korean MiG drivers, a majority of enemy fighters encountered over MiG Alley were flown by Soviet "volunteers." (Yefim Gordon Archive)

[Bottom] This frame from a MiG-15 gun camera shows VMF-311's 1st Lt. Robert W. Bell's Panther under attack by Lt. Col. Evgeniy Pepelyaev, CO of the MiG squadron and future second-ranking Soviet ace of the war. Three Marine F9Fs were jumped on July 21, 1951, by 15 MiGs. Bell became a POW and was released in September 1953. Pepelyaev identified his victim as a USAF F-94, which had not arrived in-theater.

Sabres. (The Corsair, of course, and the Douglas F3D Skyknight also shot down MiGs.)

Capt. William F. Guss was the first Marine to get a MiG, on November 4, 1951, followed by Capt. V. J. Marzelo on March 5, 1952; both pilots were on Air Force exchange duty. During a three-month tour, Maj. Alexander J. Gillis scored three times, with one probable and three others damaged. On October 6, 1952, the last day of his tour, Gillis got a MiG on two separate missions, although the second hop ended with his being shot down himself, just as he finished off the second MiG-15. He ejected over the Yellow Sea and floated for four hours in his raft before being rescued. At that time Gillis was the leading Marine MiG-killer.

A new phase of the air war in Korea opened on the night of November 3, 1952, when a crew from VMF(N)-513 shot down the first enemy jet at night with a Douglas F3D-2 Skyknight. Maj. William T. Stratton Jr. and his radar operator, MSgt. Hans C. Hoglind, shot down a Yak-15 (sometimes listed as a similarly configured Yak-17), an early-model Russian jet with a single engine buried in the fuselage below the cockpit. Major Stratton and Master Sergeant Hoglind were directed to a contact flying at their altitude of 12,000 feet at 320 knots. Stratton opened fire with his 20-mm cannon, scoring direct hits on the Yak-15, which exploded and went down.

The squadron had given up its mixed bag of Tigercats and Corsairs in June 1952 for the big twin-jet Skyknight, obtained from VMF(N)-542.

The aircraft were painted flat black, with red tail code letters and numbers. The F3Ds could have been in immediate operation after their June arrival at K-6 airfield at Pyongtaek, south of Seoul, but a shortage of parts and faulty vacuum tubes for the radar sets delayed their introduction until November 1. The big jets, with their state-of-the-art avionics, were soon tasked with escorting Air Force B-29s, which had been decimated by MiGs. From the first mission, the F3Ds proved their worth and never lost a B-29 to enemy aircraft. The MiGs would try to lure a Skyknight away from its charges to where two other fighters lay in ambush. But the additional MiGs would show up on the F3D's tail warning radar, and the Marine plane could escape before the enemy got within firing range.

On November 9, Capt. Oliver R. Davis and WO Dramus F. Fessler downed a MiG-15 with cannon fire. Maj. Elswin P. Dunn and MSgt. Lawrence J. Forten got a second MiG on January 12, 1953; Capt. James R. Weaver and MSgt. Robert P. Becker got another on the 18th. The third MiG night kill in January was scored by Lt. Col. Robert F. Conley and MSgt. James N. Scott on January 31. Conley, the commanding officer of VMF(N)-513, also claimed a "probable" in March, though that claim was never confirmed. All in all, VMF(N)-513 shot down ten confirmed Communist aircraft, the squadron's F3Ds accounting for six, including four MiGs, the one Yak, and one PO-2, more enemy aircraft than any single Navy or Marine Corps type.

A "probable" kill for the Nightmares of 513 is loosely credited to a young, aggressive Navy crew, Lt. (jg) Robert S. Bick and his radar operator, ATC Linton Smith. Normally assigned to the Navy squadron VC-4, which also briefly flew Skyknights ashore at this time, Bick evidently begged a Marine aircraft for him and the chief on the night of July 2, 1953. Approaching the end of his patrol, in deteriorating weather, Bick suddenly called in a contact to his radar controller on Ch'o-do, a small island off the Korean coast.

With very uncertain, even confusing radio calls and requests for clarification from the radar operator on the ground, Bick then called he was under attack, citing hits from "a couple of thirty-sevens." MiG-15s were armed with 23-mm and 37-mm cannon. Bick and Chief Smith were never seen again.

Navy Capt. Gerald G. O'Rourke, commanding the VC-4 detachment, later wrote, "Lieutenant (jg) Bick's aircraft did not return to base and was presumed lost. The MiG was listed as probably destroyed."[2]

It might seem as though the Marines had their fill of aerial combat in Korea, but such was not the case. In fact, the Corps gained only one ace during the three years. Former Black Sheep ace Maj. John F. Bolt, another Marine pilot on exchange duty with the Air Force, was the only Marine to gain five or more kills in Korea alone; in fact, he is credited with six MiG-15s. Born in South Carolina, he had grown up in Florida. Bolt had flown eighty-nine missions in Panthers when he wangled a ninety-day tour with the F-86-equipped 51st Fighter Interceptor Wing.

Bolt chalked up his first MiG kill on May 16, 1953, when his squadron tackled twelve enemy planes south of the Yalu. (Americans were forbidden to cross the river to pursue the MiGs, which took sanctuary in neighboring Manchuria and China, a situation very much like the stiff engagement rules laid down by an ignorant government during the Vietnam War fifteen years later.)

On his eleventh mission with the Air Force, Bolt swung onto the tail of a MiG and quickly shot it down. June 22 brought another score, as well as an additional MiG damaged. June 24 and 30 each saw him add to his tally. With four MiGs and 800 hours of jet time, Bolt had considerable experience. His chances of making ace looked good. But bad weather and unaggressive enemy pilots kept him from gaining that important fifth kill until July 11, 1953.

Leading a flight of F-86s up the Yalu—that area had become known as "MiG Alley"—he spotted four MiGs taking off across the river and heading south. Diving to the attack, he pulled behind an enemy fighter, a favorite

tactic of his by now, and his machine guns slammed the MiG into the ground from only 1,500 feet. He had five, and went after number six. Bolt later described his second kill of the day: "I made the second kill of the day when this other dude drifted over my way. I pulled up my nose and started firing into his tailpipe, getting within 500 feet of him. He started burning immediately. I was so close I was nearly blinded by the dense smoke so I pulled out and just made it in time. I watched the pilot eject himself and float to the ground."[3] In only a few minutes, Bolt had scored his fifth and sixth jet kills to become the Corps' only jet ace, to the present day. He was also the first, and one of only *two* naval aviators, to become a jet ace, the other being then-Lt. Randy Cunningham, who shot down five North Vietnamese MiGs during the Vietnam War. With six Zeros to his credit when he flew Corsairs with Pappy Boyington and VMF-214 during World War II, Bolt became the only Marine Corps pilot to make ace in two wars. Bolt enjoyed an active career after Korea, commanding his old squadron 1957–59, flying F2H Banshees and FJ-4 Furies. After retiring, he also had a satisfying second career as a community-minded lawyer in Florida until his death in 2004.

Perhaps the most famous Marine MiG-killer to come out of Korea was then-Maj. John H. Glenn. Of course, Glenn's activities as one of America's first astronauts and as a U.S. senator from Ohio are well known. But before these experiences, John Glenn was a combat pilot, first in World War II and then in Korea. He was credited with three MiG-15s while on an exchange tour with the Air Force's 25th Fighter Squadron.

Before his tour with the Air Force, Glenn had flown ground attack missions with VMF-311. A fairly senior pilot, in view of his experience in World War II, Glenn was still given to periods of recklessness, which sometimes put his life in grave danger and earned him the early sobriquet "Magnet Ass," because of his seeming ability to attract flak. On two occasions, he brought his Panther back, riddled with more than 250 holes. Once, a 75-mm Communist shell punched its way through his tail section and exited, leaving a gaping hole and shreds of twisted metal that greatly inhibited the movement of the aircraft's elevators. It was only with brute strength that Glenn was able to regain his field.

The second time Glenn screamed back up to what he thought was a safe altitude after dropping his ordnance, out of the range of most small-caliber weapons. He also quit jinking to throw off potential gunners' aim. Leveling off at 7,000 feet, he flew right into a 90-mm anti-aircraft barrage, again limping back to his base.

John Glenn could be determined and loyal, as well as aggressive. During his tour with the 25th Fighter Squadron, he flew a MiG-hunting mission with his CO, Maj. John Giraudo. Finding no MiGs, the flight began looking for targets of opportunity on the ground, as per standing orders. Glenn spotted three Communist trucks situated near a knoll and called them to his leader's attention. Giraudo responded and dove on the trucks only to be bracketed by flak from the knoll. The F-86s had flown into a "flak trap." Giraudo's aircraft was hit, and he bailed out, circled all the way down by an anxious John Glenn. There was little the Marine pilot could do for his skipper except make sure Giraudo made a safe landing.

Giraudo was almost immediately surrounded by North Koreans, who had a well-earned reputation for taking very few prisoners and violently mistreating the ones they did capture. Giraudo was beaten and even shot in the shoulder not once but three times, before a Chinese group appeared and took the American pilot themselves. (Giraudo was eventually repatriated in 1953 and rose to the rank of brigadier general.) John Glenn circled above his downed leader as long as he could, but his plane was low on fuel and he barely made K-13. In fact, he flamed out on final approach and glided to the runway. As his F-86 rolled out to a stop, Glenn leaped from the cockpit to another fighter and took off back to the scene of Giraudo's parachute descent, but it was too late.

Glenn flew Corsairs in the Marshalls campaign in 1944 and then Panthers with VMF-311, accumulating sixty-three missions in Korea in early 1953 before his Air Force exchange tour. Up to that time, Glenn had gained three Distinguished Flying Crosses for his activities in the Pacific and Korea, as well as several Air Medals. Quietly aggressive, he was anxious to go after MiGs. It was a different batch of MiG pilots he was to face than had been the case previously.

As in any "small" war, the opposing sides used Korea as a testing ground for new weapons and tactics to gain experience. The Communists were no exception, and after the free-wheeling dogfights of 1952, the MiGs to some extent withdrew, as their leaders assessed the situation and ordered more training for their pilots and uprating for their aircraft. The Chinese also discovered that the American Sabres were limited in fuel capacity and range. Having to fly up to the Yalu in search of MiGs or as escort for other aircraft didn't leave the F-86s much time to loiter or engage in heated combat once the enemy was sighted. The MiG tacticians, therefore, decided to catch the F-86s when they turned for home, cutting the U.S. jets off with MiG patrols in front and behind the Air Force formations. The tactic worked to a degree for a while.

We now know that a large number of the MiG pilots were Soviet Russians, many of whom had flown in World War II and were aces. Indeed,

[Opposite Left] Maj. John H. Glenn of VMF-311 had a reputation for attracting flak. On March 25, 1953, his Panther was hit by ground fire that covered his plane with 375 holes. Glenn was not hurt and returned to base. He has good reason to smile in the photo. Note the early jet flight helmet and oxygen mask. An ambitious MiG hunter, he eventually shot down three MiG-15s and received his fourth DFC in the process.

[Opposite Right] Maj. John F. Bolt poses on his F-86 in 1953. Flying with the USAF's 39th FIS, he shot down six MiG-15s to become the Marine Corps' only Korean War ace and the only Marine jet ace. As a member of Boyington's Black Sheep, he also scored six kills in the Pacific, one of a very few Marine aviators to have kills in two wars.

the wing of "volunteers" was led by the top Allied ace of the war, Colonel (later Air Marshal) Ivan N. Kozhedub, who had shot down sixty-two German aircraft and was the highest-scoring Allied pilot of the war. (Interestingly, he did not actually fly any missions in Korea, much to his annoyance.) One Soviet aviator tallied twenty-two kills over Korea, and others were double and triple aces, making them the highest-scoring jet-mounted aviators in the world. Although the American pilots knew they were fighting Soviet pilots, the fact was hushed up for more than forty years. But it was hard for the Americans to mistake the rapid-fire Russian coming over selected radio frequencies in the heat of a dogfight. The definitive information on this group of surrogates is still being refined years after the fall of the Soviet Union and the discovery and opening of heretofore classified files.

One afternoon, John Glenn led three Sabres up to MiG Alley, just as sixteen MiGs had taken off from their Manchurian base at Antung. Under ground control intercept (GCI), the Communist fighters swung in toward the F-86s. A fight was a certainty. Without hesitation, Glenn led his flight to the attack. (His ground crew had his F-86's fuselage emblazoned with the name "MiG-Mad Marine" in bright red letters, so well known was his desire to get MiGs and surpass his fellow Marine, John Bolt.)

He lined up on one MiG, but the enemy pilot was good and eventually got on Glenn's tail, pumping 37-mm cannon shells into the Marine's Sabre. Fortunately, one of the other F-86 pilots picked the MiG off and riddled it with machine-gun bullets, forcing the Communist fighter into a fatal spin. However, the rescuer apparently picked up some of the MiG's disintegrating fuselage, and the Air Force pilot began to experience problems with his aircraft. Glenn shepherded the damaged Sabre back to their base.

As the pair flew back, they were attacked by six MiGs that had been waiting as part of the new "box-in" tactics. Glenn succeeded in downing a MiG but then found he was out of ammunition. The Marine pilot flung his plane all over the sky, trying to bluff the MiG pilots away from the other F-86. His efforts succeeded long enough for a fresh group of Sabres to come to the rescue, the MiGs fleeing before the new formation. Low on fuel, and with both F-86s suffering from battle damage, the two pilots made emergency landings at K-13. Glenn received his fourth DFC for the action that day.

The last Marine aerial kill in Korea had a tragic ending, as Maj. Thomas M. Sellers, flying with the USAF's 336th Fighter Interceptor Squadron, 4th Fighter Interceptor Wing, on July 20, 1953, scored two MiG kills but disappeared and was initially declared missing in action. The ruling was changed a year later to killed in action. Sellers was already a veteran of many missions as a Panther pilot with VMF-115 and had received two DFCs along with the Purple Heart and six Air Medals. Some question remains as to why the original flight of four Sabres that Major Sellers led was so far north; the two MiGs and Major Sellers all crashed in Manchuria, north of the Yalu River. Nonetheless, in December 1954 his widow and daughter received Major Sellers' medals, which included a posthumous Silver Star for his last mission.

In general, air-to-air combat was not really the main activity for the air arm of the Corps. Even though Marine aviators are among the most zealous practitioners of aerial combat training, especially today, they rarely get a chance to use their training for real. Even in Vietnam, as will be seen, most of those Marines who scored kills were again on exchange duty with the Air Force. Only one Marine crew scored a kill against North Vietnamese aircraft while flying a Marine aircraft on a Marine mission, and that event did not occur until the war was nearly over.

The Flying Sergeants: Enlisted Aviators in the Marines

One area where the Corps was probably alone among the American aviation services was the degree to which it used its enlisted pilots, especially in combat. Enlisted pilots, of course, were not new. Indeed, France in World War I and the Axis powers—Germany, Japan, and Italy—in World War II had many enlisted aviators. The Royal Air Force would have been in even worse condition during the Battle of Britain in 1940 had it not been for its sergeant-pilots. For the most part, however, the United States required its pilots to be commissioned officers and, with few exceptions, that is the way it continues to be. (The Navy had instituted its Naval Aviation Pilot, or NAP, designation in 1919 because of a pilot shortage. The Marines, too, authorized selection of enlisted members to become pilots, 1st Sgt. Benjamin Belcher becoming the first Marine NAP in 1923.)

However, with the country's hurried and somewhat unexpected entry into World War II, the need for pilots transcended the niceties of rank and tradition. Therefore, all the services, at one time or another during the war, included enlisted pilots, sometimes elevating them to commissioned rank later. (Marine ace Ken Walsh, who scored twenty-one kills and earned the Medal of Honor during World War II, was an enlisted pilot until he was commissioned in 1942.)

The Marines probably had the greatest number of noncommissioned aviators (131 in 1942), and not in second-line transport squadrons; many of these NAPs flew helicopters and jets in very heavy action in Korea. Flying sergeants flew Corsairs and Tigercats at Pusan and Chosin, Panthers in close air support against the Chinese, and OYs in dangerous artillery-spotting missions. TSgt. Robert A. Hill accumulated seventy-six combat missions as an OY pilot, earning the moniker "Bulletproof" after coming home in planes that were more holes than aircraft. He received the Distinguished Flying Cross for evacuating wounded Marines near Chosin under extremely heavy enemy fire. Several of the R4D (C-47) transports that also evacuated wounded from Hagaru-ri and Koto-ri during the epic Chosin Breakout were piloted by Marine NAPs.

But, of course, the jet pilots were the glamor boys. NAPs were among the first Marine jet pilots only after 1949, taking their training in Lockheed TO-1s along with their commissioned squadron mates, providing a cadre of experienced and motivated personnel to draw on during the action in Korea. The training met some initial resistance from senior squadron commanders, a few of whom did not want enlisted pilots flying their jets.

This somewhat confusing situation had the added aspect that several NAPs had been lieutenants in World War II. However, after mustering out in 1945 and 1946, many of the former Corsair drivers regretted their decision to leave the active Marine Corps. They missed flying such powerful aircraft

as the tough F4U. The Corps also found itself short of qualified aviators to fly its new jets and to man its remaining squadrons. The Marines developed a program whereby former Marine officer aviators could return as master sergeants (E-7 was the highest enlisted rating at the time), if they re-upped ninety days or less after leaving active duty. After the ninety-day limit, the former aviator could rejoin as a technical sergeant, a grade below that of master sergeant.

When VMF-311 first brought its F9F Panthers to Chosin and Pusan, several of its pilots were enlisted aviators. MSgt. Avery C. Snow was the first NAP to complete 100 combat missions in a jet. (Snow had been a captain with VMTB-232 during World War II.)

One specialized squadron that made heavy use of its NAPs was VMJ-1, Marine Photographic Squadron One, established on February 25, 1952, flying McDonnell F2H-2P Banshees specially modified with an extended nose to accommodate several reconnaissance cameras. VMJ-1 established an enviable record in Korea, flying 5,025 sorties and processing 793,000 *feet* of film, while contributing a third of the entire UN aerial reconnaissance production during the war. Several of its pilots, who were specially trained volunteers, were enlisted men who could double as lab technicians if the situation warranted. An unusual setup.

Aerial photo reconnaissance is one of the most exacting and dangerous jobs in all of military aviation. The recon pilot must be more than just a good aviator; that's just a base from which to start. He must be a crackerjack navigator and know his camera systems inside and out, their capabilities and their limitations. And he must be resourceful, as well as having an

[Opposite] Surrounded by what appear to be Air Force crewmen, Marston Matting, and sandbag revetment, this McDonnell F2H-2P Banshee of VMJ-1 displays some 90 photo-mission symbols—small cameras—on its plane's fuselage. The squadron flew more than 5,000 such missions.

[Right] VMJ-1 NAPs stand by a squadron Banshee. These aviators, who had often been officers in World War II, were among the most experienced pilots in the Marines. L. to r.: J. R. Todd, Sam Cooper, LeRoy Copland, Marv Myers, Red Truex. MSgt. J. R. Todd accumulated 101 missions, the highest number in the squadron. He continued flying with the Marines and served in Vietnam. (via J. R. Todd)

inexhaustible supply of courage. Sometimes these last qualities are all that enable him to bring the film home and successfully complete his mission.

Most jet reconnaissance aircraft are unarmed, relying on their speed to get them home before being intercepted. During World War II, there were no specifically dedicated reconnaissance aircraft, merely modified fighters that had cameras stuck in the most convenient space, sometimes behind the pilot in the cockpit, or below him in the belly. The F6F Hellcat and P-51 Mustang are examples of such modification. Usually, these aircraft retained most, if not all, of their machine-gun armament and could therefore fight their way to and from the target if need be. During Korea, however, the dedicated photo-Banshees of VMJ-1 were toothless and needed escorts. Sometimes another Banshee would go along, both as an escort and sometimes to ensure the coverage of the target with another camera. Air Force F-86s were sometimes called on to shepherd the recce pilot. And sometimes the photo pilot found himself alone.

MSgt. Lowell T. Truex had made his photo runs against installations near the Yalu River in 1952, thinking that his F-86 escort would look out for any Communist fighters that might try to come after him. However, as he looked around, he found that the Sabres were nowhere to be seen, and he also spotted a gaggle of MiG-15s taking off across the river. Hurriedly, he finished his photo runs and ran for home. (He found later, that the F-86s had been watching from above, had the MiGs in sight, and were, in fact, ready to jump the Chinese fighters had they come after Truex.) Truex later commented, "My memories of the photo unit, which became a squadron during my tour, and all the plankowners, are good ones. We were completely self-contained and operated with field equipment from the well-point, water tank to the generators. The technicians were all superior guys, who worked with energy and diligence."[4]

A squadron mate, MSgt. Calvin R. Duke, who laid claim to being the oldest Marine NAP in Korea, was set upon by two MiGs near Chosin. In a dogfight that went from 10,000 to 30,000 feet, Duke outmaneuvered the Communist fighters and ran for home at 600 miles per hour.

MSgt. James R. Todd was the squadron's high-mission man, completing 101 photo missions before rotation home. During his time in Korea, Todd flew 51 reconnaissance missions in Banshees, 10 in F9F-2Ps, 223 in F7F-3Ps, 13 in F4U-5Ps, and 4 escort missions in F4U-4Bs. As he recalled, "The F4U-4B was used for armed escort only. The rest of the time, we relied on a .38 pistol, a can of film, and a lot of speed."

Like many others, Todd had been a second lieutenant in World War II, although he had just missed seeing combat service when the war ended, having spent much of his post-winging time as an instructor. Mustered out in September 1946, he returned in November, resigning his first lieutenant's commission and re-enlisting as a *private*. He was immediately advanced to master sergeant and sent to El Toro, then to Pensacola to learn the art of aerial reconnaissance at the Naval School of Photography.

As can be seen, Marine enlisted aviators formed an integral part of their service's capability. However, by Vietnam, there were only a few NAPs on active duty, and fewer still actually involved in flying duties. Some of these pioneers served with distinction throughout Vietnam. But by 1973 only four NAPs were still on active service with the Marines, and all four were simultaneously retired on February 1, 1973, bringing to a close a colorful era in naval aviation and Marine Corps history.

The first few months of 1951 saw a buildup by the Communists in anticipation of a spring offensive. Estimates of 750 aircraft were made for the boosted North Korean and Chinese strength. (The Air Force's B-29 crews would certainly have agreed that there were more enemy planes in the air.) On the night of April 22, 1951, the Chinese 20th Army plunged through the UN lines and by the 26th had launched their main drive toward Seoul. All of American air power was called into action to try to hold the onrushing Chinese. Navy carrier-based Corsairs and ADs struck railway lines and bridges, while Air Force F-86s battled the MiGs and mounted their own bombing effort with F-80 Shooting Stars and F-84 Thunderjets.

The Marines found themselves in action along the line of the Hwachon Reservoir north of the 38th parallel. By June the Chinese offensive drive had slowed and as the two sides faced each other at Kwachon, word came that after lengthy and secretive negotiations between Washington and Moscow, truce talks were set to begin at the old city of Kaesong, thirty-five miles northwest of Seoul. However, the truce talks made very little progress, and with the UN and Chinese forces in a stalemate, the war ground to a virtual halt. Action took place, but by mid-1952, very little real estate changed hands. As Brig. Gen. E. H. Simmons wrote, "The line had solidified and it was trench warfare now, very much like World War I. There were no general offensives or big attacks, just nasty localized actions growing out of patrols or raids, or the loss or capture of an outpost."[5]

The air war settled down to the various uses of close-air-support tactics, as dictated by the individual service. The Marines came up with the idea of using searchlights to pin-point targets at night. By July 1953, a small unit was experimenting with 3-million-candlepower lights aimed at offshore islands. The teams were working up with Air Force F-86s, Marine Corsairs, and British Meteors, when the cease-fire brought a halt to the experiment.

The Air Force tried interdiction, in an effort to cut off the North Koreans' supply routes. First MAW aircraft flew close air support for the U.S. Eighth

Army. However, by this time the Air Force had control of Marine missions. First MAW commanding generals, Maj. Gen. Clayton C. Jerome and then-Maj. Gen. Vernon E. Megee, quickly made sure that the Marines would receive top priority on arranging air strikes.

In October 1951 the truce talks were moved to Panmunjom and the laborious process began anew. The Chinese continued to throw night artillery barrages at the Marines and Army troops, which suffered hundreds of casualties in the dark, huddled in their damp, stinking trenches and dugouts.

The End of the War in Korea

During this time, several veteran Marine squadrons started to rotate home. VMA-312, now on board the USS *Bairoko* (CVE-115), left Korea in June 1953; their place and their aircraft were taken by VMA-332, made up of 80 percent reserve personnel. VMA-332's nickname was the "Polkadots," while VMA-312's was the "Checkerboards." The newer squadron lost no time in repainting their veteran Corsairs' checkered cowlings.

VMF-311's Panthers, now in company with VMF-115, continued to pound enemy positions. VMF-311 had taken delivery of six new F9F-5s and flown them to Korea in January 1953. (The Dash 5 featured a more powerful engine.) Flying on one of these ground-attack missions one day was a recalled Marine Corps reservist, Capt. T. S. Williams, better known as Ted Williams to millions of baseball fans. Williams had joined the Navy in 1942 as an aviation cadet and was commissioned a second lieutenant in the Marines when he got his wings on May 2, 1944. After a period of instructing at Pensacola, he finished the war in Hawaii and was released from active duty in January 1946. He subsequently joined the Marine reserves.

Boston Red Sox outfielder Ted Williams was one of several personalities recalled to active duty in Korea. Here, Sgt. Roger W. McCully straps in now-Captain Williams before a mission in 1953. Williams flew 38 missions and returned to major-league baseball in 1954. (TSgt. Tom Rousseau)

At thirty-four, Williams was not a young man as far as military flying was concerned when he was recalled to active duty in Korea in 1952. Of course, he was not alone in being recalled, but his visibility as a public figure made his case special. The baseball player himself took the event stoically, although he inwardly was bitter about this second interruption of his career. In a later magazine article, he said, "The recall wasn't exactly joyous news, but I tried to be philosophical about it. It was happening to a lot of fellows, I thought. I was no better than the rest."[6]

The press was not so understanding. Many could not understand the need to recall "second-hand warriors," as one reporter unkindly wrote. Most sports writers bemoaned the fact that Williams was really kind of old for a ball player as well as for a combat jet pilot. However, the Boston outfielder reported for duty on May 2, 1952, received a checkout in Panthers with VMF-223 at MCAS Cherry Point, North Carolina, and got his assignment to VMF-311, MAG-33, 1st MAW, Korea. His squadron mates got used to having a celebrity in their midst and tagged Williams with the sobriquet "Bush," or "Bush Leaguer," teasing him about his baseball activities and reputation.

On February 16 1953, Williams was part of a thirty-five-plane strike against Highway 1, south of Pyongyang, North Korea; it was his third combat mission. As the aircraft from VMF-115 and VMF-311 dove down on the target, Williams felt his plane shudder as he reached 5,000 feet. "Until that day I had never put a scratch on a plane in almost four years of military flying. But I really did it up good. I got hit just as I dropped my bombs on the target—a big Communist tank and infantry training school near Pyongyang. The hit knocked out my hydraulic and electrical systems and started a slow burn."[7]

Unable to locate his flight leader for instruction and help, Williams was relieved to see another pilot, Lt. Larry Hawkins, slide into view. Hawkins gave his plane the once-over and told Williams that his F9F was leaking some sort of liquid. (It turned out later to be hydraulic fluid.) Joining up on the damaged Panther, Hawkins led Williams back to K-13, calling on the radio for a clear runway and crash crews. The baseball player was going to try to bring his plane back instead of bailing out. With most of his flight instruments gone, Williams was flying on instinct and the feel of the plane as he circled wide of the field, setting himself up for the approach.

It took a long few minutes for the battered Panther to come down the final approach, but perhaps his athlete's instincts and control enabled Williams to do the job. At any rate, the F9F finally crossed over the end of the runway, and slid along its belly, as Williams' hand flicked switches to prevent a fire. As the plane swerved to a stop, the shaken pilot blew off the canopy and jumped from his aircraft, a little worse for wear, but alive.

Williams was awarded the Air Medal for bringing the plane back and eventually flew a total of thirty-eight missions during his time in Korea. But a pesky ear infection acted up, and he was eventually brought back to the States in June. After convalescence, Williams returned to the Boston Red Sox for the 1954 season, eventually retiring in 1960.

Ted Williams was only one of thousands of recalled reservists of all services who fought in Korea. In fact, the war became somewhat known as "a reservist's war."

John Bolt observed, "We were fighting the war with perhaps 25 percent regulars and 75 percent reserves. The reserves took a terrible beating; their losses were very high. On the other hand, the Air Force had many second lieutenants, all highly trained. They had a sprinkling of mid-ranks—captains and majors—who were far better trained than we were. We used the reserve pilots, primarily from the Boston and Norfolk, Virginia, areas. They suffered terribly. None had been flying jets before they got to El Toro and got a few hours of jet time there."[8]

Col. Richard C. Mangrum, the highly respected dive bomber skipper and Guadalcanal veteran, had helped establish the Marine Corps Air Reserve. By July 1948 there were twenty-seven fighter-bomber squadrons, flying mostly F4Us. Maj. Gen. Christian F. Schilt had refined the organization from his headquarters at Naval Air Station Glenview, near Chicago.

In January 1951, as the Korean War entered its first winter and the active forces were reeling under the Chinese onslaught of the Chosin Reservoir campaign, the Joint Chiefs of Staff authorized the Marine Corps to increase the number of its fighter squadrons from eighteen to twenty-one. And a week later, nine squadrons were mobilized. Six of the units were recalled as personnel, while three—VMFs -131, -251, and -451—were recalled as squadrons. Unfortunately, most of the recalled reserve aviators had little or no experience with jets, having flown Corsairs and SBDs in the Pacific.

Although then-Maj. Thomas H. Miller was the eighth Marine to transition to jets and was looking forward to flying Panthers with VMF-311, his time in Corsairs during World War II was considered more valuable. (He had flown with John Glenn, beginning a deep lifelong friendship that ended only with General Miller's death in November 2007.) To show support for the incoming cadre of reserve aviators, he was assigned as the executive officer of VMA-323, which was flying Corsairs. It was important, Miller observed, that the reserves see that the regular Marines flew the old, but still-effective fighters, too.

One of Miller's recalled reservists was another well-known baseball player. Capt. Gerald F. Coleman had flown SBDs in the Philippines with

Another major league player recalled for active duty in Korea, Yankee second baseman, now-Capt. Jerry Coleman sits in an AU-1, a specially dedicated ground-attack version of the Corsair. Like other Marine aviators, Coleman did not like the heavy AU-1, whose main attribute was a two-stage supercharger that allowed it to fly at lower altitudes in keeping with its dedicated mission of close air support. (via Jerry Coleman)

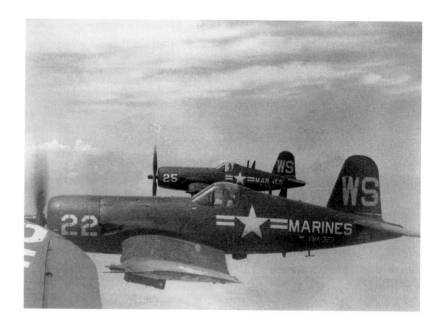

[Left] VMA-323 AU-1s fly formation. The AU-1 had a few internal changes from the F4U-4 to make it more adaptable for ground attack. An external identifier was the grouping of two dorsal antennas immediately behind the cockpit for additional FM radios.

[Opposite] Ground crew work on a VMF-312 Corsair. Although the fighter is pretty well disassembled, it still retains a couple of underwing rockets!

the "Torrid Turtles" of VMSB-341 and had received the DFC and seven Air Medals for his efforts. After the war, he had been enjoying a busy career at second base playing with the New York Yankees until he was recalled in May 1952. He and Ted Williams took their physicals at the same time in Jacksonville, Florida, but they never saw each other again while serving in Korea.

Like Williams, Coleman was stoic and understanding about the interruption of his career, saying, "If my country needed me, I was ready. Besides the highlight of my life had always been—even including baseball— flying for the Marines."[9]

After a quick refresher in SNJs, Coleman moved to VMA-251 to train in the F4U before joining VMA-323. He eventually flew sixty-three missions in Korea, to add to the fifty-seven in World War II, and he also received a second DFC and thirteen Air Medals. The squadron was flying the AU-1 ground-attack version of the Corsair. After the more agile little SBD, Coleman considered the big, gull-winged AU-1 a bit too ponderous to wheel around close to the ground.

During his time in Korea, Coleman had several close calls, including nearly running into another aircraft taking off on the same runway but from the other end, having his roommate's aircraft blow up in front of him during a weapons delivery, and then with his radio out, landing just as a battle-damaged F-86 flew right over him from the opposite end of the same runway. Coleman also crash-landed his heavily loaded Corsair when his engine failed on takeoff. Full of fuel and bombs, the fighter flipped over, the force nearly choking Coleman in his tightly clinched harness. Fortunately, a quick-thinking Navy Corpsman reached him in time.

After these wrenching experiences, Maj. Gen. Vernon Megee, commanding the 1st Marine Aircraft Wing, pulled Coleman out of the cockpit and made him a forward air controller. A newspaper correspondent quoted the general: "Jerry's got the heart of a lion, and he's done a bang-up job for us. But he's flown his share. And he's had three shattering experiences.

. . . I decided I owed it to him to keep him on the ground for a while. He'd never have asked it. He's not that kind."[10]

At first Coleman was not happy with being pulled out of flying, but as he later wrote, "It wasn't until later that I realized the toll it had taken—most visibly the hyperventilation, but also a flareup of long-standing stomach problems and a stress-induced loss of depth perception."[11]

With the direct help of the Commandant, Coleman returned to the Yankees for the 1954 season and played until 1959.

As the summer months of 1953 proceeded, the Marine squadrons of MAG-33 and MAG-12 kept up the pressure, flying countless sorties against Communist lines and pressure points, sometimes making the difference between a Communist victory and a Marine outpost remaining in Marine hands. April, May, and June were particularly active months for VMF-311. Communist anti-aircraft fire took its toll on squadron aircraft, as did the heavy monsoon weather. In July flying was completely canceled for a total of twelve days because of rain and heavy cloud cover. But there were signs of a coming cease-fire.

At the very end of the month, on July 24, MAG-33 changed hands, with Col. John L. Smith relieving Col. Arthur R. Stacy. It's not clear whether in the limited time he had the group Colonel Smith flew any combat missions. After his legendary experiences at Guadalcanal eleven years earlier, his career had had plenty of bumps and assignment to lead one of the two main aircraft groups in combat, albeit at the end of the war, should have been considered an important step.

Even with the approaching cease-fire, Chinese troops made one or two last-ditch efforts against Marine positions. On July 25, VMF-115 and VMF-311 flew strikes against enemy concentrations. Finally, word came that July 27 was to be the final day of the war. Even as the 7,000 men of the 1st MAW prepared to stand down, wing aircraft flew 222 sorties on the 27th. Capt. William I. Armagost of VMF-311 flew the last jet mission of the war against Chinese supply areas in the late afternoon, dropping four 500-pound bombs at 6:35 PM. VMF-311 had contributed 18,851 combat sorties to 1st MAW's grand total of 127,496, more than 39,000 of which had been close air support.

The final strike mission was flown by a VMA-251 AD Skyraider three hours later; the squadron had only arrived two weeks before. Capt. William J. Foster Jr. dropped *three* 2,000-pound bombs on Communist targets ahead of UN ground troops. The time was 9:25 PM, thirty-five minutes before the cease-fire was to take effect at 10:00 PM.

The wing's helicopters had evacuated more than 9,800 personnel. There were 436 Marine aircraft of various types lost. HMR-161 had flown some 30,000 hours in combat and had pioneered helicopter tactics and operations, which were to be the basis for Marine operations for years to come. The HRS-1s and newer, more powerful -3s were used after the cease-fire to shuttle repatriated prisoners of war back to their home bases.

POWs and Final Numbers

A sad but necessary area of interest concerns prisoners of war (POWs). Any conflict between nations usually produces groups of soldiers captured during engagements. Korea was no exception. There were 221 Marines captured during the war; 31 of these men were air crewmen. And 258 "air Marines" were killed in action, including 65 missing in action and presumed dead. A further 174 had in wounded.[12]

Many of the aviation POWs were piloting Corsairs during ground attack missions, and most of these were shot down by enemy ground fire. The first was Capt. Jesse V. Booker, who had launched from the carrier *Valley Forge* on August 7, 1950, in a Corsair on a photo-reconnaissance mission. His plane took a hit in the oil cooler in his left wing. Losing oil, he knew he would not make it back to the ship and decided to crash-land deep inside North Korea. Although he took refuge in a deeply wooded area, he was soon captured, the only Marine aviator to be captured until April 1951.

However, VMF-311's 1st Lt. Richard W. Bell was flying an F9F Panther when he engaged MiGs on July 21, 1951. Taking part in a strike against targets in MiG Alley along the Yalu River, Lieutenant Bell's flight was attacked by more than fifteen Soviet-flown MiGs. Although he did his best to dogfight with the MiGs and give his squadron mates a chance to escape, he soon ran out of fuel and had to eject into captivity. He and Captain Booker were the first Marine aviators to be repatriated after the cease-fire in September 1953.

The leader of the MiGs, Lieutenant Colonel Evgeniy Pepelyaev, claimed Bell's Panther as he had fired on the young Marine aviator and had seen

[Left] The end of the aviation side of the Korean War is symbolized by this VMF-311 Panther. This aircraft is credited with an incredible 445 missions and with dropping more than 400,000 pounds of ordnance, beginning in November 1950. VMF-311 flew nearly 19,000 missions.

[Opposite] An SNB-2P, one of a myriad variants of the ubiquitous Beech 18, has apparently suffered landing gear problem and crashed on one of Quantico's Brown Field runways in July 1951. The SNB became the C-45 after 1962 and continued to serve throughout the U.S. military until the 1970s. This aircraft was one of 29 SNB-2s converted to a photo trainer.

debris coming from the clouds into which Bell flew just before ejecting. The pieces could have been the canopy and ejection seat, instead of pieces of plane chopped off by the MiG's heavy cannon, which the American would have certainly felt striking his aircraft. Whatever the truth, Bell became one of the Russian's eventual tally of nineteen, making Pepelyaev the second-highest-scoring pilot of the war on either side. Humorously, he had misidentified the Marine Panthers as USAF Lockheed F-94 Starfires, an armed night-fighter variant of the T-33 trainer version of the single-seat F-80! The lack of recognition training seems to have been rife throughout the Soviet squadrons.

Predictably, the POWs suffered deprivation and torture at the hands of their captors, foretelling another such inhumane episode fifteen years in the future in another Asian war. Three Marines died while POWs, and one is presumed dead. Several attempts were made to arrange repatriation programs. The most successful were "Little Switch" in April 1953 and "Big Switch" the following August after the cease-fire.

The war in Korea had given the Marines in general, and Marine aviation in particular, a much-needed shot in the arm. Although the record of World War II spoke for itself, the air arm of the Corps had been very close to disbanding. But when the first shots were fired in June 1950, the Marines were the first to be sent. They were also among the last to leave.

10 Post-Korean Developments

THE CEASE-FIRE IN KOREA brought the inevitable post-war soul-searching peculiar to American society and also the just-as-predictable round of cost-cutting measures. The Marines, while maintaining several aircraft squadrons in Korea as peacekeepers, were somewhat protected. In 1952 a third wing, based at El Toro, had been established to support Pacific operations, with the 1st MAW in Japan and the 2nd MAW dedicated to Atlantic responsibilities, based out of Cherry Point and Miami, Florida.

The helicopter remained at the heart of Marine aviation programs, having proved its worth in Korea, and several more squadrons were created by mid-1952. By June 1952 each of the three MAWs was composed of three MAGs and a helicopter group—MAG (HR)—containing three helicopter squadrons. Each MAW also included a two-squadron transport group (fixed wing), a photo-reconnaissance squadron, a composite unit, and an observation squadron. It was quite an impressive force, obviously meant to be self-sufficient, self-contained, and self-reliant in combat.

New helicopters being considered or added to the Corps' capability included the little Kaman HOK, a twin-engine, twin-rotor design; uprated

versions of the Sikorsky HRS; as well as the HUS, a progressive development of the earlier HRS with more than twice the horsepower and capability of the HRS; and the huge HR2S, a Sikorsky aircraft that was the largest helicopter ordered for the Marines to date.

However, post-war cost-cutting finally reached the Corps, and by late 1956, the Marines Corps' total manpower strength had dropped to 200,000. Rank restructuring, particularly among the enlisted personnel, helped a bit, but the Marines found themselves in budgetary trouble once again. The Air Force was being given the role of strategic-weapons delivery, while the Army and Navy carried on their traditional roles of land warfare and sea-lane protection respectively. Even the Navy lost a round to the younger, politically powerful Air Force when its own strategic delivery squadrons were deprived of their stated raison d'être, specifically the early North American AJ Savage turboprops, the Douglas A3D Skywarrior, and the unique North American A3J Vigilante carrier-based heavy attack aircraft. The Navy, however, still kept a place in the triad of strategic weapons by maintaining a very potent force of the new underwater-launched Polaris ICBMs carried by nuclear submarines. Where, then, were the Marines?

The future lay in helicopters. In the fall of 1953, at the direction of Commandant General R. C. Shepherd, a special team met to consider specific Marine Corps problems and requirements in the amphibious-warfare area. This Advanced Research Group (ARG) also decided to consider the future role of the helicopter as part of the Fleet Marine Force. The coming HR2S was the focal point, the ARG recommending that no less than 180 of these big aircraft would meet the board's requirements for a transport helicopter capability in the late 1950s. The aircraft would equip nine squadrons. Admittedly, this figure was somewhat inflated, and the Marines had to expect considerable whittling.

[Opposite] A CH-37 of HMH-462 is inspected by a Havasupai Indian and his dog, while five of the squadron's helicopters were flying 50,000 pounds of school-building supplies to the Arizona tribe's reservation.

[Right] This unusual March 1962 close-up of a CH-37 commander talking to a crewman—note the large survival knife on the crewman's right thigh—gives a deceptive impression of the helicopter's size as well as a good view of how vehicles were loaded.

Another board, chaired by Lt. Gen. Oliver P. Smith, convened in January 1955 to consider a definitive medium helicopter. This group of senior Marine officers decided that the HR2S was overly large and required much more area to operate in a battlefield than was desirable. However, 180 of these "heavy" transport helos was still the agreed number. When the Smith Board ended in May, its recommendations included a medium helicopter to complement the HR2S, with two medium-helicopter squadrons per wing. The HUS was the prime contender for standard medium helicopter and was to equip several units.

All these meetings, boards, and recommendations, of course, really constituted a Marine "dream list," and when the cold, hard decisions had to be made, the number of HR2Ss was substantially reduced to about forty-six, but the total number of HUSs was pegged at 140 by FY 1959.

Fixed-Wing Developments in the 1950s

While the Marine Corps created a place for the helicopter, several fixed-wing aircraft were finding their way into the inventory, most of them becoming classics in the years to come. The battle-tested Grumman F9F

series continued to serve after Korea, having established a reputation for toughness in combat with VMF-115 and VMF-311, as well as several Navy carrier squadrons. As the war drew to a close, the more powerful F9F-5 was entering combat overseas. The next variant, the F9F-6, was radical enough to warrant a new name, the Cougar. (Many U.S. companies by this time had tried to establish an image for their aircraft by using a common series of names. Therefore, Grumman used "cat" names—Wildcat, Hellcat, Panther, and Cougar; Douglas used a "Sky" prefix—Skyknight, Skyray [the F4D], and the Skyhawk; and McDonnell entered the spirit world with names like Phantom, Demon [the Navy's F3H fighters], and Voodoo [the Air Force's heavy fighter, the F-101]. The routine was quite effective as a public-relations tool.)

The XF9F-6 used 35-degree swept wings and first flew on September 20, 1951. By December 1952, the straight-wing Panther had been supplemented on the production lines by the -6 Cougar, and ultimately the -7 and -8 models. There were several modifications to these aircraft, including a two-seat trainer and long-nosed photo reconnaissance variants. (The two-seater served in combat—the only model of the Cougar to do so—and only in Vietnam as a Marine recon/forward air control platform.) Although used mainly by Navy carrier squadrons, the Cougar did fly with a number of Marine units, especially in the attack role and the photo reconnaissance role, as the F9F-8P.

VMA-312 had returned from Korea in June 1953 and had been reassigned to the newly created 3rd MAW, as part of MAG-32. On February 15, 1954, the squadron was redesignated as a VMF. During this period it had traded in its veteran F4U Corsairs for the more modern F9F-4 Panther. However, by November VMA-312 had a new aircraft, the North American

FJ-2 Fury, basically a navalized F-86. The original straight-winged FJ-1 served with only a few Navy squadrons, for only a few years, with limited success. Its main purpose, along with its contemporary, the FH-1 Phantom, was to indoctrinate the Navy in jet carrier operations.

The FJ-2 was a completely different aircraft, being basically an F-86E with an arrestor hook and strengthened landing gear. Armament had also been changed from the standard Air Force battery of six .50-calibre machine guns to four 20-mm cannon. The new Fury first flew in December 1951, and the aircraft entered service with VMF-122 in January 1954. Intended as a carrier aircraft, the FJ-2 was considered a little too hot to operate from carriers and was mainly relegated to Marine units to fly from land bases, although many of these Marine squadrons periodically deployed to carriers for landing-qualification periods.

The Checkerboards of VMF-312 also received later variants of the Fury, the -3, and -3M, which was the first Navy fighter to include Sidewinder air-to-air missiles as standard armament. The Fury served with a number of squadrons. VMF-235 and VMF-323 were prime operators, along with VMF-312. VMA-223, which had remained stateside during Korea, serving as a training squadron for combat-bound Panther pilots, had also begun operating the Fury in its definitive FJ-4B model by August 1957. With increased avionics, the -4B could deliver a small atomic bomb and also carried a sizeable bombload on six wing stations, which made it an obvious candidate for close air support. VMA-212 and VMA-214 also flew the -4B, as did VMF-232, a descendant of the Red Devil Dauntless drivers of VMSB-232. VMA-334, VMF-235, and VMF-451 also flew the Fury. VMA-333 had been flying AD-6 Skyraiders but exchanged its prop-driven aircraft, along with its "attack" designation, for FJ-3s in January 1957, becoming VMF-333. The Fury also had a fairly active career in the Marine Reserves after its retirement from fleet service.

[Above Left] Maj. Ed Lefaivre stands by his F4D-1 Skyray in which he set five world climb records in 1958. Lefaivre went on to command a Marine Aircraft Group (MAG) in Vietnam. (Nick Williams)

[Above Right] A VMF-232 FJ-4 photographed in 1958. The FJ-4 had several refinements and was capable of carrying an increased payload over earlier Fury models.

[Opposite Top] A Skyray of VMF(AW)-115 taxis along the flight deck after trapping aboard USS *Independence* (VA-62). F4Ds of Marine squadrons deployed several times with Navy carriers during the early 1960s. (via Nick Williams)

[Opposite Bottom] A Skyray taxis at El Toro, November 1956. VMF-115 nearly took the F4D into combat against the Communist Chinese in September 1958 during a confrontation over Taiwan.

Another aircraft that played a major role in Marine aviation during the late 1950s was the radical delta-winged Douglas F4D Skyray, a 1947 design that set a world speed record on October 3, 1953, of 753.4 miles per hour. Maj. Ed Lefaivre also flew an F4D-1 to five world climb records in 1958. The bat-winged fighter entered Navy service with VC-3 in April 1956, but despite its spectacular performance, the short-ranged aircraft never really developed into a satisfactory carrier fighter. The only viable alternative, as it always seemed to be, was to give the Marines some of the new planes. So, VMF-115 received its first "Fords" also in April 1956.

VMF-115 unfortunately experienced an early series of accidents, which resulted in all aircraft being grounded until the problems could be solved. The faults were eventually traced to the fuel-transfer system and structural weaknesses. By the end of the year, the planes were flying again, and the squadron was redesignated VMF(AW)-115, to indicate its all-weather capability with the new radar-equipped Skyray.

The next two years saw the Marines of VMF(AW)-115 operate their planes during several exercises and also in the Far East as part of MAG-11, 1st MAW, based at Atsugi, Japan. In September 1958 the unit was put on an alert status, when the Chinese Communists caused considerable turmoil on the island fortress of Taiwan by shelling offshore islands and threatening the Nationalist Chinese with invasion. Skyrays flew from Taiwan on twenty-four-hour combat air patrols, guarding vital air-transport traffic from MiG interference. Chinese MiG-17s did tentatively challenge the Americans from time to time, running for home at the last minute. VMF(AW)-115 aircraft achieved several radar lock-ons and hungrily closed to intercept the threat, only to have the bogeys turn tail and flee.

Two F4Ds were airborne over Taiwan at dawn on one occasion, having scrambled to a threat call of thirty-two MiGs orbiting Quemoy Island. Reaching their "perch" altitude of 50,000 feet, the Skyray pilots knew it would certainly be a one-sided fight, but their mixed bag of four 20-mm cannon and two Sidewinder missiles apiece gave them some measure of confidence. Flying to within twenty-five miles of Quemoy, the Marine aviators spotted the MiGs' contrails but, to their consternation and disappointment, the quarry turned back toward the mainland, the chance of a kill immediately gone.

The squadron returned to Atsugi in March 1959, and to the United States in May, after a fourteen-month deployment. VMF(AW)-531 arrived to take their place, as well as their aircraft. Arriving back in the States, VMF(AW)-115 was reassigned to MAG-24, 2nd MAW. It was further reassigned to MAG-11, 1st MAW, in Japan during June 1960. The squadron returned to MAG-24 at Cherry Point in July 1961, having completed another overseas tour. However, the spring of 1962 saw the unit take the place of a Navy carrier fighter squadron and sail with CAG-7 aboard the USS *Independence* (CVA-62) for a Mediterranean deployment. The colorfully marked F4Ds formed an integral part of the Navy carrier air group until August.

Hardly had the men and aircraft of VMF(AW)-115 returned home than they were redeployed to the Naval Air Station at Guantánamo Bay, the American bastion surrounded by Communist Cuba. The reason for the turnaround was the October Cuban missile crisis, when the world stood perilously close to nuclear war. VMF(AW)-115 remained in Cuba until January 1963. By that time, however, many Marine units were reequipping with more modern aircraft, namely the McDonnell F-4 Phantom II or the Chance Vought F-8 Crusader. VMF(AW)-115 was somewhat behind schedule but finally traded its Skyrays for Phantoms in early 1962, also being redesignated VMFA-115 to denote its ground-attack capability with the powerful Phantom.

VMF(AW)-115 was, of course, not the sole Marine operator of the delta-winged Skyray. VMF(AW)-114, -314, -513, and -542 all flew the aircraft, although VMF(AW)-115 flew it longer than any other Marine squadron. The Skyray had been an advanced concept from its inception, but it had never found widespread acceptance during its career, either in the Navy or the Marine Corps. (The plane also saw a few years' time with reserve components.) One veteran Navy pilot wrote that the Skyray was "one of the worst Dutchrollers ever to fly [at carrier approach speeds]. . . . The vertical tail was too small, and tended to get blanked out by the wings at the high angles of attack required for slow speed flight."[1]

However, as the same aviator pointed out, the Skyray gave a lot of pilots their first taste of truly high-performance jet time: "The big manta-ray wing was great in a high-altitude dogfight, when it could be horsed around and still provide lift at almost any altitude . . . the tremendous power available could be used to climb like a rocket. . . . The APQ-50 radar was one of the first really good modern airborne sets. Its very descendants were used in almost all the F-4 Phantom models."[2]

The Skyray was also accorded the honor of serving with the North American Air Defense Command, with San Diego-based VF(AW)-3, a Navy squadron.

There was another aircraft, developed during the mid-1950s, that set a rugged, simple standard for any type of ground-attack aircraft to come after it. This small jet, the Douglas A4D series, first flew in 1954 and quickly joined U.S. Navy and Marine squadrons, forming the base for a strong attack capability. The Marines made the Skyhawk's acquaintance in January 1957, when the first aircraft reached VMA-224 at El Toro. Improved A4Ds, A4D-2s in the pre-1962 system, joined VMA-211, the Wake Island Avengers, in September. On the eve of Vietnam in 1964, twelve frontline Marine attack squadrons were flying the A-4, in addition

to various H&MS (Headquarters and Maintenance Squadron) and training organizations, as well as reserve units.

Marine Skyhawks replaced Navy aircraft on various cruises, either to give the Navy squadrons a break or to save the regular squadrons transitioning to other aircraft, as in the case of the A-6. During the early 1960s, before Vietnam, several Navy squadrons were switching over to the ultra-sophisticated Grumman A-6A Intruder, leaving their carrier air wings with reduced attack representation. The Marines were happy to oblige and sent a number of VMAs to fill in for their Navy brethren.

The F-8 and the F-4

The late 1950s was a time of transition for many Marine squadrons. By the end of the decade, plans for reequipping with the next generation of aircraft had been fairly well completed, and by the early 1960s, most of the three major new types—A-4, F-8, and F-4—were in place, their predecessors relegated to reserve units. In 1959 several fighter squadrons gave up their FJ Furies for F8U Crusaders—VMF-312 in June and VMF-333 in November, to name a couple. VMF-232 did not receive F-8s until early 1962.

The Chance Vought F8U Crusader was quite a success story for this pioneering company. Vought had had troubles connecting with a solid design after its F4U series. The company was in the forefront of jet design with some radical innovations such as the F6U Pirate, the first production Navy aircraft with an afterburner, and the big F7U Cutlass, a twin-tail bat of an airplane that, although certainly an original design, never even came close to its intended role as a missile-armed fleet defense fighter. The F7U was underpowered and dangerous, even for the Marines, who only got a chance to evaluate a single example.

So, it was with understandable enthusiasm and relief that Chance Vought greeted the first flight of its XF8U-1 in March 1955. It was an impressive aircraft and won several aviation development awards, kudos, and, best of all, pilot acclaim; the Navy and Marines lined up to place orders. Of course, the Crusader did have some initial problems, especially around a carrier. It took a fairly fine hand to fly the skittish thoroughbred down the pipe to the flight deck, and several fatal accidents occurred during beginning stages of the type's career. However, adjustments were forthcoming and by the time VMF(AW)-122 took the first Marine delivery of Crusaders in December 1957, the F-8 was well on its way to creating an enviable reputation.

Project Bullet

On July 16, 1957, a young Marine major set a speed record, flying west to east across the United States in an F8U-1P, the photo reconnaissance version of the Crusader. (The basic airframe had been modified to accommodate four

[Opposite] Maj. John Glenn in his F8U-1P preparing for his transcontinental dash in July 1957.

[Right] With the A J Savage tanker far in the background, John Glenn continues on his way across the United States during the Project Bullet flight. The Crusader's forward fuselage had been totally redesigned to accommodate a series of aerial cameras. The "hump" directly beneath the cockpit housed one camera that recorded the forward flight path over the ground. The two side fuselage windows were also camera ports. The windows on the belly served for the same cameras, which could be rotated to look either out the side or down vertically. The chevron on the vertical tail and the bands on the wingtips were Day-Glo orange. (Vought photo)

aerial cameras in the armament bay forward of the wing. The resulting F8U-1P variant was one of the most successful and long-lived tactical military aircraft in aviation history.) During the mid-summer of 1957, Maj. John H. Glenn took off with another Crusader, a straight fighter F8U-1, piloted by Navy Lt. Cdr. Charles Demmler, as part of Project Bullet. The idea was to set a record for a cross-country flight, gaining photographic coverage of the entire country along the way. The end point of the flight was Floyd Bennett Field in New York, 2,446 miles to the east.

Glenn and Demmler took off and rendezvoused with a waiting Navy tanker to refuel. However, Demmler damaged his refueling probe and had to abort the mission, leaving Glenn to continue alone. Glenn refueled three times in the air and three hours and twenty-three minutes after takeoff, touched down in New York, setting a new record, with an average speed of 726 miles per hour; this speed was little better than Mach 1, the speed of sound, at cruising altitude. It was a record that went largely unnoticed, except for some immediate press coverage.

Marine Corps Crusaders were active during the July–August 1958 Lebanon crisis, when President Dwight D. Eisenhower sent elements of the U.S. Sixth Fleet to the Mediterranean. VMF-333 was aboard the USS *Forrestal* (CVA-59), which had arrived to relieve its sister carrier USS *Saratoga* (CVA-60). However, the Crusader's finest hour in Marine colors was probably four years later during the 1962 Cuban missile crisis.

Many years later, it is perhaps a little difficult for those too young to have lived through those agonizing two weeks beginning October 14 to realize how very close the world came to nuclear war. But the Russians had gambled that the United States, under a fairly untried president, would not respond strongly to a move to insert medium-range ballistic missiles on Cuba, ninety miles from Florida.

President John F. Kennedy had not done well in foreign policy. Although he had put on a strong show of words during August 1961, when the Soviets and their East German allies threw up the Berlin Wall, precipitating

a worldwide alert, his personal credibility had suffered during the abortive Bay of Pigs invasion of Cuba earlier during the same year. To the Russians, under the colorful, mercurial Nikita Khrushchev, it seemed a calculated risk. They were not, however, prepared for total war, nor for Kennedy's rock-hard ultimatum to remove the offending missiles at once or face a showdown.

Evidence of missile-site construction had been brought back first by high-flying Lockheed U-2 reconnaissance aircraft, and the president huddled with his Cabinet to devise a course of action. Several military aerial reconnaissance squadrons, from all services, descended on the southeastern United States to fly continuous missions over Cuba. VFP-62, the East Coast Navy photo squadron, and VMCJ-2, Marine Composite Photo Squadron Two, were the senior service's contribution to the effort. The Marines were actually substitutes, called in to help VFP-62, which did not have enough

aircraft and personnel to support the massive effort because of having several detachments deployed.

The Navy/Marine operation was code-named "Blue Moon" and began on October 23rd, as RF-8As dashed over Cuba at low level to avoid radar and surface-to-air missiles (SAMs), which had already claimed at least one U-2 at higher altitude. The Crusaders landed at the Naval Air Station at Key West, Florida, where their film was quickly developed. The prints were then rushed to Washington. The combined Navy/Marine unit flew eighty individual missions during a six-week period. The last missions were on November 26, as the aircraft made surveillance runs to make sure the Russians were, in fact, dismantling the sites as they had finally promised. All the Marine and Navy pilots received the Distinguished Flying Cross for their contributions during this most difficult period.

The Mighty Phantom

One more aircraft remains to be mentioned in the pre-Vietnam era. Like its frequent stablemate, the A-4, the McDonnell Phantom earned a special place in Marine aviation. The F-4 started life in 1953 as a single-seat, missile-armed fighter, designated the AH-1, but eventually evolved into a twin-engine, two-seat, radar-equipped monster redesignated the F4H-1. Chance Vought fielded a major redesign of its F8U, the XF8U-3 Crusader III, which was a very advanced speedster with many technological innovations. However, the Phantom appeared at a time when the single-seat, gun-armed fighter was going into partial eclipse, and the McDonnell aircraft's layout was more promising for future development than the Crusader III. As a result, the Phantom won the 1958 decision and eventually became something of a legend in military aircraft design.

More than 5,000 F-4s had been produced by the time the line shut down in 1978, and even the Navy's arch-rival, the Air Force, was, at first, forced into buying quantities of the new airplane. (Of course, the junior service quickly realized what a fabulous plane the F-4 was and gladly ordered squadrons-full of the wonder fighter.)

The F-4 garnered many performance records during its initial stages of service introduction. Marine Lt. Col. (later Lt. Gen.) Thomas H. Miller set a world speed record on September 5, 1960, in an F4H-1, flying a 500-kilometer course at 1,216.78 miles per hour, 400 miles per hour faster than the previous record set in 1959 by an Air Force plane. Vice Adm. Robert B. Pirie, DCNO(Air), had become concerned that the Soviet Union seemed to be garnering a great many aeronautical performance records; others were concerned as well. Pirie, therefore, decided that the United States should attempt to regain several speed and altitude marks and what better way to do it than with the world-beater McDonnell F4H Phantom about to enter U.S. Navy and Marine service? And who better to set the records than the actual project officer/pilots in Washington, rather than some civilian test pilot?

Accordingly, Tom Miller, the F4H desk officer in the Bureau of Aeronautics, soon found himself headed to the West Coast along with other Navy pilots to make several record attempts. Miller was to try for the 500-kilometer speed record, and a triangular course was meticulously laid out that would enable him to get to the optimum altitude of 50,000 feet, punch off his underwing tanks, then finally his centerline tank, make his record dash, and regain March Air Force Base before he ran out of fuel. For above all, the speed record was actually a fuel-management exercise. A tremendous amount of gas was needed to climb to 50,000 feet, to say nothing of the amount gulped by the J-79 engines during the actual run. Miller made a number of practice runs, with Air Force pilot Jim McDivitt, later an astronaut, flying an F-104 as a chase plane.

The day of the actual attempt, Miller zoomed up to altitude and made his run, anxiously watching the rapidly decreasing fuel indicated on his gauge. The carefully calculated lines on his chart indicated that he would have less than 1,000 pounds of fuel left as he went "through the gate" and ended his run. But he would still be at 50,000 feet. As his controllers on the ground told him he was at the end of his run, the Marine aviator immediately pulled back the throttles and split-essed, rolling on his back directly over the desert town of Mojave, and pointed the nose of the Phantom straight down. The resulting sonic boom broke several whiskey bottles in the local bar, he was told later by the barkeeper.

As he approached the runway, he gave a little more throttle to bring the aircraft down safely, and as he finally touched down and began his rollout, the engines quit; he had finally flamed out through lack of fuel. It had been close. Colonel Miller received the Distinguished Flying Cross for his record flight.

During an interview, Miller told the author that the Phantom was probably never flown at its top airspeed because of the fear that its directional stability would be lost to such an extent that both the plane and its crew would have been in grave danger. In the early stages of the aircraft's career, test pilots had flown the F4H up to Mach 2.5 but had been recalled by their controllers upon reaching that speed because static tests had shown Mach 2.7 would have posed a major hazard. There was no doubt, however, that the plane could have reached that higher speed and beyond. "The F-4 was an airplane which never quit accelerating," Miller said.

VMF(AW)-314 received its first Phantoms in 1963, and the number of squadrons reequipping with the new plane multiplied rapidly. Two variants served the Marines—the F-4B fighter and the RF-4B tactical reconnaissance version, bigger and faster than the RF-8, but initially engendering some fear of flying aboard carriers because of its elongated nose, which restricted forward vision. Thus, the F-4 provided, along with the A-4 and F-8, the triangular backbone for Marine tactical aviation on the eve of Vietnam.

Marine transport aviation was due for a big boost in the early 1960s with the advent of the Lockheed Hercules. Until the first deliveries in 1960 of GV-Is (KC-130Fs), the Marines had depended on a mixture of piston-engine transports, ranging from the ubiquitous R4D(C-47) and Super-Gooney, the R4D-8(C-117), to the four-engine Douglas R5D, the Navy version of the C-54, R6D(C-118) and Fairchild R4Q(C-119) Packets of Korean War vintage. With the arrival of the turboprop C-130, the Corps not only had a highly capable heavy hauler, but a viable air-to-air refueling platform as well. The last capability allowed Marine squadrons to fly long distances with the help of their own aerial gas stations. It was a big help close to a battlefield because jets could now take the maximum bomb load, with reduced fuel, and once in the air, could top off their tanks for maximum range and effectiveness.

The C-130 had first flown in August 1954 and had quickly interested customers from all the U.S. military services, as well as several foreign countries. In fact, in the opinion of many, if ever there was a replacement for the C-47, it was the Herk. Its exploits in Vietnam, whether in Air Force or Marine colors, were legion, and it continues to serve today.

Thus, as the specter of greater American involvement in Southeast Asia began to take shape, the Corps was in the process of modernizing its air arm in every aspect, from rotary wing to fixed wing, tactical to logistical. The most important event for the Marine Corps helicopter community was a 1956 board presided over by Maj. Gen. Robert E. Hogaboom. Like preceding gatherings, the Hogaboom Board was tasked with determining

[Opposite Left] Then–Lt. Col. Thomas H. Miller in the cockpit of his record-setting F4H Phantom II. (Lt. Gen. Thomas H. Miller, USMC [Ret.])

[Opposite Right] Brand-new F-4Bs of VMFA-513 flying off the California coast in 1962. The F-4B was the first true production model and served throughout the war in Vietnam with the Navy and Marines. (Lt. Gen. Thomas H. Miller, USMC [Ret.])

[Top Left] UH-34s load Marine troops during an exercise. Vertical assault from LPH/LPDs was a relatively new doctrine, but has been steadily refined to the present day.

[Bottom Left] Troops participating in an exercise run from an HMM-261 UH-34.

[Top Right] The USS *Princeton* (LPH-5) maneuvering in 1959 with a deck load of UH-34s neatly arranged on her flight deck. Note that the ship still carries gun mounts immediately fore and aft of the island.

[Bottom Right] A UH-34 lifts off from an LPH with a cargo net underneath, while a CH-37 is serviced. These two helicopters formed the backbone of the Marine Corps' pre-Vietnam assault capability.

the requirements for the Fleet Marine Force, this time from FY 1958. The board homed in on the status and future of the helicopter and decided that although helicopters were certainly a vital part of amphibious operations, they were by no means the only recommended means for dispersing assault troops on a beach. There was still room for the traditional seaborne invasion, especially after the initial insertion by vertical assault. The board's findings also affected Marine organizational structure as well as other hardware areas and were in keeping with the new mood of austerity pervading the Corps in the late 1950s.

One aspect of Marine helicopter theory during this time period was the helicopter-carrier concept, the LPH. Anxious to have its own Navy ships, the Marine Corps eagerly accepted an offer to convert several *Essex*-class World War II carriers to meet the immediate requirement for a helicopter carrier. New, built-for-the-purpose ships were several years away. The USS *Thetis Bay* (CVE-90) had been the experimental vessel in 1956, accommodating twenty HRS helicopters. Three other veteran carriers—the *Boxer, Princeton,* and *Valley Forge*—were eventually converted by 1961, while the Marines waited anxiously for the *Iwo Jima* class of LPH to be built.

With the implementation of the Hogaboom Board's recommendations and the accompanying measures of austerity, Marine aviation was lean and trim immediately before Vietnam. Its leaders, crews, and equipment were in the best shape, many observers believed, since World War II, even better than Korea. There were even newer aircraft in the near future.

The highly capable Grumman A-6A Intruder was being touted as a sophisticated bombing and electronic intelligence (ELINT) platform, while the little Bell UH-1 "Huey," the Boeing-Vertol CH-46 Sea Knight medium, turbine-powered transport helicopter, and the big Sikorsky CH-53A Sea Stallion heavy transport helicopter were in various stages of pre-service development. They would join operations very soon. As what has been called "The Longest War" began to rumble more and more loudly in Vietnam, these new machines would be needed desperately.

Prelude to Vietnam

Before discussing the Vietnam War, which is generally dated from 1964 to 1973, it is necessary to step back to the eventful year of 1962 for some perspective. From the standpoint of Marine Corps aviation, 1962 was somewhat of a watershed. There were 341 helicopters in service in several MAGs, including MAGs -13, -16, -26, and -36, although the size of the helicopter population varied considerably from group to group. There were also several other units, including the "granddaddy" HMX-1, which had been tasked, since September 1957, with providing VIP flight service with its presidential flight. (Dwight D. Eisenhower was the first president to use helicopter service for short-range trips.)

Although there were six types of helicopters in service at this time, only three—the HUS, HOK, and HR2S—were operating with any significant numbers. Indeed, by 1962 the HUS, soon to be redesignated UH-34, was the most numerous helicopter, some 225 aircraft being in service. Originally intended as a Navy anti-submarine platform, the HUS had been gradually transformed into a useful utility type and was delivered first to HMRL-261 in February 1957. The UH-34 was to prove invaluable, because it shouldered much of the burden of early Vietnam operations, starting in 1962.

The Shufly Operation

Southeast Asia had been a battleground for centuries and had known several invaders and conquerors. By 1940 the French held much of the area, which was known as French Indochina, and had established an uneasy truce with the Japanese until Imperial forces attacked in late 1941, subjugating Thailand (then known as Siam) and much of the Indochina Peninsula. Victory over Japan reinstated French influence but another, more insidious enemy was at work. Communist rebels and insurgents began to openly fight the French and ultimately drove them out of Indochina at the climactic battle of Dienbienphu, 170 miles west of Hanoi, in 1954. As a result, Vietnam was partitioned, North and South, along the 17th parallel, with a Demilitarized

[Top] An outpost, manned by U.S. advisers, 35 miles from Da Nang. Outposts were usually placed on high ground overlooking civilian areas. (H. C. Brown)

[Bottom] Two UH-34Ds of HMM-261 return from a mission 20 miles south of Da Nang in October 1963. Marine helicopters were used as transports for the troops of the South Vietnamese Army, although toward the end of the Shufly operation, field-installed machine guns and sidearms had begun to appear as self-defense armament. (H. C. Brown)

Zone (DMZ) in between. But the area was never at peace, and by late 1961 it was necessary for U.S. leaders to consider beefing up support for the faltering South Vietnamese forces.

Accordingly, HMM-362, under Lt. Col. Archie J. Clapp, was sent to Soc Trang, eighty-five miles southwest of Saigon, the capital of South Vietnam, to increase the battlefield airlift capability then in-country. Squadron personnel began arriving in April 1962, bringing twenty-four UH-34Ds, and three OE-1 Cessnas for wing liaison duties. The fixed-wing two-seaters were borrowed from VMO-2. Other assets soon followed, including KC-130s, one of which was piloted by Maj. Gen. John P. Condon, Commanding General of the lst MAW. The Hercules were needed to bring in the heavy, bulky equipment for Marine Air Base Squadron (MABS) 16.

After the usual problems in setting up and establishing base security forces, Lieutenant Colonel Clapp's squadron began operations on Easter Sunday, April 22. The UH-34s flew missions in support of U.S. Army H-21 helos moving South Vietnamese soldiers into forward areas. The Marines were quickly involved in firefights as they shuttled supplies and troops into battle areas. (At the time, because of political considerations and concern of presenting a more hostile appearance than intended, the only weapons aboard the H-34s were those carried by the crew, namely individual side-arms and .45-caliber submachine guns.) April 24 saw the first battle damage of a UH-34, when one aircraft was hit by ground fire and forced to land with a punctured oil line. The damage was repaired in a few hours, and the helicopter returned to Soc Trang.

During these early operations, techniques were beginning to evolve that would be needed years later. One concept was the armed escort of troop-carrying helos. At times, landing zones were so heavily defended by the insurgents that it was very difficult even to get the soldiers on the ground. Initial "softening up" procedures by South Vietnamese aircraft only served to advertise the location of the landing zone (LZ) to the enemy too far in advance of the actual landings.

Therefore, the incorporation of North American T-28 prop-driven trainers from the States helped the situation. The two-seater Trojans could stay with the slow-flying helicopters flying with the troop formations and could carry bombs, rockets, and guns. As the helicopters approached the LZ, the T-28 s could zoom ahead and sanitize the area. OE-1s could also be used to reconnoiter ahead of the UH-34s. Equipped with an array of radios for communication with both air and ground units, the single-engine Cessnas could control the actual landings, especially with Vietnamese interpreters aboard.

Another improvisation was the Eagle Flight. Four Marine helicopters would fly above the main landing force, looking for Viet Cong (VC) rebels who tried to escape via alternate routes. With about fifty ARVN (Army of the Republic of Vietnam) soldiers distributed among them, the Eagle Flight aircraft would land where the ARVN troops could block the enemy's escape. Night assaults by helicopter also were tried during this early period, the first such operation occurring on July 20, 1962.

HMM-163 relieved HMM-362 on August 1. HMM-362 had flown fifty combat assaults, including 4,439 individual sorties in 5,262 combat flight hours. Through all this action, no aircraft were lost; although, of course, damage was sustained on several occasions. The new unit got right into action on August 1 but did not suffer any battle damage until August 18. It was at this time that attempts were made to arm the UH-34s with something other than hand-held weapons. Mounts for M-60 machine guns, belt-fed 7.62-mm weapons, were added and taken into battle, although the gunners were strictly admonished not to fire unless they were fired upon by a clearly identified enemy.

Redeployment North

HMM-163 moved north to the coastal city of Da Nang, arriving on September 16, having moved in by Hercules transport and UH-34. Da Nang was a larger base than Soc Trang, with an 8,000-foot paved runway. On September 19, HMM-163 aided in the evacuation of a government outpost in the mountains eighteen miles west of Da Nang. Unfortunately, this type of mission was to repeat itself many times in the coming months, as the Communists began to build up their effort, reinforced by supplies from North Vietnam. Action was heavy throughout the remainder of September. The successful Eagle Flights had been redesignated Tiger Flights and were reinstituted in early November.

There were coordination problems with the ARVN authorities from time to time as well. Unfamiliar with helicopter operations and the somewhat strict time table necessary for an effective helicopter airlift in combat, the ARVN forces were not always ready to be loaded into the UH-34s. The problem was such that a special Marine "loadmaster" was designated, usually a senior NCO, who would leave the first helicopter and hopefully get material and troops ready to go in short order.

The new year 1963 brought monsoon weather with rain and resulting mud, which hampered flight operations. HMM-163 rotated home beginning the second week in January, HMM-162 taking its place. Under Lt. Col. Robert L. Rathbun, HMM-163 had flown 10,869 hours, with 15,200 sorties.

August 1962 saw a record of 2,543 hours. HMM-162, under Lt. Col. Reinhardt Leu, was no stranger to Southeast Asia, having recently deployed to Udorn, Thailand, during the Laotian crisis in the spring of 1962. HMM-162 had arrived at Udorn in late June, around the time the crisis had eased and U.S. forces were being withdrawn. It was thus a fairly easy turnaround for the squadron to head for Da Nang.

HMM-162 joined combat operations on January 19, 1963, and participated in many helicopter assaults, losing three UH-34s in combat. The squadron also used armed helicopters with door-mounted M-60 machine guns. HMM-162 flew extensive combat until relieved in early June by HMM-261, Lt. Col. Frank A. Shook commanding. Like its predecessors, HMM-261 had moved from its base at New River, North Carolina, to El Toro en masse, to be flown to Japan where the squadron personnel were inoculated and briefed within a twenty-four-hour period.

They were finally flown to Da Nang, where they picked up the equipment and aircraft left behind by the preceding unit. Actually, HMM-261 was the first squadron to serve its full tour at Da Nang. The old French

army compound served as the new Shufly headquarters and eventually those of the lst MAW in Vietnam as well. The Officers' Club had elaborate iron doors, above which a sign greeted visitors with the inscription "Far Eastern Indochina Jungle Fighters & Combat Pilots Association LTD."

First Lieutenant H. C. Brown was a co-pilot with the unit's UH-34s, and he remembers the ever-present clouds and dampness of the South Vietnamese weather and the lush green foliage and undulating mountains over which much of Shufly's operations flew. The helicopters flew mainly supply missions to ARVN outposts, usually situated on a hill overlooking the civilian population of the individual villages. The UH-34s flew everything from livestock to people in and out of the meandering trails and rivers that flow through the area.

However, sometimes the helos and their crews were caught in vicious firefights, and Brown recalled a mission in the summer of 1963 when he took so much ground fire that he put in a call for help. Within minutes, a flight of South Vietnamese Skyraiders roared in and threw themselves at the Communist positions. Brown and his crew watched incredulously as the Vietnamese aircraft actually flew below his helicopter in an effort to put their ordnance square on target. He called the Skyraider pilots "superb."

Efficiency of ARVN forces varied considerably, the more professional units being those manned by career officers from the Air Force and the South Vietnamese Marines. The other end of the spectrum apparently included the regular field teams, which probably numbered many unwilling conscripts within their group. HMM-261 began operations and flew combat until October 2, when HMM-361 came over.

Lt. Col. Thomas J. Ross led HMM-361 and had received five DFCs for action in World War II and Korea. By the time HMM-361 arrived and began combat operations in early October, it was painfully apparent that the VC had gotten over their initial fear of helicopters and were firing on the Marine aircraft without hesitation. Shufly helicopters of HMM-361 had been hit eighteen times in just one month.

Events in Saigon, namely the overthrow and assassination of the South Vietnamese president, as well as the returning monsoon, slowly brought

Shufly operations to a halt, until at least the political situation stabilized. Of course, besides the assassination in Saigon, there had been an assassination in the United States, when President Kennedy was shot dead in Dallas in November. Kennedy's successor, Lyndon B. Johnson, immediately froze all the units in South Vietnam. Their members had begun thinking they might be rotated home. There were many rumors to that effect. It looked as if Kennedy was trying to disengage U.S. forces from Southeast Asia, but Johnson began beefing up those units and talk of returning home vanished.

On January 3, 1964, after operations resumed their previous intensity, HMM-361 sustained an aircraft loss during a medical evacuation mission west of Da Nang. Hit several times, the UH-34D crashed in the jungle and was destroyed by U.S. Green Berets to prevent its falling into enemy hands. After a month's flying, HMM-361 was relieved in February by HMM-364, commanded by Lt. Col. John H. La Voy. HMM-364 was scheduled to be the last Marine helicopter unit to fly Shufly operations, and plans were under way to train South Vietnamese crews to take over the work. Monsoon clouds still periodically curtailed flight operations until early April.

On April 14, HMM-364 suffered its first combat loss when a UH-34 was hit by VC ground fire while trying to take off after a medevac. The aircraft crashed forty miles west of Da Nang, and the crew sustained minor injuries. On the 18th, a large-scale assault by Shufly Marines, including twenty UH-34Ds and five Huey gunships, specifically armed escort helicopters, struck an area in the A Shau Valley near the Laotian border, a thick VC stronghold. Code-named Lam Son 115, this operation included air control of all aerial resources, a harbinger of things to come. It was during this and subsequent assaults that the VC tried a clever trick of lighting off smoke-signal flares at a second LZ, hoping to confuse the helo crews and catch them in a crossfire.

April 27, 1964, saw the largest airborne assault in the three-year history of Shufly, and it was also the most costly. Operation Sure Wind 202 called for the airlifting of 420 troops of an ARVN battalion in company with U.S. Army helicopters. South Vietnamese A-1H Skyraiders were assigned escort and suppression duties. (The South Vietnamese Air Force had been flying the big Douglas attack planes since 1960, when a contingent of Navy pilots and crews had come to South Vietnam to train the South Vietnamese pilots, a repeat of Marines ferrying F4Us to Saigon during the Korean War for the French.)

The first Marine helicopters, escorted by Army UH-1B gunships, approached the LZ a little after noontime and were met with a barrage of defensive fire from the Communists on the ground. The pre-assault attentions from the Skyraiders appeared to have had little effect on the enemy, and the UH-34s touched down in a storm of bullets. Several helos were hit, and one crashed in the LZ itself, although the crew was rescued.

A second wave met the same fire, although somewhat diminished because of the eventual spreading out of the ARVN troops from the first wave. Several Marine aircraft had been damaged, and only a reduced effort could be mounted for continued assault on the following morning. Sure Wind 202 was not completed until May 25, by which time HMM-364 had flown 983 sorties in 800 flight hours. The squadron rotated home in June, relieved by HMM-162.

[Opposite] Then–First Lieutenant Brown watches as his UH-34 is serviced. Note his camouflaged fatigues and flak jacket. The aircraft is equipped with a winch immediately above the cabin door, and an M-60 machine gun. (H. C. Brown)

The Shufly operation continued well into 1964, and as the situation rapidly deteriorated, with the VC attacking everywhere in the South and the August 1964 Gulf of Tonkin incident, which brought direct American involvement, it was clear that the Shufly effort had fallen far short of its expectations. What, then, did Shufly accomplish?

Lt. Col. Archie Clapp, the first Shufly squadron commander, writing in the October 1963 issue of the U.S. Naval Institute's *Proceedings*, tried to give an answer. (During World War II, Clapp had flown Corsairs with VMF-123 from the USS *Bennington* and had shot down at least one Zero over Tokyo Bay in 1945.) Although written some two years before the greater American effort of the summer of 1964, his words are worth quoting: "What did Operation Shufly add to the store of knowledge. . . ? It certainly did not produce a group of anti-guerrilla experts who have all the answers. It is believed, however, that most of the participants did come away with a keen awareness of the unique characteristics of this type combat. . . . And if an appreciation of the problems inherent in this facet of military operations is all that was gained, then the deployment can still be considered productive."

The original intention of Shufly was twofold. First, to increase U.S. presence, and particularly, as far as senior officers were concerned, Marine presence, in South Vietnam. Marines wanted first hand knowledge of the situation, though not originally as combatants, but as observers, to relay information back to Washington for political and military policy making. Second, Shufly helicopters were to be used to help the South Vietnamese move themselves around more easily in their fight against the Communist insurgents. This "taxi" service was to last only until the South Vietnamese had enough properly trained crews to operate their own helicopters.

With the above in mind, Shufly could be deemed a fair success. The South Vietnamese did gain valuable experience and confidence, proving themselves a viable force when used in conjunction with other services. The fixed-wing pilots of the South's air force were openly admired for their aggressiveness and dedication in support of the American helicopters.

In a sidelight consideration, the C-130 Hercules had proven its worth from the very beginning, bringing in heavy and valuable equipment, often into very short fields, where no other heavy transport was able to operate. Major General Condon considered Shufly "a remarkably well-planned operation" using the C-130 as an "essential tool."

The days of Shufly were vastly different from those to come, especially during the ferocious Tet offensive and battle for Khe Sanh in 1968. Lieutenant Brown later likened the period of Shufly in 1963 to "an Appalachian Family Feud." "In 1968," he said, "it was war!"[3] In cold reality, perhaps, the Shufly effort was only an early indication of just how tough the coming eight-year war was going to be for American servicemen, contending with not only weather, terrain, equipment limitations, and the confusion of their South Vietnamese allies, but also a tough, stoic little enemy who was prepared to wait it out, secure in the belief that the end would surely turn his way after all.

Training of South Vietnamese pilots had been scheduled for completion by March 1964, but an extension pushed the date into the summer. By that time the Gulf of Tonkin incident had heated things up and a call for more South Vietnamese pilots necessitated additional training. December saw Shufly renamed; its title now was Marine Unit Vietnam (MUV). By the spring of 1965, as U.S. men and material began pouring into South Vietnam, Shufly was eventually absorbed into the greater effort that was to come. The operation had given valuable experience to half of the Corps' medium helicopter transport squadrons. (March 8, 1965, can be considered an effective end-date for Shufly. On that date U.S. Marines landed at Da Nang in the first amphibious operation of the war for U.S. servicemen.) The men of Shufly had ceased to be the only Marines in the Republic of Vietnam.

The Development of the Armed Helicopter

One of the major developments to come out of Shufly was the helicopter that could shoot back. Of course, helo crewmen, from Korea onward, had carried hand weapons with which to fire back on enemy troops, but for the most part, helicopters remained unarmed and unarmored, with very little protective plating. One of the reasons for the lack of armor plate was the lack of lifting power of the early machines. The armor plate was just too heavy, and until the advent of the more powerful HR2S and UH-34, armor was a luxury that could not be afforded.

Early Shufly combat underlined the need for armor and Lieutenant Colonel Clapp immediately took steps to place protection over the more vulnerable areas of his machines, the engine and oil lines in particular. Crew protection was developed later in 1964, although all the additional weight, no matter how judiciously placed, imposed severe limitations on the UH-34's capabilities, especially in the hot, humid air of Vietnam.

Besides the obvious measure of providing armed fixed-wing escorts, the other alternative for helicopter protection was to arm the UH-34s themselves. At first, Lieutenant Colonel Clapp decided not to place machine-gun mounts in the doorway of the aircraft because of the obstruction placed in the way of ground troops as they left the helo's cabin. Clapp felt the less time spent on the ground, the better. However, as the VC began to fire with increasing regularity on Marine helicopters, Clapp realized that he had to change his ruling and mount M-60s in the doorway of the UH-34s. New instructions allowing gunners more leeway as to when to fire were also forthcoming. Additional M-60s were installed as the need was recognized, and UH-34s were carrying two to four machine guns by the spring of 1964. It was still not enough. The Communists were becoming increasingly bolder.

Arming helos was not a new thought. It had been conceived by military strategists in the late 1940s, and the British writer George Orwell had used the armed helicopter in his dark vision of the future in his novel *1984*. But like many ideas, this one had to wait until it was needed and had developed a circle of support. Experiments had shown relative success with air-to-ground anti-tank missiles launched from helicopters in the late 1950s. These experiments were conducted by Army units. The Army could not have armed fixed-wing aircraft and was therefore trying to develop its own airborne firepower. The Marine Corps' helicopter community was watching with increasing interest, but there was a lot of anti-helicopter prejudice to be overcome, especially from jet fixed-wing proponents.

Marine Corps Commandant Gen. Wallace M. Greene Jr. was very sympathetic to the need for armed Marine helicopters, and he directed that an armament kit for the UH-34s be developed as soon as possible. Since April 1963, the Marine transport helicopters had been escorted by Army UH-1B gunships in Vietnam. These Hueys were armed with four 7.62-mm machine guns and 2.75-inch rockets in pods. But Greene was in favor of the Marines providing their own protection. HMX-1 developed the TK-1 (Temporary Kit-1), consisting of two rocket pods and two machine guns mounted on platforms between the main landing gear and fuselage, the guns being placed on the right side so that the ejected casings would not strike the left-mounted tail rotor. It was a somewhat successful arrangement, but in the opinion of many crews, the TK-1 was only a stopgap until a real gunship was allocated to the Marines. The gun kits were sent to HMM-365 in November 1964, and their success was only minimal. (Even 20-mm gun pods had been tried by HMX-1 at Quantico in 1961–62.)

The only viable solution to the Marines' need for a gunship helicopter seemed to be to give them one. Therefore, Marine UH-1Es were outfitted with TK-2 kits, four electrically fired M-60s and 2.75-inch rocket pods, and sent to the Fleet Marine Force. VMO-2 took the armed Hueys to Da Nang in May 1965.

The Helicopter Pilot Shortage

The other pre-war problem facing Marine aviation was the pilot shortage of the early 1960s. Admittedly, the helicopter was not as glamorous a flying machine as the sleek, speedy jets; it took a special type of pilot to want to fly helos. Promotion possibilities for helicopter pilots were not the greatest, either. By 1962 the Marines were facing an acute shortage of helicopter pilots. Several possible solutions were considered, including recruiting from warrant officer and NAP programs. Although programs from these areas were initiated, the results were disappointing and the shortage continued. Although 40 percent of all Marine aviators was needed to adequately man the helicopter squadrons, only 29 percent was being used.

There was little to do except to force a switch. Accordingly, Maj. Gen. N. J. Anderson, in charge of Marine aviation, forwarded a plan to the Commandant whereby 500 fixed-wing aviators would be ordered to transition to helicopters. Some attempt was made to soften the impact of this edict. Pilots selected would have already finished a tour in fixed-wing squadrons and would be due for rotation, anyway. Predictably, the program was a source of consternation among those pilots selected, usually first lieutenants and captains. But by June 1964, the transition training was well under way, and many of the pilots who had approached their new tours with feelings of being "second class" soon began to change their attitude and throw themselves into their work. Their appreciation of their new trade and the different flying skills they developed were a source of great excitement and satisfaction for many, if not all. There were also new aircraft being developed for the Marine Corps helicopter community and the future appeared bright for budding helicopter aviators.

11 Vietnam: *The Early Stages*

THE GIGANTIC, PAINFUL STRUGGLE that was Vietnam burst over the American public in early August 1964. On the 2nd, American destroyers were attacked on the high seas off the coast of North Vietnam by Communist patrol boats. A second attack on the 4th prompted immediate American response in the form of retaliatory air strikes against the PT-boat bases. (Over the years, this second attack has been questioned and is currently thought to have not happened, certainly not as an actual strike by enemy PT boats.) This so-called Gulf of Tonkin incident also resulted in President Lyndon B. Johnson preparing for possible escalation. The Marines, as well as the other services, had been involved in Southeast Asia for several of the preceding years and, as a consequence, had watched the growing turmoil with more informed interest and concentration.

The 3rd Marine Division and the 1st Marine Aircraft Wing, both in Japan, were reorganized, beefed up, and alerted for duty in South Vietnam should the need arise. It was a tense period of watching and waiting. However, after the initial strikes by Navy carrier air units, the crisis appeared to ease, and the Marines were relaxed until a new period of intensive operation began late in 1964.

Actually, the Marines had been flying from selected carriers immediately before and then after the skirmishes in the Gulf. Several RF-8As, along with their pilots and ground crewmen, shuttled around the assembled carrier task forces, flying from the *Bon Homme Richard* (CVA-31) and the *Kitty Hawk* (CVA-63) almost like World War I German flying circuses, going where they were most needed to supplement Navy reconnaissance assets.

VMCJ-1 photo-Crusaders flew over Laos as well as South Vietnam, their people settling into the crowded accommodations aboard ship as best they could. The "Romeo Mike" Crusaders—the squadron tail code letters—flew aboard *Kitty Hawk* on May 22, 1964. Most of the young Marine aviators had not seen a carrier since March, a few since the previous December. Regulations dictated no more than a six-month separation from the last carrier landing, so the pilots were legal, but it was stretching things. With aircraft availability sometimes a problem, the Marines' Crusaders were a welcome boost and Navy pilots often flew their guests' aircraft.

The *Coral Sea* detachment of Marine photobirds was well settled in by the summer of 1965. Twenty-five-year-old 1st Lt. John Dodson was flying his thirteenth mission, following a strike on Vinh. The young pilot was low, maybe 100 feet off the deck, along Highway 1, going 500 knots, when he spotted a North Vietnamese truck coming toward him. Of course, the truck driver couldn't know the monster hurtling toward him was unarmed, and Dodson made the most of that lack of vital intelligence.

As he bore on toward the truck, he saw the vehicle skid, swerve, and zig-zag, as the driver desperately tried to avoid the Crusader. Dodson was satisfied to see the truck driver "bail out," leaving his truck to career off the road in the opposite direction. When Dodson returned to the carrier, his crew added a yellow truck silhouette alongside the baker's dozen camera markings.[1]

By January 1965, the Marines of the 9th Expeditionary Brigade were off the South Vietnamese coast, near Da Nang. The situation rose and fell in intensity of action. Early February saw more VC attacks, and on February 7, the 1st Light Antiaircraft Missile (LAAM) Battalion got the word to land at Da Nang. When the unit's first HAWK missiles were landed by C-130 the following day, no one could have foreseen the tremendous effort and the staggering number of men and machines that were to follow in the next eighteen months.

Four light-photo detachments plus their fighter squadron host are shown in this 1965 photo aboard USS *Coral Sea* (CVA-43). VMCJ-1 helped VFP-63's detachment, supplying aircraft and people to fly and service the large number of missions required during this early stage of the war.

As the initial programmed Navy strikes, known collectively as Flaming Darts I and II, hit the enemy from February 7–11, the Marines rode out the time in their ships off the coast. The bombing campaign, Rolling Thunder, began in early March, and on March 8, 1965, the Marines stormed ashore at Da Nang. However, there was no enemy opposition, and the bemused Leathernecks set up shop under the welcoming gaze of the South Vietnamese, who were in a festive mood. In company with KC-130s, the helos of HMM-162—transferred from HMM-365—carried the men and equipment in.

The Squadrons Begin to Arrive, and Tales of Willie the Whale

As the buildup continued, MUV was deactivated and the helicopter air group, MAG-16, took its place. By April the first tactical fixed-wing units began to arrive. The fifteen McDonnell F-4B Phantoms of VMFA-531, led by Lt. Col. William C. McGraw, flew down from Japan on the 11th and began combat operations on the 13th, twelve F-4s flying close-air-support missions in South Vietnam. A second F-4 squadron, VMFA-542, arrived later in July. VMCJ-1 arrived on April 17, bringing a detachment of EF-10Bs, the current designation of the venerable Skyknight, now used as an electronic countermeasures (ECM) platform. This type of big old jet was

known as Willie the Whale, or more colloquially, DRUT, the derivation of which can be seen with the letters in reverse order.

The DRUTs flew their first ECM mission on April 21 and were heavily used for the next two years, especially for protection against Soviet-built and -supplied surface-to-air missiles (SAMs), which began to appear in April 1965. The Skyknights retained their integral armament of four 20-mm cannon, and early in the tour crews would strafe targets of opportunity when returning from a mission. They were soon ordered to abandon this practice. The EF-10s had neither the ejection seats nor the high speeds necessary for such dangerous low-level work. The EF-10s usually flew under fairly loose control wherever they were needed. This procedure caused some problems, including a near shoot down by Navy fighters from the USS *Ticonderoga* (CVA-14).

In March 1966, a section of F-8 Crusaders of VF-51 was scrambled to investigate an unidentified aircraft off the North Vietnamese coast, near Vinh. It was night-time, and as the two Crusaders approached their bogey, its identity was still unknown. The American pilots tensed with the excitement of possible action and scanned the sky for the quarry. The F-8s were several thousand feet above the bogey and had to roll over on a wing to see when the radar controller aboard a U.S. Navy destroyer told them they should be able to see the aircraft. The section leader's radar had locked onto a target, and he sent his wingman ahead to gain a positive visual identification, as per orders. The young fighter pilot pulled up above the bogey whose straight-winged outline looked very much like an Ilyushin Il-28 jet bomber. There was a lot of expectation concerning the possible use of these aircraft in a surprise raid by the North Vietnamese, and all the pieces seemed to fit. The F-8 wingman closed in for a closer look—only to find that it was a big old DRUT motoring along. In disgust and disappointment, the Crusader driver punched in his afterburner, with a resultant boom and long tongue of bright flame, just to let the Marine crew know how close they had come, and sped away. It was determined that the EF-10 had strayed into uncontrolled airspace and no one on the ground knew it was there.

Usually, however, the EF-10's contribution was appreciated. Lt. Col. Otis W. Corman, commanding VMCJ-1, wrote how the Skyknight's use had jumped to 300 percent, a phenomenal rate. In fact, from their arrival in-country in April through the end of the year, EF-10s of VMCJ-1 flew 791 sorties in support of Navy and Air Force strikes into North Vietnam and Laos.

After North Vietnamese SAMs had destroyed several Air Force F-105s beginning in April 1965, large strike forces were sent against the missile bases near Hanoi. On July 27, 1965, a package of F-105s, escorted by F-4Cs and F-104s, was also supported by EF-10s from VMCJ-1, and after that, the Marine squadron found itself in demand for both USAF and Navy operations. The need became so great that soon VMCJ needed more radar operators, and several F-4 radar intercept officers (RIOs) were asked to volunteer their services. VMFA-513 and VMFA-542, recently arrived in-country, sent several Phantom backseaters to help out. Many of these first-generation RIOs had had experience in EF-10s.

[Opposite] Some of the first Phantoms to arrive in Vietnam land at Da Nang in April 1965. VMFA-531 F-4Bs taxi in, dragging their braking chutes behind them. The massive buildup was rapid in 1965, apparently catching the Communists off guard.

[Right] An EF-10B of VMCJ-1 sits in the rain at Da Nang. Vietnam was the Skyknight's swan song, and the big old jet served four years as a radar jammer against North Vietnamese missile defenses.

Then–1st Lt. William "Duke" Steinken, a 542 RIO, describes one mission involving a scheduled six EF-10s—the entire complement of the detachment.

I was teamed with Major Mitchell, the VMCJ-1 operations officer, but at the scheduled launch time, our aircraft (BuNo 125849) did not have all the ECM equipment installed. The other five aircraft had to depart without us to meet their IP times. About fifteen minutes later, the CO came by and said they were going to cancel our mission, but Major Mitchell said, "No, skipper, we are ready to go," and we immediately taxied out and took off north.

We had been briefed to fly over water to the Haiphong area then west to our IP near the SAM sites outside Hanoi where we would set up a race track pattern at 20,000 feet. We were about 110 miles from Danang over water abeam Vinh when I calculated we were not going to make our initial point on time on the briefed course. I plotted a new direct course and we transitioned over land toward Hanoi.

As we passed to the west of Thanh Hoa, I intercepted numerous Fire Can fire-control radars and began jamming them and breaking their radar lockon.

Major Mitchell said, "Duke, look out there," and I saw the entire area was black with heavy AAA. We got through that and arrived at our IP right on time as the F-105s began to attack the SAM sites in intervals for more than twenty minutes.

During this mission, the six Skyknights jammed GCI, fire control, and SA-2 target tracking radars as well as dispensing chaff to further confuse the enemy radars. There were MiGs reported in the area, but perhaps because of the huge jamming effort by the Marine EF-10s, they never made a move toward the strike force.

The Air Force was very appreciative of the Marines' services and wrote up all twelve Marine crewmen for the DFC. Soon the DRUTs even had their own F-4 escorts, usually supplied by aircraft from the two Marine Phantom squadrons at Da Nang.[2]

The EF-10 was remembered with varying degrees of affection by the pilots who flew it late in its life. Flying such a vintage aircraft certainly had its nostalgia value and the big airplane was rock-steady, a great vehicle for going cross-country. But it was slow and tired. By 1968 the airspeed limitation was 300 knots, and no banks greater than 90 degrees could be made. Further, no more than three Gs could be imposed on the airframe. It was, after all, a twenty-year-old aircraft, not much younger than some of the men who flew it.

Then-Maj. (later Gen.) John Dailey flew the EF-10.

Lt. Col. Ed Love was the CO of VMCJ-1. Bill Fleming actually had taken J-1 over then was relieved by Ed Love. I had been an A-4 pilot with VMA-332, MAG-12, 1st MAW, then I was on recruiting duty from 1964–66. Then, I went to El Toro and flew F-8s with VMF-334. I got combat-qualified in the F-8 and I was going to deploy to Vietnam. I made major, but the quotas had changed and they didn't need an F-8 major. They did need an RF-4 and EF-10B major.

VMCJ-3 had gone as a full-up squadron with everyone qualified. They had no residual training capability. VMCJ-3 at El Toro had airplanes but no pilots. My orders sent me to VMCJ-1 as a replacement pilot. I talked to Bill Tomlinson, the CO of VMCJ-3. I said I was going to J-1 and had no F-4 experience. He told me the orders were actually to fly the EF-10B. He told me to get fifty hours in the Skyknight and then we would talk about the RF-4.

I flew the EF-10 six hours a day to get my time in a hurry but the wing got my qualification notification. In the meantime, I was flying with a mech in the back seat of the RF-4 because there were no other qualified radar systems officers [RSOs] or pilots. I wanted to get ten hours in the RF-4 before I left for Vietnam just so I could say I was NATOPS qualified. An F-4 pilot gave me a check ride from the back seat.

When I arrived at VMCJ-1, it turned out the squadron had just won the Commandant's efficiency trophy. They had deployed with four different aircraft and had done a great job. When I checked in, Bill Fleming, the CO at the time, was surprised. He asked me if I wouldn't rather fly F-8s. I quickly said yes. He went to the group to try to fix it.

"I have bad news for both of us," he told me when he returned. "You're staying!"

So, I started flying the EF-10B. But the squadron was getting close to their time to leave. People were rotating out, going to the wing and group, and Fleming needed someone. But he didn't want to jeopardize their performance with a new guy.

I was out on a night hop, on Agony Orbit, up by the DMZ. You were up there for three hours and then called "Waterboy," the USAF ground-based radar controller, to get the weather at Da Nang before I made a penetration. Once I did that, I could not make Udorn in Thailand, which was our divert base. They told me the weather was 500 and a half. I went down and made a GCA [ground controlled approach] to 200 feet, but never saw anything.

I couldn't get to Udorn so I asked about Chu Lai but Chu Lai was under attack. I made five GCAs to Da Nang and still saw nothing. I told my ECMO [electronic countermeasures officer], Maj. Ed Perron, that I would land on the next approach. I told him he could bail out but I was going in. He stayed with me. We landed, but didn't know for sure until we started rolling! The CO was really pleased because we didn't lose an airplane. As a reward, he put me in RF-4s the next day.

When everyone rotated out, I was kind of the senior guy in the squadron. Everyone else was coming over as an individual replacement. I accumulated 300 missions in the EF-10 and RF-4 in one year. I usually flew two RF-4 hops during the day and one EF-10 hop at night.[3]

By 1969, just before its retirement, the EF-10B found itself supporting limited air strikes while orbiting off the coast safely out of reach of most of the North Vietnamese defenses. Before that, in its heyday, from 1966 to 1968, the DRUT usually was flown right into the defense envelope—where the SAMs were thickest—to protect Navy and Air Force strikes. The crewmember tasked with actually running the mission was the ECMO. These individuals, usually former enlisted technicians, spent most of the long flights looking into a scope, watching for emission indications from enemy radars. Jamming signals would then be used to confuse the North Vietnamese defenses and hopefully protect the strike aircraft entering and exiting the target area.

On March 18, 1966, the squadron lost an EF-10B (BuNo 127041) over North Vietnam, probably one of only two combat losses of the Skyknight in two wars. (A VMF(AW)-513 F3D was lost over Korea with its Navy crew, probably to MiGs on July 2, 1953.) Two EF-10s launched to support an Air Force F-105 strike near Thanh Hoa. There were plenty of SAMs nearby. Escorted by F-4s from VMFA-314, the four VMCJ crewmen headed out toward their target area.

The intel briefing had noted no active SAM sites along the route, and the Marine crews decided to split their efforts, with each aircraft taking up an orbit along the Air Force strikers' planned ingress-egress route. They would try to remain outside the fifteen-nm kill envelope of the SA-2, the main threat. It would be difficult, because not knowing the exact location of the SAM sites, as well as the EF-10's lack of an inertial navigation system, made pin-pointing the sites next to impossible.

The Druts picked up the Phantom escort over Laos and then headed north to their orbit area, about 125 miles away. As they approached, 1st Lt. Flash Whitten detected the Fansong tracking radar of a SAM off the nose. Lieutenant Whitten monitored the threat as the North Vietnamese network came alive, probing for the oncoming F-105s. Flak fire-control signals now appeared, along with the SAM signals. The EF-10 crews could only jam one or the other, not both simultaneously, a major handicap.

As the Marine ECM flight turned in the pattern, Whitten's wingman was struck by a SAM. A second missile blew up near one of the F-4s, shaking it up a bit before the pilot regained control. Flak now filled the sky, and Whitten jammed the fire-control radar, breaking the lock the flak radar had on his plane.

Thoughts now turned to coordinating a SAR—search and rescue— effort for the downed EF-10 crew, but to no avail. Without ejections seats, the Skyknight was equipped with a evacuation chute on its cockpit deck. The crew slid down the ramp to exit the aircraft, not the easiest way in an extremis situation. Unfortunately, no sign of the two men was ever seen until the ECMO's remains were returned by the North Vietnamese in 1997. Nothing of the pilot was ever found.[4]

By mid-1965, the 1st MAW would include four MAGs, with Maj. Gen. Paul Fontana, then Brig. Gen. Keith B. McCutcheon, as the commanding general. MAG-11 was the fixed-wing fighter/attack group, with VMCJ-1, VMFA-531, later VMFA-513, and VMFA-542, with later arrivals by VMFA-115 and VMFA-323. MAG-12 was the attack group, with A-4-equipped VMAs -225, -311, -214, and -211, later supplemented by VMA-223 and VMA-224. There were two helicopter groups. MAG-16, based at the Marble Mountain Air Facility, east of Da Nang, with HMM-261 and HMM-361, and HMM-161, VMO-2 with observation Hueys, and the headquarters squadron, H&MS-16 at Phu Bai. An addition in September was HMH-462, a heavy helicopter transport unit that brought six CH-37Cs to be assigned to H&MS-16. MAG-36, based across from MAG-16 at Ky Ha, south of Da Nang, included HMM-362 and HMM-364, with VMO-6 and H&MS-36. Except for the CH-37 detachment and the Hueys of the VMOs, the helicopters used by the majority of the Marine squadrons were UH-34Ds.

Additional squadrons had arrived to fill out the wing by the end of the year. MAG-11, led by Col. Robert Conley, who had gained a MiG kill in Korea flying F3Ds, brought VMF(AW)-312 and its F-8Es on December 19, the first of three Crusader-equipped Marine squadrons to fly from Da Nang. A fourth Marine F-8 squadron, VMF(AW)-212, had arrived aboard the USS *Oriskany* (CVA-34) off Vietnam on May 8. It had flown its first combat missions of the war the same day as part of Navy Carrier Attack Wing (CVW) 16. (The unit had converted from A-4s in 1963, and changed its

VMA designation to VMF.) Led by Lt. Col. Charles H. Ludden, the Lancers brought twelve F-8Es to the combat zone, flying in support of Marine and South Vietnamese ground operations. The Echos carried five-inch Zuni rockets mounted on cheek racks behind the cockpit, but no underwing ordnance. That capability would come in June, when the Crusaders were modified to carry Mark 82, 83, and 84 iron bombs on wing hard points.

From May to November, when the *Oriskany* sailed for home, the Marine aviators of VMF(AW)-212 flew 1,588 sorties in strikes ranging up and down the entire length of Vietnam, north and south. Many missions consisted of escorting A-4s in strikes near Hanoi, the North Vietnamese capital; others were solo bombing missions. Crusaders of VMF(AW)-212 were hit on twenty-six occasions, with one aircraft lost on November 5 on a raid near Hanoi. The pilot, Capt. Harlan P. Chapman, ejected safely. He was captured, however, and spent seven years as a prisoner of war.

An interesting turn of events occurred in September when the Navy wing commander, Cdr. James B. Stockdale, was shot down and imprisoned. As the senior squadron commander, it fell to Lieutenant Colonel Ludden to lead CVW-16, making him one of the few Marines to command a carrier air wing. (Of course, during World War II, the all-Marine groups [MCVGs] aboard the CVEs were led by Marine aviators.) This was the last time that a Marine squadron flew from an attack carrier for the next seven years. (Several Marine A-4 detachments, or dets, were, at this time, also deployed to the South China Sea in carriers, functioning as the ships' aerial defense. The A-4s carried two AIM-9B Sidewinder missiles when flying CAP. When not involved in these duties, the Skyhawks flew ground support missions into South Vietnam.)

Chu Lai

Outside of the actual dedication of Marine aviation assets and the subsequent buildup throughout 1965, perhaps the most important event during the year was the construction and opening of the airfield at Chu Lai, fifty-five miles south of Da Nang. The need for a second tactical jet base was readily apparent. Da Nang could not handle all the traffic pouring into South Vietnam, fixed-wing and helicopter. With the activation of Ky Ha and Marble Mountain, the helicopters had their own fields. Da Nang could host the Phantoms and also serve as a central point, but another field was needed to support the action areas in I Corps. With the planned installation of Short Airfield for Tactical Support (SATS) equipment, Chu Lai looked a likely area for development. SATS involved an aluminum plank runway, taxiways, and parking ramp as well as use of catapult and arresting gear, similar to that on a carrier, for heavily loaded jets.

Marines of the brigade hit the beach at Chu Lai on May 7, 1965, led by now–Brig. Gen. Marion Carl, one of the Corps' most celebrated World War II aces. Although it was a full-fledged amphibious landing, the Marines met only lovely Vietnamese girls offering flowers to them as they clambered ashore from their landing craft. General Carl wryly noted, "If there had been an opposed landing, the Viet Cong could have swept us off the beach with a broom."

Never one to simply sit while others were flying combat, Marion Carl flew some forty missions in Vietnam in a variety of aircraft, including Hueys, F-4s, A-4s, and F-8s. Flying with VMF(AW)-235 in early 1966, Carl went on a four-plane mission to Laos. He flew wing on the squadron's CO, Lt. Col. George Gibson. After launching from Chu Lai, the flight formed up at 20,000 feet to fly the 100 miles to the target. Dropping down to treetop level, each Crusader pilot made his run at about 200 feet and 400 knots. Using their bombs and rockets, the Marine aviators destroyed their target, which was a heavily defended staging area.

By May 31, Navy Seabees had constructed 4,000 feet of runway and installed the arresting-gear portion of the SATS apparatus. On June 1, Col. John D. Noble, commanding MAG-12, brought A-4s from VMA-225 in to a landing at the new base. That same day, four Skyhawks from VMA-311 arrived. Also on the 1st, aircraft from VMA-225 flew the first combat missions from Chu Lai. There was still a lot to be done, and Chu Lai was not declared officially complete and ready for business until July.

Rain turned the unfinished field into a sea of mud, and the A-4s had to take off with JATO (jet-assisted takeoff) and refuel in the air from orbiting KC-130s of Aerial Refueler Transport Squadron (VMGR-152) which maintained a four-plane detachment at Da Nang.

The intensity and amount of the buildup had apparently taken the VC by surprise, and they took no major action. But by July the enemy had recovered from any timidity and launched attacks against Da Nang on the 1st. Several Air Force and Marine aircraft were damaged or destroyed. August saw a tremendous effort to oust the Marines from Chu Lai. In Operation Starlite, the Americans fought an intense battle with Communist forces from August 18 to 24. Battle citations and medals were won aplenty

[Opposite] An A-4E of VMA-223 launches for a mission, using JATO in September 1966. Skyhawks flew a phenomenal number of support missions, especially at this time of the war.

[Right] The members of VMA-225 cluster around their CO in June 1965 after their arrival at the still-unfinished base at Chu Lai. They were the first of a continuing presence of Marine A-4 squadrons in Southeast Asia. (Dan Yates)

as the Marines repelled the determined attacks. Skyhawks and Phantoms from MAG-11 and MAG-12 flew day and night in support of the Marines on the ground. The helicopters of MAG-16 and MAG-36 were kept busy shuttling men and supplies in and out of battle. The fighting was the most vicious to date, but the Marines fended off the enemy attempt to retake the air base. Chu Lai remained in Marine hands and became a major part of the war effort in years to come.

Who Controls Marine Air?

As in every military action involving Marine aircraft, the subject of who controlled them in Vietnam came up early. And, as usually occurred, the Air Force laid claim to that responsibility. The Marines were understandably leery of letting their aircraft come under the junior service's control once again, as had happened in Korea. Marine air for Marines, first! Unfortunately, it was not to be, and the Air Force's Maj. Gen. J. H. Moore was designated as the coordinating authority for all aircraft, including those of the Marines.

After some political haggling by Brigadier General McCutcheon, it was decided that although overall command rested with General Moore, McCutcheon would decide which Marine units would actually be dedicated for Air Force use. This arrangement would leave specific assets readily available for Marine commanders in the field. Operational control of Marine aircraft came through the Tactical Air Direction Center (TADC), located at Da Nang. Subordinate organizations were the Tactical Air Operations Center (TAOC) and Direct Air Support Center (DASC). TAOCs provided for air surveillance and air defense coordination and, during the initial stages

[Opposite] Map 6. Vietnam

of Vietnam, relied on various radar information being plotted by hand on display boards. It would be two years before a major step could be taken with the arrival of computer-oriented, semi-automatic TAOCs.

The new Marine Tactical Data System (MTDS) was compatible with Navy systems and was set up at the Monkey Mountain complex near Da Nang. The MTDS represented a quantum leap in handling capability for the Marine controllers. Up to 250 aircraft tracks could be addressed at any one time. Eventually, information from the Air Force systems was also absorbed, making the Marine TDCC at Monkey Mountain the hub of information management in Vietnam in 1969. Of course, the growth of air control and management took time, and in 1965 the system was still very much in its infancy.

One capability that was available at this time, however, was the TPQ-10 radar, which involved ground-based radar and computers guiding receiver-equipped Phantoms, Skyhawks, and, later, Crusaders to specific areas and telling the pilots when to release the bombs. In the rain and low clouds that constantly made such missions difficult, the TPQ-10 setup proved its worth as operations began to accelerate once Chu Lai was fully operational.

As 1965 progressed, Marine aviation assets were used heavily, not only in support of ground troops but also in conjunction with other services. On May 6, the Air Force requested assistance with a rescue attempt in North Vietnam. Four Phantoms of VMFA-531 flew anti-aircraft suppression runs with Air Force planes while an Air Force helicopter recovered the downed pilot. By the end of the year, Marine F-4s had flown eighty-seven missions over the North.

In December aircraft from MAG-11 and MAG-12 struck Communist supply routes in Laos in coordination with Navy and Air Force missions. Nearly 300 sorties were flown between December 6 and December 31 in this interdictive effort. The strikes were not without losses. On December 29, 1st Lt. Thomas F. Eldridge of VMA-211 was lost while on a mission escorting helicopters. Even though his aircraft was hit and he was wounded, Eldridge dropped his ordnance through clouds and poor light and tried to get back to Chu Lai. But his A-4 crashed short of the field and he was killed.

MAG-16 and MAG-36 supplied helicopter support for resupply and troop-movement efforts in the face of heavy enemy opposition. On September 19, all seven UH-34Ds of an HMM-161 flight were hit during a helilift; one aircraft went down. Capt. Manuel O. Martinez, pilot of another helo, immediately landed beside the downed UH-34 in the midst of strong enemy fire and waited until the downed crew had scrambled aboard. Martinez received the Silver Star.

With the development of the ubiquitous UH-34 and the projected introduction of the Sikorsky CH-53, the CH-37, nicknamed the "Deuce," had not found a decent mission for itself. It was too big and temperamental to conduct vertical assaults, but Vietnam gave it a brief moment of glory and usefulness. In early September 1965, six CH-37s of HMH-461 deployed to Da Nang, where they provided heavy-lift capability for MAG-16. They airlifted damaged helicopters from battle areas, thus saving them for possible repair or at least the salvage of valuable parts. They flew the first such mission on September 12.

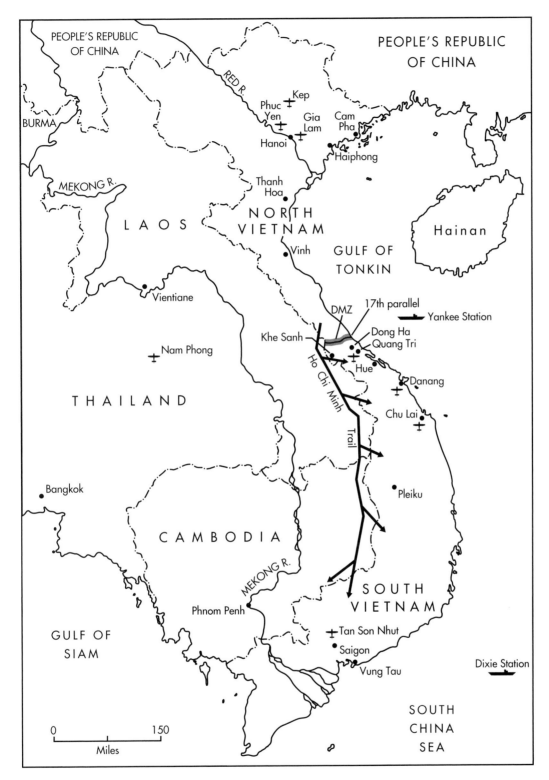

In one case, two Deuces were dispatched to lift the stripped fuselage, transmission, and rotor blades of a downed UH-34. The first CH-37 returned safely, but the second, while lifting the fuselage, was struck by enemy ground fire, which punctured the fuel lines to the port engine. The helicopter was forced to land, and another CH-37 was sent from Marble Mountain. The damaged Deuce was repaired and struggled back to its base.

By mid-1966, the end of the road was in sight for the CH-37, although the type was to soldier on until May 1967. By that time, the aircraft had flown more than 5,300 hours in Vietnam and transported 12.5 million pounds of cargo.

By the end of 1965, Marine aviation was largely in place in Vietnam. Major air facilities had been established at Da Nang and Chu Lai, and thousands of sorties had been flown in support of ground action. The VC had periodically attempted to disrupt operations. On October 27, coordinated sapper attacks had decimated the Marble Mountain Air Facility. MAG-16 flew in from Phu Bai, and MAG-36 arrived from Ky Ha, three miles north of Chu Lai, to bolster the Marble Mountain Marines. UH-1Es at Chu Lai had also been attacked, although damage was nowhere as severe as at Da Nang. The enemy penetrated nearly every security arrangement provided; it was a basic fact of life in Vietnam. But the Marine airplanes were there for the duration.

Caribbean Interlude

While events in Southeast Asia promised increased combat to come, Marine helicopter forces halfway round the world were put to combat test in April 1965. An attempted coup by army rebels in the Dominican Republic had plunged that country into civil war. Americans had to be evacuated. HMM-264 aboard the *Boxer*, now LPH-4, arrived off the coast on April 26 and the next day began evacuating civilians by airlift.

On the 28th, Marines were landed to cover the airlift, while UH-34s of HMM-264 flew shuttles between ships and Ciudad Trujillo, the capital

[Opposite] In October 1965, the only aircraft capable of retrieving downed or disabled aircraft was the elderly CH-37 Mojave. Here, a MAG-16 "Deuce" hauls the fuselage of a UH-34D hit by ground fire and forced to land.

[Right] In April 1965, Marine helicopter squadrons were sent to the Dominican Republic to evacuate American citizens during an army coup. Here, while Marines man machine guns to protect the landing field, UH-34s bring in equipment to support the evacuation.

city, using a polo field as a landing zone. An additional 684 refugees had been evacuated by midnight. Operations continued through the next day. On May 5, HMM-263 arrived aboard the USS *Okinawa* (LPH-3) to relieve HMM-362, as the flights continued, sometimes under rebel ground fire.

Fortunately, only one UH-34 was hit. Its pilot, Capt. T. P. McBrien, was seriously wounded but was able to land his damaged aircraft back on the polo field before being evacuated himself. McBrien thus became one of the few Marine aviators to be wounded in combat in the Western Hemisphere. By May 26, HMM-263 was headed home aboard the *Okinawa*. HMM-264 left two weeks later in the *Boxer*. The Marines had had a brief taste of combat in an unexpected theater before being committed to a much larger war thousands of miles away.

The Skyhawks

In January 1966, the 1st Marine Aircraft Wing was spread out all over South Vietnam. Indeed, its aircraft ranged up and down the Indochina Peninsula, participating in every capacity from close air support to cargo hauling to strategic strikes. But, of course, Marine air's main mission was close air support. Writing in the August 1967 issue of the *Marine Corps Gazette*, Major General McCutcheon, commanding the 1st MAW, said, "Marine aviation is a tactical air arm. Its sole mission is to provide support to the ground forces. It is organized, trained, and equipped to perform a spectrum of functions to accomplish this mission. . . . The 1st MAW is doing all of these today in Vietnam."

The wing was very active indeed. Perhaps the most active fixed-wing Marine aircraft were the little A-4s of MAG-12, out of Chu Lai. It is difficult to describe their role and the incredible impact they had in a few short paragraphs. When the SATS complex became fully operational, the Skyhawks of the seven squadrons that rotated in and out of South Vietnam were kept constantly on alert, if not in the air. VMAs -121, -211, -214, -223, -224, -225, and -311 all flew long and repeated tours of hard combat through early 1970.

As one writer put it, "It is difficult to single out for comment any individual sortie or mission flown by Marine A-4s, because all such missions were strictly routine close air support operations . . . Marine A-4s did perform workhorse close support missions, busting tanks with rockets or hitting enemy personnel concentrations and weapons sites with combinations of bombs, napalm and 20-mm cannon fire."[5] So important were the Skyhawk VMAs that it was finally decided to keep the squadrons continuously at Chu Lai and rotate personnel and aircraft on an individual basis. This allowed a continuity in operation, without the unavoidable disruption caused by the replacement of whole squadrons. While all VMA squadrons did their share of the work, VMA-311, with more than 50,000 combat sorties flown by the war's end in 1973, was, perhaps, the most active of the A-4 units. The Tomcats had arrived with the opening of Chu Lai in May 1965 and, in company with other MAG-12 and MAG-11 squadrons, flew the length of Vietnam.

VMA-311 had been active during Starlite, when the VC attempted to overrun Chu Lai in August 1965. Tomcat pilots flew in support of Marines on the ground in March 1966 during the vicious fighting in the A Shau Valley. It was here that the first VMA-311 pilot was lost in combat, when 1st Lt. A. M. Xavier, maneuvering in the steep mountains in predawn darkness, never pulled out of a strafing run against North Vietnamese Army (NVA) positions.

VMA-311 supported Operation Hastings, the biggest and most profitable Corps operation to date in July 1966. August saw the 7,000th combat mission and the 10,000th combat flight hour achieved. Squadron pilots were flying a combined average of 600–700 combat hours a month. It was, quite naturally, dangerous work. A-4s were hit time and again, but the simple, sturdy construction of Ed Heinemann's little "Scooter" allowed heavily damaged aircraft to reach home more often than not.

During the bloody fighting at Khe Sanh in 1968, VMA-311 A-4s supported the embattled 26th Marines. In January, the second A-4 of the squadron was shot down in as many days, its pilot, Maj. William E. Loftus, ejecting right over the besieged Marine base. Loftus landed just outside the perimeter, but a group of Marines gallantly ran to rescue the major, who had become entangled in his parachute's shroud lines, and brought him to the relative safety of the camp, where he was helicoptered back to Chu Lai.

The model Skyhawk most used by VMA-311, as well as by other Marine squadrons in Vietnam, was the A-4E, originally the A4D-5, which included a more powerful engine, increased avionics, and two additional underwing stations for greater weapons load. Five hundred Echos were produced for the Navy and Marines. However, the "Charlie" model did see service with the Marines at Chu Lai, notably with VMA-223, which apparently operated a mix of Charlies and Echos from time to time. (The squadron operated the A-4E from 1964 until 1970.)

VMA-223 had arrived in Vietnam in December 1965, operating as part of MAG-12. During the period of intense operations, the Bulldogs set a record for a day's sorties on February 3, 1966, with fifty-nine combat sorties. Milestone flight hours were rapidly achieved and surpassed. On June 16, 1966, two Bulldog Skyhawks were over a contested area where NVA activity had pinned down a Marine patrol. Capt. Lynn A. Hale, the flight leader, took his section down through the mountainous area in early morning light, and in the face of heavy enemy fire, made repeated runs with ordnance and 20-mm cannon. Having expended their weapons, the two A-4s returned to Chu Lai, were refueled and rearmed, and scrambled a second time back to the same area. Captain Hale received the Distinguished Flying Cross for his determined support of the Marines on the ground.

In 1966 operations for VMA-223 continued to be intense right through the beginning of the monsoon season in October and November. In December the squadron returned to Japan to rest and regroup. VMA-223 continued to operate in Vietnam until January 1970, when, in company with other Marine units, it left Southeast Asia as part of the planned withdrawal of U.S. forces. By that time, VMA-223 had flown more than 32,000 sorties and expended over 34,200 tons of ordnance during its six years at Chu Lai.

One other model of the A-4 was used during Marine operations, the TA-4F, a two-seater originally ordered as a trainer to replace the Navy's Grumman TF-9J Cougar, then in use as advanced trainers in the Navy's Training Command. The faithful Grummans had served long and well in several capacities and had the unique distinction of being used in combat in Vietnam at the same time they were operating in a training role. The story deserves special mention, as it is not widely known.

As the pace of U.S. participation began to intensify, it became necessary to employ aircraft in a forward air control (FAC) role. Also, helicopters were in need of a capable escort, although armed UH-1Ds served well in that capacity. Fixed-wing aircraft had the speed, range, and load-toting capability to fill the escort role more efficiently, however. With all these factors in mind, the Marines decided to try some surplus TF-9Js. Being a two-seater, the Cougar could carry two pilots, which could be an advantage in a low-level, high-speed flight in a "hot" area.

Four or five Cougars arrived at Da Nang with H&MS-13 in 1966 and operated with MAG-11 and MAG-12 for about a year, alternating between Da Nang and Chu Lai. Carrying rocket pods under the wings, as well as nose-mounted 20-mm cannon, the old jets served well, roving ahead of

[Opposite] Crewmen position a VMA-311 A-4E on the SATS catapult at Chu Lai in June 1968.

[Left] A TA-4F taxis past other aircraft at Da Nang, including an A-4 of VMA-311, an F-8E of VMF(AW)-235, and an F-4B.

[Opposite] A TF-9J takes off from Da Nang. The plane carries rocket canisters and a tiger shark nose marking. Cougars served for approximately one year as roving FACs and reconnaissance aircraft before being replaced by the OV-10 and TA-4F.

troops on the ground or beyond helicopters approaching their landing zones, to scout and sanitize the forward areas. By 1967, however, the new TA-4Fs were ready, and they began to replace the aging Cougars in Vietnam, beginning in August with H&MS-11 at Da Nang, although the Skyhawks were not integrated into the training command back in the United States until 1969.

TA-4Fs performed valuable service as escorts and as airborne tactical air coordinators (TACs) above the helicopters and accompanying escort A-4s and F-4s. Two-seater Skyhawks were also used as gunfire spotters for Navy ships, particularly the refurbished battleship USS *New Jersey* (BB-62), which arrived off Vietnam in October 1968 and which served only six months before being retired. During the big ship's tours, her giant guns pounded North Vietnamese positions to the delight and gratitude of the men on the ground. And above the *New Jersey* Marine TA-4s usually coordinated and advised the ship's gunners.

The composite squadron, VMCJ-1, based at Da Nang, received two new types during 1966. Both were highly specialized derivatives of airplanes already in fleet service. The first McDonnell RF-4B Phantoms arrived in October to replace the squadron's RF-8A Crusaders, which had been flying not only from Da Nang but also with carriers of the Seventh Fleet's Task Force 77 offshore, some since before the Gulf of Tonkin incident in August 1964. The RF-4B was born in 1961, when the Air Force put forth a proposal for a reconnaissance version of the F-4, then just entering widespread service. Actually, the RF-4B was preceded by the Air Force's RF-4C prototype. The Navy lost interest in acquiring RF-4Bs and allocated them instead to the Marines, who were only too glad to accept the long-nosed Phantoms. Forty-six RF-4Bs were turned over to VMCJ-2 and VMCJ-3 in 1965, but it was VMCJ-1 that took the aircraft into combat a year later.

The big RF-4B provided greater power, twin-engine safety, two crewmen, and a variety of imagery sensors never before available to the Marines. Additionally, the reconnaissance Phantom was capable of acquiring imagery at night, an improvement over the RF-8, whose after-dark capabilities were severely limited and seldom used.

In an example of interservice rivalry, the squadron tactical sign was changed from "Cottonpicker" to "Pigment," because the Air Force, which assigned these combat radio nicknames, apparently recalled Cottonpicker to give to one of their squadrons, which had used it as part of the squadron nickname since WWI.

Gen. John Dailey remembers:

One really good thing that the RF-4 had was true ground-track mode. There's zero (magnetic) variation in Vietnam, which helped. There was no difference between magnetic and true courses. We had a target a long way from the coast, but the only way we got there was coasting in using true ground track. There were no land marks, and the maps were so bad that you couldn't figure out even where the river bends were. Most of the charts were 1:50,000, and we would carry a whole armload of maps.

The way they'd frag you was they'd give you a bunch of missions—could be a single target or a strip—and you had to find out what the weather was and see which ones you could get in. If we didn't run out of film, we'd just keep going—we could refuel in flight, there'd always be a tanker waiting. It wasn't unusual to complete 25 or 30 missions on one flight. A mission could be just one target; each requirement had a mission number. Part of the deal was that the Seventh Air Force was fragging us, and our film had to go to them.

The A-6s were going out at night and we were flying cover for them with EF-10s. We'd go to their briefing and you'd see the imagery was three weeks old and we had just shot new stuff that morning! We started giving copies to MAG-11.

When the A-6A first arrived, we wanted to see if they were hitting their targets. They planned to have an RF-4 fly wing on an A-6 during its bomb run. We had a pilot, Maj. Jim Pierce, who was highly qualified. He had only flown photo his entire career. But he had hurt himself before this mission, so I had to fly it. We got the pictures and we could see the Intruders were *not* hitting the target. Everyone was naturally upset. They wanted to keep doing it. They'd drop bombs and break off, leaving us in the RF-4s to follow, and we were getting shot up pretty badly. But they wanted a picture of an A-6 hitting its target.

On the third try, I got really blasted over Vinh. They were bombing the bridge there. During the brief, I asked the A-6 crew, "What's your climbout speed?"

"Ahh-h, about 300," they replied.

I had three tanks on the RF-4, and was attempting a night rendezvous with dissimilar aircraft. He was doing about 250. We could fly 550 knots with the three tanks, and often flew more than 600. Those big Segreant Fletcher tanks carried 375 gallons in the wing tanks and 600 on the centerline. They were very expensive and we always brought them back instead of dropping them.

The night work was probably the most valuable stuff we did in terms of finding the enemy. They were all moving at night. You couldn't bring the night photo cartridges back because they were pyrotechnic. If you didn't use them, you went over the water and popped them all. Of course, the Navy ships off shore would think they were under attack! The IR was the primary sensor at night.[6]

[Opposite] A VMCJ-1 RF-4B in a reinforced concrete revetment at Da Nang in January 1970. Attached to MAG-11, the long-nosed Bravos were flown only by Marines. (Sgt. A. J. May)

[Right] Ordnancemen load 500-pound Mk. 82 bombs on an A-6A Intruder of VMA(AW)-533 in August 1967 (Cpl. Cowen)

Four RF-4Bs were lost in Vietnam from September 1967 to October 1968. One was a landing mishap, one crew flew into the ground, and two were hit by enemy fire.

The A-6A Intruders of VMA(AW)-242 arrived on December 1, 1966, and brought another tremendous jump in combat capability to Marine forces in Vietnam. The big, ugly Grumman two-seater, originally designated the A2F, carried a highly advanced bombing computer, as well as several more thousands of pounds of bombs than the gallant little A-4. During their first month of operations, the Bat squadron A-6s flew from Da Nang in the worsening weather of the monsoon cycle that often grounded other types. They delivered 38 percent of the total III MAF (Marine Amphibious Force) tonnage for the period.

Along with the attack version of the Intruder came the EA-6As for VMCJ-1. Identified by a big blister atop its vertical tail and the large electronic jamming pods usually carried under its wings, the EA-6A was the successor to the venerable EF-10B. The EA-6A was especially valuable against the network of SAMs, which had been growing at an alarming rate and were already responsible for a number of losses from all U.S. air services. With the arrival of the EA-6A, the strike forces had an airplane that could accompany them right into the target areas, into the deepest thickets of SAM activity, maneuver with the bombers, and bring them through the enemy defenses. EA-6s were also used in conjunction with Air Force B-52 strikes that were becoming somewhat routine.

One of the greatest threats of the Vietnam War was the growth and efficiency of the North Vietnamese radar network, especially around the major cities and industrial complexes of Hanoi and Haiphong. As American strike aircraft passed over the DMZ into the North or launched from their carriers, it was a sure bet they were being tracked and eventually locked up by enemy radar, which fed the information to the greatest array of computer-directed guns and missiles ever assembled in the history of aerial warfare. An

[Top Left] Assigned to VMCJ-1, this EA-6A takes off from Da Nang in 1970 for an ECM mission. The aircraft carries extra fuel tanks and jamming pods under the wings

[Bottom Left] As the deck crewman signals a successful trap, this F-8E of VMF(AW)-212 returns from a combat mission during the 1965 cruise of the USS *Oriskany* (CVA-34). This would be the last time a Marine squadron sailed in a Navy carrier in combat until 1971.

[Top Right] Two F-8Es of VMF(AW)-232 prepare for a mission in April 1967. The Red Devils replaced VMF(AW)-235 in November 1966 and took the departing squadron's Crusaders. The aircraft in the foreground, side number 11, carries a full load of bombs, while aircraft 5 appears to tote only a single bomb beneath each wing.

[Bottom Right] The pilot of an F-8E of VMF(AW)-235 goes through a systems check with his uniquely coiffed plane captain in May 1967. The Crusader is armed with two 2,000-pound bombs and Zuni rockets. (GySgt. Evans)

ECM platform of equal capability was desperately needed, and the EA-6A certainly went a long way to filling the requirement.

Rounding out the fixed-wing jet lineup were the F-8Es of VMF(AW)s -312, -235, and -232. This was the only use of fighter -8s made by the Marines in combat, in addition to VMF(AW)-212 aboard the *Oriskany* as already related. (The RF-8 recce bird continued to serve until completely replaced by the RF-4B, and, of course, the type formed integral parts of Navy carrier wings, in both fighter and reconnaissance versions, until the early 1970s.) The Marines had made good use of the F-8 series, but its stay in Southeast Asia was relatively brief—barely two years.

Under Lt. Col. Richard B. Newport, VMF(AW)-312 arrived at Da Nang on December 19, 1965, and by the end of June 1966, its aircraft had

flown 718 combat missions. However, that was the extent of VMF(AW)-312's operations in Vietnam. Actually, VMF(AW)-312 was scheduled to rotate back to the States just as the massive influx of Marine air squadrons gathered steam. Much to their chagrin, the pilots, officers, and men of the Crusader squadron watched as their F-4-equipped brethren of VMFA-513 and VMFA-542 prepared to go into combat. It would not do for VMF(AW)-312 to be denied a chance to fight. The squadron raised such a fuss that it was decided to extend VMF(AW)-312's tour to include two months' duty in South Vietnam, but no more, which accounts for its unusually short combat tour. The unit turned over its Crusaders to incoming VMF(AW)-235 and returned home to be redesignated VMFA-312 and be equipped with Phantoms. It never returned to Vietnam. Thus, the bulk of F-8 operations was to fall to two squadrons.

VMF(AW)-235 arrived on February 1, 1966, under Lt. Col. George A. Gibson, and was replaced by VMF(AW)-232 on November 15. Led by Lt. Col. N. M. Trapnell Jr., the Red Devils were assigned to MAG-11 in keeping with most of the fighter squadrons' duties and were equipped with TPQ-10 bombing radar receivers. The F-8Es of VMF(AW)-232 began combat in December, flying 571 sorties by month's end. The squadron's aircraft were hit by ground fire on a number of occasions. (As the only Marine aircraft capable of carrying a 2,000-pound bomb, the Crusaders were heavily involved in close air support until the arrival of the A-6s.)

On May 4, 1967, the first loss was registered, although the pilot, Maj. Edward F. Townley, was rescued. But two weeks later, on the 19th, the first Red Devil to be killed in Vietnam combat was lost when Capt. Harold J. Hellbach radioed that he was being hit over his target. The Crusader exploded before the pilot was able to eject. When VMF(AW)-232 rotated home on July 30, 1967, the squadron's record stood at 5,785 sorties. The Red Devils would return to Southeast Asia as VMFA-232 with F-4Js in 1969.

New Helicopters

While new fixed-wing jets arrived in 1966, the helicopter community also received its first examples of the CH-46 Sea Knight. The CH-46, or HRB-1 as it was called before 1962, was a Boeing Vertol design featuring twin engines with equal-size rotor blades mounted in tandem, fore and aft. After some delays, the aircraft flew for the first time on October 16, 1962, and the first production machines were delivered to HMM-265 at New River in June 1964.

The CH-46 was intended as the follow-on replacement for the faithful old UH-34, which was being used to its limit in Vietnam. The first CH-46s of HMM-164 arrived in Vietnam on March 8, 1966, when twenty-seven aircraft landed at Marble Mountain after flying off the *Valley Forge*. The Marines already at Marble Mountain welcomed the new arrivals with great expectations, and the CH-46s immediately began flying combat operations. HMM-265 arrived with twenty-four aircraft in June.

Problems with the new helicopters, capable as they were, began to arise. Two were major considerations. The gritty, dusty South Vietnamese soil infiltrated the engines with alarming alacrity, causing all sorts of maintenance

Sea Knights on their way to Khe Sanh in March 1968 at the height of the siege. Carrying a 3,000-pound load of ammunition on a cargo hook, these aircraft are from HMM-364 based at Phu Bai.

nightmares. Screens and filters were placed over the engine intakes to reduce the problem, with some success.

The CH-46 was also armed. The Shufly experiences, as well as subsequent combat, had decisively shown the need for self-protection. Therefore, Vertol-designed kits were incorporated into the Sea Knights. The kit included a .50-caliber machine gun, or the regular 7.62-mm M-60, roughly equivalent to a .30-caliber weapon. Two machine guns were placed in each aircraft, one on each side. The first kits were actually installed by the Navy, the Marines not wishing to pay the nearly $3 million total demanded by Vertol. Naturally, the extra armament and accompanying armor reduced the CH-46's performance. The troop-carrying capability was reduced from twenty-five to fifteen. The 1,000 pounds of armor also reduced the amount of fuel that could be carried, thereby decreasing the aircraft's operating endurance. It was recommended that the lighter M-60s be carried as the standard machine gun and the amount of armor be considerably reduced.

An improved model of the CH-46 was being developed that incorporated changes and modifications, many of which were the result of experience in Vietnam. The CH-46D featured more powerful engines, new transmissions, and rotor-drive components. HMM-161 took the first Deltas to Vietnam in December 1966.

Another new helicopter that arrived late in December was the long-awaited replacement for the elderly CH-37. Also a Sikorsky design, the CH-53A Sea Stallion was the largest operational helicopter in the free world. The Marines had been in desperate need of a helicopter for years, but the CH-53 did not fly until October 1964, after much political and

[Opposite] Maj. Gen. Keith B. McCutcheon, right, receives the Distinguished Service Medal from Marine Corps Commandant Gen. Wallace M. Greene Jr. on October 6, 1966. McCutcheon, then serving as Deputy Chief of Staff (Air) at Headquarters Marine Corps, was a strong force behind Marine aviation developments right up to his death from cancer in 1971. He was the first Marine Corps aviator to attain four-star rank while on active duty.

developmental haggling between Sikorsky and the Defense Department. Even after its first flight, the aircraft was hamstrung by continuous hassling. Finally, the first helos were officially accepted by the Marines in September 1966, when Maj. W. R. Beeler, commanding officer of HMH-463, took delivery of four CH-53As.

As the Sea Stallion crawled its way to operational status, plans were already being made to introduce the new type quickly to Southeast Asia combat as heavy retrievers. Accordingly, newly promoted Lieutenant Colonel Beeler took the four new aircraft to South Vietnam, arriving at Marble Mountain on December 31, 1966. Two weeks later, on January 13, 1967, the first cargo missions were flown, and four days later the first battle damage was sustained, two aircraft being hit, but not seriously damaged, by VC ground fire. From January to May, CH-53s also retrieved more than 100 downed helicopters, 72 UH-34s, 13 CH-46s, and 16 Hueys. It was a clear demonstration of the CH-53's value, and the rest of HMH-463 was hurried along in its predeployment training.

In 1966 the war continued to expand, demanding more supplies and personnel, and the combat action was both heavy and costly. Added to this was general dissatisfaction and rebellion among the Vietnamese. Anti-government demonstrations, led by Buddhist monks and nuns (some with violent, macabre displays such as self-immolation), cropped up continuously throughout the spring with resulting injuries and disorder. All U.S. military services did their best to remain clear of the civil strife but were not always able to do so.

Hampered by the lack of results of the strategic bombing campaign against the North, growing antiwar sentiment at home, and the general inability of the Vietnamese government to control its own populace, the Johnson administration began to enlarge and escalate the war on the ground in hopes of gaining at least a clear-cut military victory, if not a popular one. Therefore, 1966 became a year of constant operations, sweeps, and strikes against the invisible VC and their North Vietnamese army compatriots. Harvest Moon, Country Fair, Double Eagle, Hastings, and more operations continued to carry the war to the enemy, searching out and destroying the Communist forces wherever and whenever possible.

Naturally, Marine aviation resources were used constantly. March was a particularly active month. Several aircraft—fixed-wing and helicopter—were lost to enemy action. On March 10, word came that an Air Force A-1E had gone down in the A Shau Valley, scene of especially vicious combat, and a rescue attempt was being mounted. Another A-1E landed beside the first aircraft, and Maj. Bernie Fisher waited as Maj. D. W. Myers raced through a hail of bullets to the waiting Skyraider. Myers scrambled aboard and Fisher thrust his plane down the pockmarked strip. Fisher received the first Medal of Honor for aerial action in Vietnam.

While all this was going on, Brig. Gen. Marion Carl, now Deputy Commander of the 1st MAW and with a month remaining before his return to the United States, was being briefed by a helicopter squadron commander about the feasibility of rescuing the American and South Vietnamese garrison trapped in A Shau. The junior pilot said the weather was too bad to attempt a helilift. Carl decided to see for himself and flew his own Huey over the mountainous terrain. Carl was actually in the air and twenty minutes' flying time from the scene of the dramatic rescue by Major Fisher; he had just about decided to make his own attempt to rescue Myers when word came of Fisher's success.

Later that afternoon, Carl strongly recommended that a rescue attempt be made as soon as possible before the weather became even worse. In the evening, UH-34s of HMM-163 and Hueys of VMO-2 made the run into the valley under intense and accurate enemy fire. One UH-34 was shot down, and the crew of three was forced to hide because of the approaching darkness to await the next light for rescue. In the three-day operation, March 10–12, the defenders, Army Green Berets and South Vietnamese troops, were rescued. Besides Major Myers' A-1, an Air Force AC-47 gunship and an A-4 from VMA-311 were shot down.

As Marines assets grew, the Air Force still held overall control of the aerial activity in Vietnam. Major General McCutcheon, commanding general of the 1st MAW, furnished the Air Force with Marine support requirements with the understanding that anything in excess was left for the Air Force. There was also the continuing discussion of defense against a North Vietnamese air attack. Although the problem was discussed and agreements arrived at and promulgated, the subject of air control was always sensitive. Nearly two years passed before a "single management" alternative was introduced in the spring of 1968.

Pilot and Weapon Shortages

An insidious problem that became more apparent in 1966 was the lack of pilots and certain types of ground personnel. The pace of the overall buildup had caught the U.S. military air services short. The Marines, however, particularly the helicopter Marines, were especially hard pressed. With more than half of the Fleet Marine Force resources committed to combat in Southeast Asia, there were not enough pilots to fly the helos and jets. Pilots were rotated back to Vietnam more rapidly, or in some case, simply extended for up to a year.

It was not a morale-building situation, no matter how dedicated an individual might be. It was with ill-concealed bitter humor that Major General McCutcheon, now Deputy Chief of Staff(Air), remarked during a

1967 conference, "There is no pilot shortage; it's merely that requirements exceed resources." Part of the problem lay with the lucrative positions being offered by commercial airlines to young military aviators; another aspect was the increasing frustration many servicemen felt over the incredible restrictions placed, seemingly arbitrarily, over combat operations by a government on the other side of the world.

Arguments raged back and forth within the military and between Congressional committees investigating the problem. Solutions were generated, discussed, and reevaluated. (In the forefront of all the verbal action was the tireless, utterly dedicated Maj. Gen. Keith McCutcheon, who would spend any amount of time and effort to get his points across.) The obvious solution was to increase the number of trainees going through the pipeline, as well as drafting pilots into the helicopter community. A shortened training syllabus would also provide more pilots eventually, while decreasing such "plum" assignments as staff and postgraduate schooling would give a more immediate boost.

Aid for the Marines came from an unexpected source when in 1967 the Air Force offered to train a number of fixed-wing pilots as a result of the cancellation of a West German contract. Thus, many Marine fixed-wing aviators received silver Air Force wings, while freeing slots in the Navy's training command for rotary-wing students. Even the Army was tasked with helping the Marines, although there were several differences between Army and Marine requirements. The shortage problem had so many facets, solutions, and requirements that only an overview can be given here.

The author can recall that when he was going through Navy training in 1968 nearly one-half of the students in some classes were Marines, and that special attention appeared to be given to getting the "grunts" through. The young second lieutenants were fully aware of the situation, and those men who were encountering difficulties in training and were considering the possibility of washing out were heard to remark, "What're they going to do, send me to Nam?" There was no bitterness, just a verbal shrug in recognition that there was a problem that had no quick solution.

Another area that began to give problems in late 1965 was the shortage of armament, especially bombs. Again the culprit seemed to be the speed and intensity of the buildup. Had President Johnson and his Secretary of Defense, Robert S. McNamara, gone to war before the country and its resources were ready? Through 1966 and well into 1967, it was not unusual to see Phantoms and Skyhawks taking off with minimal underwing stores. Indeed, there were cases of completely unarmed aircraft launching from carriers merely to create another sortie for the record, "going along for the ride," because of

A Marine lieutenant, second from left, shows off his T-38 at Larado Air Force Base in November 1968. The Air Force was helping train Marine aviators to relieve the Corps shortage. (Peter B. Mersky)

"snafus on the flight deck," according to one unit's combat log. Whatever the reason, the problem became acute in 1966, and pilots of all services were troubled. One young Phantom pilot wrote, "There is nothing more demoralizing than the sight of an F-4 taxiing out with nothing, not a pair of 81s or 82s [250- and 500-pound bombs, respectively] nestled among its ejector racks." It would be a while before production could match the pace of combat employment.

1967

As 1967 opened, the war, both on the ground and in the air, began to establish its pace and intensity. It was becoming clear to both sides that the Communists could not win a decisive military victory—indeed they were losing militarily—as long as the vast might of the United States bolstered its ally, South Vietnam. Although the North Vietnamese were receiving aid from all areas of the Communist world, especially from the Soviet Union and People's Republic of China, these countries never attempted to introduce the level of personnel and machines the Americans had committed, avoiding a direct confrontation between superpowers. And yet, for all the overwhelming U.S. strength, no clear-cut victory was in sight, and the VC just kept up the pressure.

The war, with very few amphibious assaults, had allowed the 1st MAW to concentrate strictly on the sustained ground combat. Fully 50 percent of Marine aviation was engaged in supporting the III MAF in Vietnam. By this time, the wing included five MAGs and more than twenty fixed-wing and rotary-wing squadrons. MAGs -11, -12, and -13 included the VMA and VMFA assets. (MAG-13 had arrived in September 1966 and included VMFA-115, which arrived in June 1967, VMFA-314, and eventually VMFA-323 and VMFA-542.) MAG-16 and MAG-36 remained the helicopter groups, including, at the opening of 1967, seven transport squadrons and three observation units, which operated the smaller Hueys for a variety of duties.

The success of Marine air at this juncture, especially with the increased all-weather capabilities exemplified by the A-6s and the radar-directed F-4s and A-4s, was cause for some jealousy on the part of the Air Force, which was always sensitive about its supposed authority over all air operations in Southeast Asia. The continuing high level of activity along the Ho Chi Minh Trail, the circuitous 1,500-mile network along which men and supplies flowed into South Vietnam, became the focal point of Air Force attention. If aircraft were not involved in a strategic air strike against the North's industrial and petroleum, oil, and lubricants (POL) facilities, then the Air Force, under Gen. William Momyer, felt air assets, particularly those of the 1st MAW, would be best used against the activity on the trails.

As far as the Marines were concerned, interdiction was fine, but the men on the ground came first; that was the way it had always been and that was why the Marines had airplanes. The Marines' view was restated by Maj. Gen. Norman J. Anderson, USMC (Ret.), who commanded the 1st MAW for one year beginning in June 1967. Reviewing General Momyer's book *Air Power in Three Wars* in the May 1981 issue of the *Marine Corps Gazette*, General Anderson castigated General Momyer for his parochial views on air power in general, and Marine air power in particular. Addressing Momyer's charge that the Marines "employed aviation as though they were still conducting an amphibious operation," Anderson wrote, "Nothing could be further from the truth than this spurious charge of inflexibility. Marine Corps sorties were applied where needed most and frequently to other than Marine Corps units. They were diverted with caution, though, as anyone responsible for pulling support aircraft should understand, for a commander must not be suddenly stripped of expected support. . . . It was of such poppycock, however, that the infamous 'single management' was born and adopted."

Anderson believed that the Air Force's preoccupation with the so-called "single management" concept grew out of neglecting its duties regarding Army requirements. It was only when the Marines were tasked with supporting units of the 1st Cavalry Division, as part of III MAF in the northern provinces of South Vietnam in 1967 (a move designed to increase pressure on the VC infiltration routes along the border), that the problems began to take definite shape.

Acknowledging the order by Army Gen. William Westmoreland "to make certain that the needs of the Army divisions for tactical air support were satisfied," General Anderson wrote that he immediately knew Westmoreland's directive could not be implemented, because the Army could not be included in the Marines' air-control system. However, Anderson apparently prevailed on some departing units to give the 1st Cavalry some air communications equipment, which alleviated the problem to some extent. But, according to General Anderson, Marine air's reputation vis-à-vis the Seventh Air Force and its commander, General Momyer, was never able to satisfy its opponents. "In the last analysis . . . voluntary sharing which was extensive in Vietnam (although Momyer gives it very short shrift) will not effectively thwart 'single management.'" It was a battle never fully reconciled.

The Intruders also made brave forays into North Vietnam to hit strategic targets. On October 25, 1967, four A-6As of VMA(AW)-242 and VMA(AW)-533 launched against targets deep into North Vietnam. Leading the flight was the 242 CO, Lt. Col. Lewis H. Abrams and his bombardier-navigator (BN) Capt. James Anderst. The primary target was Phuc Yen airfield, which had originally been off limits to planners. But the MiG base had just been cleared for attack that day and the Air Force had already hit it. Originally, the Marines' plan called for two Intruders from each squadron, but one of the 533 crews' aircraft had a system failure and they hit a secondary target.

Supported by escorting F-4s and EF-10Bs, the strike group encountered a daunting enemy defense, including flak, SAMs, and MiGs. Flying low in mountainous terrain, which required pin-point navigation, complicated by degraded aircraft systems, the three A-6s hit their target amid a curtain of enemy fire. Maj. Fred Cone, the pilot of the second VMA(AW)-242 A-6, evaded a spread of SAMs only a few hundred feet above the ground. A third, fourth, and fifth missile came up and each time, Major Cone and his BN, Capt. Jack Wagner, outflew them, dropping their fuel tanks to gain speed and maneuverability.

Maj. Kent Bateman and his BN, Capt. Jerry Westendorf, flying the lone VMA(AW)-533 Intruder, ran into the same intense enemy defenses, including MiGs at higher altitude. Bateman descended on instruments to a lower level to avoid the MiGs and set up for his attack run. Although he lost contact with his protective EF-10, he continued on to make his delivery before exiting the area, all the while pursued by intense enemy fire.

The three A-6 pilots received the only Navy Crosses awarded to Marine jet aviators during the Vietnam War. (Of the twenty-eight Navy Crosses given to Marine officer flight crewmen, all but these three went to helicopter pilots.) Strangely, the BNs, exposed to the same dangers and riding right beside their pilots giving direction and calling out SAMs and flak, received the "lesser" Silver Star. While the Silver Star is certainly not a medal to be disregarded, no Marine Naval Flight Officer has ever received the Navy Cross. A few enlisted Marine aircrewmen have, mainly because of their intrepid actions on the ground after exiting their helicopters.

Unfortunately, Lieutenant Colonel Abrams and his BN, 1st Lt. Robert E. Holdeman, were killed in action a month later, when their A-6 was shot down as they attacked another North Vietnamese airfield at Kien An, near Haiphong. Their remains were returned to American hands in 1997.

Skyhawk Operations

In keeping with the pace of combat in 1967, the VMA units at Chu Lai accelerated their effort, often using a section of A-4s on "hot pad" alert, awaiting a scramble call: the pilots in the cockpits, the aircraft armed, and the engines turning. Sometimes the Skyhawks were already airborne. (These procedures were considered wasteful by the Air Force's General Momyer and only added to the control debate. But the Marines maintained their method of operation.)

In early 1967, MAG-12 (VMAs -121, -211, -214, and -311) flew day and night in support of U.S., Army of the Republic of Vietnam (ARVN), and South Korean army operations; every month seemed to set new records for total sorties and combat flight hours. Eventually, the idea of rotating personnel rather than entire squadrons, as previously mentioned, was instituted in 1968. VMA-311 remained at Chu Lai from mid-1967 to late 1969.

Problems with the CH-46

By mid-1967, the CH-46 was well on its way to becoming the standard Marine medium transport helicopter. There were ten squadrons equipped with the type and the improved Delta version was coming into use. (The UH-34s were to soldier on for another year, however.) The CH-46 was a welcome addition, but a series of fatal mishaps began to overtake the Sea Knight; some occurred in the United States, others in Vietnam. A "CH-46 Reliability Review Conference" was convened on August 1, 1967, at the Vertol plant in Pennsylvania. Recommendations from the conference included modification to the airframe and operating systems, especially in the aft rotor assembly, which was the main suspect. A CH-46 repair facility was established at MCAF Futenma on Okinawa. Eventually, 325 CH-46s went through the extensive overhaul program, but the result was reinstatement of a valued member of the Marine assault team.

Naturally, the grounding of CH-46s after the mishaps imposed additional burdens on the rest of the helicopter community, especially the trusty old UH-34s, which had been scheduled for retirement. "HUSSs" were shipped from the States to fill some of the gap, and ten CH-53s were sent in from California. Even Army Hueys were tasked with helping the Marines until the CH-46 problems were resolved.

It was during the heavy combat of 1967 that the action for which the only Medal of Honor to be awarded to a Marine aviator in Vietnam occurred. On August 19, Capt. Stephen W. Pless, a UH-1 pilot with VMO-6, responded to a rescue call. Four Marines were pinned down by forty-to-fifty VC on a nearby beach. Arriving on the scene, Pless made repeated strafing runs with rockets and machine guns before landing to pick up the Marines on the ground. After the four men had scrambled aboard his damaged Huey—Pless had sustained shrapnel hits from debris of his ordnance, so low had he flown—the intrepid pilot tried to take off. Pless attempted liftoff four times before his overloaded helicopter remained in the air, all the while under heavy Communist fire. He made it on the fourth try and brought his helicopter and men home.

Captain Pless was presented with his Medal of Honor in 1969 at ceremonies in the White House. (In a unique and very well-deserved simultaneous recognition of their efforts, his two crewmen and co-pilot were awarded the Navy Cross.) At the time, he was serving as the military department head for the Navy Aviation Schools Command in Pensacola, Florida. The author remembers Pless as a compact, beribboned, tough major—he had been promoted after his exploit as the youngest major in the Corps—complete with swagger stick. He epitomized the tough, professional, no-nonsense aviator for the sweaty young hopefuls going through precommissioning training. Unfortunately, Pless was killed in an accident riding his motorcycle shortly after receiving his award.

We should make note of the only Vietnam Medal of Honor given to a Marine aircrewman, HMM-263's PFC Raymond M. Clausen, the aircraft crew chief. On January 31, 1970, answering a desperate call for help from beleaguered Marines on the ground, he guided his pilot, Lt. Col. W. R. Ledbetter, squadron CO, around the craters of the battlefield to a touchdown spot in a *mine* field, all amid heavy enemy fire. Then, although his CO told him to remain inside the aircraft, Claussen repeatedly braved more withering enemy fire to rescue wounded Marines, making several runs from the helicopter to drag or carry the infantrymen to safety. The entire CH-46 crew was decorated. Colonel Ledbetter received the Navy Cross; 1st Lt. P. D. Parker, the Silver Star; and the two door gunners, Sgt. Maj. M. S. Landy and Cpl. S. M. Marinkovic, the Distinguished Flying Cross, itself a rare medal for an enlisted Marine to wear.

Clausen died in 2005; however, his Sea Knight, nicknamed "Blood, Sweat and Tears," had carried on well after Vietnam and even served during Operation Iraqi Freedom, this time with HMM-161, thirty-five years after its exploits in Vietnam. It was only as they prepared to deploy to Iraq that the squadron realized they had such an important aircraft on their roster.

However, upon arriving in-theater and beginning operations, the veteran helicopter suffered a hard landing and was judged to be "hors de combat," only suitable as a cannibalization airframe, a somewhat ignominious end for

A Medal of Honor crew. Then-Capt. Stephen W. Pless, far right, earned the Medal of Honor during a 1967 mission in which he and his crew picked up ground troops from a Communist ambush. Pless' co-pilot and two crewmen received the Navy Cross.

such a gallant, long-lived Marine. But all was not lost, and the Sea Knight, BuNo 153389, was wrapped and shipped back to the States, where it was restored to its former glory. After restoration, and on loan from the Marine Corps' Museums Branch, it will go on display at the Carolinas Aviation Museum in Charlotte, North Carolina, one of only a mere handful of treasured Medal of Honor aircraft that survive today.

As the 1967 holiday season approached, the customary truces and standdowns were initiated. It was hoped that the Communists would honor this American idealism, but this hope was dashed as reconnaissance missions showed violation after violation of the Christmas truce. For the men of the reconnaissance squadrons ashore and aboard the carriers in the South China Sea, there was no holiday that year; Christmas 1967 came and went with barely a notice from the hard-working photo-interpreters. The trails were clogged with men and supplies all heading south. The biggest, bloodiest, and most costly period of the war was about to erupt.

Realizing they could not win a military victory, the North Vietnamese, led by General Vo Nguyen Giap, victor of the battle of Dienbienphu in 1954, which forced the French out of Indochina, had planned a major military and psychological offensive against the towns and hamlets of South Vietnam in an effort to convince the South to join in the war and throw the Americans and their Saigon allies out. It was a desperate but well-planned gamble.

Tet and Khe Sanh

Chronologically, the offensive began with a series of probes against the outpost at Khe Sanh in the extreme northwestern corner of South Vietnam in January. After the loss of the A Shau Valley in 1966, Khe Sanh had taken on major importance, and the Americans were constantly on the alert against a Communist attempt to overrun the base. The 26th Marines were about to fight for their lives over a period of seventy-seven days, while all the assets of American air power in Southeast Asia were brought into play.

Along with the battle for Khe Sanh, the Communists also launched a series of devastating attacks to coincide with the Lunar New Year—Tet— which began on January 27, 1968. Throughout the holiday truce, there were repeated violations and rocket attacks against the major U.S. air facilities at Da Nang, Marble Mountain, and Chu Lai. The real hell spot, however, for the men on the ground, was the old Imperial Vietnamese capital of Hue, near Phu Bai. It was here that the VC conducted some of the most intensive and bloody battles of the entire war. The walled inner city became a killing ground for both Communists and Americans. At least eight battalions of North Vietnamese Army troops, along with VC sympathizers, were arrayed against three undermanned U.S. Marine battalions. More than five thousand NVA combatants were killed in house-to-house fighting; 142 Marines died in action. But the Communists were eventually repelled, as they were all over South Vietnam, their gamble lost.

While the Tet Offensive was mainly ground combat, the battle for Khe Sanh, essentially a confrontation between ground forces, involved major elements of air support. On the ground, Khe Sanh was largely a Marine operation. However, although Marine air power was used to the utmost during the siege, so were air assets of the Navy and Air Force.

Khe Sanh had always been an objective for Communist forces, for it represented a major military and political roadblock to victory in the South. As long as Khe Sanh remained in American and South Vietnamese hands, it would hinder movements into South Vietnam from Laos. Marines repelled a three-week siege in April and May 1967, but the stakes increased considerably when the second, and final, battle for Khe Sanh began in late January 1968. The intensity and frequency of NVA attacks made it obvious that air power was needed, fast and constantly. Supplies were the first concern. The isolated base would not last for long without massive airlift support. VMGR-152 and the helicopter groups, MAG-16 and MAG-36, were the Marine units first used in the multiservice operation to keep Khe Sanh operating.

Problems were compounded by the horrible weather, because the battle had begun at the height of the infamous monsoon season. More often than not, aircraft flew into Khe Sanh on instruments, the clouds and surrounding mountains making approaches and takeoffs tests of piloting skills, to say nothing of the intense ground fire from the NVA gunners nearby. The C-130s were especially vulnerable as they flew down the ground control approach path to the airstrip, and several aircraft were hit by Communist gunfire.

On February 10, CWO Henry Wildfang was approaching Khe Sanh in his C-130, loaded with bladders of fuel, when his Hercules was hit and began to burn. His 15,000 flight hours gave Wildfang, one of the last NAPs on operational duty, the experience to bring in his blazing transport. As the plane slid along the runway, crash crews raced to cover it with foam. Wildfang and his co-pilot were able to escape, but several others inside the heavily loaded C-130 were killed. Wildfang received his fifth DFC.

Because of this and other damage to C-130s, landings at Khe Sanh for the big four-engined turboprops were suspended until a way could be found to decrease the danger to the transports. A partial solution came in

A Marine C-130 at Chu Lai in late 1968. Hercules from Navy, Marine, and Air Force squadrons made a great effort to resupply the desperate base at Khe Sanh but were withdrawn for a time because of highly dangerous ground fire.

the form of an Air Force procedure, the Low Altitude Parachute Extraction System (LAPES). Approaching from the east, which would put the aircraft nearer the loading area of the camp, the Hercules pilot would open his tail ramp doors, and as he neared the planned touchdown point, an electrically operated parachute would be deployed, pulling the pallet-mounted cargo out. The C-130 never actually landed and thereby kept to a minimum its exposure to gunfire.

Another method was to simply airdrop by parachute, which called for close coordination between the men on the ground and the transport crews. There was the danger of the supplies being damaged or scattered by a hard landing. The helicopters were also part of the Khe Sanh airlift. Helo crews flew day and night on medevac and supply missions, continuously exposing themselves to enemy fire.

VMO-6 helicopter crews were in the thick of the fighting. February saw several aircraft hit, some seriously, as they flew low-level escort and medevac missions. But resupply of the Marine outposts around the main base was critical, if Khe Sanh was to remain in American hands. The crews of the UH-34s, CH-46s, and CH-53s, escorted by Huey gunships, were in a class by themselves. But a more effective escort was needed. The operation known as the Super Gaggle was developed. A-4s were pressed into service from MAG-12 at Chu Lai.

The first Super Gaggle went off on February 24, 1968, and involved twelve A-4s, twelve to sixteen CH-46s, four UH-1E gunships, and one TA-4F for coordination. The TA-4F would scout the area for weather information. If the ceiling was sufficiently high, the two-seater would call in the A-4s and, simultaneously, the CH-46s would launch from their bases. The slower speed of the helicopters would allow enough time for the Skyhawks to sanitize the immediate area with everything from napalm to tear gas and 20-mm cannon fire.

As the helicopter transports descended to the landing zone, they would be followed by the gunships, which would scoop up crews that were shot down at this point. Of course, the Super Gaggle depended on timing, weather, skill, and luck, but the operations were more successful, more so than before its introduction. Everything, water, ice cream, soda pop, and mail, as well as the necessary war supplies, was flown in in an effort to support the Khe Sanh defenders.

Lt. Col. David L. Althoff was the executive officer of HMM-262 during that Sea Knight–equipped unit's activities in the Khe Sanh airlift. In a later

account of the helicopter operations at Khe Sanh, he described Super Gaggle mission planning as follows:

> Each night we'd pick the hill we were going into the next morning and brief the fixed-wing people. We planned all the takeoff times so that when the fixed-wings arrived from Chu Lai, the Huey slicks would be there to control them. Meanwhile, we'd have launched the twelve CH-46s from Quang Tri, gone into Dong Ha, picked up our external loads and be heading for the objective.[7]

Questioned about the weather and the high rate of instrument flying, Lieutenant Colonel Althoff gave a good picture of the conditions:

> Normally during that time of the year the weather would be socked in at Dong Ha, and then clear, or at least broken, at Khe Sanh. So we had to climb out IFR . . . with our . . . loads. We'd line up at Dong Ha, pick up our loads one at a time, and take off into the soup. We'd break out at six or seven thousand feet, regroup and fly on up to Khe Sanh.

He also detailed how GCA approaches were tailored for the environment at Khe Sanh:

> You had to stay above the glide slope. I remember four different nights I got in there with the weather below GCA minimums. People

would come up to Quang Tri, where my squadron was based, and drop off supplies that were needed urgently at Khe Sanh . . . we'd just have to go.

I'd get to where Khe Sanh had me on radar and I'd ask the controller there to bring me down paralleling the glide slope, about 700 feet above it. The North Vietnamese would hear me coming and open fire, but it would mostly go below me.

I'd have the controller tell me when I was over the threshold of the runway. He'd lose me on radar at this point, so then it was up to me. I'd slow down to about 20 knots and start a very slow descent to the runway. I watched my radar altimeter, and when I got to 100 feet if I wasn't visual then, I'd just take it around. . . . The CH-46 is a real stable instrument ship and she handles very nicely under these conditions.

Even though the American camp at Khe Sanh would be dismantled in June, action around the area in northern Quang Tri Province remained high throughout the summer months. Former Shufly pilot, H. C. Brown, now a major, had arrived at Khe Sanh in early May with HMM-262, the same outfit with which Lieutenant Colonel Althoff served as the executive officer. Brown flew several resupply missions during the final stages of the siege, and his CH-46D was hit on several occasions.

During a mission in August, Brown was called on to insert a Marine ground reconnaissance team near the Laotian border. After dropping the team, Brown stood off in his helicopter waiting for the routine message that everything was all right and the team was proceeding. He waited anxiously, as the minutes went by with no sight or sound from the men he had just deposited in extremely hostile territory. An hour went by and still nothing. By this time, the two Huey gunship escorts were running low on fuel; so was Brown. He dispatched the gunships back to an outpost with a refueling capability, and when they returned, he, himself, left to refuel. Upon returning, he found the team had immediately run into heavy enemy action and could not call for fear of being heard, so close were they to the VC.

During the same month, Major Brown participated in a major effort to insert a battalion of Marines near Con Thien and the DMZ. So important was the operation that the pre-insertion landing-zone sanitizing was conducted by Air Force B-52s! As Brown and his squadron mates waited at Quang Tri, they could see the big bombers off to the north pounding the area. It was a strange feeling knowing that they would soon be headed directly for that area. In company with aircraft from HMM-161, Brown led a flight of four CH-46s, using an old church as a landmark over which the helicopters would turn and head directly north toward the landing zone.

The HMM-161 flight turned over the church and was immediately caught in heavy ground fire, two of the Sea Knights being so badly damaged as to be out of action. The leader of the flight, who was also the commanding officer of HMM-161, passed the lead of the entire operation to Brown, who found himself in charge of some twenty-five aircraft. The battalion was dropped off, to be picked up that afternoon.

The afternoon pickup proved to be just as interesting as the morning's mission. (Brown did not fly that afternoon.) The flight leader of the

[Opposite] An HMM-262 CH-46A. Helicopters were hard to maintain in the dusty, wet atmosphere of northern South Vietnam and thus looked tired and dirty even when they were operational. Note the squadron tiger on the tail. HMM-262 was based at Quang Tri in early 1968. (H. C. Brown)

afternoon pickup was hit by a radio-controlled mine and had to land. His wingman was hit by a similar weapon and nearly blown apart. The two pilots escaped miraculously, but the crew chief was killed. The helicopter aircraft commander (HAC), Maj. Harvey Britt, and his co-pilot immediately joined the Marines on the ground, awaiting rescue.

After spending some time thinking about their predicament, Britt looked at the first downed chopper, which had landed intact and was covered with dirt from the mine explosion. Acting on a hunch, Britt collected the surviving members of his squadron, and together the Marines cleaned off the CH-46, climbed in, started the engines, and to everyone's surprise, took off. (Britt had gained something of a reputation for being an extremely capable and daring pilot and was given the moniker "Blades" because he always seemed to bring his aircraft back from dangerous escapades with the rotors damaged and in need of repair.) The battalion could not be airlifted out of its position, and it remained for them to literally walk out from Con Thien.

Operation Niagara

The aerial defense of Khe Sanh was given the code name Operation Niagara, and it was a veritable deluge of support. Not only the 1st MAW aircraft, but also all the other air services, including mammoth B-52s, were called in. Generally, close air support, B-52 Arc Light strikes, and radar-directed bombing were the three types of missions flown during the operation.

Tactical aircraft from the Navy's Task Force 77 or 1st MAW were available around the clock and were usually under a tactical air controller (airborne) TAC(A). Although sometimes the TAC(A)s were flying TA-4Fs, the versatile little Cessna Birddog, a single-engine, tandem-seat, conventionally landing-geared airplane, which had been around since 1950 and had seen action from Korea onward, was the usual mount of the TAC(A)s. Marine O-1C pilots, according to one source, controlled nearly 95 percent of air strikes around Khe Sanh.

The Birddog carried three radios, two FM for communication with ground units and a UHF set for communicating with aircraft. Birddogs controlled strikes day and night, from Chu Lai to inside North Vietnam. There was never a problem getting air power for Khe Sanh. Indeed, the problem was just the opposite. The controllers had their hands full with literally stacks of aircraft from all the services orbiting—sometimes up to 35,000 feet, awaiting the call to come down and drop their ordnance. (Pre-1967 photos show the area around Khe Sanh to be dense foliage, a jungle. But by late 1968, the terrain had taken on the appearance of a Martian landscape, the thick carpet of trees killed by defoliants and the bare red clay pockmarked with bomb and shell craters.)

A-4s of VMA-311 and F-4s of VMFA-323 were especially active during the actual siege. Lt. Col. Harry T. Hagaman, commanding officer of VMFA-323, and his radar intercept officer, Capt. Dennis F. Brandon, had a close call in late January when their Phantom was mortally hit by enemy fire. Brandon, with more than 300 combat missions, knew the sound of a fatal hit and did not wait and ejected immediately. Lieutenant Colonel Hagaman stayed a while longer, fighting to maintain control of the F-4, but finally he, too, punched out, as the stricken aircraft began to roll and tumble a scant 100 feet above the ground. The two Marines aviators sustained minor back injuries from their ejections but were eventually rescued by helicopters. Captain Brandon went on to amass 400 missions, the first RIO to do so.

The TPQ-10 radar system really showed its value during the battle for Khe Sanh. The weather was rarely even fair, and the TPQ-equipped aircraft, such as the A-6s, were invaluable. Their heavy loads could be released from ground-control positions without their crews ever seeing the actual target. A-6s and F-4s were used to complement the B-52 Arc Light missions, and, as a result, the enemy took a tremendous pounding almost daily from the massive air strikes.

A Cessna O-1C Birddog of VMO-6 flies low over a Marine company in February 1967. Aircraft scouted ahead for enemy activity, ready to call in air support. Note triple rocket launchers, one under each wing. O-1Cs carried six smoke rockets to mark targets for air strikes.

By April successful ground sweeps had all but driven the NVA from the main area, and Khe Sanh was officially declared secured, although mopping-up operations continued for the next two months. Outside of the strategic-bombing strikes of Rolling Thunder, the aerial umbrella over Khe Sanh had been the largest and most successful air operation of the war. General Westmoreland said that more than 300 sorties were flown daily—one every five minutes—and some 35,000 tons of ordnance expended during the seventy-seven-day period of January 22–March 31, 1968.

Air Force General Momyer later wrote: "Khe Sanh was probably the turning point in the enemy's strategy for Tet. If Khe Sanh had fallen, the regular NVA forces would have moved against the major cities that were initially assaulted by VC local forces. The fact that there were no significant actions by regular forces indicated the enemy backed away from a combined military-political offensive."[8]

VMO-6 acquired its first fixed-wing aircraft sometime in July 1968, the Cessna O-1C Birddog. The pilots who flew the O-1 were TAC(A)s. O-1s had been very active during the Tet offensive of January 1968 and had controlled air strikes throughout South Vietnam and just above the DMZ into North Vietnam, day and night.

The O-1 detachments used the radio call sign "Fingerprint" and served until 1969, when the Birddog was retired from first-line service. The O-1C carried two FM and one UHF radios, acting as an airborne link between air and ground forces. They also conducted low-level reconnaissance missions with hand-held cameras. Sometimes the O-1s, on a seemingly quiet recce mission, would spook Communist troops in an "abandoned" bunker into firing on the aircraft, thereby revealing their position. The O-1 would then spend the rest of its time directing air strikes against the enemy.

Single Management Arrives

March 10, 1968, saw the controversial control doctrine known as "single management" put into practice, the Seventh Air Force obtaining complete control of air assets and operations in Vietnam. One of the more practical aspects of the Khe Sanh fighting was the realization that this method of controlling tactical air power could work. The Marines had fought long and hard against its implementation, but control of 1st MAW's fixed-wing assets, as integrated into the massive effort of Operation Niagara, was imperative. Basically, the Marines were directed to convey to the Seventh Air Force their daily capabilities, as opposed to the previous method of detailing their own needs first and then allowing any additional aircraft to be tasked by the Air Force. The Air Force, apparently in an attempt to smooth ruffled feathers, did its best to take care of Marine requirements, especially those of helicopter escort and landing-zone preparation. The system took a little getting used to, mainly from the Marines' point of view; but both sides tried to make it work and, as seen at Khe Sanh, generally succeeded.

OV-10As Become Operational

On July 6, 1968, a new aircraft arrived at Da Nang with VMO-2. After a lengthy development period, the LARA (light armed-reconnaissance aircraft) of 1962 arrived in Southeast Asia. Looking something like a World War II fighter with its twin propellers and twin tailbooms, the North American OV-10A Bronco was the result of a call for a lightly armed aircraft capable of operating in the counterinsurgency (COIN) role. The Navy, Marines, and Air Force were all subscribers and the first aircraft flew in 1966. (The Navy's VAL-4 "Black Ponies" operated the type for four years as the last Navy fixed-wing squadron in South Vietnam. The Air Force probably used the Bronco more than did the other two services.)

The Marines, however, used the Bronco as a helicopter escort, a TAC(A) vehicle, and general reconnaissance aircraft. VMO-6 took delivery of the plane in the summer of 1968 while attached to the Provisional MAG-39, based at Quang Tri, home of many of the helicopter squadrons that participated in the Khe Sanh airlift. (Quang Tri was a veritable beach, though far inland from any coastal area. The base was built upon gritty white sand, which caused constant maintenance headaches, as well as permeating everything from clothing and bedding to food.) MAG-39 had been the command-and-control element of MAG-36's Det Alpha until it was redesignated on April 15. VMO-6 had been attached to MAG-39 at the same time.

Having the ability to loiter on station with a variety of weapons, the Bronco was a welcome addition to the ground war waged by the hard-pressed helicopter crews. Four M-60 machine guns were fixed armament, and the high-tailed aircraft could also carry Zuni air-to-ground rockets, as well as Sidewinder air-to-air missiles, although the latter were rarely used. The Bronco, although it had a high degree of maneuverability, was not at its best in a high-threat area with large-caliber flak guns, or even the possibility of interception by enemy MiGs. As an air-to-ground weapon, the Bronco could carry additional guns and rocket pods in a variety of combinations.

The Bombing Halt

For the U.S. government, 1968 was a difficult year. Civil unrest at home, spurred on by the seemingly endless involvement in Vietnam, constricted the president's abilities to decide and act. Indeed, the pressure on Lyndon Johnson was so great that he decided in the spring not to seek reelection in November. It was a stunning disclosure, and set would-be candidates scurrying to make up for lost time. Johnson had been under constant advice from his Cabinet and some of his senior military strategists to disengage all U.S. forces from combat, bring the men home, and come to some sort of terms with the North Vietnamese.

It was a hard and bitter pill to swallow. Militarily, American strength could not be disputed; but a peaceful end to the war in favor of South Vietnam was impossible. Some sort of inducement had to be offered to the Communists. Therefore, on October 31, Johnson announced a unilateral bombing halt, effective the next day, November 1. All strike activity north of the DMZ would cease, except in the case of retaliatory measures against enemy violations, and unarmed reconnaissance flights. The North Vietnamese responded on November 3 by saying they would go to Paris to talk peace. Like most of the Communist diplomatic activities throughout the war, these peace talks would turn out to be a series of ploys to gain time.

With the bombing halt, the first phase of the Marines' involvement in Vietnam came to an end. From the first, tentative Shufly operations to the initial buildup in 1965, Marine aviation in Southeast Asia had by 1968 become a compact and powerful force. The Marine close-air-support doctrine, the raison d'être of Marine air, had been restated and restructured, but was still an important aspect of combat operations in Southeast Asia.

New aircraft such as the A-6/EA-6A, the OV-10A, CH-46, and CH-53 had shown themselves to be valuable members of the Marine team. The older veterans, like the F-8, UH-34, and CH-37, were passing from the scene, but left their own brilliant records. Of course, the two workhorses of the conflict had been the A-4 and F-4. These sturdy, yet flexible, aircraft met each and every task, got their crews home again despite devastating battle damage, and had plenty of room left for development for future requirements. The two could be compared to the SBD Dauntless and F4U Corsair of World War II. They were a team that enabled thousands of flight crewmen to cut their teeth in combat and come home.

In 1968, 47,436 combat sorties were flown by fixed-wing aircraft, while helicopter sorties had doubled since the previous year, from 388,000 in 1967 to 639,194, reflecting greater support of the effort on the ground to seek out the enemy. Yet, for all the high numbers, the sorties, the tonnage, and the thousands of enemy soldiers killed, the war had realized very little. To be sure, some areas in the South had been pacified, the Communists thrust out (for the moment), but the rejection never lasted. For those military personnel in Vietnam, hamstrung by foolish political policies emanating from an ineffective government and vocal minority, the war was becoming an impossible situation.

The North Vietnamese gleefully observed the travesty of the Democratic presidential convention in Chicago during the summer of 1968 and knew that their policy of watching and waiting would ultimately bear fruit. The great military giant was being ripped apart from within; all the Communists had to do was wait. They were good at that.

12 The Communist Waiting Game Pays Off

IN NOVEMBER 1968, the Republican Party, under the leadership of Richard M. Nixon, regained control of the White House. It was not an overwhelming victory; Hubert Humphrey and the Democrats gave a good fight. But at the center of the election was the war, and the country was tired of the war. Perhaps a change of administration would help. At any rate, Nixon was inaugurated in January 1969 and quickly set new directives into motion. A gradual phasedown and phaseout of U.S. military presence would begin by June. Troops and aircraft would begin to leave South Vietnam, and by the end of the year, many units had departed, leaving a rapidly decreasing nucleus of their comrades to continue advising the South Vietnamese. The intent was to give the war back to the South Vietnamese, who had been bolstered with huge amounts of aid and training so that they could carry on themselves with minimal U.S. assistance and presence.

For the 1st MAW, the new orders had some effect. There was still to be a considerable Marine air presence in Southeast Asia. But some of the units in-country would be redeployed to Japan, while the remainder would be consolidated. Provisional MAG-39 was deactivated, and MAG-36 departed, leaving MAG-16 in control of Marine helicopter assets in Vietnam. Most of the fixed-wing squadrons remained, MAGs -11, -12, and -13 still playing a large role in the continuing combat operations.

Perhaps the single most important event in 1969 for Marine aviation was the arrival of the first Bell AH-1G Hueycobras, the first designed-for-the-purpose gunships to be placed in production. The UH-34 and UH-1 had been merely makeshift developments to fit the need for an armed helicopter. Successful as they had been, they were only stopgaps. What was needed was a real attack helicopter. By the mid-1960s, several companies had been involved with a gunship, but it was Bell's Model 209 that showed the most promise. With a two-man crew, and a slim, shark-like profile, the first AH-1Gs entered Army service in early 1967 and deployed to Vietnam in late August, flying their first combat missions on the 31st. Used in company with Army ground forces and helicopter units, the new Bell soon proved its worth. The Marines were very interested.

The Corps wanted some changes in the Cobras, especially an additional engine that was essential for overwater flights from LPHs. It would be

two years, however, before the twin-engine AH-1J Sea Cobra would enter service. Therefore, thirty-eight AH-1Gs were sent to the Marines. Four of the Cobras joined VMO-2 at Marble Mountain Air Facility in April 1969. Used in concert with the OV-10, also a recent arrival, the Cobras served as escorts and flew fire support and armed reconnaissance missions. The new gunships were received with enthusiasm. Writing in the May 1968 issue of the *Marine Corps Gazette*, Capt. W. L. Buchanan, a highly decorated Huey pilot, stated: "The secret of helicopter escort is instantaneous fire suppression; not in ten or twenty seconds, but instantly. The Emerson TAT-101, a movable gun turret, gives the Cobra this capability . . . it is undoubtedly the best helicopter escort aircraft on the market."

The OV-10, he wrote, was a worthy companion to the Cobra. "The OV-10A and AH-1G are not bombers. Their weapons systems were designed for two jobs; fire suppression and target marking. We have the best attack aircraft and close-air-support pilots in the world, and if we don't use them at every opportunity we are missing a bet."

A newer, more powerful model of the Sea Stallion arrived in 1969 with the introduction of the CH-53D, while the faithful old UH-34 was finally retired. The HUSS had been retired when the CH-46's problems had been rectified, but the plan was somewhat premature. Plans to give remaining UH-34s to the Reserve were rescinded when rising combat losses in 1967 necessitated the reinstatement of the UH-34 to full operational status. Every military facility was scavenged for UH-34s; only the training command was allowed to retain its helicopters.

Once the Marines had gained operational experience with the CH-46 and CH-53, the UH-34 could finally retire gracefully. Oddly, and perhaps appropriately, the type's last combat flight was with HMM-362, the first Shufly squadron back in 1962. On August 18, 1969, in ceremonies at Phu Bai, a HUSS' rotor blades were folded for the last time. (HMM-362 later left for the United States and reequipped with CH-53s as HMH-362.)

By September, all UH-34s were gone from Vietnam. Although several "last" flights were claimed, UH-34s flew in the United States until October 3, 1973, when the really last flight took place at MCAS New River. Another old-timer that left the scene in 1969 was the EF-10B. "DRUT," "Willie the Whale," or Skyknight, the old jet aircraft retired from VMCJ-1 after four years of service in Vietnam.

Early Withdrawals

Throughout 1969 troop withdrawals had continued, and the men and equipment remaining were consolidated. Ground combat was still going on, however, and the Marines were in the thick of the fighting. From January 22 to March 18, 1969, Operation Dewey Canyon covered the A Shau Valley in northwestern South Vietnam, scene of some of the war's bloodiest fighting. The 3rd and 9th Marines, complete with supporting artillery, were airlifted by helicopters from Quang Tri. Dewey Canyon was a real tribute to helicopter support. For two months, at the height of the monsoon, the Marines sought out and destroyed the Communist camps along the Laotian border, denying much-needed supplies and food to the NVA troops coming across. With the help of Marine helicopters, the mud-Marines hopscotched the area to attack enemy bases. Killed were 1,617 Communists and more than 500 tons of food and supplies were confiscated.

VMO-6 was heavily involved in Operation Dewey Canyon. All three types of aircraft in the squadron—Hueys, Birddogs, and Broncos—saw

[Opposite] Two Bell AH-1G Huey-cobras, possibly of VMO-2, newly arrived in Vietnam in 1969. Their slim profile and chin-mounted turret are evident in this view. Twin-engine AH-1Js arrived two years later and were specifically designed for the Marines, who wanted the safety of an additional engine for overwater operation. The Juliets were quickly put into operation during Lam Son 719, the American-supported South Vietnamese incursion into Laos.

[Bottom Right] Marine UH-1Es touch down at a fire support base during Operation Dewey Canyon in early 1969. Dewey Canyon was one of the most successful Marine endeavors of the war and became a showcase for helicopter support.

heavy action throughout the operation. Hueys were used as escort for supply and medevac aircraft, while the two fixed-wing aircraft operated in the reconnaissance, artillery-spotting, and FAC(A) roles.

It was during this period when 1st Lt. Joseph P. Donovan of HMM-364 won two Navy Crosses, one of only two individuals, Navy or Marine, to be so honored in the war. (Capt. Martin L. Brandtner of the 5th Marines received two awards for two ground actions a week apart in September 1968. Lt. Col. Van D. Bell Jr. and Col. Stanley S. Hughes, both of the 1st Marines, received their second Navy Cross, having won the first in Korea.) Flying a CH-46 on February 22, 1969, First Lieutenant Donovan was originally part of a medevac flight of two Sea Knights, escorted by gunships, but the lead helicopter had to abort because of mechanical problems.

Pressing on, Donovan, encountered heavy enemy fire as he approached the pickup site. Although badly wounded, the young aviator landed and picked up the wounded Marine. He then took off and headed for a medical facility, where he had his wounds bandaged. He then took off again on another medevac, without gunship support, to retrieve eight badly injured Marines.

Again flying through heavy Communist fire, he picked up the Marines and took off, only to learn that more casualties had made it to the site he had just left. Undaunted, First Lieutenant Donovan flew back and picked up the additional wounded and flew them to the medical facility.

Barely two months later, on April 21, Lieutenant Donovan launched on another medevac. After bringing the wounded to safety, dodging enemy fire all the way, he inspected his CH-46, and realized the helicopter was no longer flyable. Accordingly, he took another Sea Knight and headed back to the pickup site he had just left to retrieve more casualties. The Communist defensive fire was intense. He picked up a few of the waiting Marines, but the Communist fire was intensifying and had, in fact, wounded Donovan's right gunner. The intrepid Marine aviator took off to assess his gunner's condition, and deciding the man's injury was not that serious, he called the men on the ground to say he was coming back in. However, they replied that another helicopter was inbound, and he could leave.

By the early part of 1970, many Marines had left Vietnam, rotating either to Japan or back to the United States. The 1st MAW lost four squadrons: HMH-361, with its CH-53s; A-4-equipped VMA-223 and VMA-211; and VMFA-542, which took its F-4s back to El Toro. The wing now consisted of MAGs -11, -13, and -16. MAG-11 at Da Nang included VMCJ-1, VMA(AW)-225, and VMA(AW)-242, which had A-6As, along with VMO-2 with its OV-10As. MAG-13, based at Chu Lai, contained VMA-311, the faithful "Tomcats," and VMFAs -115, -122, and -314. The helo-equipped MAG-16, located at Marble Mountain, consisted of four medium helicopter squadrons with CH-46s, one HMH with CH-53s, and two light squadrons, one with UH-1Es and the other with AH-1Gs. In all, 170 fixed-wing aircraft and 210 helicopters.

In July 1970, more departures saw VMCJ-1 leave for Japan, having flown 4,500 combat sorties since 1965, and VMA-311 leave Chu Lai for Da Nang to become part of MAG-11. HMM-161 took its aircraft back to the United States, as did VMFA-122, VMFA-314, and VMA(AW)-242. Chu Lai was turned over to the U.S. Army. MAG-13 redeployed to El Toro, too. By

September 1970, sixteen tactical squadrons had left Vietnam, and only two groups, MAG-11 and MAG-16, remained in-country. At the peak of Marine activity in 1968 and 1969, there had been twenty-six aircraft squadrons in Southeast Asia.

1971

In 1971 the South Vietnamese launched Lam Son 719, a massive incursion into Laos, ostensibly to attack VC staging areas. Ideally, the operation was meant to demonstrate the effectiveness of the Army of the Republic of Vietnam (ARVN) forces acting on their own with little or no American aid. Marine ground forces were to provide security for various areas along the invasion route, and CH-53s of HMH-463 were to airlift equipment and troops.

Accordingly, on February 8, ARVN forces crossed into Laos. CH-53s, escorted by AH-1Gs, or the newly arrived twin-engine AH-1Js, airlifted heavy artillery pieces into position. The AH-1J Sea Cobra, four of which had arrived for HML-367, was a heavily armed gunship, the kind for which the Marines had begged for many years. The AH-1Js flew their first combat mission on March 2, escorting Sea Stallions.

VMA-311 was in action throughout Lam Son 719, flying hundreds of interdiction strikes against Communist trails and supply routes, hitting trucks and tanks. Air Force FACs in OV-10s controlled the strikes. Navy aircraft from the carriers were also involved.

Lam Son 719 was a costly operation for the South Vietnamese, although they inflicted heavy casualties on North Vietnamese Army (NVA) forces. The Air Force estimated fully one-third of the helicopters involved were destroyed; Army numbers were somewhat less. Nevertheless, the estimates do indicate the ferocity of the action. Thus, while Lam Son 719 did show some favorable results for the South Vietnamese and for Vietnamization, it was clear that the ARVN could not sustain itself on the battlefield without large amounts of American air power.

The might and breadth of the U.S. air umbrella was the one thing the VC and North Vietnamese feared and respected above all else. Its withdrawal in 1971, at a fairly critical stage of the war, allowed the Communists to finally contemplate massive invasion of the South and final victory. On May 26, 1971, the last Marine air combat unit, HML-167, redeployed to New River in the United States. All American squadrons had left Vietnam; the last Navy squadron, VAL-4, had taken its OV-10 Broncos out in April. MAG-11 departed on May 21, and MAG-16 left on June 1. Five hundred Marines were left in-country to provide transitional support for the Vietnamese. But the withdrawals were largely complete. President Nixon had made good on his promise to bring Americans out of combat. In doing so, he had left the South naked.

The 1972 Easter Invasion

As the American withdrawals were completed and the Communists sat at the Paris peace talks, they were plotting the invasion of South Vietnam, now

divested of U.S. air power and support. On March 30, 1972, Good Friday, a massive mortar barrage signaled the beginning of the offensive. North Vietnamese Army troops flooded across the DMZ into Quang Tri Province supported by tanks and heavy artillery. Surface-to-air missiles followed the Communists into the south. Along with ground-launched SA-2 and SA-3 missiles, the NVA brought the shoulder-launched, highly mobile SA-7 heat-seeking missile, which played havoc with low- and slow-flying aircraft like transports and helicopters. The surprised ARVN forces were routed by the ferocious enemy assault. There was little to do but fall back to safer ground and wait for help.

U.S. air power in Southeast Asia had, of course, been greatly reduced during the withdrawals, until only Air Force units in Thailand and a pair of aircraft carriers patrolling up and down the coast were all that remained. The 1st MAW had been redeployed back to Japan and the United States. As U.S. forces were once again hurriedly mobilized for the trip back into South Vietnamese combat, air units joined the flow of men and machines.

MAG-15, under Col. Keith O'Keefe, was ordered to bring VMFA-115 and VMFA-232 back to Da Nang, while VMFA-212 flew in from Hawaii and joined the other squadrons. MAG-12, led by Col. Dean C. Macho, took its A-4E squadrons, VMA-211 and VMA-311, to Bien Hoa air base, fifteen miles northeast of Saigon. The Skyhawks arrived on May 17 from Japan and by the 19th were ready for combat operations.

The aircraft of both groups flew sorties along the Cambodian and Laotian borders in an effort to interdict the flood of North Vietnamese supplies. VMCJ-1 and VMCJ-2 brought their EA-6As to Cubi Point in the Philippines, operating a combined detachment, rotating in and out of Da Nang as well as staging directly from their Philippine base with the inflight refueling services of VMGR-152. Arriving in April, the composite squadrons flew ECM missions in support of Navy and Air Force strike groups. Orbiting offshore, the EA-6s of the six-to-seven-plane detachment put in a performance which was one of the minor miracles of this hectic period.

From April to January 1973 they flew a sustained period of operations that earned the detachment a Navy Meritorious Unit Commendation. Staging out of Cubi and Da Nang, the Intruders operated against enemy SAMs. April 13 saw the first loss of a crew and aircraft when Pigment 08—the aircraft call sign—failed to return from an Alpha strike near Thanh Hoa in North Vietnam.

Part of the success of the EA-6As of the VMCJ-1/2 group resulted from the Marine aircraft being the only platforms capable of jamming the new I-band frequency guidance radar of some of the North Vietnamese missiles. Another aspect was the tremendous maintenance and support effort that enabled as many as seven EA-6s to be airborne simultaneously on different missions.

One other unit of Marine aircraft that responded to the call for air power was VMA(AW)-224, one of three Marine squadrons aboard Navy aircraft carriers in the South China Sea. It had been seven years since Marines had flown into combat from carriers, but the A-6As of VMA(AW)-224 were aboard the USS *Coral Sea* (CVA-43) as part of Air Wing 15. In all, VMA(AW)-224 operated through six line periods on Yankee Station, the northern area of operations for carrier air power.

Arriving on line in early January 1972, CAW-15 flew strikes against major passes in Laos. The A-6As of VMA(AW)-224 also flew as pathfinders, leading other aircraft down through the low clouds to the targets, or alone at night against North Vietnamese trucks on the Ho Chi Minh Trail.

During the third line period in March, VMA(AW)-224 received three A-6Bs, variants equipped with the Air Force-developed AGM-78, Standard ARM (anti-radar missile) for use against SAMs. The new mission was approached with some uncertainty, but eventually ninety-five A-6B sorties were flown. More than forty-seven Standard ARM missiles were fired, with a 39 percent success rate, against the Fansong guidance radars of the SA-2 sites.

VMA(AW)-224 lost four Intruders in combat beginning in April when the squadron flew in support of Operation Pocket Money, the mining operation of May, and Operation Linebacker, the initial major reaction to the North Vietnamese invasion. On May 9 the air wing commander, Cdr. Roger E. Sheets, led three A-6As and Navy A-7s on a mining mission into Haiphong Harbor, the main North Vietnamese port. The mining of the principal ports of North Vietnam had been a bone of contention for military planners for almost as long as the war itself. The prevailing military view was that to mine the ports would effectively close off the supply of the Communist effort

[Opposite] CH-46Ds of HMM-164 depart on a mission to deliver South Vietnamese marines of the 4th and 6th battalions to the front lines at LZ Columbus, north of Phu Bai and south of Quang Tri during the hectic fighting in late May 1972. The South Vietnamese civilians in the foreground are actually local farmers tending to their land.

in the south at its source. The timid Lyndon Johnson administration had balked at what it considered such a drastic step. However, Richard Nixon was more daring and, by May, Haiphong, Cam Pha, Hon Gai, Thanh Hoa, and Vinh had been sealed up.

VMA(AW)-224 continued its combat tour, losing a third aircraft on May 29. After their Intruder was hit by flak, but after they had made their bomb run, Lt. Cdr. Philip Schuyler (pilot) and Marine Capt. Lou J. Ferracane (BN) ejected over the Gulf of Tonkin, where they were rescued by a SAR helicopter. Relieved by USS *America* (CV-66), the *Coral Sea* left the line in July after its sixth period, taking the Marines of VMA(AW)-224 back to the United States. The Bengals had flown 2,800 combat sorties, accumulating 4,500 hours of flight time.

The MARHUKs

A unique operation began in June 1972. A month after the mining operation, it became clear that the North Vietnamese were going to continue pressing men and supplies south to support the new offensive. Actually, the situation had evolved to an extent from the fact that merchant ships, whose captains were afraid to try negotiating the newly mined areas to come into port, were offloading their much-needed cargo onto lighter vessels such as sampans and barges. Some interdiction mission had to be created to intercept these deliveries.

Normal offensive missions had to be further augmented, and a special Marine unit was stood up using the newly arrived AH-1J Sea Cobras of HMA-369. The Marine Hunter/Killers, or MARHUKs, would interdict the supplies that were coming south from merchant ships from third-world countries. Because of the obviously highly secretive nature of the operation, its security was of utmost importance, especially as the main focus would be the Hon La anchorage south of Vinh in North Vietnam, one of only three deep-water anchorages in the small country. It was obvious that Hon La would be heavily defended with flak sites surrounding its pocket-like geographical formation.

Forming first at Okinawa and tending to several administrative problems that included building up the pilot roster, the MARHUK contingent embarked aboard USS *Denver* (LPD-9), flagship for the Commander, U.S. Seventh Fleet, Vice Adm. (later Adm.) James L. Holloway III, who had first taken the nuclear-powered carrier *Enterprise* to war in 1965. Arriving on station on June 20, the squadron flew its first missions two days later, scouting the anchorage and predictably generating defensive fire from the batteries ashore. From then on, the pace was quick, and the MARHUKs expended a lot of ordnance against various ships they discovered in the little bay. They also acted as low-flying FACs for Navy carrier strikes.

The North Vietnamese were always quick to respond to any intrusions, and on July 12, the first battle damage occurred, although it wasn't too serious.

By the end of the month, the squadron had to transfer to another ship, because the *Denver* was due to take a break. USS *Cleveland* (LPD-7) relieved her and the MARHUKs flew aboard, flying their first missions from the new ship on August 4. However, bad weather prevented the Cobras from completing their missions and actually shut down the operation for the next two days.

The squadron maintained a busy night-time schedule and eventually was cleared to carry the highly useful Zuni five-inch rocket, which was carried by many fixed-wing aircraft to use against ground targets of opportunity like trains and waterborne traffic. Ideal for the MARHUKs' purpose. The Zuni's size and weight required a four-shot pod that actually only carried two of the six-foot-long rockets.

Denver was eventually relieved by USS *Dubuque* (LPD-8) at the end of November. The squadron kept flying and even participated in the Linebacker II series of strikes that eventually brought the foot-dragging North Vietnamese to the peace talks, resulting in a cease-fire and an end to the fighting. By that time, HMA-369 had flown 981 combat sorties and destroyed or damaged 123 sampans and their combined cargo of 5,444 100-pound bags of rice. Admittedly, the last number is open to conjecture. Whatever the actual number, the MARHUKers had certainly contributed an important effort by interdiction and enemy surveillance at a pivotal stage of the war.

A Marine Crew Scores a Kill

The chances for Marine aerial victories in Southeast Asia were next to nothing. As has been shown in the preceding pages, nearly all the assets of the 1st MAW were committed to close air support or peripheral support of larger strike groups (as in the case of the EF-10s and EA-6s of VMCJ-1 and VMCJ-2). Although most Marine aviators would have gladly paid large sums of money for a shot at a MiG, the Marines scored only three times against enemy aircraft in Vietnam. Two of these kills occurred while the Marine pilots were on exchange duty with the Air Force.

The first action took place on December 17, 1967, when Capt. Doyle D. Baker, serving with the Air Force's 13th TFS out of Udorn, Thailand, shot down a MiG-17 with 20-mm cannon fire from a SUU-23/A gun pod, and finally an AIM-4 Falcon air-to-air missile. Flying an F-4D (66-8719), Baker

[Opposite] Intruders of VMA(AW)-224 just before their deployment in the *Coral Sea* in early 1972. Marines flew as part of Air Wing 15, losing four aircraft in combat.

[Bottom] While on exchange duty with the Air Force, Capt. Doyle D. Baker got a MiG-17 in December 1967. Baker stands before a 13th TFS F-4D at Udorn, Thailand. He eventually transferred to the USAF and retired as a colonel before entering corporate aviation. (via Doyle Baker)

was on his thirtieth mission over the North, escorting F-105 fighter-bombers. (He had already served a tour flying F-4Bs with VMFA-513 in 1965 and would eventually fly 242 missions in two tours.) His backseater was Air Force 1st Lt. John D. Ryan, the son of the Pacific Air Force Commander, later USAF Chief of Staff. (Lieutenant Ryan would be killed in a crash two years later.) Captain Baker eventually joined the Air Force with the help of Lieutenant Ryan's father and retired as a colonel, entering the world of corporate flying.

The second Marine aerial victory did not occur until August 12, 1972, when Capt. Larry Richard, flying with Navy Lt. Cdr. Mike Ettel, in an F-4E of the 58th Tactical Fighter Squadron, claimed a MiG-21. Richard got a GCI call on two MiG-21s. The enemy aircraft soon came into view, and as Richard blew off his underwing fuel tanks, a slow-turning dogfight developed, with Richard shooting a Sparrow AIM-7 first at one MiG then at the other. The first North Vietnamese evaded the American missile, but the second MiG had its tail blown off.

VMFA-333—the Fighting Shamrocks, Trip Trey (the unit enjoyed several nicknames)—had been the first Marine F-4J-equipped unit to deploy as part of a carrier air wing. Basically an Atlantic Coast squadron, VMFA-333 nonetheless had become part of CVW-8 in the USS *America* (CVA-66) in January 1971, along with another East Coast squadron, Navy VF-74. *America* arrived on Yankee Station in July 1972, and its air wing, including VMFA-333, immediately began flying group strikes, photo escort, and various CAP missions.

During the carrier's third line period in September, the opportunity for a MiG engagement arose. On September 11, two VMFA-333 F-4Js were on patrol near Phuc Yen. The lead aircraft, flown by the squadron executive officer, Maj. Lee Lasseter, and Capt. John Cummings, the RIO, got a radar call on two MiG-21s. Turning rapidly into the oncoming enemy aircraft, Lasseter shot a missile that quickly destroyed one of the MiGs. The second MiG retreated some distance away from the Marine flight. However, as the two Phantoms turned back toward their ship, the MiG made a run on Lasseter's wingmen, Capt. A. S. Dudley, and his RIO, 1st Lt. J. W. Brady.

Lasseter fired off another Sidewinder, which apparently damaged the MiG, although not downing it. The enemy plane turned away, and the two Phantoms again turned for home. Coasting out, the pair waded through some heavy flak. Lasseter's aircraft was hit by a SAM; Dudley's F-4 had been damaged by flak and was in probable danger of running out of fuel. Both crews ejected south of Haiphong, were picked up by a helicopter, and were flown back to their carrier.

Even though the mission resulted in the loss of two aircraft, the first and only all-Marine kill of Vietnam was a milestone, and Major Lasseter was awarded the Alfred E. Cunningham Award as the top Marine aviator of 1972. He also assumed command of VMFA-333 when Lt. Col. J. K. Cochran and his RIO were shot down by flak during a photo-escort mission on December 23.

The Shamrocks returned to Beaufort, South Carolina, in March 1973, having flown throughout the final stages of the Vietnam War, gaining the Meritorious Unit Commendation for its work with Task Force 77. (Unfortunately, Lt. Col. Lee Lasseter died in March 1980, after being medically retired from active duty the previous year.)

The Rose Garden

In mid-May, the remote base at Nam Phong in Thailand began receiving Marine squadrons. VMFA-115 with F-4Bs and VMFA-232 with F-4Js arrived from Da Nang in June, as did VMA(AW)-533 with its A-6As. Nam Phong was 300 miles from Hanoi and had never been completed. So austere were the surroundings that the Marines called it the "Rose Garden," in wry reference to a popular song and current Marine recruiting slogan. The Red Devils of VMFA-232 and Silver Eagles of VMFA-115 flew missions into

[Top Left] North Vietnamese MiG-17Fs (Fresco-Cs) of the 923rd Fighter Regiment are readied for a mission at Kep, west of Hanoi, in 1967. MiG-17s were highly maneuverable, especially against the ponderous Phantom, and carried three fuselage-mounted cannon. (via Dr. Istvan Toperczer)

[Bottom Left] An F-4J of VMFA-333 aboard USS *America* during workups before the 1971–72 deployment. The squadron scored the only all-Marine (all-Marine crew in a Marine aircraft) kill during the war.

Laos and North Vietnam, VMFA-232 losing three F-4Js between August and November; two crewmen were lost.

One of the Phantoms lost was actually shot down by one of a pair of MiG-21s that had come at the American fighters head-on on August 26, 1972. Acting as a barrier contact air patrol (BARCAP) protecting orbiting tankers for a strike into North Vietnam, the section of VMFA-232 F-4Js heard a threat call from Red Crown GCI. The MiGs were closing, but the F-4 crews had not made radar or visual contact by the time Red Crown called merged radar plot, meaning that the two opposing sides had overflown each other and were now headed in outgoing directions.

Standard procedure was to unload for maximum airspeed and extend with the aim of reattack if the bogey was not seen at merged radar plot. However, the wingman (1st Lt. Sam G. Cordova, pilot, and 1st Lt. D. I. Borders, RIO) hauled their heavy F-4 (155811)—each Phantom was flying with *three* underwing fuel tanks!—around to engage the oncoming MiGs. The section was at 26,000 feet, not the best operating altitude for heavily loaded F-4s. The Phantom slowed enough for one of the North Vietnamese pilots to shoot a missile. The lead saw the fireball as his wingman exploded. The young, inexperienced pilot was killed, but his RIO was rescued. Lieutenant Cordova had had to eject from his F-4 only a few weeks before, on August 2, when he lost power while on final approach to Nam Phong following a training flight. The MiG-21 pilot has been identified as Nguyen Duc Soat, a six-kill ace with the 927th Fighter Regiment of the Vietnamese People's Air Force. (The Marine Phantom may have been his fifth kill.)[1]

The two F-4 units only flew daytime hops, leaving night flying to the crews of VMA(AW)-533, who flew singly or in pairs against the truck traffic on the darkened trails. Flying with no lights, the Intruder crews exhibited considerable skill and daring in the mountains and hilly terrain of Laos and North Vietnam.

Life at Nam Phong was straight out of *M*A*S*H*, with wooden, tin-roofed hangars and tent-huts for living quarters. Having come from the much more modern and commodious base at Da Nang, the Marines were in for quite a shock when they arrived at their new base in Thailand. Making the best of the situation, the F-4 crews flew interdiction missions, usually under Air Force control, hitting targets in South Vietnam, Laos, North Vietnam, and later, Cambodia, taking enemy ground fire nearly 70 percent of the time.

To their credit, the Marines never stopped flying combat missions even during the move to Nam Phong. On the day of the redeployment, MAG-15 aircraft launched on interdiction missions from Da Nang, recovered at Nam Phong, where they were reloaded with bombs that had earlier been delivered to Nam Phong, and continued to fly combat missions, all the while as the main body of the aircraft group continued to arrive at the Thai base.

The Marine Phantoms took off from Nam Phong, checked in with an orbiting C-130 control center, which handed them off to a FAC in an OV-10, which would actually pin-point the targets. Occasionally, the Phantoms would double cycle, flying from Nam Phong to Da Nang and back to Nam Phong, including two missions. It was a hectic time and the only way to be sure of the date was to check a calendar watch.

[Opposite] During a 1972 mission from Nam Phong, a Silver Eagle Phantom delivers its bombs through the clouds, probably on signal from Air Force F-4s, which frequently accompanied Marine aircraft. Air Force planes carried Loran radar and could tell the Marines when to release their loads. Note the open chaff dispenser door above "MARINES." (Joe Rice)

[Below] VMA-311 A-4Es at Da Nang in June 1972 as part of MAG-15. Having left Vietnam only a year before, the Tomcats were back in response to the North Vietnamese invasion, flying from Da Nang and then Bien Hoa.

Sometimes, the Air Force would provide Loran bombing fixes when the weather got so bad that targets were obscured and visual bombing was impossible. Marine aircraft did not carry Loran, and one or two Air Force F-4s would fly up from Udorn and accompany the VMFA-115 or VMFA-232 birds to the target area, getting the necessary radar fix while the Marines dumped chaff to confuse the enemy defenses.

The action did not stop with the January cease-fire, as many missions were flown into Laos and Cambodia after the war had stopped in Vietnam. VMA-311 pilot 1st Lt. Charles G. Reed flew his squadron's 50,000th combat sortie of the war on August 29. The unit would eventually total 54,625 sorties by January 29, 1973. VMA-211 and VMA-311 flew in support of the ARVN forces still trying to counter the NVA thrust. On

August 12, two VMA-311 A-4Es flew close air support sixty miles southeast of Saigon, hitting an enemy command post. Briefed in the air by an orbiting FAC, the two Skyhawks immediately dove on the target, bracketing it with 500-pound bombs. Several local positions were destroyed during this typical sortie. VMA-311 would deliver the last Skyhawk war load on January 28, 1973, during a mission into Cambodia. Four A-4s took off in the late afternoon, armed with specially painted red, white, and blue bombs, just for the occasion, with suitable inscriptions and messages for the VC. A little more than an hour later, the aircraft returned to Bien Hoa in a diamond formation. First Lieutenant Thomas Boykin was the last to land. He reported taking hits in the Mekong Delta area. "I dropped the last one," he reported, "I'm glad it's over."

VMFA-212 returned to Hawaii and did not deploy to Nam Phong from Da Nang.

At the end of June, the ARVN forces were ready to begin their own counteroffensive. Driving north toward Quang Tri, the Saigon forces eventually pushed the Communists back, and South Vietnam was fairly well secured once again by late September.

Linebacker II and the Cease-Fire

There was still a lot of combat, and much of it was to take place directly over Hanoi in October and December, as waves of Air Force B-52s, in company with Navy aircraft, pounded the North Vietnamese capital. At one point the Communists seemed to call for peace, and President Nixon stopped the strategic-bombing campaign. But the enemy was only stalling, and the giant Stratofortresses were unleashed in a massive bombing offensive named Linebacker II. Throughout the week of December 18, Hanoi and Haiphong reeled under strategic bombardment. The Air Force and Navy aircraft waded into the biggest, most sophisticated network of aerial defenses in the history of warfare. The mining of the harbors had had a distinct effect, but there were still plenty of SAMs and flak to go around. The courage and skill of the B-52 crews over Hanoi in those night raids of December 1972, against flak, SAMs, and MiGs, deserves telling in any account of Vietnam combat.

As has been said, the main Marine contribution during this period was VMCJ-1 and VMCJ-2's ECM support. Together with Navy EA-6B Prowlers, four-seat versions of the Intruder, which had entered combat in June, the Marines provided indispensable anti-SAM support for the strikes. So great was the need for Marine ECM support that a four-plane detachment of VMCJ-2 operating from the carrier USS *Saratoga* (CVA-60) was dispatched on April 20, 1972, to NAS Cubi Point in the Philippines to assist the growing force of Marine "electric" Intruders. The EA-6As would fly to Da Nang before a mission for refueling, briefing, and other necessities before launching to support the Navy and Air Force strikes for the day. The work of both VMCJs was deeply appreciated at every operating level and generated many expressions of gratitude and congratulations.

Finally after a week of intense action, the North Vietnamese sued for peace. An accord was signed in Paris for a cease-fire to take effect on January

27, 1973. Prisoners of war would be returned and the mines would be cleared from North Vietnamese harbors.

Marine squadron HMH-463 was tasked with providing its CH-53As for Project Endsweep, the mine-clearing operation. HMM-164 and HMM-165 brought their helicopters along as well, for SAR services.

On February 24, the first units arrived in Haiphong Harbor, with the Navy's HM-12 and HMM-165 aboard Navy amphibious transport docks. The first sweep was conducted on February 27 by HM-12, while HMH-463 flew additional sweeps. A Marine CH-53 was lost on March 18 near Hon Gai because of mechanical difficulty, but its crew was rescued. The operation continued until mid-April when it was halted because the North Vietnamese slowed the POW repatriation process. Eventually, the mine-clearing was resumed and was completed on July 27, after the Navy and Marine helicopters had made 3,554 sweeping runs.

On January 29, 1973, MAG-12 under Col. Dean Macho, the last American combat aviation unit still in-country, left Vietnam. The official figures for combat losses in Southeast Asia for Navy and Marine squadrons were 529 and 193 fixed-wing aircraft, and 13 and 193 helicopters, respectively. These figures, of course, reflect the greater use of helicopters by the Corps. The strides in all phases of aviation had been tremendous, from in-flight communication and air-ground coordination to blind-bombing techniques and new equipment. However, sadly, neither the Marines nor the rest of the American military services, were through fighting in Southeast Asia.

Navy carrier strikes continued throughout early 1973 against targets in Cambodia and Laos, as the Communists still harried the governments in these countries. In March, the Communist Khmer Rouge forces were closing in on the Cambodian capital of Phnom Penh, tying up traffic on the vital Mekong River, the main water highway to South Vietnam. It was imperative to withdraw American citizens from the city. Under Operation Eagle Pull, Marine Corps aircraft from MAG-15, including F-4s from VMFA-115 and VMFA-232, and Intruders from VMA(AW)-533 struck Communist positions beginning on May 11.

By August, the U.S. Congress had had quite enough of the endless drain of Vietnam and voted to cut off U.S. support in any form. Thus, the last actual missions of Southeast Asian combat were really flown on August 15 by Navy and Marine aircraft from carriers and from bases in Thailand. By September 1, all the Marine Corps' aircraft and support assets had left Nam Phong and headed for home in the United States.

South Vietnam Falls

Ground combat in Southeast Asia never really halted with the 1973 Paris Accords. The wily North Vietnamese had effectively duped then–national security adviser Henry Kissinger and the United States, and, as always, bided their time. In January 1975, the NVA, which had been allowed to remain in the South, struck out in a bold new offensive. Without U.S. presence, the South Vietnamese were nearly helpless. By late April, the Communists' long-awaited victory was all but assured. All that remained was the final evacuation of American personnel from South Vietnam.

The end came on April 29 when orders were given to execute Frequent Wind, the evacuation of Saigon. HMH-462, HMH-463, and HMM-165 began shuttling back and forth, carrying evacuees out to the assembled ships offshore. CH-53s and CH-46s kept up the flow, while an umbrella of Air Force and Navy jets flew protection overhead. Even EA-6As from VMCJ-1 contributed their special talents. Originally assigned to the *Midway*, two aircraft and three crews had been transferred to the *Coral Sea* and orbited the area around Saigon, jamming enemy signals, especially the gun control radars of the Communists' 37-mm flak guns.

The pace was hectic, as the helicopters kept up a steady stream of flights back and forth from the ships to the landing pads in South Vietnam. That there were no midair collisions was a minor miracle, the traffic was so heavy. Because of the late start of the rescue flights—they did not get under way until 1300—the operation was still going on until well into the early morning hours, several pilots totaling up more than eleven hours of flight time when they finally left their cockpits.

One humorous story to come out of the operation concerned the rescue of the U.S. ambassador, Graham Martin, who was to be the last to leave the embassy in Saigon, thus signaling the end of the rescue. When the ambassador was safely aboard a helicopter and the aircraft airborne, the pilot was to transmit the supposedly secret call "Tiger, Tiger, Tiger," and nothing else. The rescue of the ambassador and his staff was accomplished, and as the young Marine pilot flew his airplane back to the carrier, he transmitted "Tiger, Tiger, Tiger," as per instructions.

The airborne controller responded, "Roger, confirm Tiger, Tiger, Tiger?" The excited helicopter pilot came back, "Affirmative. Tiger, Tiger, Tiger. I have the ambassador!"

HMA-369 returned with its AH-1Js aboard the USS *Midway* (CVA-41). The Sea Cobras served as escorts and pathfinders for the transport helicopters, as well as tactical air controllers (TACs) for the overall effort. In more than forty sorties during the "Night of the Helicopters," the Marines brought out 2,000 people. On the 30th, the last frantic flights left Saigon just as the Communists rolled into the fallen city. The Vietnam War was finally over.

A final action in Southeast Asia involved Marines, although not specifically Marine aviation. Barely a month after the fall of Saigon, an American container ship, the SS *Mayaguez,* was captured by Communist forces from Cambodia on May 12, 1975. Efforts to recapture the pirated ship were eventually successful, although not without loss of American lives and aircraft. Air Force HH-53s airlifted Marine troops into battle on Koh Tang, an island off the Cambodian coast. They freed the *Mayaguez* and its grateful crew.

13 Post-Vietnam Future

WITH THE FALL OF SAIGON, and the ultimate loss to the Communists, the Americans left Southeast Asia for a while. Losing a long, important war, at the expense of more than 50,000 lives, was a hard experience. Yet, for the most part, those who served in combat came home with their heads high, even if the public was not as welcoming as it had been in previous wars. Again, as in earlier conflicts, the military, including the Marine Corps, reduced itself, let people go, retired squadrons and aircraft, and generally tried to bring itself down to a more traditional peacetime physique.

Still, there were thousands of highly experienced aviators whose skills could not be wasted. This new influx of hard-won expertise predictably found its way into the Reserve components of all the military services, and nowhere more directly than the Marine Corps Reserve.

The Reserves

Like all the U.S. military aviation services, Marine aviation has a shadow complement of men and equipment: its Reserve force. The Reserves are an important part of the U.S. military, more important, perhaps, than would initially appear. In reality, the active-duty forces of any nation are usually compact; it is the strength of the Reserves that usually determines a country's ability to fight a long-term war successfully. The regulars are the first line, the first to fight, and it is the Reserves, upon mobilization, who allow the fight to continue.

Marine Reserve aviation had its beginning soon after the formation of a regular Marine Reserve in 1916. Many of the first Marine aircrews to see combat in World War I were reservists, the first USMCR aviator being 2nd Lt. Allen H. Boynton. These men flew long anti-submarine patrols in the Azores, as well as the more publicized supply and bombing missions over the lines in France. Indeed, the first Medal of Honor to be awarded to a Marine aviator went to a reservist, 2nd Lt. Ralph Talbot, whose exploits have been detailed in earlier pages.

Post-war demobilization allowed the deactivation of much of the Reserves. By March 1919, only forty-one reservists were flying in the

Marines. Five Marine reservist pilots were recalled to active duty in 1928. These World War I veterans were tasked with forming an active Marine Air Reserve. The program allowed for the training of ab initio aviators who would be obligated for one-year tours of active duty, upon completion of flight training and receipt of their commissions.

In 1935 legislation was passed that created the grade of aviation cadet in the Marine Reserve, providing for the training and pay of such individuals. Among the future "greats" who were part of the cadet program were Gregory Boyington and Robert Galer, both of whom received the Medal of Honor for their service in World War II.

In 1938 the Naval Reserve Act increased the pay and benefits for Marine reservists as well, and by the end of that year, more than 700 Marine pilots, crewmen, and ground personnel were drilling at various sites around the country, Quantico and San Diego being the most active locations.

World War II brought the complete integration of the Reserves into the active forces; 75 percent of all servicemen were reservists. Six of the eleven Medals of Honor awarded to Marine aviators went to reservists. After the war, the Reserves were reactivated with a headquarters at NAS Glenview, Illinois. Bolstered by the large number of World War II veterans, Marine Reserve aviation could boast more than 6,300 officers and enlisted men, associated with forty-two squadrons, by 1949.

During the Korean War, there was a call-up of many U.S. Reserve units, with eleven Marine Air Reserve squadrons eventually mobilized. Relatively few actually saw combat duty; one that did was VMA-121. With the 1st Marine Division saddled with the brunt of the Korean action, other resources of the organization had to be called upon. The Organized Reserve was mobilized in July 1950. Most of the men in the Marine Reserves were combat ready. The infantry reservists were in combat by the fall of 1950, and the 1st MAW had received mobilized reservists by September. Six Marine fighter squadrons had been called up, as well as three ground-control intercept squadrons. The reservists were to be integrated into the regular squadrons already in combat or on the way.

The first Marine air reservists had just returned from their regular two-week annual stint of active duty. It involved a major exercise at Cherry Point, North Carolina. VMF-235, located in Boston, Massachusetts, flew its Corsairs to El Toro to join VMF-232 from NAS New York. VMF-143 reported to NAS New Orleans in early 1951, bringing its Corsairs to retrain many of its members who were going to the regular 1st MAW squadrons in Korea. Throughout the late 1950s and early 1960s, the Marines updated their aircraft as well as struggled to maintain flying proficiency. In July 1962, the 4th Marine Aircraft Wing was established at Glenview to replace the Marine Air Reserve Training Command. The 4th MAW consisted of eight MAGs and one support group. During Vietnam, no 4th MAW units were recalled, but the end of the war saw a great influx of seasoned combat veterans into all-Reserve components, and the Marines got their share.

For the most part, Marine Air Reserve squadrons flew fairly modern aircraft, the F-8 Crusader and A-4 Skyhawk providing much of the tactical jet equipment. Eventually, the Crusader was replaced by the Phantom. VMFA-321, based at the Naval Air Facility, Andrews Air Force Base, got the first F-4Bs in 1973.

VMFA-321 was a fairly representative Marine Air Reserve squadron, and a closer look at such a unit will give an idea of the heritage of Marine Reserve aviation. The Hell's Angels of VMFA-321 had their roots in a World War II Corsair squadron, which enjoyed a good record, shooting down thirty-nine Japanese aircraft during that conflict. In the immediate post-war years, VMF-321 flew several aircraft, especially the Grumman F8F Bearcat and Vought F4U Corsair. While the squadron remained based at NAS Anacostia during Korea, several squadron members were recalled and saw combat duty; a few did not return.

Capt. Warren York, a Washington, D.C., native, was killed in action on October 29, 1951, while serving with VMF-214. A highly decorated veteran, with two DFCs, York was flying a Corsair on a night mission when his aircraft was hit by flak and crashed. A Corsair flown by Capt. Herman L. Bushong Jr. was also hit by enemy flak late in 1952, but the recalled reservist managed to make it home with a two-foot hole in his F4U's tail.

[Top] Grumman F8F Bearcats of VMF-321 fly over the Jefferson Memorial and the Tidal Basin in Washington, D.C., in 1949. Fast and highly maneuverable, the stubby little Bearcats, the last Grumman prop fighters, were turned over to the French for use in Indochina.

[Bottom] Corsairs replaced Bearcats. VMF-321 was based at NAS Anacostia, just south of Washington. This F4U-4 carries the orange Reserve band on the rear fuselage.

In 1953 the squadron's Bearcats were replaced with F4U-4s because the French desperately needed more F8Fs in Indochina. When the 4th MAW was established, VMF-321 was assigned to MAG-42, and in 1959 it was reassigned to MAG-41. Until 1968, Navy and Marine Reserve pilots in Washington took turns flying the Crusaders at Andrews. This sharing accounts for the pictures of various Reserve aircraft carrying both Navy and Marine markings. But in 1970, the Naval Air Reserve was drastically reorganized, largely because of its poor showing during the 1968 *Pueblo* crisis. With two tactical carrier wings, the Navy also established two Reserve light-photographic squadrons, VFPs, which flew the RF-8G variant of the Crusader. Use of this specialized version released several F-8Ls to the Marines, and VMF-321's complement rose to nineteen aircraft. Painted with distinctive black dorsal areas and tails, spangled with white stars, the Crusaders, later F-8Ks, were an eye-catching lineup on the ramp. VMF-321 also changed its name to the "Black Barons."

By late 1962, the entire Marine Air Reserve had transitioned to tactical jets. VMF-321 at Anacostia had flown AD-5N Skyraiders, as VMA-321, through the late 1950s, but by 1962 had begun receiving FJ-4B Furies and had also moved just across the river in October 1961 to the new Naval Air Facility at Andrews Air Force Base. By January 1965, the Furies had begun

to be replaced by F-8B Crusaders, and the Vought aircraft was destined to serve the longest of any type with the Marine Air Reserves.

In December 1973, VMF-321 turned in its F-8Ks for F-4Bs and became VMFA-321. Transition to the Phantom, obviously a more complex airplane than its predecessor, went fairly smoothly. A big help was the large number of pilots, RIOs, and ground crewmen who had operated the type in Vietnam. One of the F-4Bs had a MiG-17 kill to its credit while it was serving as a Navy fighter with VF-51 in the *Coral Sea* (CV-43) in 1972. The F-4B gave way to the updated F-4N in 1976.

VMFA-321 not only served as the focal point for Marine Air Reservists from the Washington, D.C., area, but also provided various services for components of the regular services, especially in the air combat maneuvering (ACM) training role. Over the course of a year, detachments of VMFA-321 crews would take their aircraft all over the United States and Canada, or host a detachment from other units, even Air Force, for several days of intensive flying and training.

In the Reserves, each squadron member drills—works at the squadron spaces—for two days per month, usually more, and also participates in an annual two-week period of active duty with the squadron going out to a fleet base, such as MCAS Yuma, Arizona, where there are bombing and electronic ranges. The time each reservist devotes to his job and position within the squadron is important in the overall status and importance of the Marine Air Reserve.

Until the period following the 1990s, and certainly the terrorist attacks of 9/11, Reserve components were facing a budgetary crunch but in the first decade of the twenty-first century, with American military forces engaged in a multifront conflict across the globe, the military groups took on a new importance, and the Marine Air Reserves were soon engaged. The 4th MAW was changed, and squadrons and people deployed to the frontlines in Iraq and Afghanistan.

[Opposite] VMF-321 progressed to F-8K Crusaders after sharing F-8Bs with the Navy Air Reserves at NAF Washington. The F-8Ks were given black trim with white stars and the squadron called itself the "Black Barons," abandoning the original "Hell's Angels" sobriquet for a time. Note the extended in-flight refueling probe above the national marking.

[Top] VMFA-321 F-4s went through several color schemes. This 1979 photo of two F-4Ns (the "N" was an uprated version of the "B") shows vestiges of the 1976 markings: a blue vertical tail, white stars and lettering, and a red pitchfork. The squadron had returned to its earlier "Hell's Angels" nickname.

The Future

After the experience of Vietnam, the Marines, as in nearly every post-war period, found themselves in a battle for survival. Equipment, personnel, and responsibilities were all being scrutinized. Marine air was coming in for a major share of reorganization and orientation. The Marines still felt that having their own air arm was essential to support amphibious operations and provide helicopter airlift for supply and troop movement, as had been emphatically proven in Vietnam.

Fixed-wing aircraft were an essential part of the Marine air effort, giving direct support when and where needed. However, being officially part of the overall Navy establishment, the Corps was caught in the traditional squeeze of Navy budgetary planning. Fortunately, one program that was already fairly well established was the V/STOL AV-8A Harrier. Developed from a British design of the late 1950s, the Harrier took off and landed vertically, like a helicopter, but could then rotate its engine nozzles and fly like a normal fixed-wing jet. Britain's Hawker-Siddeley Company had created a unique military aircraft, and the Marines saw immediate applications of the Harrier for their special needs.

The plane could operate right behind frontlines or from the deck of an LPH, which usually accommodated only helicopters. The Harrier offered tactical jet speed and weapons delivery, yet the ability to operate right with the troops. It was a long-sought combination, and in 1968 Maj. Gen. Keith McCutcheon sent to England two experienced Marine aviators, Lt. Col. Bud Baker and Col. Thomas H. Miller, to gain first-hand experience with the Harrier. The two Marine pilots spent two and one-half weeks flying the British jet and returned to Washington determined to sell the Corps on the new airplane. Fortunately, they found ready ears in both McCutcheon and Gen. Leonard F. Chapman Jr., the Commandant. Appropriations were sought to purchase the Harrier from England "off the shelf," but Congress balked at buying foreign machinery unless a good deal of future production could take place in the United States.

Two key individuals who were difficult to recruit were Dr. Alain C. Enthoven, Assistant Secretary of Defense (Systems Analysis), and his assistant, Russell Murray II. Both men had a history, during their tenure under Secretary of Defense Robert S. McNamara, of denying the Marines were having problems, either in personnel or equipment procurement. In 1967 it had been extremely difficult to convince Dr. Enthoven that the pilot shortage was real. He eventually was won over after much discussion, education, and haggling by both Chapman and McCutcheon.

However, Russ Murray developed into something of an "enemy" of the Marines in the aviation community, and especially where the Harrier was concerned. For some reason, he challenged the Corps' decision to buy the British aircraft, saying the plane would not be cost effective, a watchword in military spending. He convinced his boss, Dr. Enthoven, to oppose the purchase, even though leading aeronautical engineers gave the Harrier high marks, favoring its acquisition by the Marines.

Senator Stuart Symington of Missouri was also opposed to the purchase, because the funds to buy the British planes would have to come from money set aside to purchase seventeen new F-4s. McDonnell

Douglas, the manufacturer of the Phantom was, of course, based in St. Louis; Symington's son was a congressman from St. Louis. It was getting very sticky; $58 million was a lot of money to take out of American pockets and give to a foreign, albeit friendly, nation. Fortunately, Colonel Miller had visited McDonnell and discussed the situation with the McDonnell family, with whom he enjoyed a great rapport. The McDonnells agreed to support the foreign purchase because they believed it would be a shot in the arm for American V/STOL hopes and would provide the Marines with a unique aircraft. Of course, McDonnell would also be involved in future manufacturing rights. Miller suggested that the irate senator from Missouri place a call to McDonnell. No more complaints were heard about buying British over American goods.

A licensing agreement was subsequently worked out between McDonnell Douglas (McDonnell had merged with Douglas in 1967) and Hawker-Siddeley, but by 1971 the Congress had reversed itself and refused to fund further money for moving production of the Harrier to America. Thus, the British filled the entire order of 110 aircraft by 1976, including 102 single-seat AV-8As and eight TAV-8A two-seat trainers.

The mark the Marines obtained was comparable to the GR Mk 3, redesignated AV-8A in U.S. service. Minor modifications were made, including avionics and a different ejection seat. The first aircraft were delivered in February 1971, while the first Harrier squadrons were formed soon afterward, VMA-513 in April and VMA-542 in December 1972. VMA-231 followed in October 1973 and the training squadron VMAT-203 in 1975.

The first AV-8As actually went to the Naval Air Test Center at NAS Patuxent River in southern Maryland for initial service trials, including compatibility tests aboard LPHs and LPDs. January 1972 saw the first deployment of the Marine Harriers as VMA-513 embarked in the USS

Two AV-8A pilots from VMA-231 discuss their flight as they walk across the *FDR's* flight deck in November 1976. (PH3 Greg Maas)

Guam (LPH-9) for the North Atlantic. VMA-231 and VMA-542 traveled to Japan in 1976 and 1977, as well as serving aboard the carrier USS *Franklin D. Roosevelt* (CV-42) during the same period, on various Mediterranean cruises.

But problems with the V/STOL program toward the end of the 1970s, plus the development program surrounding the so-called Super Harrier, the AV-8B, caused concern. Aside from what some considered an inordinate number of crashes, it was found that the AV-8A could not carry a satisfactory payload; either more power or greater lift was needed. The AV-8A was a demanding aircraft. It incorporated a powerful engine in a light-weight airframe, and it flew through a wide spectrum of flight regimes, which demanded a high degree of motor skills and reflexes from its pilots. With cutbacks in flight time, leave, or other responsibilities, Harrier pilots had a greater need to stay current than, say, their A-4 counterparts.

A proposed AV-16A design was abandoned because of the development costs for a new airframe and Rolls-Royce engine. McDonnell Douglas redesigned the aircraft, incorporating a larger wing and various lift improvement devices. The Pegasus 11 turbofan of the A remained. The new aircraft's payload and radius were doubled and the Harrier became a true V/STOL airplane. In fact, the AV-8B carried one of the heaviest payloads in modern tactical jet aviation.

When President Jimmy Carter took office in January 1977, twenty-eight AV-8As had crashed since the introduction of the type, and although this number was not as catastrophic as would appear at first glance, given the total number of flight hours achieved, criticism of the entire V/STOL program was hot and heavy. Russ Murray led a group opposed to the AV-8B and succeeded in convincing Secretary of Defense Harold Brown to delete the AV-8B from the FY 79 defense budget. In a hard-hitting paper, Murray called the AV-8B "a small, single-engine, subsonic aircraft of British lineage, developed as an improvement over the Marines' current AV-8A. The Harrier is a relatively undistinguished aircraft in all respects save one—its unique ability to use very short runways . . . at some sacrifice in range and payload."[1] Murray claimed that the forthcoming F/A-18 would be a much better acquisition than the AV-8B, and his group pointed to the B's high cost and relative weakness in the field of air-to-air combat. They downplayed, however, the type's obvious advantages in tactical proximity to the battlefield.

The Marines fought alone. The Navy, occupied with its floundering F-14 program, did not lend any support, and the Air Force and Army chose not to show much concern, either. Besides, the Air Force was having enough problems keeping its own B-1 program afloat. Chief champion was, of course, now–Lieutenant General Miller, now D/CS (Air). He talked to anyone and everyone who would listen, and eventually assembled a group of influential supporters at the Congressional level, as well as Commandant Gen. Louis H. Wilson. Through Miller's efforts and those of his allies, funding for the AV-8B through FY 81 survived.

The YAV-8B first flew in 1978, after some budgetary problems, and the first pre-production prototypes flew in November 1981. There were currently plans for over 300 AV-8Bs to be produced, though not before 1984.

The Marine use of the British aircraft fostered public interest; certainly the plane's unique flight characteristics were reason enough for attention. (Use of British aircraft, though rare, was not unheard of. During World War II, Army Air Force units reaching Europe flew Spitfires, Mosquitos, and even Beaufighters, until U.S.-manufactured equipment arrived in strength.) The Harrier, while primarily employed as a ground-attack aircraft, was also well equipped for air-to-air combat. Armed with Sidewinders and cannon, and having an unusual ability to "turn square corners," through VIFFing (vectoring in forward flight), the rapid control of the moveable engine nozzles to quickly decelerate and almost stop in midair, the Harrier boasted a true air-superiority potential. This potential was finally realized in the 1982 Falklands war between Britain and Argentina, when British Harriers destroyed twenty Argentine aircraft with guns and missiles without the loss of a single Harrier in aerial combat.

The introduction of the AV-8A brought new demands for the Marine aviators selected to fly it. They had to learn new terminology and skills before even getting into the aircraft. Proponents of the plane saw limitless possibilities in the roles of close air support and air combat. All was not rosy, however. The AV-8A's lifting power, particularly with any useful combat load, was not all it could be, and steps were taken to improve it. These steps resulted in the AV-8C, which incorporated lift improvement devices and additional avionics. The "Charlie" model filled the performance gap until the AV-8B entered service.

The Skyhawk Continues Serving

No tactical jet aircraft had come to mean as much to the Marines as the tough, capable little A-4 Skyhawk. There was a certain empathy between the A-4 and the Corps. Indeed, they were quite similar in background and experience: small, but ideally suited to their combat roles and endowed with a durability born of long service. In the post-Vietnam period, the Marines were loath to retire the A-4, although the number of fleet squadrons

operating the aircraft was reduced to five—VMA-211, -214, -223, -311, and -331. Although the older Echo and Foxtrot models were still retained, a new development soon began to appear in strength.

The Marines had considered obtaining the Vought A-7 Corsair in the late 1960s to replace the Skyhawk, but in the final analysis, it was decided that the Corsair was too sophisticated for the close-air-support mission flown by Marine aviators and that funds would be better used to further develop the A-4.

Designated A-4M, the new Skyhawk flew in April 1970. It incorporated a larger engine and cockpit canopy, nose-mounted bombing radar, and other internal refinements. VMA-324 received the first A-4Ms in 1971; 158 were finally produced. On February 27, 1979, the Skyhawk reproduction line finally closed with the delivery of the 2,960th aircraft to VMA-331, at MCAS Cherry Point, North Carolina.

A new variant entered service in 1979 with the introduction of the OA-4M, a reconfigured TA-4F, to be used as FACs by headquarters squadrons. The OA-4M incorporated a laser spot tracker, a device that "sees" a target illuminated by a laser beam pin-pointed by a ground facility. This capability allowed the FAC to see his target more readily. Eventually, however, the Skyhawk also retired from both the Navy and Marine Corps.

[Top Left] The OA-4M was the last version of the Skyhawk to see Marine service. Developed from the TA-4F, this variant carried a laser spot tracker below the nose and was briefly used as a FAC aircraft. (Harry Gann)

[Bottom Left] An A-4M of VMA-223 just before the Bulldogs transitioned to the AV-8B Harrier II at MCAS Cherry Point, June 1985. The "Mike" was the last U.S. model of the Skyhawk and had a relatively short career, going to the Reserves for an equally brief time before the valiant little Scooter was eventually retired from service altogether. (Peter B. Mersky)

[Right] The Bell UH-1N was a twin-engine development of the earlier UH-1E, which had one power plant. Here, a UH-1N flies off Okinawa in 1980. (Fred Lash)

Helicopter Developments

The Marine Corps continued operating the same four basic helicopters it used in Southeast Asia: UH-1, AH-1, CH-46, and CH-53. Of course, development of these versatile helicopters continued as well. The single-engine UH-1E was given an additional engine and redesignated UH-1N. The first UH-1Ns were delivered to the Marines at New River in North Carolina on April 7, 1971. Some actually flew in the last frantic stages of the Vietnam War.

The AH-1 had gone from the single-engine, Army-funded "G" to the twin-engine "J" built expressly for the Marines. A postwar development was the AH-1T, fifty-seven of which replaced Marine AH-1Gs. The "T" carries TOW (tube-launched, optically guided, wire-controlled) anti-tank missiles manufactured by Hughes, as well as Sidewinder missiles for an air-to-air capability against Soviet gunship helicopters.

The A/D versions of the veteran CH-46 continued to serve the medium-helicopter community. A new development was the Echo, which incorporated more powerful engines, a more effectively armored interior, engine exhaust suppressors to decrease vulnerability to heat-seeking missiles, and other internal refinements. CH-46Es arrived in Fleet Marine Force (FMF) units in October 1977. Other developments for the Sea Knight included a new

infrared (IR) paint scheme, which reduced sun reflections and thereby IR signatures, various radar warning receivers and jammers, and modified cockpit lighting for better night-time operations. The metal rotor blades were also replaced by those of fiberglass, which promised longer life. With all these improvements, the CH-46 was certain to serve past the turn of the century.

The last member of the Vietnam quartet of helicopters was the Sikorsky CH-53 Sea Stallion, the largest production helicopter in the free world. Ever in need of a versatile heavy-lift helicopter, the Marines had made the new CH-53E their best bet in the 1980s. Based on the Delta, the Echo still incorporated many changes, the most advantageous of which was the addition of a third engine. With its name changed to Super Stallion, it offered the capability of lifting any tactical aircraft used by the Corps, including another CH-53E. This "retriever" capability was the CH-53A/D's forte in Vietnam and remained a very desirable asset.

Development of the Echo began as early as 1967 and preliminary studies were concluded in early 1972. The Department of Defense had authorized

[Top] The Marines are responsible for maintaining the helicopters of the presidential flight. Here, a VH-3A flies past the Washington Monument. When the president is aboard one of these helos, its call sign is "Marine One."

[Bottom] A brand-new CH-53E flies over the water during a test flight. The aircraft's seven-blade main rotor is evident. The Super Stallion is powered by three engines, one more than the earlier aircraft's two.

further development and the first prototypes flew on March 1, 1974. On August 10th, a YCH-53E lifted an external load of 17.8 tons into a hover, for a total gross weight of 71,700 pounds, the heaviest load ever lifted by a helicopter in the free world. Production problems at the Sikorsky plant, however, prevented the introduction date of May 1980 from being met. But HMH-464 was established at MCAS(H) New River in March 1981 to receive fifteen new Echos in June. A second squadron, HMH-465, received its first aircraft in February 1982 at MCAS(H) Tustin, near El Toro.

Fixed-Wing Fighters

Two types of Marine Phantoms: the F-4N (left) serving with VMFA-323 and the RF-4B of VMFP-3. (Harry Gann)

Perhaps no area of Marine aviation generated so much concern, developmental and administrative, as that of a tactical jet fighter to replace the F-4 Phantom. The F-4 reached Marine squadrons in 1962/63, served throughout Vietnam and into the 1980s. But a replacement was necessary. From an air-superiority standpoint, the Grumman F-14A Tomcat seemed a likely candidate. This ultra-sophisticated weapons system first flew in 1970 and began reaching Navy fleet squadrons in 1973.

The Marines, at one point, in the person of then–Brig. Gen. Philip D. Shutler, D/CS(Air), tried to strike a deal with the Navy for the purchase of Harriers and Tomcats. Shutler believed the Navy and Marines should operate the same aircraft, either on carriers or from shore bases. Why, argued Shutler, could not the Marines fly Harriers from land bases, in advance of the main forces, while the Navy operated the AV-8s from carriers. (The AV-8A had nearly the same attack capability as the F/A-18; indeed, their ranges were nearly equal.) With wing folding, nearly twice as many Harriers could be accommodated on current ships as could A-7s, the standard Navy light attack bomber. It was an interesting concept, but given the rivalry that has always existed between Navy and Marine air, it was stillborn.

The F-14, with its huge, highly capable radar, could also serve as an advanced early-warning system, able to defend itself, something which the E-2s and Air Force E-3 AWACS could not do. If there were a real hot

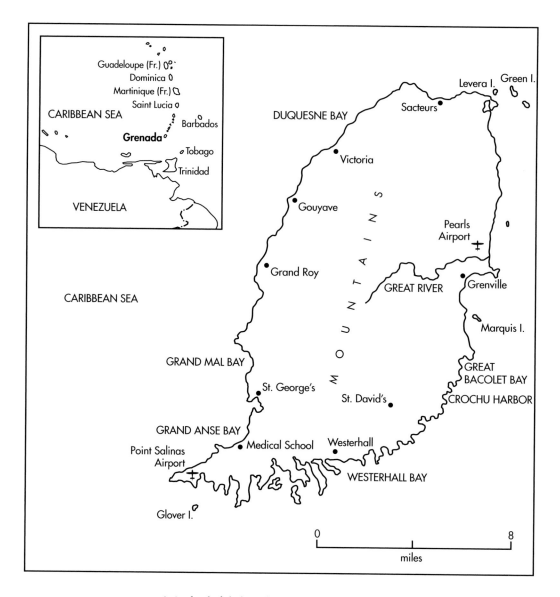

war, it is doubtful that the expensive AWACS aircraft would be sent right into the high-threat areas. The risk of their being shot down, by missile or interceptor, would make such use prohibitive. The Tomcat, however, with Phoenix missiles and integral cannon, would not be at a disadvantage.

Initially, the Marines had asked the Secretary of the Navy, John Warner, himself a former Marine, for a number of F-14s. Discussions and counterproposals naturally followed. The F-14 was too expensive, too difficult to maintain in the rough field conditions in which the Marines usually found themselves. Too many squadron personnel would be needed just to maintain the weapons systems, let alone the aircraft itself. The money would be better spent on the F-4, a proven aircraft, while the F/A-18 was being developed. However, as money became scarce and the per-unit cost of the F-14 seemed to be running away, the decision was made to take nearly $600 million earmarked for Phantoms and put it toward F-14s for the Marines.

The first F-14 squadron was to be VMFA-122 at Beaufort, South Carolina, with three other units to follow. It was somewhat of a strong-arm method, as the Commandant was forced to purchase the Tomcats, nearly seventy in all. However, to those who had originally wanted the Grumman fighter, it was a blessing to be embraced enthusiastically. But when James R. Schlesinger became Secretary of Defense, he decided to get the Marines out of the F-14 controversy. On July 2, 1975, Gen. Louis H. Wilson announced that the twelve VMFA F-4-equipped squadrons would continue to operate the Phantom until the F/A-18 became available.

The F/A-18 Hornet

The Marines knew what they needed: a moderately fast, capable yet simple aircraft, with room for development, but without the overpowering avionics and systems that distort the plane's mission, namely to operate in a fast-paced, hazardous environment in defense of the ground troops. The ability to dogfight at 30,000 feet would be a secondary advantage.

The twin-engine, twin-tailed Northrop-designed YF-17 Cobra, the losing competitor to the General Dynamics F-16 in the Air Force's Air Combat Fighter (ACF) runoff, now became the front-runner for the Navy/Marine new fighter/attack aircraft, the VFAX. Having lost a major Air Force and NATO competition for the next-generation light fighter, the YF-17 was quickly developed, with McDonnell Douglas's help, into the F/A-18 Hornet. This aircraft was to have both superb light-attack and air-combat capabilities, thereby eliminating both the F-4 and A-7 from the Navy's inventory, as well as the F-4 and A-4 from the Marines' lineup.

Opponents of the Harrier, among them Russ Murray, quickly pointed to the F/A-18 as the only choice for the Corps against the AV-8B. Of course, the Hornet had its own share of detractors, including the Secretary of the Navy, John Lehman, who demanded that McDonnell Douglas reduce the cost of the aircraft or face cancellation of the production contract. But the Hornet did not deserve of a lot of the "bad press" it received. VMFA-314 took official charge of its Hornets in January 1983, while VMFA-323 and VMFA-531 prepared for deployment by July 1983. Initial reports indicated widespread acceptance of the Hornet by Navy and Marine personnel. Its serviceability and combat capability gave it the highest marks of any new aircraft in the past twenty years.

[Opposite]
Map 7. Grenada, 1983.

[Bottom] Subject of much controversy, the McDonnell Douglas (now Boeing) F/A-18 Hornet was developed from the Northrop-designed YF-17A. Here is an F/A-18A of VMFA-314, the first Marine squadron to transition to the Hornet. (McDonnell Douglas)

[Top] An OV-10D aboard USS *Okinawa* (LPH-3). The OV-10D carried night sensors and a 20-mm gun turret.

[Second from top] The Douglas C-117, a super C-47/R4D, flew with the Marines in Japan until the last three were retired in June 1982. Note the squared tail of the C-117. (Hideki Nagakubo)

[Third from top] The McDonnell Douglas C-9B served the Marines as a long-range transport.

[Bottom] Marines supply the transport for the Navy's Blue Angels flight demonstration squadron. Their KC-130 follows the team's F/A-18 Hornets, transporting ground crews and maintenance equipment. (Peter B. Mersky)

The Hornet has a self-starting capability, because of its auxiliary power unit (APU), which released the aircraft from dependence on a massive ground-support facility. It can take off, depending on the load, from a 2,600-foot roll, with a 600–900-foot maximum performance takeoff also within its capability.

An engine change was also made much easier by the aircraft mounted accessory drive (AMAD), which shortens the disconnect/connect time for most of the engine accessories, an area that is a tedious and time-consuming part of mounting a new power plant. Marine Hornets also included forward-looking infrared radar (FLIR) and a laser designator (LSD), giving the Marines their first night and marginal-weather capability in a fighter/attack airplane. The integral cannon is palletized for ease of maintenance and loading.

Combat in the 1980s

In August 1982, Marine air was part of the task force of ships and planes that covered the landing of 800 Marines at Beirut, Lebanon, a replay of such an occasion in 1958. Throughout the tense months that followed, Marine

A Marine UH-1N flies over Beirut International Airport during a patrol for the multinational peacekeeping force in September 1983.

[Top] Marines board a CH-46 for the flight back to their ships as the 22nd Marine Amphibious Unit leaves Lebanon in February 1984. (PHC Chet King)

[Bottom] A CH-53 operating from the USS *Guadalcanal* (LPH-7) off the coast of Lebanon in May 1983.

helicopters stood by aboard the ships, ready to support the men ashore, as well as evacuate civilians and embassy personnel. The catastrophic bombing of the Marine barracks in late October 1983, with the loss of 241 Marines and Navy personnel, raised tension to the highest level of the deployment.

However, Marine aviators had been more actively engaged in the Caribbean. Supporting the U.S.-led invasion of the tiny island of Grenada, Marine helicopters flew their first combat missions since the *Mayaguez* rescue mission eight years before. Only one Marine aviation squadron was involved, HMM-261, a composite squadron from MCAS New River, North Carolina. Embarked in USS *Guam* (LPH-9), HMM-261 used CH-46E Sea Knights, CH-53D Sea Stallions, and UH-1N Hueys to move men and weapons into and out of the battle zones during the operation, code-named Urgent Fury. Four AH-1T Sea Cobras were also assigned to HMM-261 for the invasion.

Action was sporadic, but occasionally intense, especially during the first hours of the invasion. The four Sea Cobras from HMM-261 were heavily

[Top] A Marine AH-1T of HMM-261 prepares to launch from USS *Guam* on the first day of Operation Urgent Fury, the invasion of Grenada in October 1983. (PH1 Dave Wojeik)

[Bottom] An AH-1T heads toward the beach during the invasion of Grenada. The helicopter carries a three-barreled 20-mm cannon in the nose turret, and TOW anti-tank missiles and 2.75 unguided rockets in pods on the stub wings.

engaged covering the initial assaults on October 25. One AH-1T was hit by ground fire in the mid-afternoon. Capt. Tim Howard crash-landed the Cobra well within sight of the Cuban defenders. Howard had his right forearm severed by the intense fire, and his right leg badly wounded. He barely managed to bring the helo down. As the aircraft landed, it began to burn, and Howard yelled, trying to rouse his co-pilot/gunner Capt. Jeb Seagle, knocked unconscious by the initial defensive fire.

Seagle regained consciousness, and both men jumped from their burning plane amid a hail of fire from the Cuban positions only forty yards away. Pinned down, the two Marine aviators were trapped. Howard yelled for Seagle to save himself, but Seagle said he would try to run for help. He had barely covered forty yards before Cuban machine-gun fire killed him.

A second Sea Cobra, orbiting the scene tried to suppress the Cuban fire while directing a rescue helo toward Howard. This Cobra, too, was hit, and it crashed into St. George's Harbor, killing both pilots, Capt. John P. Giguere and 1st Lt. Jeffrey R. Scharver.

Finally, a CH-46 landed near Howard and its crew chief, GySgt. Kelly Neidigh, carried the injured Marine to safety under enemy fire. Captain Howard recovered and remained in the Corps, despite the loss of his right arm. Captain Seagle was awarded a posthumous Navy Cross and Air Medal. Captain Howard received the Silver Star and Distinguished Flying Cross.

[Opposite] A CH-53 of HMM-261 lifts off after depositing Marines near Pearls Airport during the invasion of Grenada.

[Right] A CH-46 departs after landing Marines in a field during the Grenada operation.

[Top] A pilot from VMFA-323 makes last-minute adjustments to his flight gear before manning his F/A-18A at NAS Norfolk in August 1985. (Peter B. Mersky)

[Bottom] The scene on the flight deck of USS *America* (CV-66) just after midnight on April 15, 1986. An EA-6B of VMAQ-2 is ready for launch from the no. 4 waist catapult. The Marine Prowlers provided ECM services for Air Force and Navy strike aircraft during attacks on the Libyan cities Tripoli and Benghazi.

Working with Army helicopters, and supported by fixed-wing aircraft of CVW-6 from the carrier USS *Independence* (CV-62) detoured from a Mediterranean deployment, the Marine helicopters contributed to the success of Operation Urgent Fury, which resulted in the denial of Grenada to Soviet and Communist Cuban forces, and the rescue of nearly 1,000 U.S. citizens, including the medical students at St. George's University.

The continuing conflict in the eastern Mediterranean increased U.S. Navy carrier presence, and along with those carriers, U.S. Marines made the first Atlantic deployment in the F/A-18A. Learning their new aircraft was a full-time job for the Marines in the carrier. The Hornet's futuristic avionics and capabilities combined tremendous potential with problems concerning a pilot's ability to keep up with the aircraft. This situation was not limited to the Navy and Marines and was an unwelcome by-product of the great advances in aircraft design and avionics of the late 1970s and early 1980s.

Nevertheless, by the time *Coral Sea* entered the Med, her air wing was ready, just in time. Something had to be done to control the terrorists, who seemed to be getting aid and instructions from the Libyan dictator, Colonel

An EA-6B Prowler of VMAQ-2 flies off the Libyan coast in April 1986. These ECM aircraft provided coverage for the Navy and Air Force strikes against Libyan targets in March and April of that year. (Dave Parsons)

Moamer al-Khaddhafi. Threats by Libya, whose leader drew a so-called "line of death" across the Gulf of Sidra, could not be long ignored.

Accordingly, on March 24, 1986, after Libyan ground forces fired a spread of Soviet-supplied SA-5 SAMs at Navy aircraft, the U.S. carriers present—*Saratoga, America,* and *Coral Sea*—launched selective strikes during a two-day period against the SAM sites and Libyan patrol boats, which approached too close to the task force. Navy and Marine F/A-18s flew combat air patrols with the F-14s of the *Saratoga* and *America.*

Three weeks later, on the night of April 14th, aircraft from the *America* and *Coral Sea* launched strikes against the Libyan city of Benghazi, while Air Force F-111s attacked Tripoli. Alongside the Air Force strike, Navy and Marine F/A-18s fired HARM missiles, against anti-aircraft sites, standing off from the main attack. Thus, the Hornet had flown its first combat missions. More Hornets with Navy A-7s hit additional targets an hour later. EA-6Bs of VMAQ-2 aboard *America* also provided valuable ECM services for both the Air Force and Navy strikes.

14 Fighting Terrorism in the 1980s

FOR THE LAST HALF OF THE 1980s, American foreign policy focused on the volatile Middle East and Southwest Asia. After having left Lebanon in 1984, the United States became concerned with the on-going bloody war between Iran and Iraq, which began in September 1980. Though generally kept ashore in the vast desert between the two countries, the fighting sometimes spilled out to the adjacent Indian Ocean and Persian Gulf. ("Persia" is an ancient name for Iran, and political sensitivities sometimes require the name to be changed to the more generic "Arabian Gulf." Iranians do not consider themselves Arabs.)

Since a great deal of the world's oil supply flowed in and out of this vital region, the free conduct of the tanker fleets was of great concern to the United States. Coupled with a rising rate of terrorism, which was sponsored by both rogue states, the Iran-Iraq conflict took on major international importance.

Iran began threatening tankers (one source lists 111 attacks), mining approaches to the Gulf, and harassing water traffic. On March 7, 1987, the United States agreed to reflag Kuwaiti tankers as American ships and thus provide escort and protection in the dangerous tanker channels. On May 17, the frigate USS *Stark* (FFG-31) was hit by two Exocet anti-shipping missiles fired by an Iraqi Mirage F.1 eighty miles northeast of Bahrain. Thirty-seven sailors were killed. There were many repercussions to the tragedy, several of which focused on the ship's lack of preparedness to meet the threat. But questions about the Iraqi pilot's true intentions—and those of his government—persisted after the official investigation. Four years later, this incident was recalled by some as a disregarded warning and perhaps an opening shot of the Persian Gulf War.

In late July, Operation Earnest Will, the escort of reflagged tankers, began. Although protected by American task forces, the tankers still encountered threats in the form of mines, and several ships were damaged by these underwater weapons. In September Army helicopters attached to Navy ships discovered a small Iranian ship laying mines and attacked it with rockets and machine-gun fire. The situation continued to escalate, and on October 19, 1987, the U.S. task force attacked two Iranian oil platforms that were being used as communication centers. But even with this confrontation, the Iranians continued their operations. On December 12, a Cypriot-flagged tanker was sunk by Iranian speedboats.

The final straw came when USS *Samuel B. Roberts* (FFG-58) struck a mine on April 14, 1988. No one was killed, and the badly damaged ship was towed to Dubai for repairs and eventually returned to service. Operation Praying Mantis was the answer to this accumulation of terrorist attacks, and on April 18, Navy and Marine units fought what was termed the largest purely naval action by American forces since World War II. A combination of naval gunfire and rockets from Marine Corps AH-1T gunships of HMLA-167 struck armed Iranian oil platforms in strategic positions in the Gulf. A Cobra and its crew were lost, although the reason was never clear. A month later, the bodies of Capt. Stephen C. Leslie and Capt. Kenneth W. Hill were recovered. Both pilots received posthumous Purple Hearts and Distinguished Flying Crosses.

The Iranians tried to respond, sending several Boghammar speedboats and an F-4 Phantom toward the American task force. Aircraft from the nuclear carrier USS *Enterprise* quickly attacked the speedboats and the Iranian frigate *Sahand*. Another Iranian frigate, the *Sabalan*, was also badly damaged and dead in the water. The delay in authorizing a coup de grâce, however, allowed Iranian units to rescue the *Sabalan* and tow her to the port of Bandar Abbas. By December Operation Earnest Will was concluded. Some 270 merchant ships had been escorted through the Gulf.

While events around the world took center stage, other milestones in Marine Corps aviation included the deaths of Lt. Gen. Christian F. Schilt on January 13, 1987, and of Pappy Boyington on January 11, 1988. Schilt had received the Medal of Honor for action in Nicaragua in 1927 and had risen to three-star rank by the time he retired in 1957. He was ninety-one. Boyington was seventy-five when he died of cancer. He had also received the Medal of Honor for his record as an F4U Corsair ace in the Pacific during World War II.

In 1987 Marine aviation celebrated, albeit somewhat quietly, its seventy-fifth anniversary, and on January 5, 1987, VMA-331 began the first extended deployment with the AV-8B Harrier II, sailing in USS *Belleau Wood* (LHA-3) to the Pacific. The Harrier II was already involved in a lengthy development program, and the first night-attack AV-8B made its first flight at St. Louis on June 26, 1987.

VMA-211 celebrated a thirty-year anniversary of flying the A-4 on September 9, 1987, and on October 1, VMFAT-101, the Marine's fleet training squadron for F-4s, officially transitioned to the F/A-18 Hornet. The Phantom was in the waning days of its great career with the naval service. The Navy had long ago relegated the big fighter to reserve squadrons, fleet defense being taken over by Grumman's F-14. Light-attack and strike duties were the responsibility of A-7E squadrons, but by 1984 an increasing number of squadrons were equipped with the Hornet. The FMFPAC squadron VMFA-235 had retired the last F-4s in October 1989, moving to the Hornet and leaving only VMFP-3 flying RF-4Bs in the fleet.

"P-3," as it was affectionately called, had taken over tactical reconnaissance duties on some carriers when the Navy retired the venerable RF-8G photo-Crusader from the fleet in 1982. The long-nosed photo-Phantoms cruised aboard *Midway* and *Coral Sea*. However, by the late 1980s, even

[Top] Ordnancemen load an AIM-9 Sidewinder onto the starboard weapons pylon of an AH-1W aboard USS *Guadalcanal* during operations in the Persian Gulf, August 1987. The uncertainty of operating close to Iran gave rise to the necessity of carrying air-to-air weapons for possible use against Iranian fighters. (PH3 Cleveland)

[Opposite] Armed with Sidewinders, this AH-1W of HLA-169 flies up the starboard side of USS *Okinawa* (LPH-3) in the Persian Gulf in 1987. (Carl. D. Siegmund)

these long-serving variants of McDonnell's masterpiece were looking at the end of the road. Only the reserve squadrons, VMFA-112 at Dallas, and VMFA-321 at NAF Washington, D.C., flew the F-4. And finally, even the Reserves retired their last Phantoms in January 1992.

There were many changes afoot as the 1980s gave way to the 1990s. Old aircraft that had served long and well continued giving way to new types, and with drastic funding reductions and drawdowns, the entire U.S. military service faced incredible face-lifts in both the number of squadrons and also the number of bases that hosted them.

A major organizational change at the Marine Corps squadron level occurred in 1988, when the Headquarters and Maintenance Squadrons (H&MSs—usually pronounced "Hams") became Marine Aviation Logistics Squadrons (MALSs). The MALSs gained a more sharply defined mission and new responsibilities. Concerned that the H&MSs had developed a "garrison mindset," which could only support a specific aircraft (e.g., H&MS-31 could only service MAG-31's F/A-18 Hornets), HQMC redesigned the concept as a contingency support package. MALSs could now deploy with their MAGs, allowing the group to bring their "house" with them.

Perhaps the most important changes involved a helicopter and the tactical-jet side of Marine aviation. The Boeing Vertol CH-46 Sea Knight had been the true medium-lift workhorse of the Navy and Marine Corps since its introduction in June 1964, when HMM-265 took delivery of the first CH-46As. The first Sea Knights arrived in Vietnam with HMM-164 in March 1966, and the helicopter served throughout the war.

Inevitable development and changes in capability accompanied the twin-rotor Sea Knight, often called "Phrog." By 1982 all Marine Corps squadrons were flying the CH-46E, while the Navy continued operating several variants. Upgrades and close inspection of existing aircraft could not keep the Sea Knight from aging, however, and as the mid-1990s approached, the need for a replacement for the faithful Phrog became more immediate with every deployment.

On May 13, 1990, the Marine Corps grounded its CH-46 fleet. The Navy followed on July 3. A lot of interest, therefore, was shown toward a revolutionary aircraft from Bell, the V-22 Osprey, which offered the combination of vertical takeoff and landing capabilities, with the greater speed of the traditional fixed-wing aircraft. The first V-22 was rolled out at the Bell facility in Arlington, Texas, on May 23, 1988, with the first flight taking place on March 19, 1989.

Built largely with composite materials and using fiberglass rotor blades, the boxy V-22 soon attracted its share of proponents and detractors. The various military services lined up for a closer look, each seeing the V-22 as the next generation of its own particular mission aircraft. For the Marine Corps, the need was straightforward: a replacement for the Sea Knight. But, even as the V-22 made its first flights, Congress began slashing the defense budget, including continued funding of the Osprey's development. On September 4, 1989, the V-22 made its first flight in the traditional aircraft configuration.

As the helicopter question plagued the Marines, the Corps was also trying to modernize its fixed-wing fleet. Thus, the A-6E Intruder was scheduled for retirement in the early 1990s, with a gradual, but steady phase-out of the few remaining Marine A-6 squadrons.

The Intruder's replacement was already well established. On February 14, 1989, VMFA-225 had received the first F/A-18Ds, a two-seater variant of the Hornet. Previously, the F/A-18B had been a two-seat trainer version for transition training. But the F/A-18D retained much of the single-seater's weapons capabilities, and in fact, included several avionics upgrades, which gave the new Hornet the ability to act as FAC as well as deliver its own ordnance. The Delta thus boasted a light- to medium-attack ability that promised a replacement for the Intruder.

The new F/A-18D squadrons were redesignated VMFA(AW)s and also provided a place for the cadre of Marine naval flight officers (NFOs), who had seen their career paths disappear with the demise of the F-4 and A-6. Using the Air Force term "weapons system officer"—or WSO (pronounced "Wizzo")—the Hornet backseater became an integral part of the mission. Other Delta squadrons stood up quickly. VMFA(AW)-121 got its aircraft in May 1990. VMFA(AW)-242 soon followed. The new Hornet would soon get to test itself and its new mission in combat.

The Marines also began their long farewell to another veteran aircraft, the Douglas A-4 Skyhawk. On February 27, 1990, VMA-211 sent its last A-4Ms to MAG-42 of the 4th MAW, the Marine Corps Air Reserve. The little jet bomber flew with Reserve squadrons in Massachusetts, Tennessee, and California, but even these second-line units' time was growing short. By 1992 only one of the former Reserve A-4s had survived to transition to F/A-18s. There were more reorganizations and decommissionings to come, but first, the Marines had to fight alongside an international coalition in a major unpredicted war in the desert of Southwest Asia.

15 Taking the Measure of Saddam

THERE HAD BEEN VERY LITTLE public indications of the action to come. U.S. intelligence officers had been watching, and a few even tried raising warning flags, but the Iraqi invasion of Kuwait on August 2, 1990, caught the world largely by surprise. America's military had been piecing together the results of its operation in Panama in December 1989. Operation Just Cause had deposed strongman Manuel Noriega, whose resume included conflicting, almost double-agent activities such as working as an operative for the CIA while selling drugs.

The two-week action rid Panama of the dictator, and several components of the American military took part. The Marine Corps sent 700 troops, losing one in action. The invasion of Kuwait presaged something infinitely bigger, however. Iraq had long maintained that Kuwait was its nineteenth province and constantly threatened its smaller neighbor to the east.

On August 3, President George H. W. Bush sent the USS *Eisenhower* (CVN-69) and USS *Independence* battle groups into the Red Sea and the Indian Ocean. As the two forces rushed to the Persian Gulf, diplomatic messages and charges flew. Iraq then threatened to invade Saudi Arabia. Its million-man army would have made short work of the smaller army of the wealthy sheikdom.

The following weeks brought several escalations, including the taking of hostages by Iraq, closing of embassies, military buildups, economic sanctions, threats, and counterthreats. The entire Southwest Asia region was boiling over. President Bush, determined not only to free Kuwait but also to keep its oil and that of the Arabian Peninsula out of Iraqi hands, began hammering together a surprising coalition of improbable allies, not the least of which were several Arab states that had seldom worked together and had often made war on each other. The Egyptians and Syrians cautiously joined the alliance, as did several European and Asian nations that relied on oil shipments from Iraq.

Operation Desert Shield became the most massive buildup of military men and materiel since World War II, all aimed at facing down one apparently deranged, or dangerously wily, dictator. While Desert Shield gathered steam, the Marines answered another call. The West African nation of Liberia had

In August 1990, Marines guard supplies that a CH-46E of HMM-261 has just delivered to the U.S. embassy in Monrovia, Liberia. A few days later, these Marines and helicopters evacuated people from the war-torn African country. (JO2 William G. Davies III)

been fighting a civil war for nine months, and three different factions were tearing the country apart.

By May 1990, it was clear that the action endangered American citizens, and a four-ship amphibious ready group, with 2,100 Marines, prepared to extract them. On August 4, with the situation ashore quickly deteriorating—one of the rebel leaders had threatened to take American hostages—the president issued the order to start Operation Sharp Edge. Elements of the 22nd Marine Expeditionary Unit (MEU) launched from USS *Saipan* (LHA-2). Covering the operation were Sea Knights (HMM-261) and Sea Stallions (HMH-362), escorted by four Sea Cobras (HMLA-167) and two Harriers (VMA-223).

The transports brought Marines to reinforce the embassy compound and help the evacuation. On the first day, 72 people were rescued, and eventually more than 1,600 people, including 132 Americans, were taken out of the country. The helicopters then flew in medical supplies, fuel, and water. The operation continued through August, finally concluding on December 3 after a cease-fire in Liberia on November 28. A total of 226 American citizens and 2,200 other nationals had been rescued.

Desert Shield Gathers Momentum

On August 12, President Bush announced a naval quarantine of Iraq to reinforce a UN-established economic embargo. Six days later, the first incident saw two Navy frigates confront two Iraqi tankers. The next two months included several other incidents as more supplies and people poured into bases in the region, building a wall around Iraq and its leader, Saddam Hussein. Marine aviation was in the buildup immediately, along with every other component of the Corps. Older veteran aircraft and their squadrons accompanied the latest types to the Gulf area. Two A-6E squadrons—VMA(AW)-224 and VMA(AW)-533—arrived in Bahrain in August and December, respectively. VMO-2 flew its OV-10A/D Broncos 10,000 miles from California to Saudi Arabia. VMO-1's Broncos hitched a ride across the ocean on board USS *America*, while VMAQ-2 transpaced two-thirds of its complement of Prowlers, twelve EA-6Bs deploying to Sheik Isa Air Base in Bahrain. For many of the Leatherneck Prowler crews, this unexpected combat deployment was an exciting introduction to real-world operations.

[Top] An OV-10D of VMO-2. Although the OV-10 had seen much action in Vietnam, serving with the Air Force, Navy, and Marines, Desert Storm was its swan song. The Marines had difficulty finding the right use for the evocative little twin, and it soon left U.S. service.

[Bottom] The Playboys arrive. VMAQ-2 Prowlers inbound to Sheikh Isa, 1990, during Desert Shield, the buildup to Desert Storm.

"I had about 500 EA-6B hours," Capt. Joel Strieter said. "My two junior ECMOs—1st Lts. Daniel Friedel and John Fulp—had arrived in VMAQ-2 in the spring of 1990. My senior ECMO, Capt. William Fiser, was on his second tour with the squadron."

Marine CH-46 and CH-53 squadrons rode over on LPHs and LHAs, accompanied by AH-1T/Ws, and even older AH-1Js from two reserve squadrons. Reserve HMM and HMH squadrons also made their way to the Gulf. Reserve KC-130 tankers supplemented FMF VMGRs. Every community contributed. FMF Hornet squadrons transpaced, including an F/A-18D squadron, VMFA(AW)-121.

Maritime interdiction missions were some of the first offensive operations in the Gulf and usually involved intercepting various tankers, freighters, and smaller ships that might be carrying contraband. There was always the chance of a hostile reception by the boarded ship's crew, and the Navy SEAL and Marine teams were, in turn, always ready to meet any threat. There were few incidents, although contraband was occasionally discovered.

In one case, however, an elderly Swedish passenger seemed to have a heart attack after a SEAL team had boarded her ship. She needed immediate medical attention, and the CH-53E squadron on board USS *Iwo Jima* got the call. Capt. Rick Mullen and his crew flew the woman, who was later determined to have a bad case of food poisoning, to Muscat. Captain Mullen did his best to calm the woman's fears about riding in his huge, noisy helicopter. He wrote her a letter explaining who he and his crew were and what their mission was. An avid photographer, he included a photo of his

helicopter. When they landed, the woman grasped Captain Mullen's hand and said, "Thank you. You people are so kind. Thank you."

"It felt especially good to be an American that day," he recalled.

By January 1991, the enormous coalition of 500,000 men and women representing some thirty-five countries was in position, waiting as the diplomatic clock wound down to the inevitable. Yet, even as the Marines and their coalition compatriots prepared to face down the Iraqis, another sideshow developed.

As in Operation Sharp Edge only six months before, Operation Eastern Exit was launched to rescue U.S. citizens caught in a civil war in Africa, this time in Somalia. Although the ten-day operation in early January 1991 was overshadowed by events in the Gulf, it resulted in the rescue of 281 people from thirty countries. USS *Guam* and USS *Trenton* (LPD-14) received orders on January 2 to head for the waters off the Somali capital, Mogadishu. The CH-53Es of HMH-461 in *Guam* would provide the primary lift support.

Three KC-130s from VMGR-252 and VMGR-352 left their Desert Shield base in Bahrain to provide aerial refueling services for the big Sea Stallion helicopters. Allowing for the low-grade, but very real threat of SAMs, the Marine crews planned a low-altitude approach to the American embassy.

On January 5, at 2:45 AM, two CH-53s of HMH-461 launched from *Guam* with sixty Marines and nine SEALs, refueled from orbiting KC-130s, and headed toward Mogadishu, 460 miles away. The helicopters crossed the beach, avoiding the northern areas of the city, where the fighting was reported to be the heaviest.

The helo crews ran into trouble picking out their objective because of old, out-of-date maps. Maj. Dan Schultz, the detachment commander, decided to fly back over the water to get his bearings. As they headed back

[Opposite] CH-53Es line the stern of USS *Iwo Jima* (LPH-2) while the amphibious assault ship is moored at Manama, Bahrain, in December 1990. Many of the large helicopters were transported to the Gulf lashed to the decks of whichever ships could carry them. (PH2 Susan Marie Carl)

[Right] KC-130s—this one from VMGR-252—continue to provide airlift and aerial refueling services for the Corps. The Hercules is the Marines' oldest aircraft type.

over the city, the two Marine helicopters flew over a band of Somali trucks, several of which were armed with .50-caliber machine guns. The operators, however, jumped off their vehicles and ran.

Finally, the pilots spotted the embassy, which seemed to be under attack by a group of Somalis. These people also ran as the helicopters approached.

Setting their aircraft down inside the compound a little after 7:00 AM, the Marine crews waited for an hour, loading sixty-one people, before taking off for the safety of their ship. After depositing the evacuees on the *Guam*, the two CH-53s headed for the *Trenton*, their home ship, to the enthusiastic greetings of the ship's crew.

Alerts continued throughout the day, with CH-46Es from HMM-263 and HMM-365, and armed UH-1Ns from HMLA-269, ready to fly back to the embassy. *Guam* and *Trenton* had steamed to a point where the CH-46s, which lacked in-flight refueling capability, could launch to get the remaining civilians. The final wave retrieved the remaining Marines and SEALs out of harm's way, leaving the building to the violent attentions of the Somali populace, who rocketed, then looted, the embassy.

Back to the Gulf

One gap in Marine Corps support in the Gulf was tactical reconnaissance. For three decades, VMFP-3 had flown its RF-4Bs. The photo-Phantoms had become the last fleet Phantoms in naval service. But P-3 decommissioned on October 1, 1990, incredibly, leaving the Corps without a valuable set of eyes on the eve of what would be the largest military action since Vietnam. The squadron had once flown as many as twenty-one RF-4Bs and included some 800 people on its rolls.

The hole left by P-3's retirement was to be filled to an extent by unmanned aerial vehicles (UAVs), specifically Pioneer reconnaissance drones. These small unmanned aircraft, originally obtained from Israel and delivered to the Marine Corps in 1987, could be launched from ships or from shore launch points close to the battlefield. Their size limited the number of sensors, and thus they could not offer the RF-4B's depth of coverage. But in the coming months, the drones, used by the Navy and the Marine Corps, would sometimes be the only battlefield reconnaissance assets available.

UAVs flew with Marine, Navy, and Army units and generally received high marks for their performance. Crews became intensely loyal to their little aircraft, and since the war, were great boosters of the UAV program, citing their slogan, "No widows, no POWs with UAVs."

Marine Corps UAV battalions used all three types of UAVs: the Israeli-manufactured Pioneer, the Pointer, developed by and for the Army, and the new BQM-147A Exdrone, which was still under development but was taken from testing units because of the great need for them in the Gulf.

Writing in the September 1991 issue of *Marine Corps Gazette*, Maj. Christopher P. Gutmann, an experienced RF-4B backseater, made several telling observations:

> VMFP-3 for years played an unsung and unglamorous role in Marine aviation . . . the RF-4B did not represent our only

reconnaissance asset, but surely it was our most significant and most capable reconnaissance asset. . . . P-3's greatest problem was its lack of visibility within the Marine Corps. . . . At the time of its retirement, the RF-4B, still very capable, had long past seen its best days. The airframes and reconnaissance systems were tired and subject to excessive failure. . . . What was difficult for officers within the reconnaissance community to understand was how the RF-4B could be retired with no replacement in sight. My feeling was that unmanned aerial vehicle (UAV) employment . . . must have existed for the Corps to disband its only reconnaissance squadron. . . . Undeniably UAVs are very important . . . but they can't currently replace manned aircraft.

This CH-46E of HMM-264 stands on an airfield near the first tent city constructed as part of Operation Provide Comfort in April 1991. (JO1 Greg Snaza)

Lt. Gen. Royal Moore, commanding general, 3D MAW, commented on the intelligence problem in the Gulf: "Our own aircraft supplied us with the best intelligence. We had 177 airplanes at Sheikh Isa, both Air Force and Marines, and some Air National Guard RF-4Cs. I retired the last Marine Corps RF-4Bs two days before I left California in August 1990. We looked very hard at bringing those RF-4Bs back; we just could not do it."[1]

General Moore also assessed the UAV contribution, saying, "We used the Pioneer system extensively. We had all the Pioneer companies out there . . . the RPVs caught some SA-6s coming down the road to Jabar, and we knocked them stiff."[2]

16 Desert Storm

THE BOLDNESS OF THE IRAQIS, and particularly their dictator-president, seemed to many observers a sign that they would not leave Kuwait, and thus, a conflict was inevitable. With his coalition in place and prepared after six months of training in the Saudi Arabian desert, President George H. W. Bush delivered a final deadline for the Iraqis to agree to UN demands, namely retreat back to their traditional borders, vacate Kuwait, and avoid war. The January 15 deadline passed, and the first strikes of the war were launched in the early hours of January 17.

Captain Strieter commented that Marine Corps aviation activities were divided into four phases during Desert Storm. Preplanned waves, which lasted for the first four days, strikes on high-value targets such as air defense, command and control, air fields, and logistics areas, battlefield interdiction, then close air support.

"During Phase II," he said, "we would receive the Air Tasking Order in the evening, and plan for the next day's missions. This was different from Phase I where we had received the ATO months before."[1]

Phase III included artillery raids and border skirmishes, which the Playboy (VMAQ-2) Prowlers supported. At 3:00 AM, Playboy Prowlers were in the air to cover the first coalition raids into Iraq and along the border of Saudi Arabia and Kuwait. One Prowler crew could shield six different missions at once with its jamming facilities, as well as with HARMs, fired against enemy SAM and anti-aircraft radars. Captain Strieter and his crew helped defend a force of more than forty Marine F/A-18s as well as Navy strike aircraft as they headed into and out of Iraq.

Strieter observed, "My orbit's southern point was the 'crotch' of the Iraq-Saudi-Kuwait border. . . . We had no dedicated CAP—alone, unarmed, and unafraid! Looking left, right, and out front, all we could see were AAA and SAM launches. It wasn't any better turning around."

Strieter tried to call his wingman, but after several attempts without a reply, he feared the worst. Happily, they regained contact with the other Prowler as they were heading back to their base. He recalls, "In retrospect, holding to land was probably the most dangerous phase of the flight. All aircraft coming home were not under positive control, so there were about

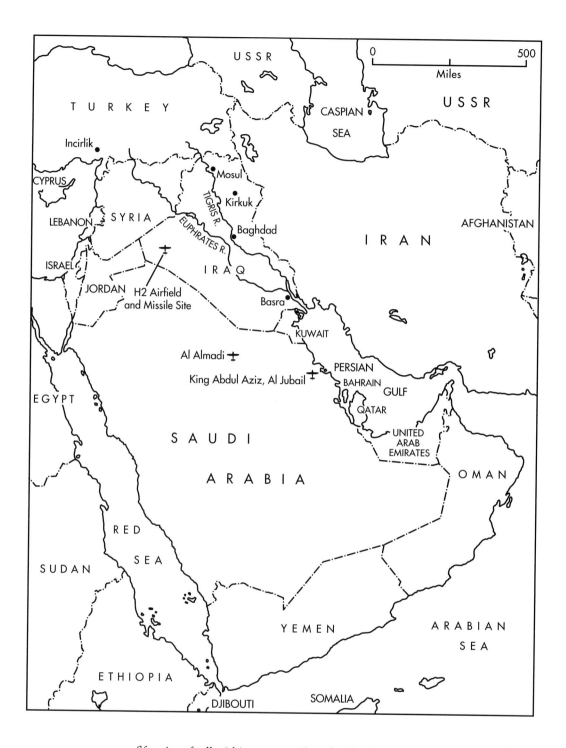

fifty aircraft all within twenty miles of each other. . . . It seemed like everyone was out to kill you!"[2]

The squadrons of the four MAGs that made up 3rd MAW—which had come from redesignating and reorganizing MAG-70—flew from shore bases and ships. MAG-70 had been the air combat element (ACE) of the 7th Marine Expeditionary Brigade (MEB) and was what retired Brig. Gen. E. H. Simmons had called a "pocket air force . . . flying a great variety of aircraft."[3]

In reality, however, the shore-based Marine squadrons reported appropriately to the senior Marine commander, Lt. Gen. Walter E. Boomer,

[Opposite]
Map 8. Desert Storm, 1991.

[Top] VMA-542 Harriers at King
Abdul Aziz Naval Base, Jubail,
Saudi Arabia. The AV-8Bs all
carry Rockeye canisters, the
weapon of choice for most of the
V/STOL squadrons.

[Bottom] AV-8Bs of VMA-331
prepare to launch on a mission
from USS *Nassau* in February
1991. (Joe Doyle)

commanding the I Marine Expeditionary Force (I MEF). However, the
various helicopter squadrons and VMA-331, the AV-8B squadron on board
USS *Nassau*, were under the control of Vice Adm. Stan Arthur's Seventh
Fleet organization.

It was a somewhat disjointed arrangement brought on as much by
Marine Corps stubbornness as by more traditional interservice rivalries. As
usual, the Air Force wanted a large piece of Marine Corps aviation assets
and so did the Navy. The Marine Corps, of course, wanted to fly its aircraft
in support of its Marines on the ground, with a distinct secondary role in
support of other services. It was an argument as old as Marine Corps air,
itself, and like so many times before, the situation was never satisfactorily
resolved, even when the shooting started.

The Marines also wanted to be ready to support any amphibious
operation that might be launched, which, after all, was at the heart of Marine

air's raison d'être. But, in truth, the massive from-the-sea invasion of Kuwait that so troubled the Iraqis was never planned. It was considered for a short time but never really given any more thought, primarily because such an operation would have been much too costly for what it might have gained.

The depth of the Marines' resentment of having to split their forces showed up during General Royal Moore's interview in the November 1991 issue of the U.S. Naval Institute's *Proceedings*. When the interviewer noted that the Marine Corps had lost five Harriers to enemy action, the 3rd MAW commander quickly and strongly corrected him: "First we did not lose five; we lost four, and the 4th Marine Expeditionary Brigade, which was under the Naval Commander, Central Command control, lost one on the last day."

It may have been a fine point, but it was one that the Marines felt strongly about. (VMA-331, embarked in USS *Nassau*, had lost the last AV-8B during combat operations. Although considered a combat loss, the reason was never specifically determined to be the result of enemy action.)

The first offensive mission by Marine Corps aviation in the Gulf began at 4:00 AM on January 17. Forty-eight Marine aircraft from Sheikh Isa and Bahrain International Airport, along with twenty other allied planes, hit Iraqi airfields and SCUD missile shelters. As dawn broke, MAG-13 Harriers and OV-10s went in against targets in southern Kuwait. By the end of the first day of Desert Storm, Marine aircrews had flown 144 combat sorties, the first of more than 18,000 during the war.

While largely successful, the Marines did have losses. On January 18, an OV-10A from VMO-2 was shot down, its two-man crew interned as POWs.

The pilot was the squadron CO, Lt. Col. Cliff Acree, and the observer was CWO-4 Guy Hunter.

The Leatherneck Intruder squadrons were also at work, flying day and night missions in the terrible weather that enveloped the region. These precision bombing missions led the A-6 crews into Iraq and Kuwait against convoys of armored and supply vehicles, as well as troop concentrations. Even when the Iraqis used ecological terrorism and torched hundreds of Kuwaiti oil wells, releasing towering plumes of thick, black smoke that eventually curtained off the region, the Intruders responded.

VMAQ-2's Prowler crews were constantly in demand to support coalition strikes. It was not uncommon for the Playboys to be jamming for raids involving more than fifty aircraft. On February 21, Captain Strieter and his crew defended twenty-five separate flights of Harriers and Hornets. Strieter's Prowler was carrying three ECM pods and two HARMs. It had been less than a week since Marine Prowlers had fired their first anti-radar missile on February 15. The controller told the Marine Prowler to support a B-52 raid near Al Jaber. An Iraqi mobile SAM's radar came up near the target, and Captain Strieter shot a HARM at the enemy site, gaining a possible kill.

Magill's MiG

One Marine fighter pilot continued a long-established tradition by shooting down an enemy MiG while flying an exchange tour with the Air Force. Capt. Charles Magill was assigned to the Air Force's 58th Tactical Fighter Squadron, flying the F-15C Eagle, which was, along with the Navy's Tomcat, one of the world's premier air superiority fighters.

A Hornet pilot by trade, Captain Magill launched as part of an eight-plane escort early in the afternoon of January 17. By this time, the war's first strikes had yielded the first kills by other F-15 pilots in the predawn darkness over Iraq. As Magill and his four-plane division topped off from an orbiting

[Opposite] An A-6E of VMA(AW)-224 with a load of Rockeye at Sheikh Isa. The Intruder will launch on a mission to support the coalition advance. The ground war in Desert Storm is one day old.

[Below] Capt. Charles Magill, on exchange duty with the Air Force, shot down an Iraqi MiG-29 on January 17, 1991, the only Marine aviator to score a kill in Desert Storm. He sits in the cockpit of his F-15C, which now carries a small black star indicating his kill below the windscreen. (via Charles Magill)

tanker, the omniscient AWACS aircraft warned of Iraqi MiG-29s over the target airfield at A1 Taquaddum.

"As we drew nearer the target," Magill commented later, "I directed the second division to continue their sweep to the north while I led three Eagles toward the south."[4]

He bore down on the MiGs, just as he saw two SAM launches. The F-15 pilots jettisoned their external fuel tanks, but the missiles flew past without detonating. The two blue MiG-29s had turned south toward Magill's flight, and as they approached the F-15s, Magill fired two AIM-7 Sparrows. His wingman, Capt. Rhory Draeger, also fired a missile. For the Marine and Air Force fighter pilots, time slowed down as their missiles seemed to hang in midair. Finally, the Sparrows' rocket motors lit off, and the missiles sped toward their targets.

Draeger's Sparrow got to his MiG first, blowing it into a huge fireball. Then, Captain Magill's Sparrows struck another MiG, one right after the other, sending the Iraqi fighter toward the desert below. The elated Eagle pilots turned back toward their strike group of F-16s, avoiding a spread of SAMs. Arriving back at their base, Magill and Draeger indulged in the traditional victory roll to the delight of their ground troops. (Draeger, who would get another kill—a MiG-23 on January 26—was one of eight Air Force pilots to score two kills.)

Marine Air in the Ground War

The strategic air campaign against Iraq continued throughout most of February. The results were a mighty confirmation of air power's role in modern war, but the ultimate action of the war was yet to come: the ground war. Everything else had been in preparation for confronting the enemy on the desert floor.

All coalition factions prepared for the kickoff of the ground war, the main act of which would include lifting massive numbers of coalition troops into fighting areas. All squadrons would be used to cover the battlefield, from AH-1Ws to CH-46s and CH-53s.

The long-awaited ground war began at 4:00 AM on Sunday, February 24. Coalition forces thrust deep into Iraq and Kuwait, cutting into Iraqi positions with surprising ease that caught the Allies off guard as much as the Iraqis. HMLA-367 Cobras were in the thick of the action. On the morning of February 24, after flying several armed reconnaissance missions, they took out several enemy 120-mm mortar batteries that were firing on advancing Marine tanks, and then went after three Iraqi tanks, destroying them as well. Seeing their comrades' fate, the remaining Iraqi troops quickly surrendered to the Marines, who were quickly advancing toward the Iraqis.

As thousands of Iraqi POWs stretched the limits of the coalition's ability to detain and care for them, the push quickly went far ahead of schedule, and coalition units scrambled to catch up with those who had gone before them.

Capt. George Caulkins, a Cobra pilot with HMLA-367, proudly recalled his squadron's record. "There is really no doubt that Scarface was the best. I am as susceptible as the next guy to unit pride, but we feel that we went

beyond that. We did not have the most assets in theater, but no one answered the call the way we did."

At the cease-fire on February 28, HMLA-367 had accounted for ninety-six kills against Iraqi equipment, as well as being directly responsible for thousands of Iraqi POWs who surrendered to the approaching Scarface Cobras.

Maj. John S. Stollery Jr., USMCR (FTS), had arrived with HMM-774, a Reserve CH-46E squadron from Norfolk, Virginia. The squadron was originally scheduled for an exercise in Norway that year, but now it was one of several Marine Reserve squadrons mobilized for duty in the Gulf. HMM-774 loaded its Sea Knights onto USAF C-5s, and their people and material onto eight C-141s. They landed at Jubail, the main Marine Corps helicopter base in Saudi Arabia, on January 5, 1991, having left the United States on January 3.

For the next two weeks, the squadron reassembled and flight-tested their aircraft, set up their operations, acclimatized to the desert, and practiced with their new ANVIS-6 night-vision goggles (NVGs). They had had no chance to train with the new NVGs in the States, but the new goggles were easier to use then the PVS-5 models the squadron had used at home. The ANVIS-6 was also more capable than the earlier model.

HMM-774 moved to the forward base called Lonesome Dove on February 22 to be ready for the ground war. Lonesome Dove was eight miles southwest of the Kuwait-Saudi border, merely a point in the desert known only to the Bedouin nomads as a cross point. It was chosen because of its proximity to Kuwait and to projected "breech" points for the ground war through which Marine ground forces would pour into Kuwait once the ground war began. Stollery called it "a mixture of gravel, and camel and goat turds."

Unlike Jubail, which featured a terrain of small hills, Lonesome Dove was flat and allowed the squadron to practice "turfing" flying at fifty feet above the desert with little fear of running into an unexpected hill, especially while using NVGs.

Stollery tried to calm his pre-combat jitters by reading and walking. He read a book while sitting in the cockpit of his helicopter the day before the ground war. He wore his full NBC MOPP gear; however, as long as he did not move too much, the gear was not too uncomfortable. Communication was a problem, though, and could only be done on ICS.

On February 24, Stollery launched with forty-six other Marine helicopter-transports (CH-46s and CH-53s) and their Cobra escorts. He was in Red group, a four-plane section from HMM-774. They had gone to LZ Sandy at 3:00 PM on the 23rd and slept in their helicopters, waiting for a white star shell, which would signal that they had twenty minutes before launch.

The launch was briefed to start at noon on the 24th, however, by 3:00, no signal had come. Finally, at 3:30 the shell was fired. The crew got into their NBC gear. Stollery's co-pilot was nervous and furiously tapped his fingers. Fortunately, it was not too distracting through all the NBC gear. They would be hauling a two-man TOW-missile team and their jeep-launcher. A sergeant drove around to all the aircraft in a jeep to tell the crews that it had been determined that there was no NBC threat and that they could, thankfully, discard their cumbersome protective gear. The messenger also warned they would launch in eight minutes.

The wind had shifted from the west to the north. As the large gaggle of helos lifted, the rotor wash stirred up the sand and dirt, mixing it into a huge cloud that obscured vision for the helo crews, especially those in the rear of the formation. A half mile ahead of Stollery's aircraft, one plane rolled over as its pilots lost ground reference in a brownout. No one was killed, although the H-46 incurred strike damage.

Stollery lifted off and gingerly sidled off to the right to clear the cloud directly in front of him. His torque warning horn blared in the cockpit. His aircraft was fully loaded at maximum gross weight of 24,000 pounds. He had fuel for an hour and forty-five minutes of flight—1,200 pounds—and besides the TOW team and their jeep, he had two door-mounted M-60 machine guns with 700 rounds per gun.

The Marine helicopters joined up, and the huge formation headed toward the Kuwait border. The sun was setting in the late afternoon, and what was to have been a daylight operation was becoming a night-time hop, complete with night-vision goggles. Whereas the sun could be a problem as it sank below the horizon, the hazard was replaced by the glare of the raging oil fires that made seeing the aircraft around him difficult for Major Stollery. He likened the scene with NVGs to taking a picture directly into the sun: he could only see a featureless silhouette of the aircraft in front of him and could not tell how far away the next helicopter was from him, except as the profile changed in size. He made slight movements with his H-46 to keep the formation in sight as they flew at 200 feet.

The radio frequency was clobbered. Everyone was talking, making communication difficult. Since there was no threat from the Iraqis, precautions were dropped. Escorts were having a tough time staying with their transports. Stollery's lead announced that he would abort the flight unless control cleared up the confusion.

"The fog of war," Stollery said, "made it hard."

The formation crossed into Kuwait directly over a breech line. The word came that the ground forces were having great success. Stollery and his four-plane formation decided not to deliver their troops because of the confusion and obscured visibility and turned around for home.

As they recrossed the border, the MAG-16 aircraft broke off and headed for Tanijib, their home base, while Stollery's formation flew toward Lonesome Dove. Everyone was low on fuel. The MAG-16 choppers would try to make the forward air refueling point (FARP), while the Reserve planes pressed on. It was a dangerous point in the flight, because aircraft broke away from the formation and struck out in new directions. HMM-774 recovered at Lonesome Dove in an open space near their tents.

SSgt. William Chambers, a regular Marine assigned to HMM-774, was in a CH-46E in the third string. They were to carry a jeep and its four-man crew to the landing zone, but the mayhem of the brownout ahead of them made it nearly impossible. Chambers, a designated aerial gunner manning a .50-caliber machine gun, eventually flew into Kuwait International, his pilot touching down by the passenger terminal. HMM-774 had been the first Marine aviation squadron into Kuwait City, just behind the exultant ground troops who liberated the city. The reserve helo crews had taken replacements for the lead troops into the city, which Chambers remembers as "war torn, gutted."

For Staff Sergeant Chambers, the strongest memory of Desert Storm was of the oil fires. "You could see the fires as soon as you crossed the border. Everything was black from the fires. You could see the smoke from fifteen miles away."[5]

Capt. G. J. Mazenko, flying CH-46s with HMM-268 from USS *New Orleans*, also considered the fires and smoke the most troubling part of any mission. When the plans for an amphibious assault changed to supporting the ground war, the Red Dragons moved ashore to the airfield at Tanajib, Saudi Arabia.

"The most dangerous enemy we faced," Captain Mazenko reported, "was not the Iraqi Army, but the thick, dense, black smoke from the hundreds of oil fires. High-tension power lines across the open desert were sometimes masked by the smoke."

On one occasion, a flight of eight helicopters, including six CH-46s and two Cobra escorts, entered what appeared to be a thin cloud of smoke. The visibility in the smoke, however, quickly dropped to zero, and with the tight formation often within two or three rotor diameters of each other, the danger of a midair collision was great. Fortunately, the Marine helos got out of the cloud before such a tragedy could happen. Marine gunship helos were busy during this last phase of the war. At 4:00 AM on February 26, six UH-1Ns from HMLA-269, armed with 2.75-inch rockets and machine guns, launched from USS *Nassau* and headed for Iraqi-occupied Failaka Island. The raid was meant to be part of a feint to keep the enemy off guard while diverting attention from the real invasion further inland.

Flying on night-vision goggles, the Huey crews flew the seventy-two miles to the island. The smoke and flames from Kuwait's burning oil wells and from Kuwait City were plainly visible, as was random flak from Bubian Island to the north. But the Huey crews pressed on, arriving at their pre-attack position. Flak from Bubian was still peppering the sky around them, but after making a night tactical turn, all six helicopters fired their rockets at targets along the northwest beach of Failaka.

The Iraqis quickly responded with defensive fire, and the sky was lit with bursts from both sides. The Hueys spread out, finally reversed their direction, and headed back to their ship, having reinforced the bogus threat of an amphibious invasion of Kuwait in the minds of the Iraqis. AH-1W crews of HMLA-169 had brought an experimental system to the Gulf. The Nite Eagle laser identification system had literally been taken from its testing laboratory for a combat evaluation with Hellfire laser-guided missiles. The enthusiastic Viper pilots scored several kills against Iraqi tanks with the new system.

It was on February 26 that Lt. Col. Michael M. Kurth, the commanding officer of HMLA-369, earned one of only two Navy Crosses given to Marines during Desert Storm. Having led five AH-1Ws from Lonesome Dove to Al Jaber, he then launched in a UH-1N to scout for the ground forces. Contending with near-zero visibility because of the smoke from oil well fires, he repeatedly flew near and sometimes under power lines. Eventually, he located the Marines on the ground, then returned to the AH-1s he had left at Al Jaber, and soon the Cobras were providing support for the ground forces, using laser designation from Lieutenant Colonel Kurth's Huey.

Maj. Gen. J. M. Myatt, who commanded the 1st Marine Division during the war, commended Lieutenant Colonel Kurth during a magazine interview: "So here's . . . the 3rd Armored Division . . . needing some help, and you've got Mike Kurth flying from the area south of all the smoke, in a Huey, guiding a division of helicopters under three big high-tension wire systems, flying under them, going north to support Task Force Ripper."[6]

Besides the EA-6Bs and A-6Es, two other fixed-wing tactical jets flew with the squadrons of MAG-11, 3rd MAW, the AV-8B Harrier II, and the F/A-18C Hornet. Derived from the preliminary, quick-reaction organization of MAG-70, 3rd MAW, under Maj. Gen. Royal Moore, carried the brunt of Marine Corps aviation activities in the war in the Gulf. During the forty-two days of the war, MAG-11 aircraft posted more than 7,500 sorties in 16,500 flight hours. MAG-11 aircraft dropped more than 17,000,000 pounds of ordnance, including Mk-80 series bombs, Maverick, HARM, and Rockeye.

Perhaps the most anticipated sorties were those of the highly touted AV-8B, flying in its first combat since the AV-8A entered USMC service in 1971. Four full squadrons (VMAs -311, -542, -231, and -331), and a six-plane detachment from a fifth (VMA-513 Det B), of Harrier IIs flew in the war, most from shore bases. VMA-331 flew from USS *Nassau*, however, eventually making the first ship-launched missions for Marine Corps Harriers, beginning on February 20. The V/STOL attack squadrons mainly flew the CAS missions for which they were designed, ahead of advancing Marines on the ground.

Harrier missions were not without cost, however, and five Harriers were lost in combat. Two pilots ejected and were captured. (Capt. Michael C. Berryman of VMA-311 and Capt. Russell A. C. Sanborn of VMA-231 were eventually released with other coalition POWs in March after the cease-fire.) Another ejected after nursing his crippled plane close to friendly lines. But two Harrier pilots died in action, one while attacking an enemy tank at night, and the second in unspecified circumstances during a mission.

Captain Berryman described his experience to a reporter for *Marines* magazine. Now a major, he told of the beatings and deprivations during his thirty-seven-day captivity. His mission on January 28, 1991, had been to destroy a FROG missile site that had been a danger to Marines in Khafji. The site was protected by another SAM site. Berryman and his wingman could not find the primary target, so they chose to hit the secondary, a convoy snaking along the coast.

As he set up his attack, Berryman's Harrier's aerial refueling probe popped out, sending the AV-8 into a sideways skid. The Marine aviator aborted his run and set up for a second approach. The enemy on the ground fired a SAM. It hit the Harrier, which quickly flipped over at 10,000 feet and spun toward the ground. Berryman couldn't know that his aircraft's tail had been blown off, but he quickly made the decision to eject.

"When I pulled the ejection handle," he reported, "I knew it should take 1.2 seconds until I had an open parachute. That was the longest 1.2 seconds of my life."[7] Although the chute did blossom above him, his troubles were far from over, and he was quickly captured by waiting Iraqi troops, who immediately began beating the Marine.

Taken to a camp north of Baghdad, Berryman was moved to two other camps during his time as a prisoner. At first the interrogations and beatings were light, but they increased as the Iraqis became more frustrated and insistent.

"There were some things I was willing to die for. I was never going to tell them where my squadron was based. I didn't want to be responsible for the deaths of fellow Marines. If I had to die, so be it. I was willing to take that information with me to the grave."[8]

Berryman was thrown into solitary confinement, spending thirty of those thirty-seven days alone, listening to the screams of other POWs undergoing torture and beatings.

Eventually, he and his fellow prisoners were released and were flown out. "I was thinking, 'They're going to let us get airborne, then they'll shoot us down again.' I didn't believe it until we punched through the clouds and we had two American F-15 Eagles roll up on either side of the airplane. They did victory rolls, lit their afterburners and went straight up. It was a very emotional moment. . . . I'll never forget it."[9]

U.S. Marine Corps AV-8Bs were not the only Harriers in-theater, although they alone saw combat. Britain's Royal Navy stationed the carrier HMS *Ark Royal* with a complement of Sea Harrier FRS.1s of 899 Squadron in the Red Sea along with other coalition ships. The British Harriers were held in reserve, however, as the Royal Navy's helicopter units were that service's most active aviation groups.

The Royal Air Force was in the middle of a major transition from its old GR.3 Harriers—comparable to AV-8As—to the GR.5 and GR.7. Since the RAF had sent many other types of aircraft to the Gulf, and because Vice Adm. Stanley Arthur, commanding the U.S. Navy's Seventh Fleet and U.S. Naval Forces Central Command, decided that he did not need the British Harriers, the RAF aircraft remained at home.

The first major Harrier actions involved the battle for Khafji on January 28–29. Originally thought to be an Iraqi feint, the attack on the border town quickly became the first full-fledged ground battle of the war, with probes, thrusts, and artillery duels. On the night of January 29, the Iraqis took the lightly defended town. Harriers from VMA-542 flying from King Abdul Aziz East airfield, ninety miles from Khafji, responded to the call.

Maj. Jim Lee and his four-plane flight headed toward an Iraqi column of personnel carriers, which were right in the middle of Khafji. Major Lee and his wingman, Capt. Dennis Hass, made the first runs, dropping their Mk-82 500-pound bombs. Capt. Dan Claney and his wingman followed with Rockeye anti-tank cluster bombs. Angered by the first attack, the enemy was waiting for the second section of AV-8Bs. The Iraqis fired at least seven SA-9 heat-seeker SAMs at the oncoming Harriers, whose pilots evaded all of the missiles.

Harrier attacks against Khafji continued throughout the following day, disposing of a number of Iraqi tanks and FROG surface-to-surface missiles. Shortly after dawn, VMA-311 AV-8Bs hit an Iraqi artillery battery that had been shelling the town and an adjacent oil refinery. An orbiting OV-10 crew called in the Tomcat Harriers, which obliterated the enemy position with 1,000-pound bombs and cannon fire. Eventually, the Iraqis were evicted from Khafji.

The battle of Khafji also saw widespread use of Marine AH-1W Cobra gunships from the beginning of the Iraqi attack. HMLA-367 crews constantly engaged Iraqi tanks and armored columns, destroying several vehicles.

Harrier pilots flew their own missions or in company with another important Marine Corps jet, the F/A-18 Hornet. No less than seven VMFAs flew in the Gulf as part of MAG-11 (VMFAs -212, -232, -235, -314, -333, -451, and VMFA(AW)-121, with its new two-seat F/A-18Ds). The single-seat Hornet squadrons flew both F/A-18As and F/A-18Cs, staying mostly within the Kuwait Theater of Operations (KTO) after the first week of the war. Following extensive training in Desert Shield, the MAG-11 Hornet squadrons were ready for Desert Storm, flying strike missions as well as CAPs in the northern Gulf, and a single mission against targets close to Baghdad. Marine Hornets flew more than 5,100 combat sorties during the forty-three-day air campaign, and although several aircraft were hit by Iraqi ground fire and missiles, none was lost in combat.

Capt. A. Morrison, an F/A-18A pilot with VMFA-333, reported that the Shamrocks had a young Navy intelligence officer "who did a superb job and probably saved several pilots."

Recalling various missions, Captain Morrison remembered that the Iraqis "threw 'orange pumpkins' at us—flak." But unlike Vietnam, where getting permission to go after the flak sites was complicated, the Marine F/A-18 pilots in the Gulf War, after finding the sites, would actually troll for fire. When the flak guns—usually 85-mm–100-mm weapons—opened up, the Hornet drivers went after them, frequently with Rockeye cluster-bomb canisters, a very effective weapon against stationary ground targets.

Having traded its A-6Es for the two-seat Hornets in April 1990, VMFA(AW)-121 barely had time to get to know its new mounts before heading out to the Gulf on January 7, 1991, little more than a week before the shooting started. With six aircraft and 118 people, the squadron set up at Sheikh Isa, followed by six more Hornets and flight crews. Their mission was largely battlefield preparation and reconnaissance in the KTO. Carrying 2.75-inch rocket pods, 20-mm cannon, and white-phosphorous marking rounds, the Green Knights flew among the oil fires, scouting Iraqi positions for the coalition ground units. The first mission came on January 18, when, after topping off from KC-130s, squadron Hornets marked targets for a strike group. As the war continued, the 121 crews flew around the clock, using NVGs during night missions, spotting the muzzle flashes of Iraqi artillery, and quickly either directing strikes against the artillery battery, or going after the enemy position themselves.

Like their Harrier compatriots, the F/A-18D crews helped defend the town of Khafji, in one case stopping an Iraqi armored column threatening a Marine position. Capt. Robert Turner (pilot) and his weapons system officer,

[Opposite] An F/A-18D of VMFA(AW)-121 flies over a field of oil-well fires shortly after Desert Storm. Even though the Iraqi air-to-air threat had disappeared by this point in the war, this Hornet still carries wingtip-mounted Sidewinders. The two-seat Hornet, relatively new to service, quickly got its baptism of fire during the first Gulf War, taking over the role of Fast FAC and battlefield interdictor. (McDonnell Douglas–Boeing)

[Top] Two Reserve squadrons brought their older AH-1Js to the Gulf during Desert Storm. This Sea Cobra from HMA-775 frames the smoke and flames from numerous oil-well fires. (R. S. Doty)

[Bottom] An AH-1W of HMLA-269 prepares to head out on a mission during the ground war in 1991. The Cobra is armed with Hellfire anti-tank missiles and pods carrying 2.75-inch air-to-ground rockets. (R. S. Doty)

Maj. Michael Pedersen, used rockets and their cannon to strafe Iraqi tanks, which came as close as 1,500 meters from the Marines on the ground.

Lt. Col. Stephen F. Mugg, the commanding officer of VMFA(AW)-121, remarked: "Every crew flew every day, and each crew was paired up. They got to know their relatively small area very well."

The surprisingly fast pace of the ground war brought a quick end to the overall conflict. By February 28, the Iraqis had retreated from Kuwait, back across the extreme southeastern border with their "nineteenth province." Even when the Iraqis could muster and launch an offensive or counterstrike of their own, it did not last long. Allied air power would usually pull the plug. Marine Corps fixed- and rotary-wing squadrons roamed free to give whatever support was needed.

AH-1W Super Cobras were especially active during the ground war phase, using TOW anti-tank weapons and their turret-mounted 20-mm cannon to good effect. AH-1T and AH-1J (the Juliets were from the two Marine Air Reserve squadrons, HMA-773 and HMA-775) escorted transport helicopters over the battlefield. The cease-fire announced by the United States on February 28, 1991, ended the immediate hostilities, but there was a lot of cleaning up to do, and the Iraqis still had a few scores to settle.

Provide Comfort

The United States had hoped that one of the results of its victory over Iraq would be the deposition of Saddam Hussein by his own people. The Kurds, tribesmen who composed 20 percent of the Iraqi population, had been oppressed by Saddam for years and had been the victims of bombing raids and gas attacks. The United States hoped that the Kurds would be the driving force behind an uprising, but after a few days of rebellion, the Iraqi army, which had been decimated and demoralized by the coalition's

A Pioneer reconnaissance drone or UAV stands ready for a mission in Saudi Arabia.

overwhelming conquest, reformed and went after the Kurds with a vengeance that could only come from the frustration of being defeated by a more powerful enemy.

The Kurds fled into the mountains bordering Iraq and Turkey, some 750,000 of them flooding refugee camps by late March. The disheartened, sickened Kurds soon presented a massive humanitarian problem for the allies of the coalition. With 1,500 refugees dying every day, the United States, which was still dismantling its huge war machine, assessing the results of Desert Storm and the frustrating continuing presence of Saddam in power, knew it had to help.

Along with units still in the Gulf, the Marine Corps ordered other Marines from around the world to head for the area to participate in the largest humanitarian effort in Marine Corps history. Besides its own CH-46Es, many of which were battle-scarred veterans of Vietnam more than twenty years before, HMM-264, a composite squadron embarked in USS

Guadalcanal (LPH-7), brought elements of HMH-461 (CH-53Es) and HMLA-167 (UH-1Ns and AH-1Ts) to what had been labeled Operation Provide Comfort.

As they began flying missions on April 15, the Marines struggled to establish primitive landing zones and base camps among the inhospitable mountains and hills of northern Iraq. They also had to contend with the seas of humanity that pressed forward to meet each helicopter, little caring of the danger from whirring rotor blades and heavily laden helicopters.

For the next two months, the Marines of HMM-264 and of various ground units helped the huge allied operation of first resuscitating the Kurds and then trying to relocate them back in Iraq. Fighting weather, Kurdish fears, and the vengeful Iraqis were no easy tasks, but by mid-June, when the Marines left the hills of Kurdistan, the tribesmen were much healthier and the future held promise, even among the ruins and tensions of Saddam's country.

In addition to helping the Kurdish refugees, Marine aviation participated in another large-scale humanitarian effort, Operation Sea Angel, a massive relief operation to help survivors of a huge cyclone in Bangladesh. The storm struck the impoverished country on April 29, 1991, and the country's prime minister appealed for help. Soon a worldwide rescue involving thirty-two countries was mounted. President Bush sent in elements of III MEF, including 5th MEB and MAG-50. The squadrons of this aircraft group were looking forward to returning home after the Gulf War, but their homecoming would be delayed. HMLA-169, HMM-265, VMA-513's Det B, and HMH-772, a Reserve squadron, were sidetracked to the Bay of Bengal. From mid-May to early June, the MAG's heavy- and medium-lift helicopters brought food and medical supplies to the devastated countryside.

Much has been written and said about the overall contribution of Naval Aviation during the Gulf War of 1991. The USAF usually claims the lion's share of credit so far as the impact of air power on the Iraqis, pointing to the effect of its strategic air campaign and the success of its F-15 pilots against Iraqi MiGs, whose pilots seldom flew their advanced aircraft in an aggressive or knowledgeable manner. However, while the USAF and other coalition partners certainly did well in the one-sided war, the Navy and Marine Corps did not spend the conflict on the sidelines.

For the Marines, the war was a chance to exercise, much like the wish of an athlete who has spent a lot of time and effort training in a gym and who longs to try himself in competition. Indeed, it may be argued that Marine Corps aviation found itself more of a tangible role than did the Navy's vaunted carrier-based squadrons, whose dedicated crews had to deal with the Air Force's complicated air-tasking order and fight for the junior service's aerial tankers.

The Marines, with their highly trained Harrier and Hornet crews, as well as their own KC-130 tankers, were more independent, and in more demand by the ground units, who, after all, ultimately fought the ground war that was the centerpiece of Allied strategy.

Col. John P. Oppenhuizen had been serving as the deputy commander of the Naval Safety Center in Norfolk, Virginia, when he was asked to volunteer to serve as the air officer for I MEF. An A-4 pilot in Vietnam with VMA-223, he commented on Marine aviation in the Gulf: "Marine air was probably

[Opposite] CH-53Es of HMH-464 at LZ Lonesome Dove sported names and low-visibility paint schemes. (Rick Mullen)

An AH-1J of Reserve squadron HMA-775 skirts the smoke columns of oil-well fires in Kuwait during the ground war, February 1991. (R. S. Doty)

not used as much in the CAS role before the ground war. There were CAS missions since we had people along the border the whole time. . . . Harriers were definitely used at Khafji. . . . Marine air was used a lot for interdiction and SEAD—most of it was interdiction."[10] Colonel Oppenhuizen was correct in assessing the use of Marine aircraft as battlefield interdictors, a role that Marine aircrews seldom trained for. Maj. William R. Cronin commented in the March 1992 issue of *Marine Corps Gazette*: "The release of Marine air for Marine use was delayed . . . by a spate of bad weather over many of the strategic targets in Iraq and northern Kuwait, and by a lack of confirmed bomb damage assessment assets."

Bomb damage assessment was a problem that was never resolved during the war. Major Cronin concluded, "Unlike deep air support and armed reconnaissance, battlefield air interdiction (BAI) is a mission seldom practiced by Marine tactical aviation, and prior to Desert Storm, was most often associated with Air Force tactical doctrine."

17 New Challenges for All

DESERT STORM and its fortuitous conclusion was only a pause in the larger activities that involved all the U.S. military, including the Marine Corps. Hard budgetary considerations in Washington forecast a shrinking lineup of squadrons and people. And even though squadrons may have participated with distinction in the Gulf War, they were not protected from the ax. Several aviation squadrons were decommissioned by 1993, with more to follow by mid-decade.

Important programs like the MV-22 Osprey were never safe, especially when crashes and operational mishaps seemed to dog the Navy and Marine Corps. Safety standdowns, by the direct orders of the Chief of Naval Operations, the Commandant, and their respective heads of aviation programs, strove to reorient people's attention toward safety and making do with a declining budget and supply chain.

Seventy AV-8Bs were grounded for five days in March 1996 after two mishaps. A similar grounding followed in June of all Navy and Marine Corps CH-53E and MH-53E helicopters to permit inspection of the big helos' main-rotor heads. Concern developed after the fatal crash in May of a CH-53E, which killed four Sikorsky employees on the pre-delivery flight.

The Harrier community, however, also scheduled a partial grounding of the AV-8B fleet—90 of 170 aircraft—in October after another series of fatal mishaps, which brought the number of AV-8Bs lost in 1996 to seven. The investigations focused on the Harriers' new 406 engines. By October sixty-eight Sea Stallions remained grounded because they were waiting for parts to prevent crashes like the one in May.

Veteran aircraft finally left the inventory. The unique OV-10 Bronco and its squadrons—VMO-1 and VMO-2 in the FMF, and VMO-4 in the Reserves—retired in 1993. Entering Marine Corps service in 1964, the big A-6 Intruder also retired in April 1993, VMA(AW)-332 having the nostalgic honor of flying the last Leatherneck sortie with Grumman's attack bomber. And Reserve squadron VMFA-112 at NAS Dallas held a retirement ceremony in January 1992 to bid farewell to McDonnell's F-4 as it left naval squadron service.

Other changes included the deactivation of VMAQ-4, the Reserve Prowler squadron in September 1992, followed by its immediate reactivation as part of a four-for-one split in the USMC EA-6B community. In an unusual move, the Marines reconstituted their sole VMAQ, the Playboys of VMAQ-2, with three detachments (X, Y, and Z) into three separate squadrons, VMAQs -1, -2, and -3. The Reserve 4th MAW's VMAQ-4 was disestablished, then stood back up as the fleet's VMAQ-4. The reorganization occurred on July 1, 1992, and permitted better coverage around the world and throughout the Navy and Marine Corps.

Besides the changes in hardware and organization, the Marines also found themselves changing geographic location in some cases. Service-wide base closings and realignment necessitated Marine Hornet squadrons on both coasts to shift. MCAS El Toro would be closed, and the West Coast Hornets would have to move south to the Navy's tactical jet base at Miramar, outside San Diego. Likewise, VMFA(AW)-533, having given up its A-6s after the Gulf War, had transitioned to the F/A-18D and would take up residence at MCAS Beaufort, South Carolina.

Marine Corps aviation had a full plate with new missions, new squadrons, new groupings, and new responsibilities. But the world went on, and new crises in different parts of the globe required that Marine squadrons participate.

The Marines also dealt with the sociological changes affecting the entire American military. Women were now entering naval flight training for the express purpose of becoming Marine aviators. By August 1996, two women had pinned on their wings of gold, one as a pilot and one as a naval flight officer. First Lieutenant Sarah Deal would fly CH-53Es, while 1st Lt. Jeanne Buchanan would fly EA-6Bs as an electronic countermeasures officer (ECMO).

Back to Africa

For the third time in two and one-half years, the Marines were called to action in Africa, and once again, the place was the strife-torn, famine-ridden coastal nation of Somalia, where rival factions were ruled by avaricious warlords who plundered their country and kept the rest of the civilized world at bay. More than 300,000 Somalis had died since the Marines' last visit in January 1991. The United States and other UN member countries wanted to send in medical supplies and food but could not risk entering the unsecured ports and airports. Thus, it fell to the Marine Corps' 15th MEU(SOC) to land on December 9, 1992, launching Operation Restore Hope.

The uncontested landing was carried out in a light atmosphere in front of enthusiastic news cameras. However, the risk was real, and on January 12, 1993, a Marine was killed during a gun battle near the airport at Mogadishu.

HMM-164 (REIN) from USS *Tripoli* (LPH-10) provided air support with CH-46Es, CH-53Es, UH-1Ns, and AH-1Ws. On December 12, 1992, a Huey took small-arms fire, and shortly afterward, two AH-1Ws came under fire from armed Somali trucks, called "technicals," near the road to Baledogle, a few kilometers inland. The Cobras returned fire, making short work of the light trucks and their foolish drivers.

[Top] A CH-53E and CH-46E of HMM-263(REIN) land in a field of scrub in famine-ridden Somalia in 1993. (CWO2 N. H. North, USMC)

[Bottom] Somalis bear bags of precious food from a CH-46E of HMM-263(REIN). (CWO2 N. H. North, USMC)

Soon, other Marine squadrons arrived, including HMLA-169, HMLA-369, HMH-363, HMH-466, and VMGR-352. By December 23, Marines had set up radar and a control tower at Mogadishu airport. Although action was heavy in the first weeks, by late February Somalia was sufficiently secure to allow some squadrons to leave. When they happened, firefights between American forces and Somali irregulars could be vicious. One such encounter led to the downing of an Army helicopter, the entrapment of its crew and Army Rangers, and eventually, the awards to two Army troopers—albeit posthumous—of the first Medals of Honor since Vietnam.

Operation Deny Flight over Bosnia

The world had changed greatly since the start of the 1990s. There had been an unpredicted war in the Persian Gulf, which had changed the way the United States and the rest of the world saw the pecking order in the rank of

[Left] WK 505 and its two-man crew get last-minute checks before heading out for a mission over Bosnia from the Italian air base at Aviano.

[Right] AH-1W Super Cobras and CH-53E Super Stallions of HMM-263 (REIN) lift off to carry out the TRAP mission for USAF Capt. Scott O'Grady in June 1995. (Sgt. Dave A. Garten, USMC)

international standing. Another, arguably more substantial and indicative change was the collapse of Communism in Europe and the demise of the world's second superpower, the Soviet Union. Marine Corps helicopters helped evacuate U.S. citizens from former Communist Albania in March 1997, as well as in the war-torn African countries of Zaire and Sierra Leone in April and May.

As the regions of the former USSR fell to squabbling among themselves, establishing their own new independence and ranking, they also faced periods of frightening internal strife, perhaps none so dangerous as in the always volatile nation-state of Yugoslavia. Loosely constructed and barely held together, because of surging ethnic, racial, and religious differences, this area had always been a simmering pot, ready to boil over at a moment's notice. (It was, after all, the assassination of a minor Austrian archduke in Sarajevo in 1914 that led directly to World War I, the cataclysmic struggle that changed world history forever.)

Finally, factional problems became too great and the country was quickly torn apart by an especially bloody civil war. There were old scores to settle, some harkening back to World War II, before the Communist takeover of the late 1940s, and although the United States and NATO tried desperately to monitor the situation, find solutions, and simply prevent violence, it was soon clear that the warring parties would not be ruled by outside interference.

NATO, working for the UN, could moderate the war in one area, however. In much the same way as they tried to prevent Iraq from mounting aerial attacks against its ethnic minorities such as the Kurds, NATO and the UN imposed an embargo in Yugoslavia, primarily against the Serb faction, which had the best-equipped air force.

In July 1993, eight F/A-18Ds from VMFA(AW)-533 arrived at Aviano Air Base in Italy to participate in Operation Deny Flight, the enforcement of the so-called no-fly zone over Yugoslavia, now called Bosnia-Herzegovina. VMFA(AW)-224 would also bring its F/A-18Ds to Aviano. The Marine fighters patrolled the skies over the Adriatic, and on April 11, 1994, two F/A-

18Cs from VMFA-251 attacked Serb targets outside the town of Gorazde, which had been besieged by the Serbs. Other Hornet squadrons from MAG-31 would participate in Deny Flight.

On November 21, 1994, a major strike involved more than thirty NATO planes from eight Italian air bases. The force, which included six F/A-18Ds from VMFA(AW)-332 at Aviano, hit Ubdina Air Base in Croatia, which had been used as a staging field for Serbian air attacks in Bosnia. The Moonlighter Hornets were the first in, launching HARMs against SA-6 sites. VMAQ-4 Prowlers, which had only arrived at Aviano and Sigonella the previous day, provided electronic countermeasures support. For the next two months, Seahawk crews flew more than 220 missions, which included firing several HARMs.

On May 25, 1995, a NATO strike hit Serb positions, and a week later, on June 2, a Serb missile downed an F-16. The young Air Force pilot, Capt. Scott O'Grady, hid from the Serbs trying to find him. They sometimes passed within a few feet of where O'Grady was crouching in the underbrush. Efforts to recover him failed. Finally, early on the morning of June 8, the tired and hungry F-16 pilot made contact with a member of his squadron on a patrol, and the rescue force was sent in.

The Marines of the 24th MEU(SOC) had trained for just such a mission, and they were ready. HMM-263 (REIN), on board USS *Kearsarge* (LHD-3), provided three CH-53Es (from HMH-464), three AH-1Ws (from HMLA-269), and four AV-8Bs. Two F/A-18Ds of VMFA(AW)-533, out of Aviano, also joined the flight, as did two Navy Prowlers from USS *Theodore Roosevelt* (CVN-71). The EA-6Bs were crewed by members of VAQ-141 and recalled Naval Air reservists of VAQ-209. Maj. Bill Tarbutton led the overall mission from the lead Sea Stallion.

[Left] Assigned to HMM-264 and flying from USS *Wasp* (LHD-1) in 1995, this AH-1W carries fuel tanks and LAU-68 7-round rocket launchers. Note the IFOR marking on the starboard engine, meaning Implementation Force, a NATO group that relieved UN protection forces. IFOR aircraft and troops helped maintain the cease-fire with helicopters flying CAS missions. (Paul Croisetiere)

[Top Right] An AV-8B prepares to launch from USS *Wasp* during operations in the Adriatic. (Paul Croisetiere)

[Bottom Right] An F/A-18D of VMFA(AW)-332 heads out on a mission over Kosovo. The "Moonlighters" were one of two Delta squadrons that flew from the Hungarian Air Force Base at Taszar, some 120 miles southwest of Budapest in May and June 1999 during the Kosovo Crisis, involving a short, bitter conflict with Serbia on one side and the NATO factions on the other. Serbia had invaded Kosovo, which had a large Muslim population. The two Hornet squadrons saw considerable action during this little-publicized tour. (via Istvan Toperczer)

The Cobras, led by Maj. Scott Mykleby, escorted the CH-53Es toward O'Grady's position. Launching at 5:05 AM, the helicopters were feet dry by 5:49, heading into Croatia from the Adriatic, then into Bosnia. By a little after 6:00 AM, the Harriers had launched to provide further escort. The F/A-18Ds flew passes to check for SAMs and to try to contact the young F-16 pilot. The Marine Hornet crews pin-pointed O'Grady's position, and at 6:40, as the AH-1s circled the area to defend against enemy action, the CH-53Es landed in a rocky landing zone.

The F-16 pilot dashed from his cover, and as the Marine troops hauled the bedraggled Air Force captain into the shuddering helicopter, the pilots lifted off, heading west toward the coast. However, still over Serbian territory, the rescue force came under fire, several rounds from small arms fire hitting the helicopter carrying Captain O'Grady. Surface-to-air missiles were also fired at the rapidly departing CH-53Es. Except for a few holes in their aircraft, and momentarily elevated heart rates, the Marines and their thrilled evacuee were safe. It was a happy ending to a tense week for the F/A-18 squadron, several of whose crews had befriended Captain O'Grady at Aviano.

Despite the success of Captain O'Grady's rescue, NATO's patience was wearing thin, and on August 30, it was finally exhausted. When the Serbs lobbed a shell into a busy marketplace in Sarajevo, killing thirty-seven innocent civilians, NATO decided the time had come for a strong show of force and resolve. Accordingly, a sustained air campaign called Operation Deliberate Force began, which lasted until September 14, with several breaks to allow the Serbs to come to the peace table. Hundreds of sorties blasted the Serb position, and Marine Hornets were in the thick of the action. VMFA(AW)-533's two-seater Hornets flew 180 sorties, which included suppression of enemy air defenses (SEAD) and interdiction.

VMFA-312 flew its single-seaters from the *Roosevelt* against the Serbs, delivering HARMs and bombs. VMFA-251, flying from USS *America* as a part of CVW-1, also participated in the latter stages of Deliberate Force. Having departed its homeport of Norfolk in late August, *America* received orders to steam ahead of its battle group to arrive in the Adriatic to relieve *Roosevelt* and also to provide additional support for the intense campaign over Bosnia. Arriving on September 8, CVW-1 quickly began combat operations, with Thunderbolt Hornets delivering the wing's first ordnance during a CAS mission.

The four-week air campaign finally got the Serbs to agree to a round of peace talks in the improbable locale of Dayton, Ohio. Administered by the U.S. State Department, the talks produced a cease-fire agreement, which if not the ideal solution for all parties, at least gave each faction a portion of its goals, allowed them to agree to stop the fighting, and permitted a NATO force to enter the country to prevent a resumption of hostilities.

Assigned to VMFA(AW)-533, this Delta
fires flares over Serbia. Serbian defenses
were occasionally quite heavy and not to
be taken lightly. The "Hawks" were the
second squadron to fly from Hungary.
(via Istvan Toperczer)

Development of existing aircraft as well as new types continued, but at a slower pace in the mid-1990s. The night-attack version of the Harrier II began arriving in squadrons in 1991. Using forward-looking infrared (FLIR), night-vision goggles (NVGs), and a digital moving map, the AV-8B(NA) also received an engine upgrade, with 15 percent more thrust. VMA-211 got its first night-attack Harrier in March 1991. The AV-8B Harrier II (Plus) brought continued improvements with a characteristic bulbous nose, which added seventeen inches to the standard Harrier II airframe, to house an improved bombing radar, the Hughes APG-65.

Included in the program was the remanufacture of seventy-three older Bs to II (Plus) standard, thereby saving 22 percent of the cost of a new aircraft. The first rebuilt AV-8B II (Plus) made its first flight on November 29, 1995. Only twenty-seven new aircraft have been built.

The Troubled Osprey

To consolidate CH-53D lift resources, all Delta squadrons migrated to Kaneohe in Hawaii, while a new squadron, HMH-366, joined them on September 30, 1994.

"It's no secret that the CH-46 is in trouble," wrote Maj. Jay Anderson in the November 1995 issue of the U.S. Naval Institute's *Proceedings*. "By the time the MV-22 is fielded in sufficient numbers . . . around 2008, the CH-46 will have been in service approximately forty years."

In March 1994, with the MV-22 Osprey still having funding problems, the Marine Corps began a modernization program to keep its remaining Sea Knights flying up to the 12,500-hour level, some 4,000 hours more than what most airframes had logged. The program involved replacing rotor heads, drive systems, transmissions, and rotor-control systems within the coming five years.

By the middle of the decade, the Marines were becoming anxious, if not downright desperate, to find a replacement medium-lift helicopter. Maj. Frederick J. Whittle lamented in the spring 1995 issue of *Wings of Gold*, the quarterly journal of the Association of Naval Aviation (ANA): "[If] the USS

Guam possessed the MV-22 . . . during Operation Eastern Exit in January 1991, the rescue of 300 diplomats in Mogadishu, Somalia, (we) could have completed the mission in under eight hours, vice the eighty-four it took."

The MV-22 was a battle-scarred veteran even before the first full-scale aircraft took flight. Intended as a multiservice aircraft, the Osprey lost one third of its USAF sponsorship in 1986. Defense Department support also wavered and finally disappeared when Secretary of Defense Richard Cheney canceled the program in April 1989, even though it had such important supporters as retired Colonel, now-retired Ohio U.S. Senator, John Glenn, and retired Lt. Gen. Thomas H. Miller, who was, after all, responsible for the Marine Corps AV-8 program.

There were, however, five development aircraft flying, and the flight-test program continued. But, on June 11, 1991, a V-22 test aircraft crashed at Wilmington, Delaware. The remaining four Ospreys were grounded but returned to flight status in October. On July 20, 1992, MV-22 No. 4 was destroyed when it crashed into the Potomac River near Quantico after a long ferry flight from Florida. Seven civilian and military crewmembers were killed. In May 1993, a board of inquiry determined that the Potomac mishap involved faulty maintenance and design flaws, but not the tilt-rotor technology at the heart of the MV-22's design. The flight program began again.

On October 22, 1992, Bell and Boeing got a $550 million contract for testing and development, including four new MV-22s and a modification of two existing Ospreys.

Finally, in December 1994, DoD made a commitment to produce the MV-22 for the Marine Corps and the Air Force's special operations units, with a tentative service introduction of 1999. Four special operations aircraft would be initially built along with thirty-three MV-22s for the Marines. Navy combat search and rescue (CSAR) would eventually receive forty-eight Ospreys. Ultimately, the production run will see some 400 aircraft manufactured from 1997 to 2021.

On December 5, 1995, Osprey No. 7's wing was mated to its fuselage. This example was the first engineering-and-manufacturing-development MV-22, basically the first production Osprey. All internal and external features should be the same as on those aircraft that will follow. DoD budgetary cuts had decreased the initial production lot of MV-22s. The Marine Corps' request for 425 MV-22s, including 65 so-called "attrition aircraft," has been reduced to 360. However, an accelerated production program would see thirty Ospreys a year by 2004. Delivery schedules called for the first MV-22Bs to reach the redesignated VMMT-204 training squadron by 1999, with an initial operating capability by 2001. These dates proved to be off, however, by several years.

Changes in the Reserves

As with the U.S. Naval Air Reserve, the Marine Reserves were dealing with downsizing and restructuring in the late 1990s. Several Marine Air Reserve squadrons—mostly helicopter units (but also various support units and two VMGR aerial refueling squadrons)—were mobilized for combat duty in 1991. Although very few air reservists saw actual combat, and of those, none saw sustained action, they were very much a part of the overall Corps participation in Desert Shield and Desert Storm, providing support and backup when needed.

However, with their return home, the Reserves had to deal with the business of force restructuring, base closings, and squadron decommissionings. As noted earlier, VMAQ-4, while on duty during Desert Storm to replace the single FMF VMAQ squadron, was decommissioned, then immediately reconstituted as a regular squadron. VMO-4 retired altogether, along with its OV-10s. Other Reserve squadrons that retired by the mid-1990s were VMA-133, VMA-322, VMA-124, and VMA-131, along with their trusty A-4s. VMFA-112, VMFA-134, and VMFA-321 gave up their Phantoms for Hornets, while VMA-142 traded its A-4s for F/A-18s and moved from Cecil Field, near Jacksonville, Florida, to NAS Atlanta, Georgia. Several helicopter squadrons also retired, or were redesignated and given different missions.

The Marine Air Reserve adversary squadron, VMFT-401 at MCAS Yuma, Arizona, flew leased Israeli Kfirs, indigenously produced modifications of the French Mirage, from 1987 to 1989. After returning the delta-winged Kfirs to their owners in September 1989, the Snipers have flown the F-5E and F-5F and will do so for the foreseeable future, one of the few survivors of the U.S. military's once mighty adversary program.

Altogether, twelve fleet and eight Reserve squadrons decommissioned after 1989, with an additional two fleet and two Reserve units in 1997. More followed in the coming years. Many squadrons moved—from El Toro (near Los Angeles) to Miramar (San Diego) or Hawaii, or from Cherry Point to Beaufort. Several of the survivors changed equipment and missions as noted above. As with some Naval Air Reserve squadrons, Marine Air Reserve units were also being tasked to support the huge anti-drug effort in the Caribbean and South America.

In September 1995, HMLAs -773 and -775 sent detachments to Trinidad and Tobago for a joint drug interdiction exercise in the island nation's forests. AH-1Ws and UH-1Ns carried the Marine Corps reservists into the so-called "marijuana belt" to help destroy the illicit crop, which enjoyed a street value of $3,000 per pound. The two-week "Weedeater" operation destroyed $500 million of marijuana plants, according to the American ambassador.

Various communities also saw changes and upgrades as the new century approached. Marine Corps helicopter squadrons continuously upgraded their aircraft, including new cockpit systems, radar and weapons systems, and ECM suites. To give the light-attack helo units (HMLA) more punch, they received more Cobra gunships, with a proportion of eighteen AH-1s to nine UH-1s. UH-1Ns and AH-1Ws also benefited from major upgrades. The remanufacturing of 280 Hueys and Cobras gave these veteran helicopters more powerful engines and four-blade main and tail rotors. Increased weapons and fuel capacity would also be included in these models, the AH-1Z and UH-1Y.

There were six CH-53E and four CH-53D squadrons in the fleet, and they consolidated and improved their equipment, too. The two Reserve squadrons flying RH-53Ds, HMH-769 at El Toro and HMH-772 at Willow Grove, transitioned to CH-53Es by the end of 1997. The Echo was the only heavy helicopter still in production in the United States, and there were no

plans for a replacement. The CH-53E's use in Somalia and during the rescue of USAF Captain O'Grady in Bosnia pointed out the Echo's long range and load-carrying capabilities.

Incredibly, the CH-46 was scheduled to serve for another twenty years, by which time its career would have spanned some fifty years. This extension came even with the introduction of the MV-22.

The Marines' two main tactical fixed-wing jets—the AV-8B and the F/A-18A/C/D—while still at the heart of the CAS mission, already faced replacement by the end of the first decade of the twenty-first century, at least on paper. However, events put those plans on hold, and the Harrier and Hornet remained vital members of the Marine Corps' aviation community.

USS *Inchon* under way in the Caribbean off the coast of Haiti during Operation Support Democracy, June 1994. (PH2 John Sokolowski)

The F-35 Lightning II joint strike fighter—more than 600 of which are planned to be built for the Marines—would eventually consolidate the Harrier and Hornet roles, as well as fly in other services.

Other types of aircraft, namely the KC-130 Hercules and EA-6B Prowler, continued to serve, again, with the help of upgrades in systems and instrumentation. The Navy's projected EA-18G Growler, a two-man ECM variant of the Hornet scheduled to replace its aging EA-6B fleet, will not enter Marine Corps service. Current plans call for the Prowler to fly on for another ten years.

The KC-130T is the Marine Corps' oldest type, and had equipped three fleet and two Reserve squadrons. The tankers are much in demand, and can be found across the globe. However, an important upgrade, the KC-130J, with its distinctive six-bladed propellers, entered service in June 2002 with VMGRT-253, the training squadron, and is currently replacing the "T" in the fleet.

UAVs have also reorganized and are now part of Marine aircraft groups, just as any other squadron. Whereas until January 1996, UAVs served in companies—1st Remotely Piloted Vehicle Company 1 and 2—providing aerial reconnaissance services for all four elements of the Marine Air-Ground Task Force, they have since been redesignated VMU-1 and VMU-2 (Fixed-Wing, Marine, Unmanned 1 and 2). A third squadron was activated in September 2008.

As Marine Corps aviation headed toward the new millennium, there were many obstacles to be faced and overcome. The world was not what it was even twenty years ago when this book's second edition appeared, or twelve years ago with the third edition's publication, to say nothing of after World War II more than sixty years ago. Old enemies were now cautious allies, and old scenarios against which we all trained no longer held true, or at least completely true. The dangers and threats were still out there, but they had different names and faces. Just how new and different would be tragically demonstrated with the crashes of four American airliners on a bright, clear Tuesday morning, September 11, 2001, and as they did for everyone else in the world, the Marine Corps' frames of reference would be changed forever.

18 Fighting in the New World of Terrorism

WHO OF US WAS READY FOR THE NEW WORLD that burst upon everyone that late summer Tuesday morning? Even the players, the hijackers of the four airliners and their "handlers" in Afghanistan, Pakistan, and Saudi Arabia, could barely understand what their actions would bring, thrusting the entire world into a new society, where all references would now be pre-9/11 and post-9/11.

Certainly, the U.S. armed forces were not ready. The best that could be said would be that some inklings of accelerated activity could be discerned in the troubled area known collectively as Southwest Asia. (Strange, that so much of post–World War II—a large one-half of which was an Asian war–military action—had been ranged in Asia, and then concentrated in the Southeast, and now Southwest portion of that vast territory. Is it us against the Asians, and now the Muslims?)

Intelligence warned of increased planning and testing exercises but nothing concrete or definite. Thus, on September 10, what could be considered the last day of normalcy or peace throughout the world, there was little to alert American forces and their military and civilian leaders to anything in the wind of the next twenty-four hours. But the storm was building rapidly and would break over the densely populated American northeast corridor like ten Hiroshima bombs.

As the millennium turned to the heretofore science-fictional twenty-first century, American military attention had been largely focused on the turbulent world of the Balkans, the little enclave of nation wannabes that had troubled the planet since the late 1800s. Indeed, it was here that World War I had begun, precipitating a century of bloody unrest that frequently exploded into unbridled war that took millions of lives.

While most of the land conflict involving U.S. forces was fought by Army troops, the aviation support included a large portion of Navy carrier-based squadrons, of which some numbers included Marine units, specifically F/A-18 Hornet and AV-8B Harrier squadrons. Navy carrier air wings required an influx of light attack units, especially as the veteran F-14 Tomcat, now equipped to fly in the role of a medium bomber—the A-6 Intruder having long since been retired—was also scheduled for reductions in quantity and ultimate retirement itself. The hard-pressed Navy Hornet squadrons needed help from their Marine Corps compatriots, and once again, the question of Marine tactical squadrons serving aboard carriers came up. But now there was little time for discussion; the Marines were definitely needed, and thus they would come aboard. The conflict that would explode over the world in 2001 was barely discernable as the Marine flight crews dove on targets hidden in the Yugoslavian forests and dueled with Serbian SAMs and flak in the late 1990s.

America has often been derided for relishing the role of "policeman to the world." Some Americans like seeing themselves in that position, but most do not. Yet, the twentieth century, even perhaps going a few years earlier with the Spanish-American War of 1898, and certainly beginning with the Banana Wars of Central America in the early 1900s, gave a more definitive form before World War I. By this time, when America entered the war in 1917, U.S. actions began a hundred years of what has become the American intervention in and protection of older, longer-established countries than the United States.

By 1941 Europe was either under Nazi domination or exhausted, waiting only for the final German assaults. Indeed, perhaps the greatest mistake of the war was that of the Japanese, who, with their attack on Pearl Harbor that December, brought America into the war and ultimately sealed their fate and that of their Axis partners. Twice in barely thirty years, American resources, industrial might, and fighting spirit had saved the world from attempted domination by a small coterie of draconian dictators.

Wars in Korea and Vietnam were campaigns to protect those countries from communism. Vietnam established a sequence where America had to step in to take the place of a defeated European country—in this case France—to keep Communist forces at bay, if only for a time. In 1979 the great military resources of the Soviet Union were brought to bear in Afghanistan. The Soviets quickly became mired in their own "Vietnam-style" conflict for which victory seemed a distant hope. Twenty-three years later, the United States followed its Russian nemesis into the area. However, Americans had a more definite reason and a much clearer purpose: to rout out the Taliban rulers and punish the perpetrators of 9/11.

It might be said, however, and given the incredible shock of the attacks on the American psyche, that national paranoia ran high for the first six months. Even a national hero like Joe Foss was not immune. He had battled the best the Japanese had to throw at him in the skies over Guadalcanal, and a then-grateful nation had given him its highest decoration, the Medal of Honor. Yet, sixty years after receiving it, Joe Foss was accosted and detained at the Phoenix airport before he boarded a flight to Washington.

The surviving Marine Corps' ace of aces, a retired brigadier general in the South Dakota Air National Guard and a former governor of that state, wore the blue ribbon and imposing medal around his neck as he tried to go through the gate on January 11, 2002. Under-educated gate guards stepped forward and held him for forty-five minutes because they were afraid of this eighty-six-year-old's medal! The fighter ace stood his ground, maintaining he would not board the plane if he could not wear the highest medal of the country he had fought so hard to defend.

Although he normally did not travel with the medal, Foss was taking it with him for special reasons, to show to the Army cadets at West Point, where he was to be a guest speaker. Foss noted that his one-way ticket and his big ten-gallon hat may have caused some suspicion for airline personnel, and eventually, after an intense security search, Foss was allowed to board. The incident made the news wire for the next few days, and it caused many veterans, this author included, to wonder just where the country's education system was headed when its younger citizens did not know what such a device was and what it represented for both the individual wearing it and the cause for which he fought at a time when the country was mobilizing to confront nearly the exact same menace all over again.

The first direct participation by Marine air following the attacks was very local: VMFA-321, the Reserve squadron at Naval Air Facility (NAF), Washington, D.C., a tenant command on Andrews AFB south of the city, joined with other squadrons in patrolling the skies over the capital. The operation was called Noble Eagle, and teaming with its neighbor, the 113th FW of the Washington, D.C., Air National Guard, with which they had shared the flight line for many years, the Hell's Angels flew over the area armed with Sidewinders.

In the meantime, the planning and assignments were in high gear. Planned returns to the United States by long-deployed ships, squadrons, and their members were placed on hold. Ships were turned around and redirected to stations in the eastern Mediterranean and the Persian Gulf. At first, the way seemed relatively simple: destroy the base the terrorists had established in the distant country of Afghanistan. A second, more involved and trying objective was to capture the leaders who had taken refuge in the mountains strung along the dangerous border between Afghanistan and Pakistan. Though simple, the tasks would not be easy.

For centuries, Afghanistan had been at the center of trade routes and had been the target of invasion and foreign domination. Yet, the exotic country had survived and had even managed, with what was now an embarrassment, the help of American arms and advisers, to repulse the vaunted Soviet war machine in a long, bloody war that eventually ended with the invader's withdrawal.

To make things more difficult, Afghanistan was landlocked and far from any ocean that supported naval carrier strike groups. Like the 1991 Gulf War, long missions would have to be flown for only a few minutes over target. Another daily string of aerial tankers, much like Desert Storm ten years earlier, would have to be conceived and assigned.

The small Afghani Air Force—the Taliban claimed 250–300 aircraft, an assortment of obsolescent MiGs, Antonov transports, and Mil helicopters—would not pose any credible threat. So, as there would be little or no aerial opposition, Operation Enduring Freedom (OEF) became a campaign of ground combat that made great use of close air support, a large portion of which would be supplied by the Marine Hornets and Cobra gunships.

Much like the period of the first half of the preceding twentieth century we had just left, Americans and their coalition allies would have to return to the general area they had left a little more than a decade before to fight one new enemy, and very soon, the old enemy hiding in his palaces and in the dusty streets of the towns of his oppressed nation.

Harriers and Hornets to the Front

It took a month after the attacks of 9/11, but the first retaliatory strikes of OEF came on the night of October 7, 2001, as coalition aircraft hit a wide assortment of strategic targets in Afghanistan. U.S. Air Force bombers flew long missions, while the Navy sent F-14s from the carriers USS *Enterprise* (CVN-65) and USS *Carl Vinson* (CVN-70). The following days and weeks were a succession of attacks, hitting the Taliban and preparing for a major ground operation to capture the country and destroy the ruling government.

On the night of October 18, the first Marine strikes were flown by F/A-18Cs of VMFA-251 aboard USS *Theodore Roosevelt* (CVN-71), which had just arrived on station, having left Norfolk on September 19th, along with her battle group.

A Thunderbolt pilot received one of the war's first Distinguished Flying Crosses. Maj. Brant Bond and his division of five Hornets were up on October 25 when they got a call that Marines were under heavy Taliban fire. At first, the enemy was so well camouflaged that the Marine aviators couldn't pick them out from the rocky terrain. But Bond saw his first target, and he and his squadron mates destroyed several enemy anti-aircraft emplacements.

Strikes continued for the rest of the month, and on November 3, USS *Peleliu* (LHA-5) launched the first Harrier strikes of the war against targets in southern Afghanistan, the four Marine jump jets of VMA-211, assigned to HMM-163, delivering 500-pound bombs. The ship's air combat element (ACE) was part of the 15th MEU(SOC) (Marine Expeditionary Unit [Special Operations Capable]).

Soon, the V/STOLs were operating ashore from an abandoned airstrip, which the Marines dubbed Camp Rhino. Located in the desolate area west of Kandahar, it had been used by the Taliban and their al-Qaeda masters. Marine helicopters and gunships, escorted by Harriers, cleared the base, allowing KC-130s to bring in ground troops and their supplies. They were followed by Air Force C-17s bringing in heavier equipment. The Marines were in to stay.

More than a thousand Leathernecks came in during the following days, and they occasionally had to repel Taliban forces bent on retaking their base. But Cobra gunships and F-14s and F/A-18s helped ensure Camp Rhino remained under its new American ownership.

The USS *Bataan* (LHD-5) soon brought its 26th MEU(SOC) and its VMA-223 AV-8Bs, part of HMM-365, and CH-53E Sea Stallions, which quickly went ashore to Camp Rhino. More Marine Hornets had also arrived aboard USS *John Stennis* (CVN-74). VMFA-314's F/A-18Cs joined the Thunderbolt Hornets in flying continuing strikes against Taliban positions in the mountains.

The KC-130s of VMGR-252 and VMGR-352 were very active flying supplies in and out of the forward operating bases and also providing aerial refueling services when needed. One Hercules was lost on January 9, 2002, when a VMGR-352 transport crashed in the mountains of Pakistan. Seven crewmen died.

The KC-130 fleet was aging rapidly, yet the aircraft was without peer and there were no plans to field a new design. However, on September

7, 2001, the Marines accepted the first examples of a new C-130 when KC-130Js arrived at VMGRT-253 at Cherry Point, North Carolina. The remaining seventy-nine KC-130s—Fs, Rs, and Ts—were all scheduled to be replaced by the highly upgraded model, which featured more powerful engines driving six-bladed propellers that provided nearly 30 percent more thrust than earlier models, as well as a 15 percent increase in fuel efficiency. The new Hercs would soon join operations in OEF.

In the meantime, the existing transports were heavily engaged supporting the rapidly accelerating war. VMGR-252 would be the first Marine squadron to deploy with the new "Battle" or "Super Hercs," taking them to Iraq in 2004 and conducting operations not only in Iraq but also in support of OEF in Afghanistan. The new tanker's high-tech avionics and engines, plus their aging refueling pods, required a lot of attention from the squadron maintenance troops, especially in the area's periods of high heat and dust-laden winds.

The Harrier complement built quickly, and soon some seventy AV-8Bs were serving in OEF, alongside Harriers from Great Britain, Spain, and Italy. It was a unique situation that harkened back to the days of World War II, when a huge coalition of nations used equipment from only one or two major producers—namely the United States and Great Britain. But this time, a very unique aircraft was fighting under four different national colors.

The Italian Harriers, flying from their carrier, *Giuseppe Garibaldi*, were the first AV-8s to carry the Litening II FLIR pod, which allowed their pilots to designate their own targets for their laser-guided bombs. Eventually, the Italians flew 131 OEF missions.

USS *Wasp* (LHD-1) arrived on station in March 2002, bringing the 22nd MEU and its HMM-261 ACE. The *Wasp* Harriers were making the AV-8 deployment with the Litening II system, and their pilots soon put the pod to use against enemy targets above the envelopes of Taliban air defenses.

The massive influx of Marine aviation assets, some on ships, others by air, began flooding the region as squadrons and their support groups began arriving en masse. The tanker squadrons were hard pressed to meet all their requirements, and the maintenance sections worked day and night to ensure vital helicopter sections were ready.

Operation Anaconda

One of the earliest major engagements of OEF began in March 2002. It had become obvious that the terrorists whose capture was at the heart of the entire campaign were holed up in the mountain and valley hideouts in the Afghanistan hinterlands. Capturing them was not going to be easy. On March 3, Anaconda aimed at routing them out from the Shah-e Kot Valley in southeastern Afghanistan. Some 1,200 troops from the U.S. Army, the Australian army, and other coalition forces were sent in to block escape routes. They encountered stiff enemy opposition and called for help.

Early on March 4, atop a 10,000-foot mountain, a U.S. Army Chinook helicopter—the largest in the Army inventory—was shot down, beginning a desperate fight to retrieve the crew and the contingent of Navy SEALs that was aboard. Covered by Navy and Marine jets, another Chinook ran in and picked up the survivors, but the fight was not over.

Early the next morning, Marine Cobras and Sea Stallions from the 13th MEU(SOC)'s HMM-165 (REIN) launched from USS *Bonhomme Richard* (LHD-6). The 730-nautical-mile trip required in-flight refueling. The helicopters arrived over their target in the early evening and struck the Taliban targets. Marine helicopters quickly established a much-appreciated link with coalition troops, especially the U.S. Army forces, whose vaunted Apache attack helicopters were having maintenance problems and could not always respond to the calls for help from the ground.

There were also problems with fuel and ammunition supplies, the Army choppers having to travel long distances to rearm and refuel. The Marine CH-53s used their tactical bulk refueling system, taking fuel from orbiting KC-130s and returning to the forward area arming and refueling point (FAARP) to service the waiting Cobras. Ordnance and ammunition had to be brought in from Bagram. As one CH-53 squadron CO commented, "It was the classic USMC rapid response to the man on the ground. . . . They were able to provide continuous fire support to the soldiers on the ground, who were ecstatic."[1]

The engagement lasted for several more days and eventually involved most of the Navy and Marine Corps aviation units in-theater. The AV-8Bs were heavily engaged. Anaconda lasted until March 18. It must be said that the Harrier fleet enjoyed a large amount of press immediately after this initial period. Magazine articles were published in many American and British publications, while the equally hard-working helicopter communities saw little "ink." For many observers, it was not an unexpected situation. The Marine Corps was not known for tooting its horn while its operations were on-going. After the fighting had finished and the units and people had been brought home, there was time to write the formal histories, an activity in which the Corps shines. But it does take time.

One of the Harrier squadrons had also seen a lot of action in Korea, using a variety of aircraft and even accomplishing the first night jet-to-jet kill. VMA-513, the Flying Nightmares, flew their six AV-8Bs into Bagram Air Base in Afghanistan, thirty-five miles north of the capital of Kabul, on October 15, 2002. It was an old Soviet field, and the conditions were pretty bad. The runways and taxiways were strewn with debris. Even with the Harrier's touted vertical takeoff capabilities, it was important that the operating surfaces be cleaned up.

The Marines named their base Camp Tuefel-Hunden, harkening back to World War I when the Germans quickly named their Leatherneck foes Devil Dogs, a moniker all Marines quickly took to their hearts.

Quickly establishing an operating routine, the Nightmares soon found themselves flying a large number of night missions, requiring night-vision goggles (NVGs) and the new wonder tool, the Litening II targeting pod, always mounted on the Harrier's station 5, the inboard starboard wing pylon. The missions were flown lights out. As one pilot remarked, "We face danger as soon as we take off and until we land. It's not like we have the luxury of taking off far behind enemy lines and then prepare ourselves for combat. We're smack dab in the middle of it."[2]

On the night of November 14, a Nightmare Harrier joined an Air Force A-10 in engaging the enemy during a firefight near a U.S. special-operations base.

On-going Programs Stretch Things

While the first campaigns of the War on Terrorism were evolving, programs and plans were also continuing. The Navy and Marine Corps considered three innovative ideas: putting AV-8s aboard CVs, putting Marines and their helicopters aboard CVs, and integrating Marine squadrons—primarily VMFAs with Hornets—with the Navy carrier air wings. The first concept didn't work because of the amount of maintenance and berthing spaces required. The second idea was used to a limited degree. The third idea called TacAir (tactical aviation) integration boded ill and promised to constrict both Navy and Marine carrier squadrons right when they were most needed in their traditional roles. Basically, the plan called for assigning at least one Marine Hornet squadron to each of the ten Navy carrier air wings and a Navy VFA to fill in for one of the three Marine VMFAs normally assigned to ground-attack duties in Japan.

Admittedly, the Navy's carrier air wings were occasionally hard pressed in meeting their responsibilities across the globe. Six-month deployments stretched out for another month or two, and quick turn-arounds hurt families and individual members. Besides placing undue burden on the Marine units, it also became clear that maintaining such a hard-driving schedule would soon completely disrupt the VMFAs' ability to service the Marines on the ground simply because the Navy's schedule was different than those of the aircraft groups that had to deploy to Japan, or now to Southwest Asia, while still meeting the Navy's time tables.

As late as mid-2005, the Navy Department was still trying to adopt the TacAir integration program. In mid-2004, Navy squadron VFA-97 had been temporarily assigned to duty with the Marines in Japan, sending its regularly assigned Hornets to other Navy squadrons at Lemoore and taking Marine

A Silver Eagle F/A-18+ launches from USS *Harry S. Truman* on an OIF mission in January 2005. VMFA-115 was one of the very few squadrons still flying the older so-called "legacy" Hornets. (PHAN Ricardo J. Reyes)

Hornets from VMFA-212 already at Iwakuni. After lengthy maintenance and operation training, the Warhawks of VFA-97 began making their way west. But the press of the War on Terrorism and its two-front war in Southwest Asia, OEF, and Operation Iraqi Freedom (OIF), made the arrangement too cumbersome.[3]

Finally, in August 2008, the Navy and Marine Corps decided to "shelve" the program. Things had just become too complicated. The Marines were waiting for their V/STOL F-35s and were sticking with their veteran F/A-18s to save money, which they would put toward other programs. The Navy's intent was different from the Corps, and the cost of training and reassigning Navy squadrons to Marine Corps groups was too prohibitive.

Quoted in an article in the *Navy Times* newspaper, defense analyst Loren Thompson opined, "Marine and Navy aviators have different training and orientation, which means they are suited for different missions. . . . The Navy aviators are into strike warfare, [and] what the Marines are saying, based on experience in Iraq, is that there are operational limitations to integration. It looks better on paper than it works in practice."[4]

What has lasted is the integration of Navy and Marine Corps EA-6B Prowler squadrons. This accompanied the Air Force retirement of its own tactical electronic warfare (EW) squadrons, which flew the EF-111A Raven in Desert Storm in 1991. The Air Force came to rely on the Navy and Marine VAQ and VMAQ squadrons for tactical electronic attack support. Air Force

EA-6B Prowlers continued to be vital components of any mission during OIF and OEF. This EA-6B is assigned to VMAQ-1 based at Al Asad in July 2005. (Sgt. Juan Vara)

officers were even assigned, and in a few cases, even rose to command land-based, not carrier-based, Navy VAQs. Indeed, the Navy's training squadrons have occasionally also "enjoyed" the unique philosophies and skills of USAF COs, primarily in the primary training squadrons and the main undergraduate NFO (naval flight officer) training squadron, VT-10.

For a time, OEF CVWs included one, occasionally two, Marine squadrons. Although they greatly aided the overall effort, very few VMFAs participated in OEF, leaving the task to the CVWs, forced to fly hundreds of miles inland, and to the detachments of Harrier VMAs and Cobra and Huey combined units. When OIF began in March 2003, the war in Afghanistan quickly became the forgotten war in the minds of the public, but not the participants still struggling to contain a resurgent Taliban. The Navy and Marine Corps were being stretched incredibly thin, and for the man on the ground, it might have appeared that getting Saddam was more important than supporting their efforts in the rugged mountains of Afghanistan. The dedicated public affairs professionals in the Navy were generally prohibited from going into the OEF war zone as well and were sent to Iraq in much greater numbers. Thus, the amount of coverage that would come from OIF was, indeed, greater, than that emanating from Afghanistan.

Meanwhile, aircraft programs involving a highly improved Huey and Cobra, and the tri-service MV-22 Osprey tilt-rotor, which the Marine Corps desperately required to replace its Methusalian CH-46 Sea Knight, struggled in the funding campaigns being waged on Capitol Hill. Originally, the Navy was considering the Osprey for combat SAR (search and rescue), but decided against it, leaving the Air Force and the Marines to continue the program. A new model of the CH-53 Sea Stallion, the CH-53K, was also under development. It would be the largest and heaviest-lift helicopter in the west.

Finally, a science-fiction newcomer was making a name for itself. The unmanned aerial vehicle (UAV) was being flown by many U.S. services, as well as the CIA, and the Marines were heavily involved. A bewildering number of UAVs and their manufacturers made keeping track of them all difficult. Yet, there was growing satisfaction in how these pre-programmed and radio-controlled aircraft performed, delivering real-time imagery, protecting positions and seeking out targets, both strategic and human. Marine UAVs included hand-thrown and sling-shot-launched vehicles to look over the next hill as well as micro-UAVs, a little larger than insects, equipped with a mini-TV system, that could literally fly into the door or window of a building and look for people hiding in the darkened rooms. Thus, Marine companies and even platoons could have their own air arms while support for larger formations was provided by the Air Force and Army operating their larger Predators and other UAVs.

19 Persian Gulf War II: *Taking Saddam, Again!*

FOLLOWING DESERT STORM IN 1991, the U.S.-led coalition found itself burdened with maintaining a standing patrol in the air to assure that no Iraqi aircraft would violate established boundaries and corridors and that, especially, the oppressed near-nation of Kurds in the north would not be subjected to the oppression that had characterized Saddam's draconian rule. Established in August 1992, Operation Southern Watch (OSW) took advantage of all the assets available, French, and British, as well as all the American air services. The Kurdish patrol had been established in January 1997 as Operation Northern Watch (ONW). Operating alongside their Navy compatriots, Marine aircrews racked up an impressive number of missions in Hornets. Between 1995 and 2003, Marine Hornet squadrons VMFA-251, -312, -314, and -323 gained valuable combat experience that would stand them in good stead a few years down the road.

The most intense action was the four-day campaign labeled Operation Desert Fox, which began on December 16, 1998. The premise was Iraq's stubborn refusal to permit inspection of its weapons facilities. American concern over the question of whether Saddam possessed or was developing weapons of mass destruction finally came to a head and then-President William J. Clinton ordered strikes from the carriers USS *Enterprise* (CVN-65) and USS *Carl Vinson* (CVN-70). *Enterprise*'s CVW-3 included Hornets from VMFA-312, and Checkerboard Hornets delivered the first AGM-154 Joint Stand-Off Weapons (JSOWs), along with several AGM-88 HARMs and laser-guided bombs. Trying to target the Iraqi leadership, their targets were a presidential palace and several buildings assigned to Iraqi Republican Guards units.

Results of Desert Fox were inconclusive, and the Iraqi dictator remained defiant. For the next five years, occasional U.S. strikes included Marine squadrons reacting to occasional "painting" by Iraqi SAM and flak radars during OSW missions. From March 2000 to March 2001, coalition aircraft were tracked more than 500 times. In February 2001, VMFA-312, now part of the USS *Harry S. Truman*'s (CVN-75) CVW-3, again struck Iraqi positions.

OSW missions were also flown by shore-based Marine Hornets, mainly the two-seat F/A-18Ds of several VMFA(AW)s. Flying from Al Jaber air base in Kuwait, the Green Knights of VMFA(AW)-121 were succeeded by VMFA(AW)-225, followed by VMFA(AW)-332 and a detachment of F/A-18Cs from VMFA-212, forward deployed in Japan.

Following the 9/11 attacks, American carrier air power took station in the northern Arabian Gulf (NAG), and the stage was set for OEF, to be followed by OIF. In December 2002, flying from USS *Constellation* (CV-64), a division of F/A-18Cs of VMFA-323 assigned to CVW-2 struck Iraqi targets in an area that would soon see lots of ground action, namely An Nasiriyah. A number of these small-scale strikes were only rehearsals for the larger campaign to come.

First OIF Strikes

Operation Enduring Freedom had the headlines to itself for nearly a year. But there was occasional intrusion by news from Iraq as the United States struggled to determine if the Iraqis and their diabolical leader, Saddam Hussein, a thug in the mold of Josef Stalin, Adolf Hitler, and Benito Mussolini, had nuclear weapons. Hussein maintained he did not throughout the last years of his life. However, America was not satisfied and ultimately gave the Iraqis an ultimatum to come clean and allow proper international inspections, or face the combined wrath of the coalition of most of the countries that stormed across the desert in 1991.

Predictably, Hussein remained unintimidated, and Present George W. Bush (ironically, the *son* of the president who fought Desert Storm, Gulf War I, in 1991) ordered the huge armada waiting on Iraq's doorstep to go in.

Elements of I Marine Expeditionary Force Headquarters Group (I MHG) were among the first in action, beginning on March 19, and continuing for the next several days. Crossing the Euphrates River and the Tigris River—vital waterways in both ancient and modern times—at the city of An Nasiriyah southeast of Baghdad, Marine ground forces made good time while engaging various enemy forces at several industrial sites. As they drove on to Baghdad, Iraq's capital city of six million people, the troops on the ground came under a massive close-air-support (CAS) umbrella provided by fixed-wing jets from several carrier air wings, as well as a dedicated F/A-18D Hornet squadron and Marine Corps helicopters from the 3rd Marine Aircraft Wing. It was the largest deployment of a Marine air wing since Vietnam, including supply ships, men, and material, as well as the squadrons, aircraft, and their personnel.

On the night of 20–21 March, I MEF Marines crossed the Kuwait border into southern Iraq in the first push to Baghdad. They encountered stiff opposition from Iraqi forces in armored personnel carriers. The Marines destroyed the two enemy vehicles and kept going toward the important Iraqi oil fields at Rumeila.

Marine Hornet and Harrier squadrons of Marine Aircraft Group 11 and Marine Aircraft Group 13 flew more than 4,000 CAS sorties and air interdiction sorties, delivering more than 3.8 million pounds of ordnance. Marine UH-1 Hueys and AH-1 Cobras contributed helicopter CAS services, often flying much closer to their target than was possible with the fast-moving jets.

An Nasiriyah was one of many intense battles in the beginning of the campaign. Marines on the ground faced a determined enemy in several

pitched battles among the city's buildings. In the late afternoon of March 23, the crew of a CH-46E of HMM-162 dropped onto the street amid heavy fighting to pull a badly wounded Marine out of action.

The venerable CH-46 was fighting its third major war since its introduction during Vietnam nearly forty years earlier—besides numerous skirmishes and brush-fire actions. Its service life painfully strung out because of the MV-22 Osprey's equally painful gestation period, the "Phrog" began contributing to the War on Terror almost from the start. Although it was hard put to operate in the higher altitudes of Afghanistan's OEF campaign, it was right there in the initial operations, especially in the Casualty Evacuation (CASEVAC) missions that were so vital to the survival of wounded coalition troops. Usually armed with two .50-caliber door guns, the Phrogs, many of which were much older than their young crews, flew into hostile territory to retrieve badly injured Marines, giving them a more than equal chance of surviving their wounds once they got to the operating table. HMM-162,

HMM-165, and HMM-268 were just a few of the squadrons involved in these early stages of the war.

The campaign continued, and as the carrier air wings found their groove, the Marine Hornet squadrons contributed their fair share. On March 23, despite a sand storm, a feature of war in the desert, four F/A-18Cs of VMFA-323 each dropped three 2,000-pound Joint Direct Attack Munitions (JDAMs) on Iraqi buildings on the vital airport outside Baghdad. The hits helped Allied forces soon capture the important enemy facility.

A single Marine carrier-based Hornet squadron, VMFA-115, was flying in the eastern Mediterranean, from the nuclear-powered carrier USS *Harry S. Truman* (CVN-75). (Naming the huge ship after the 33rd U.S. president was an honor that would have brought a quizzical smile from the acid-tongued president from Missouri, arguably one of the Navy's—and Marines'—harshest post–World War II critics, and actually, a World War I Army veteran, who had seen action in France.) Operating refurbished, and upgraded, F/A-18A+s, the Silver Eagles and their CVW-3 teamed with CVW-8 aboard the *TR* to support strikes against fixed targets in the so-called "Shock and Awe" strategic campaign. Their initial tasking was made more difficult when Turkey and Saudi Arabia, supposedly staunch U.S. allies, refused to let American forces come through their airspace, unlike the 1991 Desert Storm campaign, when the area's countries were much more united against Iraq. Eventually, however, Saudi Arabia relented to a degree, and the eastern Med air wings launched eastward to strike Iraqi targets near Al Taqaddum air base west of Baghdad, one of the most important, and dangerous, targets of the Desert Storm fighting.

Hornet Recce

One of the mistakes of Desert Shield/Desert Storm was the premature retirement of the Marine Corps' only dedicated tactical air reconnaissance unit, VMFP-3, and its RF-4B Phantoms just before the campaign started. Frustrated field commanders often found themselves without adequate photographic intelligence. In the years following Gulf War I, several Marine F/A-18Ds were outfitted with the Advanced Tactical Aerial Reconnaissance System (ATARS). Basing from Al Jaber, these aircraft flew some of the most important pre-war missions before OIF over southern Iraq. VMFA(AW)-225 and VMFA(AW)-121 had varying degrees of success with the systems, but the overall contribution of ATARS was generally well accepted.

The nose-mounted ATARS requires the deletion of the normal 20-mm cannon as well as the installation of different nose-gear doors. ATARS Hornets still retain the rest of their offensive capabilities.

It might be argued that tactical aerial reconnaissance has always had its dark side, juxtaposed against its obvious benefits. Sensitive cameras and later computer links were subject to the effects of weather and flying at altitude and recovering aboard ship, not to mention the long-term degradation of a six-month deployment. In Vietnam, the boiling Southeast Asian climate or the hot, humid, salt-sea environment of the aircraft carrier did little to help maintainers keep the systems of their RF-8s, RF-4s, and RA-5Cs in working order.

For the Umpteenth Time: Who Owns Marine Air?

From World War II, the thorny question of who tells Marine aviators what to do at any particular point in a war has immediately raised its head whenever a new conflict begins. It happened in Korea, in Vietnam, and in Desert Storm, and it threatened to do so again in OIF. Hoping to head the matter off and come to a reasonable solution *before* hostilities began, the Marines hosted a conference with Air Force leaders at MCAS Miramar, which had changed hands from the Navy in October 1997. The change came as a result of the closing of the Marines' longtime jet base at El Toro, near Los Angeles, and the ongoing consolidation of the Navy's Pacific F-14 and F/A-18 squadrons. The Tomcat fleet was on the retirement track, and several squadrons had already been decommissioned, while others were to follow or transition to the Hornet and become VFAs.

The Air Force wanted to come up with a way to manage 3rd MAW assets without appearing to take over Marine Corps air operations completely. USAF Gen. T. Michael Moseley, who would run the aviation side of the coming war, made it known he wanted all the services to come together. (Moseley would later become USAF Chief of Staff only to be fired—along with Air Force Secretary Michael W. Wynne—by Defense Secretary Robert M. Gates in June 2008 because of several well-publicized problems, including the unauthorized transport of nuclear bombs aboard a B-52.) After briefings from various officers, Moseley and his staff worked for four hours to come up with "an informal pact. All Marine aircraft would be placed on the ATO [air tasking order] although the CFACC [combined force air component commander] would not have tactical control of organic Marine air assets."[1]

At the center of this hopeful grouping was the direct air support center (DASC). There was some initial overloading and cumbersome procedures that bogged things down. The Air Force, predictably, worked with its usual heavy hand, often claiming credit for things going well and warning of the possible demise of Marine air. Things it had done since 1945. "The OIF experience raises a larger question about the future of Marine air in the MAGTF [Marine Air-Ground Task Force]: how to ensure that future joint force commanders can count on a swift and productive integration of organic Marine air assets with the larger air war."[2]

Gen. Michael W. Hagee, commanding I MEF, and later, the 33rd Marine Corps Commandant, commented, "Buzz Moseley understood how we fought and how we used our aviation. What he needed was the ability . . . he did not disagree with how we did it. What he needed was the ability to go after high-value targets and not have to do a lot of coordination. . . . He promised to keep all his colonels in line."[3]

Maj. Gen. James F. Amos, commanding the 3rd MAW, noted, "We got to fight, the Marine aviation piece of the MAGTF, for the very first time in the history of Marine aviation, the way we always said we wanted to be able to."[4]

Hornets Ashore

On April 15, 2002, six F/A-18Ds of VMFA(AW)-121 became the first aircraft to arrive at the coalition air base in Kyrgyzstan, once part of the Soviet Union, to participate in early OEF missions. After more than five months, the Green Knights returned in October to MCAS Miramar, having flown more than 4,800 hours without a single mishap. The squadron's rest was short. Barely five months later, in February 2003, 121 was headed out once more for action in OEF.

The Marine Hornet squadrons from Al Jaber were kept busy for the second half of March and into April. They supported coalition forces, which included U.S. Marines and British troops throughout the theater as they engaged Iraqis, often in street-to-street fighting. The two-seat F/A-18Ds were especially active, VMFA(AW)s -225 and -533 delivering a variety of bombs and rockets.

The F/A-18D, manned by a FAC(A)-qualified crew, quickly became the "go to" asset in OIF when it came to running open kill boxes. Performing the strike coordination and reconnaissance (SCAR) missions, MAG-11 F/A-18Ds would cycle back and forth from the tanker to the kill box, providing on-going control and marshalling other strike assets expeditiously into areas where they had located targets.[5]

The two-seater Hornets were indeed busy in the first few months of the war, running their own missions, leading other aircraft like bombed-up F-14s and carrier-based Navy and Marine Hornets onto their targets. Fuel was always a concern for the short-legged F/A-18s, no less for the two-seaters, and they usually got head-of-the-line privileges behind the duty tanker.

MAG-11's aircraft's main enemy was the infamous Republican Guards, the huge elite force of the Iraqi army, whose reach was enormous and throughout the country. They defended cities, or streets, often with unexpected ferocity that required immediate CAS from the orbiting Marines. Crews from Air Force and Navy squadrons were always glad to work with the Hornet D FACs.

Tony Holmes wrote, "Indeed, USAF pilots were so keen to work with the FAC(A)s that they would regularly press them for future mission details at Al Jaber."

Quoting one Hornet CO, "I had A-10 'drivers' I knew on base come up to me in the mess hall to find out when I'd be up as a FAC(A), and what kill box I'd be running."[6]

Another shore-based Marine type was the EA-6B Prowler. VMAQ-1 brought their aircraft to Prince Sultan Air Base in Saudi Arabia and contributed an amazing 1,850 hours and 395 sorties flying SEAD missions. Although there was no aerial opposition during the campaign, the Iraqis still possessed an impressive number of SAMs and anti-aircraft guns that often made their collective presence known to the incoming aircraft of the coalition.

VMAQ-2 Prowlers were in on the first missions of OIF, with crews flying eight-to-ten hours a day. Early on, the Prowlers were on demand to support the Air Force B-2s and F-117s as they waded into the heart of Baghdad's defense systems on their night missions. Flak and SAMS quickly rose to confront the Prowler crews. The SA-6s were especially active. The

Iraqis would fire a spread of the dangerous missiles at the incoming strikers. Often the EA-6B crews had little choice but to fire their HARMs and split-s away from the threat.

Capt. Marlin Williams, an electronic countermeasures officer, or ECMO, with VMAQ-2, commented, "I can't believe how much ammunition or stuff is in the air going at these guys and they make it through!"[7]

The Helicopter Story

While the fast jets were taking care of business, their slower-moving compatriots in the helicopter squadrons were certainly contributing their share to OIF's pace. There were the occasional diversions such as the move to the West African coastal nation of Liberia in July. The 26th Marine Expeditionary Unit (MEU), including HMM-264 (REIN), was ordered to steam aboard USS *Iwo Jima* (LHD-7) to protect American interests in the area. The on-going civil war in the small nation threatened American citizens and interests. HMM-264 (REIN)'s complement included detachments of CH-53Es, AH-1Ws, UH-1Ns, and AV-8Bs, and all were on standby. However, the end of the threat came on August 14 when the country's president was removed and Marines began maintaining security at the port facility.

Eventually, HMM-264 (REIN) returned home to North Carolina in October, having been deployed for 232 days.

By early April 2003, Marine HMHs had begun using an important upgrade to the defensive armament, the ramp-mounted weapon system (RMWS). HMH-461 and HMH-465 took the new machine gun into action aboard their CH-53Es. RMWS gave the helicopters a 180-degree field of fire from their loading ramp, using a .50-caliber machine gun. In earlier missions in the 1990s, the need for a heavy weapon facing aft, to cover exits from hostile territory—such as the operation in Somalia and the Capt. Scott O'Grady rescue in the Balkans—gave rise to crews strapping guns on their aircraft. In early missions in Afghanistan, troops were often lashed to the ramp to fire their personal M16 assault rifles to provide support. The formal design of a gun installation promised greater flexibility and protection.

HMLA-267 was one of several Cobra/Huey squadrons that served in the early stages of OIF. Arriving in-theater in late February 2003, the squadron soon found itself engaged in all the firefights, including the intense battle around An Nasiriyah. They took on Iraqi tanks, personnel carriers, and various artillery emplacements.

HMLA-167 was another veteran combined squadron that saw action, bringing seven AH-1Ws and two UH-1Ns to fight alongside sister squadron HMLA-269 in the opening days of the campaign. Relying on night-vision goggles (NVGs), the crews flew mainly at night. HMLA-169 and HMLA-369 also saw action. The "Gunrunners" of HMLA-269 had made the trip, along with the other units assigned to MAG-29, aboard USS *Saipan* (LHA-2) and USS *Ponce* (LPD-15). The transplant took ten days and when they arrived at Al Jaber air base, the squadrons became part of 3rd MAW, which was accumulating quite an impressive number of aircraft.

The Cobras were involved in the fighting around An Nasiriyah, which initially centered around capturing two vital bridges on two waterways.

Aircraft of the assembled HMLAs shuttled back and forth to support the ground troops surging toward the bridges. Enemy ground fire was occasionally intense and several Cobras and Hueys were hit, causing varying degrees of damage and resulting in the loss of two Hueys and Cobras. Of the fifty-four Marine Cobras deployed, forty-four sustained a degree of battle damage.

One of the contributing factors to the overall success of the Cobra mission was the forward arming and refueling point (FARP). These forward-placed "oases" provided fuel and ammunition for the gunship crews who would have otherwise had to return all the way back to their main base after using their ordnance or their fuel. The FARPs were given the names of American baseball parks—Fenway, Camden—and provided the unique service to keep the operations going.

A Colorful Rescue

One of the most publicized operations of the early OIF war was the rescue of Army PFC Jessica Lynch. Captured during a bloody ambush, she was hidden away by her captors for several weeks. Eventually, Iraqi informants disclosed her position to their American "friends," and during a well-coordinated raid on the night of April 1–2, she was rescued along with several other American prisoners. Marines provided the transportation for nearly 300 Army Rangers with MAG-16 helicopters, including seven CH-46Es of HMM-165 and three CH-53Es from HMH-465. PFC Lynch was the first American POW to be rescued since World War II. (A few individual aviators escaped their captors during the Vietnam War, but these were on their own.)

The Reserves Get Their Call

Perhaps one of the greatest individual successes in the post-9/11 military story has been that of the Reserve component, especially that of the Marine Corps. The greatest need was in the helicopter category, and several Marine Air Reserve helo squadrons were mobilized in the largest such recall in history. In February 2002, HMH-772, from Willow Grove, Pennsylvania, was mobilized and arrived at MCAS New River, North Carolina, with nine helicopters and its complement to begin deployment training with the 24th MEU. This was the first time Reserves would help ease the increased demand for heavy-lift helos in OEF, as well as make up an entire component of an MEU's composite helicopter squadron. The squadron participated in operations in East Africa, flying from USS *Nassau*, then was sent out as part of OIF, operating in Kuwait.

The AH-1W Cobras and UH-1N Hueys of HMLA-269 had departed MCAS New River on January 13, 2003, sailing aboard USS *Saipan* and USS *Ponce* as part of Amphibious Task Force (ATF) East. Making their way across the world, the squadrons were in place when OIF began and quickly became involved in the intense fighting. On March 20, Gunrunner Cobras and Hueys flew in bad weather to support ground troops advancing toward the Iraqi town of Safwan. The squadron's Cobras were the first unit to fire the new "November" variant of the AGM-114N Hellfire missile, with devastating results. During the next week, the squadron was involved in CAS missions. Several helos were hit by small arms fire, although none was lost during the entire deployment.

The Cobra reserves were also greatly involved, especially in the on-going fighting in Afghanistan. They had served in Desert Storm, flying AH-1Js, but now, twelve years later, the Red Dogs of HMLA-773 and the Coyotes of HMLA-775 were flying AH-1Ws and UH-1Ns, right along with their regular counterparts. HMLA-773 left its home in Atlanta, Georgia, in October 2003 and arrived in Afghanistan. On New Year's Eve, the squadron got its first kills, to become the first Reserve HMLA squadron to do so. Two Cobras were providing cover for an Army convoy that, according to local intelligence, might be ambushed.

A half hour after sunset, the Marine crews spotted enemy gun emplacements firing on the convoy near the border with Pakistan. Rolling in, the Cobras began firing their 20-mm cannon, hitting the targets. After another pass, the guns were silent. However, the Red Dog crews soon spotted a third gun firing at the middle section of the convoy and rolled in again, taking that position out. Now, the crews saw an observation post and took that out with rockets.

KC-130Ts of Reserve squadrons VMGR-234 from Texas and VMGR-452 from upstate New York contributed to the constant requirement for aerial refueling, as well as for ground refueling activities when necessary.

The AV-8s' Contribution

The Harrier's story entered a new phase when the final AV-8B II Plus was delivered to VMA-231 on September 30, 2003, at MCAS Cherry Point. The aircraft was the 230th AV-8B produced by Boeing since December 1983. (Boeing bought out the "real" manufacturer, McDonnell Douglas in 1997. McDonnell had merged with Douglas in 1967.) The date was also significant because of the retirement of the "straight" AV-8B day attack Harrier, giving place to the much more capable Harrier II Night Attack upgrade, which included a more powerful engine and a forward-looking infrared system. By the time OIF began, virtually all of the so-called day-attack Harrier IIs had received the upgrades and modifications to make them the night-attack variant.

The Harrier contingent was extremely active, and truth be told, much of the STOVL action in the early stages of the war had emanated from several ships, validating the so-called Harrier-carrier concept. In Desert Storm, the half-dozen Harrier squadrons had largely operated from shore bases, with only a few launching from ships. Twelve years later, the cycle was reversed.

Some sixty MAG-13 AV-8Bs—out of a total of seventy-six in-theater—flew from LHDs, equipped with the Litening II targeting pod that made things a lot easier for the Marine aviators tasked with providing CAS and interdiction services to the advancing coalition forces. Indeed, the initial figures showed that in twenty-six days of combat operations, Harrier squadrons flew nearly 2,000 sorties, delivering more than 750,000 pounds of ordnance in support of I MEF. *Bonhomme Richard*'s Harriers of VMA-311 destroyed the Iraqi

Republican Guards' Baghdad Division, the only tank battalion threatening the Marines on the ground. In a rather odd situation, the Tomcats divided their resources, creating a detachment for the *Bonhomme Richard* and one for the *Tarawa*. The Harriers worked day and night as required, sometimes basing from an airfield ashore to be closer to the action and able to respond that much quicker to frantic calls for help from coalition troops in contact with the enemy.

A Premature Victory?

As April dawned, the Marines were headed for Baghdad, perhaps taking up where they had left off some twelve years ago in Desert Storm. By April 4, they were at the capital city's outskirts, and five days later, Iraqi resistance collapsed, allowing coalition troops to occupy the city outright.

OIF was a freewheeling, though controlled campaign, with plenty of action for all the Marine Corps air and ground units involved. Although pockets of stubborn Iraqi resistance occasionally made the fighting hard and often bloody, the outcome was seldom, if ever, in doubt. Thus, it could be understood that with the fall of Baghdad, as well as the well-televised "fall"—aided by enthusiastic Marines—of a prominent statue of Saddam, that President George W. Bush erroneously declared victory on May 1, 2003.

Map 9.
The War in
Afghanistan

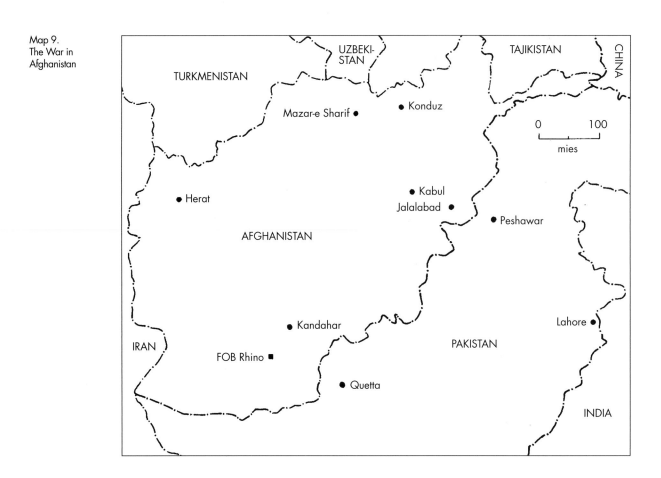

In another understandable, but charitably described ill-advised demonstration, he played co-pilot in a Navy S-3 that flew out to the home-coming carrier USS *Abraham Lincoln* (CVN-72) as it neared San Diego on May 1, 2003. Strutting around the flight deck in full flight gear (Bush had been a sometime Air National Guard F-102 pilot) greeting enthusiastic sailors who clamored for photos with the commander-in-chief, the president declared, "Mission accomplished," and that "major" action in Iraq had ended. It was an ill-timed, ill-conceived appearance that would come back to haunt him and ultimately prove to be a false and tragic misreading of the facts. OIF was definitely not over. Indeed, it had just begun! And truth be told, OEF was not buried, either.

20 Continuing the War That Was Finished

IN THE RUSH TO DECLARE THE VICTORY won in a six-week struggle, America's leaders failed to take into account the presence and strength of a large cadre of rebel insurgents who refused to acknowledge they were beaten. Taliban operatives found ready followers in a decimated Iraq. While the Taliban had been thrown out of power in Afghanistan and replaced by a democratic government supported by the U.S.-led coalition, there were still deep pockets of Taliban planners and fighters, all too prepared to foster fear and insurrection in Iraq's dirty, powerless cities, towns, and villages. And if the Iraqis themselves would not follow the rebels, there was always simple, direct, bloody execution, accompanied by home invasion and abduction, or bombings of marketplaces and roadside explosives.

It was a strategy America hadn't considered, and for a long while, it would work. The frustrating culture of Vietnam-like protests and demonstrations would also rear its head, displaying growing American dissatisfaction with the war and its leaders. Like their predecessors of the 1960s, these occasionally large demonstrations gave erroneous signals to the enemy that American resolve and ability to fight the war were weakening.

For a time, again echoing the tumultuous history of the Vietnam War more than thirty years earlier, America sought to bring its troops home as soon as it could. The main contingent of the I MEF boarded ships or flew its aircraft to distant staging areas. While the Iraqis had welcomed—more or less—the fall of Saddam's terrible rule and the deaths of many of his hated henchmen, including his two diabolical sons, there was a reluctance to embrace the Americans as the victors and liberators Washington saw them. Except for the unforgettable scene of the destruction of the big statue of Saddam and the subsequent joyous dancing by the Iraqi populace around the broken symbol of their hated ruler, there were no sustained demonstrations of welcome and embracing thank-yous that marked the liberation of Kuwait in 1991. The restraint was ignored by the people on Capitol Hill, but the people in the Pentagon were on edge . . . and with good reason.

With growing unrest, as well as the breadth of the on-going war on terrorism increasing throughout the world, I MEF Marines were again sent into Iraq in March 2004, relieving the Army troops that had been in place. Whatever hopes the Marines had of holding down the insurgents were sorely tested in the city of Fallujah, forty miles west of Baghdad. A base for enemy activity, the city had been a problem for coalition forces as they headed for Baghdad in 2003.

Soon after the arrival of the I MEF Marines, die-hard followers of Saddam ambushed a convoy driven by American civilians. They killed four of the truckers, and on April 2, as part of Operation Vigilant Resolve, Marines entered the city to begin one of the most intense and bloody engagements of the war so far. The Coyotes of HMLA-775 were busy flying alongside HMLA-167 in Iraq.

"When fighting broke out," Maj. Fred Allison later wrote, "Marine Corps Cobra and Huey squadrons provided CAS. These pilots wanted nothing more than to support their ground brethren at war on Fallujah's mean streets."[1]

On-going and frustrating enemy activity throughout the year made it clear there was no easy way out. By mid-October, what became known as Fallujah 2 was under way, with Marines again attacking the battered city. The largest military operation since the opening days of OIF began on November 8 with thousands of U.S. and Iraqi troops attacking the insurgent positions in Fallujah. Operation Phantom Fury combined Marine and Army battalions to fight against a well-prepared insurgency. The city had been in enemy hands since April after the Marines were ordered to stop all offensives. Eventually, a week-long engagement resulted in a Marine victory and the return of Iraqi control, but the cost had been high: eighty-three Marines and one Navy corpsman had been killed in action, with hundreds more wounded in the November fighting. The ground campaign had received tremendous air support from Navy and Marine squadrons, including Cobra and Harrier units like VMA-542, which had flown 150 sorties a week in support of the campaign.

A Heavy Lift Mission in OEF

The war in Afghanistan also began heating up once more, and Marine aviation was in the thick of the renewed OEF campaign. Marine Reserve crews flew Cobras and CH-53s in and out of the mountainous terrain. HMH-769 from California had deployed in March 2004. Desert Storm veteran now–Lt. Col. Rick Mullen had done his best to prepare his squadron for its combat deployment with lectures from other veterans and renewed studies of their powerful helicopters. "The thing I had always instilled in my squadron mates was that the H-53, because of its range and payload, was very often called upon to fly missions of national importance and on an urgent timeline . . . certain missions would most likely be given to the Special Ops Forces, but if they were not available or the timeline too urgent, we had to always be ready."[2]

Based in the high desert of Edwards Air Force Base, the Titans had experience in high-altitude operations. Their Echoes were equipped with AN/AAQ-29 forward-looking infrared radars (FLIRs), a third-generation FLIR technology that endowed the H-53s with extra capabilities that might be useful in Afghanistan's mountains. One particular advantage was a Doppler capability that was particularly advantageous in hovering.

The Titans found themselves involved in "stability operations" until local elections were completed. Their flights became mainly resupply and transport from the main base at Bagram out to the various Provision Reconstruction teams and combat bases in the hinterlands.

"This was a Marine H-53 dream come true," now-Colonel Mullen recalls. "We were doing long-range, heavy-lift missions that were truly capitalizing on the unique capabilities of our aircraft. We weren't just following H-46s around like in a composite squadron. There wasn't an H-46 in sight."[3]

The faithful CH-46 had had difficulty operating at the high altitudes of the Afghani terrain, and so the three-engine CH-53E had become the workhorse heavy lifter in the theater.

On June 17, a battle erupted between rival warlords in the north central part of the country, halfway between Bagram and Herat. The town of Chagcharan had also been the site of an outpost of a UN mission whose election workers had become increasingly concerned for their safety. A task force of U.S. helicopter units, including Marine Cobras from HMLA-773 and Army H-60 Black Hawks and AH-64 Apaches was tasked with keeping order. With its long range, HMH-769's CH-53Es were also sent out to the town, some 200 miles away. In a scene reminiscent of a call to a fire house— Colonel Mullen is a firefighter, himself, in civilian life—the squadron sprang into action, leaving dinner and personal activities to download maps and load navigational gear. The squadron's maintenance troops turned to and quickly got two aircraft mission-ready, no small accomplishment in so short a time.

"We did a running takeoff, "Colonel Mullen remembered, "and lumbered off the ground, going by the east river range to test fire our weapons." Turning west in the dark night, they headed for Chagcharan. The climbout was slow because the aircraft were heavy with fuel and Marines. Although they were familiar with the initial route, the crews were soon past that comfort point, struggling at 13,000 feet altitude but with the actual terrain only a few hundred feet below them.

Colonel Mullen noted, "It had the eerie feeling of a strange world we had never seen before. The scale of the mountains was way out of proportion to what we were used to in the Sierras of California. This was the Hindu Kush, and as I looked at the small silhouette of the lead aircraft with its pulsating infrared, anti-collision light weaving along against the backdrop of this spectacular starlit geography, it was as though we were intergalactic explorers venturing onto a strange planet like a scene from the move *Alien.*"

The long distance was well beyond the range of the Cobras, and so Mullen's section had no helicopter escort. As it was, he and his other pilots had to strictly maintain the power settings to obtain maximum efficiency for the big helicopters' engines. Oddly, there was an escort of sorts well out of sight, high above. An Air Force B-1, call sign "Bone 52," trailed them, ready to provide reconnaissance and fire support if needed.

As they approached the landing zone, the Marine helicopters came down to 100 feet above the ground, finding the riverbed that would eventually guide them to their landing area. The UN people were assembled, waiting for their rescuers. They reported that the landing zone was mainly grass. Colonel Mullen remembered the debacle of Desert One in the ill-fated mission to rescue the American hostages in Iran in 1980. Several of the CH-53s assigned to the mission collided with each other in the dust storm that developed, with terrific loss of life. He, therefore, agreed with the mission commander's decision to land one at a time. He remembered to switch the satellite guidance system from automatic to manual, keeping the indicator needle locked on the landing site.

Carefully making their approach, the crews strained to see the signal lights from those on the ground, who had been strictly instructed to not illuminate the area until they heard the sound of the helicopters. Someone spotted the lights and the section turned toward the LZ only to have it disappear in a swirling cloud of sand thrown up by the rotor wash.

Long hours of training paid off as the Marine crews quickly backed off to stabilize their situation. Finally, the other crew reported they saw the LZ and began their final descent. The pilots instructed the Marines in the cabin to remain on board. The rescue of the Air Force F-16 pilot Scott O'Grady in Bosnia had resulted in some initial confusion as the bedraggled young captain ran from his cover to the helicopter. Mullen and his men wanted no repeats of that mission's difficulties.

The second crew sent one grunt down the ramp to find the UN people; they were barely fifty feet from the whirling rotor blades! The Marine escorted them into the trembling aircraft, which quickly took off in another huge cloud of dust and sand. Releasing the USAF B-1, Mullen and his crews landed at Bagram to deposit their charges, with blinking low fuel lights all around.

As a result of the mission, which was considered a great success, the UN decided to remain in Afghanistan to supervise the elections, which were, after all, a major sign of the overall success of OEF in the first place.

And, as Colonel Mullen remarked, somewhat wryly, "Like many successful missions, it was quite un-spectacular. Things often get spectacular when they do not go as planned or they are unsuccessful. . . . We spent time reviewing other missions . . . and we paid attention to the lessons and applied the small things that help ensure success."

The Red Dogs Keep the Pressure On

Like many of their Reserve compatriots, the Red Dogs of HMLA-773 maintained a cycle of rotation in and out of the war zone, flying right alongside their regular counterparts. It was the thing all reservists had been training for all their careers. The squadron had arrived in Afghanistan in late October 2003 and joined the U.S. Army command known as Combined Joint Task Force 180. The Marine Cobras were subsequently designated Task Force Red Dog. After area familiarization flights, the squadron was integrated into daily operations and flew their first mission on November 17.

[Opposite] Two CH-53Es of HMH-769 fly over a base near Gardez on a resupply mission some 50 miles south of Kabul, Afghanistan. (Rick Mullen)

In December the Red Dogs supported the Army's famous 10th Mountain Division. The reservists flew security missions, escorted convoys and medevac flights, as well as providing CAS and armed reconnaissance services. On the last day of the year, the squadron actually engaged the enemy for the first time while responding to a call for help by a U.S. Army ground convoy that had been ambushed by Al Qaeda terrorists.

The section of Reserve helicopters attacked four separate enemy positions, eventually claiming eleven confirmed kills, and allowing the convoy to clear the ambush zone with only three casualties.

The new year saw increased action for the Georgia Marines as a number of operations made wide-ranging use of their capabilities. In April, during Operation Dragonfly, HMLA-773 Hueys and Cobras helped defend an embattled border control point (BCP). The large enemy force was advancing on the Allied position, but Red Dog Cobras kept them at bay, while UH-1Ns inserted a special operations force and two air controllers. The result was a breaking up of the enemy force and its attack with heavy casualties.

June was a particularly busy month. Three Army UH-60s were added to the mix, making the first time since Vietnam that a Marine CO also had operational control of a joint service unit in combat. On June 22, insurgents rocketed Forward Operating Base (FOB) Salerno, wounding three Army troopers as well as four local interpreters. During the forty-five-minute attack, seven 122-mm rockets hit the base.

In less than ten minutes, Red Dog Cobras were heading for the enemy position some eighteen kilometers away. Four two-plane sections eventually converged on the target. After expending their ordnance, and in need of fuel, the first section, led by Maj. John Currie, turned over to the next incoming group, led by the squadron CO, Lt. Col. Lance Maffett. As Lieutenant Colonel Maffett checked the area, the men on the ground called that communication intercepts reported the enemy was preparing to shoot RPGs at the Marine helicopters.

The Marines began working to insert an Army platoon to kill or capture the enemy force. However, another intercept revealed the enemy was calling they were pinned down by Cobra fire, unable to escape. The Marines kept up a cycle of attacks as each section—the first section had now returned—required rearming and refueling. Eventually, a report determined that as many as eight enemy terrorists had been killed, including the possible head of the local Al Qaeda cell, who had coordinated the attack.

This engagement had dealt a severe blow to local Al Qaeda operations and provided a wealth of intelligence.

In August the squadron was involved in the largest engagement against the Taliban since Operation Anaconda. On the night of August 1, some 300 Taliban struck a BCP on the border between Afghanistan and Pakistan. Outnumbered four to one, the BCP defenders were soon in dire straits. At 2:00 AM, a section of Red Dog Cobras launched and attacked the enemy position, quickly silencing a gun emplacement. The Marines were then directed to a ridgeline to the west of the BCP.

The helicopters came under RPG fire, which they noted was coming from the perimeters of the BCP. Apparently, the enemy had overrun that section of the BCP. The Cobras engaged the Taliban forces with rockets and 20-mm cannon fire, eventually making the enemy break their hold and disperse, thereby saving the lives of every coalition and Afghan soldier at the BCP. Each of the four Red Dog crewmen received the Distinguished Flying Cross for that night's work.

September continued the pace as Red Dog helos engaged the enemy regularly. On the afternoon of September 20, a patrol had been ambushed with heavy casualties that required medevac services. HMLA-773 Cobras launched with two Army UH-60s. Upon arriving at the scene, the Cobras swung into action to protect the Army UH-60s as they tried to land to recover the wounded. During the four-hour engagement, the Cobras battled Taliban positions with TOW missiles, 2.75-inch rockets, and 20-mm cannon fire. They also provided laser marking for Air Force A-10s called in to assist. Eventually, eight enemy were dead and several stockpiles of munitions were destroyed.

Map 10.
The War and
Insurgency
in Iraq

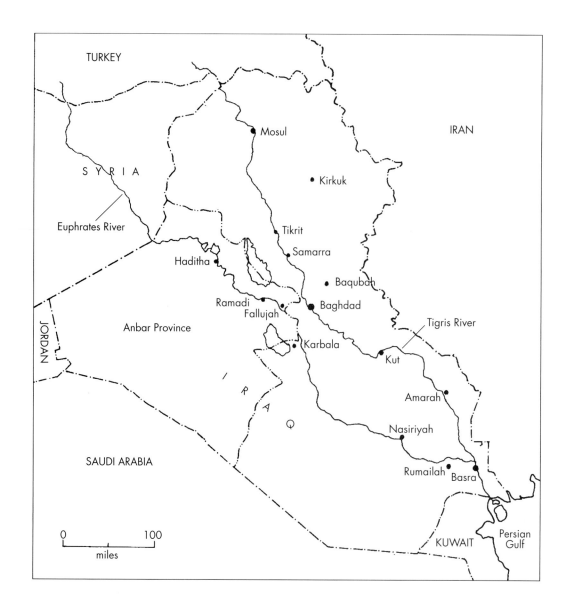

The remainder of the year kept up the cycle of launches and confrontations. It was far beyond what any Marine AH-1 unit had ever experienced, even in Desert Storm, or Vietnam. The Reserve Cobras were in almost continuous action.

On February 24, 2005, a platoon-sized enemy force entered Afghanistan from Pakistan and ambushed an Afghan convoy and the nearby BCP almost simultaneously. After several rounds of RPGs and heavy machine-gun fire, four Afghan soldiers were badly wounded, and once again, the Red Dogs responded, escorting a UH-60 for medevac. Maneuvering through heavy defensive fire from the ground, the Cobras poured their own bullets and rockets into the enemy positions. Finally, twenty enemy terrorists lay dead on the ground, and a significant amount of classified intelligence, communications equipment, and weapons was captured.

The Coyotes of HMLA-775 were also heavily engaged in OIF operations during this period. It was during this deployment that the squadron suffered the only loss of a Reserve Cobra or Huey pilot in OEF or OIF. On July 28, 2004, Lt. Col. Dave Greene from Vergennes, Vermont, and his co-pilot, Maj. Joe Crane from Overland Park, Kansas, were flying a CAS mission over Ramadi. Greene was in the back seat while Crane was forward operating the telescopic sight unit, radios, and navigational aids. Marines on patrol on the east side of the town began taking fire from several buildings. Lieutenant Colonel Greene maneuvered his section of Cobras toward the fight.

After making a targeting run and turning away from the town, Greene and Crane took massive amounts of small-arms fire from AK-47s and possibly RPKs.[4] Five rounds hit their helicopter in various places, including the engine, which failed. The aircraft rolled level momentarily then began a left diving turn toward power lines.

Crane took control, narrowly avoiding crashing. Getting no response from the man behind him, he flew back to Al Asad as the wingman, Lt. Col. Bruce Orner, the squadron CO, and his co-pilot, 1st Lieutenant Hardin, called for medical personnel, who quickly found that Lieutenant Colonel Greene had been hit in the neck and had died in flight. Greene, who was also a native of upstate New York, had graduated from the Naval Academy in 1986. After flying Hueys and Cobras in the fleet, he left active duty and went to work for the Goodrich Corporation while maintaining his Reserve affiliation. He became the most senior Marine killed in OIF.

Disasters at Home and Abroad

Although embroiled in a two-front war, Marine aviation had other assignments around the world, perhaps none more important than helping civilians in time of dire trouble and need. The normally happy, family-oriented time of the Christmas holidays was tragically disrupted on December 26, 2004, in the faraway country of Indonesia, when a massive tsunami struck the island nation, killing hundreds of thousands of people, including Indonesians and foreign tourists. The towering wave washed away fishing villages and inundated and changed coastlines in minutes, leaving death and destruction as it receded. The world community stepped up to offer aid, and included in the U.S. effort were Marine Corps and Navy helicopter crews and their ships.

Elements of the 15th Marine Expeditionary Unit (special operations capable; MEU[SOC]) aboard the *Bonhomme Richard* (LHD-6) airlifted supplies and medical assistance to the beleaguered victims, using CH-46Es from HMM-165 (REIN). Other ships and squadrons from the Navy and Marine Corps assembled off shore, shuttling badly needed supplies into the decimated areas. USS *Essex* (LHD-2) relieved the "Bonnie Dick" on January 18, and besides its own 31 MEU assets, also gathered additional helicopters from Bahrain and Okinawa.

Cdr. Ted Williams, XO of VAQ-131, the Navy Prowler squadron aboard the carrier USS *Abraham Lincoln* (CVN-62), was part of the overall effort. He spent three days ashore at Banda Aceh, one of the worst-hit towns. In a lengthy e-mail to his family, he probably spoke for most of his compatriots, Navy and Marine. "I have never been so proud to be a member of the U.S. military. We are often focused on keeping the peace and deterring evil acts. To

now have a direct impact in saving lives and attempting to rebuild a society is a testament to the United States' amazing resolve and capabilities."[5]

Eight months later, disaster struck closer to home when, during a very active hurricane season, Katrina paid a visit to the U.S. Gulf Coast on August 29. Waterfronts along the coasts of Louisiana, Mississippi, and Alabama were flooded, and several naval air stations soon became staging bases for Navy, Marine Corps, and Coast Guard helicopters as they flew rescue missions and dropped supplies and food to the affected areas. Three amphibious ships also arrived quickly to serve as control points and reception centers for the victims.

Three Marine squadrons from New River sent six CH-53Es and two CH-46Es, while HMH-772, the Reserve squadron at Willow Grove, outside Philadelphia, contributed four more CH-53s. At the height of the rescue operation, there were more than 350 military helicopters and more than 70 fixed-wing aircraft involved in the relief effort, which was further burdened when another huge storm, Hurricane Rita, slammed into the area on September 24. HMLA-773's Hueys flew reconnaissance missions over the affected areas.

The Fighting Continues

As disappointing and frustrating as the fact was, OIF and OEF were far from being won, and America had to send its troops back into Afghanistan and Iraq. Ships carried grunts back, along with the squadrons of aircraft and personnel. The parallels between these operations and Vietnam were strong. Some thirty years earlier, Marine aviation had left Vietnam by 1971, and Marine Corps ground forces had been greatly reduced to no more than individual advisers to help the South Vietnamese fight the war themselves. Indeed, when the North Vietnamese invaded the south during the Easter Invasion in March 1972, it was the South Vietnamese marines, with the American Marine advisers, who saw most of the initial action, meeting the hard-charging enemy in fierce engagements in northern South Vietnam, just below the DMZ.

Now, in South*west* Asia, the indigenous forces of Afghanistan's new government and army, and Iraq's greatly reorganized military service, had to rely on their American sponsors to teach and lead them as they dealt with the still-dangerous terrorist groups that operated, seemingly without interference, in the cities of Iraq and in the mountains and valleys of Afghanistan. More coalition forces had to be recalled.

Part of the resuscitation of the Iraqi government was the holding of free elections after the ouster of Saddam. Accordingly, on January 30, 2005, the first such elections in more than fifty years signaled the country's new status. However, the concern was great for just how representative the elections would be and how easy it would be for the general population to participate without interference from the insurgents. Al Anbar Province, which included the recently liberated cities of Fallujah and Ramadi, was of particular concern. The United States wanted to assure the Iraqis in that province that they would be able to come to the polls and cast their vote without fear of harm or reprisal. Approximately one thousand poll workers were needed in the province and VMGR-452, the Reserve KC-130 squadron from New York transported the workers from Najaf, landing at Al Taqaddum Airbase, where they would receive training and support before they were flown to the various polling centers in Al Anbar by CH-46s. On voting day, thirty-three polling stations opened throughout the province. Turnout was especially high in Fallujah.

VMGR-252 made the first deployment of the new KC-130J in February 2005, with six aircraft basing out of Al Asad in Iraq. The KC-130J was seeing increasingly more use, each of the five fleet and Reserve VMGRs (flying a mix of 130Js and the so-called legacy KC-130Ts) contributing personnel to maintain a detachment at Al Asad. The missions were of the usual aerial delivery type and occasional battlefield illumination, using flares to light up the night-time terrain. These missions were especially important to illuminate dark roads that sheltered insurgents as they planted roadside bombs. When a "Battle Herc" dropped its flares, the ground below immediately gave up its shield for the rebels and, in turn, protected the coalition ground forces as they patrolled their area.

The 130s and their crews also continued their traditional aerial refueling role, often taking over from other tankers to gas up returning strike aircraft. Although normally dedicated to Marine aircraft, the KC-130s serviced carrier-based Navy aircraft in need of a fill-up.

As the fighting continued, encounters developed into the horrific roadside bombings that engulfed convoys or individual neighborhood patrols, destroying one or two vehicles and killing or maiming their young crews. It was a terrible time. Over the streets of Baghdad and other Iraqi cities, Marine helicopters and fast jets orbited and then swooped in to attack insurgents wherever they could. The 3rd MAW completed its longest deployment in March 2005, returning home after a thirteen-month stay in Iraq. Its relief, 2nd MAW, would spend nearly a year in place before it relinquished control of air operations to 3rd MAW once again in February 2006.

In July 2005, VMAQ-4 returned to MCAS Cherry Point following a six-month deployment after being relieved by VMAQ-1. Other squadrons came and went, their deployment through, or others just beginning. It was a seemingly never-ending cycle that evoked feelings of a long war. The Banshees

of "Q-1" were kept busy responding to tasking to support many operations. The squadron's maintenance division, like all the other Prowler squadrons, had their hands full keeping their four aging jets and their systems mission capable. The heat and sand permeated all areas, and it was a real task to keep at least three aircraft always ready.

By the time 2007 dawned, many squadrons were on their fourth or fifth deployment to the combat zone. But as HMH-362 began its fourth overseas deployment since 2002 on April 3, arriving at Al Asad Air Base in Anbar Province, it also began its first OIF deployment. (Al Asad quickly had taken on the nickname of "HMH West," painted in huge white letters on an old paraloft tower on the flight line.) Descending from the Shufly squadron of early Vietnam action, HMH-362 was relieving their sister squadron, HMH-363. Both squadrons were unique among the H-53 community because they were flying CH-53Ds. The crews immediately took up where HMH-363 had left off, cargo and personnel transport, insertion of infantry units, and aerial reconnaissance and occasional raids.

The Hornets Keep Flying

Besides the rotating AV-8 and various helicopter squadrons, Marine Corps aviation's presence was clearly exhibited by the many two-seat Hornet squadrons. The F/A-18Ds were always on call, orbiting the battlefield or suspected areas of terrorist activity.

After an OIF mission, Capt. John Bailey (l.) and his WSO, Capt. Chad Cipparone, head for debriefing. The VMFA(AW)-224 aviators had flown as part of Operation Spear, fighting insurgents near the Syrian border, a major crossing point for enemy fighters. (Cpl. Alicia M. Garcia)

Assigned to 3rd MAW's MAG 16, the Bats of VMFA(AW)-242 had made their first combat deployment since Vietnam in August 2004, taking their F/A-18Ds to Al Asad, the huge former Iraqi MiG-29 and MiG-25 fighter base 100 miles west of Baghdad. The base boasted thirty-three hardened aircraft shelters and runways that stretched 14,000 feet. Al Asad had been captured by the Australian Special Air Service (SAS) at the end of OIF I, then handed over to the I MEF. Like their fellow VMFA(AW)s, the Bats' missions included FAC(A) aerial reconnaissance with the Advanced Tactical Aerial Reconnaissance System (ATARS), and for the first time, the use of Litening II pods for targeting. VMFA(AW)-242 had been in action during Fallujah II in November 2004, and then the following January to support the elections during Operation Citadel. Al Asad was close enough to Fallujah that the Hornet crews could drop their ordnance and return to be rearmed and refueled, then fly back to Fallujah within forty-five minutes.

On November 8, the squadron helped Marine ground forces begin Operation Phantom Fury, delivering four GBU-31 2,000-pound Joint Direct Attack Munitions (JDAMs) to breach a fifty-foot berm north of the city. Marine Hornets kept the CAS stream flowing for days on end, prompting one ground officer to comment appreciatively, "it felt [like] a continuous faucet, a continuous flow of airplanes. I never knew a time in November when I had [troops in contact] when I didn't get an airplane without about a minute."[6]

The ground war that OIF became was the ground war that most people feared in Desert Storm and what looked like a tumultuous climax with the invasion of Baghdad in late February 1991. But that desperate house-to-house battle never developed, because President George H. W. Bush stopped the fighting and brought about a cease-fire just as the coalition forces were literally on the capital city's doorstep. But this second time, it was all the way, and then some. And soon, the men on the ground found themselves in almost daily contact with well-equipped and formidable insurgents who knew how to fight and inflict grievous harm and destruction on their opposition.

The war developed into a classic ground assault supported by aerial close air support, which in the close-in fighting usually included Marine air.

As Maj. Fred Allison wrote, "[I]t was a joint fight, both on the ground and in the air. Ground and aviation units from other Services and nations participated. . . . There were lots of good guys fighting in Fallujah—10 battalions worth crammed into a 5-kilometer square city composed of look-alike and densely packed, low-slung, brown/gray brick buildings."[7]

Using strike jets like the Hornet and Harrier called for great finesse, because allowing fast-moving strikers to drop huge bombs on an urban target ran the risk of casualties other than the intended combatants. In this area, the Air Force and Marine Corps differed the most. Involved with supporting Army units, Air Force F-16 pilots were increasingly frustrated as they were kept from dropping their bombs near the men they were trying to help. However, Marine jets were called in, taking great care to hit their intended victims. It was, admittedly, a close-run thing.

A unique Hornet squadron was VMFA-142, a Reserve outfit from Atlanta, Georgia. The Gators were the first Marine Corps Air Reserve fighter squadron to see combat since Korea, more than fifty years before. Their F/A-18A+ Hornets were updated aircraft that carried Litening II pods, making them a valuable tool for battlefield commanders. Like many Reserve squadrons that took advantage of their highly experienced pilots and ground troops, VMFA-142 could count several aviators with more than 2,000 hours flight time as well as senior rank.[8] Whereas fleet squadrons might have a couple of such experienced aviators, Reserve units naturally become high-time organization, whose members have often been with the squadron for five to seven years.

The squadron was, for a time, the only single-seat Hornet squadron based ashore. The squadron flew more than 2,500 sorties, totaling 5,000 flight hours, and delivered thirty-three tons of ordnance before returning home in September—to be placed in cadre status the following May! (Cadre status is not the same as being decommissioned and means the unit could be reactivated in the future time. For instance, several Hornet squadrons that were recently placed in cadre status are scheduled for reactivation in a few years to fly the oncoming F-35B STOVL fighter.)

VMFA-142 shared its tour with VMFA(AW)-224, the Bengals, which were relieved by VMFA(AW)-332 in early August 2005. Flying a uniquely striped F/A-18D, bureau number 164884, as the group commander's assigned "00," the Bengals had arrived in January. VMFA-142's complement included the father of another Marine serving with 224, thus giving the two men the unique chance of serving together on the same flight line. Sgt. Timothy

[Opposite Right] U.S. Marine Maj. William D. Chesarek earned a singular accolade when he received the RAF's DFC in 2006. Here, he poses with his Lynx crew at Basrah during his exchange tour. L. to r.: Lieutenant David Williams, RN; Major Chesarek; and Lance Corporal Max Carter, RM.

[Opposite Left] Following the formal investiture, Major Chesarek displays his unique medal outside Buckingham Palace. He is already wearing the corresponding striped ribbon on his uniform.

Toborg was an electrician with 142, and his son, Cpl. Travis Toborg was a plane captain with 224.

The senior Toborg had worked with A-6s during his eight-year stint on active duty. He had joined the Reserves when his son chose to follow in his father's footsteps and enlisted in the Marines. The inspiration was mutual, and after a fourteen-year break, Timothy joined the Reserves. When VMFA-142 was mobilized for duty in Iraq, the son volunteered to go with the Bengals, transferring from another assignment, so that he could be with his father when they went overseas.

Another example of close relatives serving in the same area at the same time was that of Capts. Richard and Christopher Allain. Richard flew F/A-18Ds with VMFA(AW)-225, and Christopher flew F/A-18Ds with VMFA(AW)-121. While their father flew F-16s with the Air Force, both brothers chose Marine Corps aviation, with older brother Richard encouraging his undecided younger brother to follow him. Although their individual tours did not overlap completely, the two men did manage to fly several combat sorties together.

Marine single-seat Hornets continued flying from carriers, including those of VMFA-115 and VMFA-323. VMFA-232 assigned to CVW-11 aboard USS *Nimitz* (CVN-70), was making its first combat cruise with the F/A-18. These squadrons were operating in the Northern Arabian Gulf (NAG), a theater that had seen little press coverage but was no less an important area.

Another Delta squadron, VMFA(AW)-533, flew their twelve aircraft from MCAS Beaufort, South Carolina, more than four thousand miles to Al Asad, arriving on February 10, 2006. It was the squadron's second combat deployment in OIF, the first tour having occurred right at the opening of the campaign in 2003. During the second tour, the Hawks dropped more than 803,000 pounds of ordnance and flew more than 1,500 flight hours.

The final months of 2007 were relatively quiet. In March 2008, the Vikings of VMFA(AW)-225 were relieved by VMFA-115, the first single-seat Hornets to serve ashore since VMFA-142's six-month tour in 2005. Like the Gators, the Eagles brought F/A-18A+s. The decision was meant to spread the flight time and resulting airframe stress around the Hornet fleet.

The War Goes On . . . and On

The Harrier was still very much in the fight, and on November 9, 2006, four VMA-211 AV-8Bs were the first Harriers to deliver JDAMs. The Avenger Harriers carried two different bombs, 1,000-pounders and 500-pounders, against buildings in Ramadi. In September and October 2007, VMA-223 AV-8Bs assigned to the 22nd MEU(SOC)'s aviation combat element, HMM-261 (REIN), were aboard USS *Kearsarge* (LHD-3), providing CAS for ground units with a wide variety of ordnance as well as the Harrier's 25-mm cannon.

Harriers returned to the fight in Afghanistan as part of the 24th MEU(SOC) aboard USS *Iwo Jima* (LHD-7). Between September 9 and 21 2006, AV-8Bs from the VMA-542 detachment flew 136 sorties supporting

coalition forces. To speed up time between the missions, a small detachment was also set down at an airfield in Kandahar.

Maj. Peter Lee, who led the AV-8s into Afghanistan, said, "Our Harriers were invaluable in filling the gaps of coalition air cover. We would regularly show up when no other aircraft were on station and coalition forces were engaged with the Taliban, and we would deliver lethal fire on the enemy. Our presence on more than one occasion resulted in the destruction of the Taliban and their weapons."[9]

By early 2006, most Marine Corps aviation squadrons and their support units had made at least two tours in OIF. The Gunrunners of HMLA-269 returned to Al Asad in February, flying "mixed" sections with AH-1s and UH-1s to best use the Cobra's strike capabilities with the Huey's fixed weapons and FLIR, as well as its ability to carry passengers. The combination provided the ability to handle a wide range of missions from CAS to casualty evacuation (CASEVAC).

The veteran CH-46 still had an important role: ferrying people and cargo around the theater. On occasion it even moved coalition forces. On December 19, 2005, HMM-266 lifted the "new" Iraqi Army's 1st Brigade into battle, along with Marines from 3rd Battalion, 6th Marines. It was during Operation Moonlight, the first planned large-scale operation for the Iraqi brigade, and the objective was to disrupt insurgent activity along the Euphrates River. In November the Griffins of HMM-266 lifted another Iraqi force into battle near Al Qaim.

The rapidly aging "Phrog Phleet" enjoyed a little resuscitation in 2006. After all, the forty-year-old veterans required *some* modernization. With that in mind, lightweight composite armor, pilot and co-pilot crashworthy seats—something that had been of major concern in recent years—upgraded engines, avionics, and structural improvements not only strengthened and improved the overall aircraft, but also reduced its weight by some seven hundred pounds.

In a story that might be called, "A Yank in the Royal Navy—21st Century-Style," Maj. William D. Chesarek Jr. earned a unique citation from a grateful British Queen and her government. A Cobra pilot, Major Chesarek was on an exchange tour with the Royal Navy's No. 847 Squadron, flying the Lynx Mk 7 helicopter, which might be loosely compared to the U.S. Sikorsky SH-60.

On the evening of June 10, 2006, Major Chesarek and his crew were providing radio communication relay service for a British ground unit near Amarah in Iraq. (The British had been closely working with U.S. forces since the very beginning of OIF and often hitched rides into battle with Marine helos.) During the course of an engagement with insurgents, a British vehicle had become disabled and surrounded by enemy insurgents, who were firing at the British troops. The situation looked desperate.

As Major Chesarek flew low over the scene, he could see that the insurgents were too close to the British for him to safely use his machine guns. He made a number of low passes to disrupt and harass the enemy to hopefully disperse them. But the men in the vehicle called that the Lynx was now the target of the rebels' small-arms and rocket fire, and that, in fact, a rocket-propelled grenade had just passed behind the helicopter.

The previous month, the British commander of the squadron, Lieutenant-Commander Darren Chapman, RN, and his crew had been shot down by a shoulder-launched SAM over Basrah while flying the incoming CO of Joint Helicopter Force, Iraq, and his adjutant on a reconnaissance of the battle space. All five men had been killed.

Talking to the men on the ground, Major Chesarek learned that one of them was hurt with a life-threatening head injury. He quickly decided to try to medevac the British soldier, although the Lynx was not configured for such a mission. When he landed, his door gunner, Lance Corporal Max Carter, Royal Marines, jumped out and pulled the injured soldier into the helicopter. Because of the June temperatures, the extra man presented problems and concern for engine overtemps. Thus, the Royal Army captain, who was flying as on-board liaison to the ground force, remained behind in the LZ.

Nine months later, on March 23, 2007, wearing his Dress Blue Bravos, Major Chesarek stood before Queen Elizabeth II at Buckingham Palace to receive—or be "invested with," as the British say—the British Distinguished Flying Cross. He thus joined a very select group of Americans. Only 21 in World War I, 264 in World War II, and 8 in Korea were so honored. Only one other Marine aviator received the award, then-Maj. Robert E. Galer for action at Guadalcanal in August and September 1942.

The Osprey Deploys

Constant attacks by insurgents and resulting American and coalition casualties were reminders too strong to ignore. OIF was in trouble, and the American public as a whole was becoming dissatisfied with the lack of progress in bringing the campaign to a conclusion and bringing U.S. troops home. The commanders in the field as well as their troops knew that more "boots on the ground" were needed. Finally, the president ordered a "surge" in manpower to help bring the insurgency under control. With a relative decline in insurgent activity as a result of the surge, Marines were sent to Afghanistan, where the resuscitated Taliban was making things very difficult for the coalition forces that remained, including U.S. Army and Marine units.

As the renewed OIF and OEF campaigns gathered momentum, a milestone occurred: the long—too-long—awaited MV-22B Osprey tilt-rotor made its first combat deployment. With newly redesignated VMM-263—Marine Corps Medium Tiltrotor Squadron 263—aboard, USS *Wasp* (LHD-1) departed North Carolina in mid-September 2007. The ten-aircraft squadron landed at Al Asad on October 4. The "Thunder Chickens" quickly flew their first operational missions between Baghdad and western Iraq bases, even airlifting somewhat quizzical Iraqi soldiers to their LZ at the start of a mission. It was obvious the Iraqis had never seen such an unusual aircraft and probably didn't know they had the honor of being among its first operational passengers.

On March 18, two MV-22s airlifted soldiers of the 27th Iraqi Infantry Brigade for the Iraqis first heliborne operations. On December 6, the Ospreys again airlifted Iraqi troops 150 miles away from Baghdad for a raid on suspected insurgent positions.

The Osprey had gone through so much development, criticism, and counter-criticism, and it was often hard to know if the revolutionary aircraft would ever enter production, much less squadron service. Following 263's redesignation, two other CH-46 squadrons were tapped for transition: HMM-162 and HMM-266. A fourth tilt-rotor squadron, VMMT-204, had been established at MCAS New River to train new Osprey crews.

HMM-263 had a long, colorful history, which included having one of the very few Vietnam Medals of Honor received by a Marine flight crewman, officer or enlisted. As described earlier, PFC Mike Clausen had rescued several injured Marines who had wandered into a minefield during a firefight on January 31, 1970, running in and out of his CH-46 six times until all the troops were aboard the shuttering helicopter, all the while under heavy enemy fire. A maverick by nature, Clausen had ignored the orders of the helo commander to stay in the helicopter.

The Osprey took twenty-five years to reach the fleet, an incredible amount of time. In the meantime, the aircraft it was intended to replace, the CH-46, carried on in stellar Marine fashion. Yet, with all its credits and accomplishments, the Sea Knight had just about reached the end of its career. The tilt-rotor MV-22 can carry twenty-four Marines or 20,000 pounds of cargo at speeds more than double those of the CH-46. A new test and development squadron, VMX-22, had even been established to establish the Osprey's operating parameters, missions, and prospects.

The second Osprey squadron, VMM-162, arrived in early April 2008. The Golden Eagles set up shop at Al Asad, after taking advantage of USS *Nassau*'s transport to the eastern Mediterranean. A vanguard of two Ospreys then launched from the ship and flew 200 miles to the island of Crete. After preparing for the 1,200-mile trip to Al Asad, the Ospreys headed inland, escorted by VMGR-252 KC-130Js. The squadron soon got into flying operational missions, including direct support and troop insertion. One such mission involved four Ospreys and a variety of support from other Marine

squadrons, including VMFA-115 F/A-18+s, Hueys and Cobras from HMLA-167 and KC-130Js from VMGR-352. The year being a presidential election year, the two main candidates even visited troops in the field courtesy of the Marines' new aircraft. VMM-263 hosted Republican Senator John McCain, and later, VMM-162 ferried Democratic hopeful Senator Barack Obama.

The Eagles were relieved by the third Osprey squadron, the Fighting Griffins of VMM-266 in the fall of 2008. The Griffins got right into the swing of things, moving troops and equipment to and from forward operating bases. As with any new weapon, use and tactics were always evolving. The MV-22B had little in the way of defensive armament, only a single rear-mounted 7.62-mm machine gun, although the design original called for a forward-mounted gun. The crews took advantage of the Osprey's great climb capabilities to get them out of the range of small-arms fire. At $64 million per aircraft, protecting the major investment was a prime concern.

Lt. Col. Christopher Seymour was the CO of VMM-266 during the squadron's first combat tour in Iraq. "I used to fly the CH-46 and we couldn't do nearly what we do now in terms of weight, cargo, distance or speed. [The Osprey] is a gorilla. The ability to accelerate to speeds is so strong. Like a bat out of hell, you're at altitudes safe from small arms fire."[10]

Predictably, there were problems and critics of the new aircraft. Parts endurance and mission availability rates made many opponents of the Osprey question its existence as they had throughout its development. Indeed, sand and heat affected many items throughout the theater in Iraq. The objectors also questioned how effective the tilt-rotor had been, and also whether it could operate from a ship's flight deck.

The Marines rebutted point-paper objections saying that the Osprey had performed satisfactorily in all missions, often in high-threat areas. The

Corps also declared that the new aircraft could operate from a carrier, along with other types like the Harrier and helicopters, the way it was intended. Only time will tell just how well the MV-22B ultimately fits in with the existing aircraft.

The Reserves Meet the Osprey

The Reserves continued to support the effort and the Red Dogs of HMLA-773 returned to Al Asad in September 2007, relieving HMLA-269. Now assigned to 2nd MAW, the reservists had volunteered for this somewhat unusual additional seven-month deployment to the combat zone, having largely fulfilled the requirements for Reserve deployment. The complement was composed of Marines from Marietta, Georgia; Belle Chasse, Louisiana; and from HMLA-775 at Camp Pendleton, California. Also, because of the somewhat top-heavy rank structure of the Reserve unit, seven lieutenants and one captain were assigned from the regular squadron HMLA-167, plus *one* flight instructor from the advanced training squadron in Florida, HT-18. The group that arrived in mid-summer 2007 was truly a cross-section of the 4th MAW's spirited Reserve makeup.

The Red Dogs quickly began rolling up the sortie numbers with their Hueys and Cobras, ranging from Al Asad up to the Syrian border. HMLA-773 participated in the newly developed Aero Scout missions, which were devised to monitor suspicious activities in the deserts of Al Anbar Province. While HMH squadrons had responsibility for lifting troops to areas of interest in the vast reaches of the desert, the Red Dog gunships contributed armed reconnaissance capabilities as well as communications with the CH-

[Opposite] The second Osprey squadron to deploy to Iraq was VMM-266. Here, a squadron aircraft loads troops and mail. (via Bell Boeing)

[Top] Two Marines fan out from an MV-22B Osprey during an Aero Scout mission in October 2008. The Osprey is from VMM-263, making the new tilt-rotor's first deployment. (via Bell-Boeing)

53Es. The newly arrived MV-22B Ospreys were also quickly integrated into the operation.

The Aero Scouts discovered thousands of pounds of homemade explosives, as well as capturing many insurgents and oil smugglers and providing supplies to the indigenous population that included Bedouin nomads. VMM-263's Capt. Jonathan H. Brandt commented,

> The [Aero Scout] mission is basically insertion and extraction of a small ground force to a location not known until moments before landing. With the ground force embarked, we fly low-level behind the "skids" [the helicopters] scouting out suspicious vehicles, personnel, possible weapons caches, or improvised explosive devices; and if something of interest is discovered, the force is inserted for further exploitation. . . . Findings ranged from nothing of significance to thousands of pounds of homemade explosives that an EOD [explosive ordnance detail] team destroyed to prevent their use against coalition forces or Iraqi civilians.[11]

The development of the Aero Scout mission created a force within the force, with the helicopter squadrons devising their own tactics and logistics, including the Tactical Bulk Fuel Dispensing System (TBFDS). Basically, TBFDS permitted the establishment of a temporary forward-area refueling and support base with a CH-53. Maj. Owen M. Coulman of HMLA-773 wrote, "With the enormous area that is covered on any given Aero Scout, this ability is critical since without it, some on-station times would be as little as five minutes. The ability to refuel the skids allows for missions in excess of six hours. This critical capability has hampered the inclusion of the Osprey, as they do not have that capability in theater [without] a nearby fixed FARP or the CH-53s anyway."[12]

By the time VMA-311 returned to Yuma, Arizona, from the war zone in October 2008, the situation had changed. There were no plans to replace the Tomcats with another Harrier squadron, because the need for CAS had dwindled to light or safer conditions. There was also increasing hope that the Iraqi army would be able to shoulder more of the burden. Cpl. Joshua Ortega had commented that, "We were loading the bombs, but the pilots weren't dropping any. But that is a good thing."[13]

Maj. Jerome Whalen, squadron XO, added, "This is certainly a milestone for the Harrier community. To my knowledge, this is the first time we haven't been replaced by an AV-8B unit since we started deploying to Al Asad, and in my opinion, it's a sign that we are definitely winning the fight."[14]

21 Dealing with the Present, Planning for the Future

AS IT HAS THROUGHOUT ITS NEARLY 100-year history, Marine Corps aviation has a lot to collectively think about. The approach of the second decade of the new century brings a lot of satisfaction with what has been accomplished, but also concern and hope for the years to come. The world of post–Soviet Union, post–Cold War worries has not panned out as had been hopefully expected. Although the old USSR is gone, the ersatz ally of Russia has taken on a lot of the characteristics of the old enemy, blocking American attempts to found a new order in Europe and helping the new collection of would-be contenders in various parts of the world contest U.S. influence.

These new enemies, including Iran, North Korea, and China—and perhaps a resurgent Russia—present a viable threat to the peace and stability of the world, often in ways that people feared in the 1950s and 1960s. Only now, combined with a worldwide war-without-end on terror—essentially a conflict between Muslim extremists and the rest of civilization—the stakes and prospects appear higher and less well defined than that against the Kremlin some twenty years ago. It's a dangerous world, perhaps far more dangerous than we could have ever contemplated at the time. And Americans have to be ready to combat the ever-increasing numbers of prospective enemies that seem to be growing as third world concerns for hunger and other global matters such as energy use and supply push the have-nots into the armed camps of the extremists.

With that in mind, the Marine Corps, and especially Marine Corps aviation has to look to the future to maintain its present. The Corps has seen a lot of beginnings in recent years in hardware and in social programs. Unmanned aerial vehicles (UAVs); new aircraft, specifically, the Osprey and the F-35B STOVL fighter; and the introduction of women into combat squadrons are arguably the most important developments in the next decade.

The Rise of the UAV

Unmanned aerial vehicles are not new. Experiments with radio-controlled aircraft began during World War I and proceeded sporadically in World War II. Even during the Korean War, surplus aircraft like F6F Hellcats were loaded

[Top] This stalwart Pioneer UAV of VMU-2 is ready for launch from Al Taqaddum, Iraq, in June 2006. (Sgt. Jennifer L. Jones)

[Opposite] A VMU-2 ScanEagle UAV is readied for a mission in Iraq by a Marine and a civilian representative of the Insitu Group, which manufactures the UAV. The 40-pound ScanEagle can remain airborne for more than 10 hours. (GySgt. Shannon Arledge)

with explosives and flown by remote control into various Communist targets. There is the tragically famous example of Lt. Joseph P. Kennedy, brother of the future martyred president, who was flying Navy PB4Y-1s heavily loaded with explosives into German V-1 missile sites. The Navy Liberators were flown by a reduced crew, which bailed out after takeoff, allowing the bomber to be guided to its target by a controller aircraft. Kennedy was killed in August 1944 when his PB4Y exploded prematurely after takeoff.

In Vietnam, unmanned drones were occasionally used as reconnaissance platforms to be recovered by specially equipped C-130s. The second generation of viable UAVs, pushed along by intense work by the Israelis, was developed in time for the First Gulf War in 1991. Looking more like big model airplanes, these largely reconnaissance vehicles were flown from ships and from shore fields, providing dramatic imagery for planners.

After Desert Storm, UAVs became part of the established arsenal available to all services, especially the Marine Corps. By 9/11 several of the newer UAVs had been equipped to carry many of the air-to-ground weapons currently used by frontline aircraft. Naturally, these armed unpiloted aircraft often became attractive alternatives to sending manned aircraft to strike potentially dangerous targets. They could fly longer and could be flown by qualified "pilots" from safe bases far from the battlefield.

Initially, in the mid-1980s, the Marine Corps used the Mastiff, which had seen service with the Israelis. When the Pioneer appeared, it became the Marines' main UAV, operated by two dedicated UAV squadrons that became VMU-1 and VMU-2. These small 450-pound UAVs flew at 100 knots with an endurance of five hours and could operate from frontline strips or launch from rails, much like launching a conventional aircraft from a carrier by catapult.

Having flown in Desert Storm as well as in the Balkans' conflicts of the late 1990s, the Pioneers proved themselves to be reliable and productive. Pioneer

A Marine prepares to hand-launch a Raven UAV in Anbar Province, Iraq, April 2008. Raven provides real-time video of the battlefield. (Cpl. Ryan Tomlinson)

crews called in artillery fire as well as provided almost instantaneous bomb damage assessment (BDA). Early in OIF, VMU-2 UAVs discovered a cache of Iraqi SAMs, which was destroyed by USAF F-15s and Navy F/A-18s. The UAVs sent in immediate BDA. Throughout OIF, VMU-2 UAVs scouted out targets that were then attacked by Marine Cobras.

VMU-1 Pioneers flew during Operation Phantom Fury, the battle of Fallujah, a nonstop eleven-day aerial campaign that saw the unmanned drones coordinate strikes and provide streaming video that identified targets.

A newer UAV, ScanEagle from Boeing, also participated in the battles of Fallujah in 2005. Originally designed to track fish for commercial fishermen, ScanEagle was modified for the Marine Corps as their Pioneer fleet began aging. Rail launched, the four-foot-long ScanEagle is retrieved by snagging a rope suspended from a fifty-foot pole.

Former VMU-2 CO, Col. Robert Rice, wrote, "The future of UAVs in the Marine Corps . . . is bright. While the total number of manned aircraft, particularly strike fighters, will continue to fall, the number of UAVs in the inventory will climb, more than doubling by 2012."[1]

By 2008 VMU-1 was operating two different UAVs, or to use the current acronym UASs (unmanned aircraft systems), the RQ-7B Shadow and the ScanEagle. With the headquarters in Al Anbar Province, three detachments move around the theater of operations. Originally developed for the Army, the Shadow was an attractive changeover from the Pioneer for the Marines, who made the transition in ten months.

VMU-2 had originally formed in June 1984 and two months later had been designated as the 1st Remotely Piloted Vehicle Platoon, headquarters Battalion, 2nd Marine Division. Training in Israel on the Mastiff, the unit then moved to the Pioneer, eventually arriving at Al Jubail, Saudi Arabia, in January 1991 for operations in Desert Storm. During the campaign, they flew fifty-five combat sorties in 192 flight hours without any UAVs being lost to enemy action. Redesignated VMU-2 in January 1996, the squadron deployed to Kuwait in February 2003 in time for OIF.

A third VMU was established in September 2008. VMU-3, based at Twenty-nine Palms, California, flies the RQ-7B Shadow.

The newly developing story of the UAV is constantly growing and changing. In the short time that a viable aircraft has been in operations, the number of different UAVs has grown to the point that it has become difficult to keep them all sorted out. Different UAVs fly with different services depending on the individual service's responsibility. For the Marine Corps, whose need for immediate battlefield scouting and imagery is ongoing and insatiable, the smaller UAVs have become the focus. The start of continuous campaigns like OIF and OEF provide a constant proving ground for these systems and the people who fly and maintain them.

Women Marines in the Cockpits

Female Naval Aviators have been around since the 1970s, the first getting her wings in 1974. All the U.S. military services now include woman pilots and WSOs, particularly after Congress lifted the ban against women flying in

combat in 1991. Even then it took a while, and the women who flew in Desert Storm were, for the most part, helicopter pilots who, nonetheless, found themselves occasionally operating in-country and often exposed to enemy fire.

In 1990 a female aviator first took command of an aviation squadron, and the first woman CO of a fleet Hornet squadron assumed command in 2007. However, the Marines were slower in allowing women to enter flight training. And then they were only allowed to fly helicopters and as NFOs in jets. Recently, however, women have been flying all types of Marine Corps aircraft and have also seen combat in OIF and OEF.

Maj. Sarah M. Deal became the Corps' first female aviator in April 1995, eventually flying CH-53Es with HMH-466. In August

[Top] Capt. Nicole Aunapu gets ready for a mission over Iraq in September 2006. She was assigned to VMFA-251, flying from the big base at Al Asad. (LCpl. Nikki M. Fleming)

[Bottom] After flying CH-46s with HMM-263, Capt. Elizabeth A. Okoreeh-Baah became the first female Osprey pilot and served with now-VMM-263.

1996, Lt. Jeanne M. Buchanan received her NFO wings at Pensacola, eventually being assigned to the EA-6B program. Shortly afterward, 1st Lt. Keri L. Schubert became the first woman Hornet NFO in February 1997. The first Marine female strike pilot was Lt. Karen F. Tribbett, who received her wings in October 1997. Another Marine female Hornet aviator is Capt. Nicole Aunapu, who, assigned to VMFA-251 and flying with CVW-1 aboard USS *Enterprise* and ashore from Al Asad, participated in OIF in 2006 and 2007.

Capt. Elizabeth A. Okoreeh-Baah served with VMM-263 as the first woman Osprey pilot and flew missions in Iraq during the new aircraft's first combat deployment.

The Cobra community numbered several woman pilots, among them Capt. Jessica M. Moore, flying with HMLA-167, and Capt. Vernice Armour, assigned to HMLA-169, both of whom have seen action in Iraq.

And a final milestone to note, Maj. Jennifer Grieves arrived at HMX-1 in October 2005—only the second female Marine aviator to get orders to the squadron. She eventually became the first woman to earn the designation of helicopter aircraft commander (HAC) in the Presidential Flight, flying the VH-3D known as Marine One when the president was aboard. In recognition of her achievement, she flew newly-elected President Obama from the White House to Andrews Air Force Base—a short flight—with an all-female crew on July 16, 2009. Maj. Jennifer Marino was the copilot and Sgt. Rachael Sherman was the crew chief.

New Life into Old Helicopters

There used to be a constant cycle of developing new aircraft to replace older, obsolescent types. However, after Vietnam, and certainly by the turn of the twenty-first century, requirements and financial considerations slowed this continuing turnover. Indeed, very few tactical jets followed the F/A-18 Hornet and F-16 Fighting Falcon. The Air Force struggled to field its F-22 Raptor stealth fighter and B-2 Spirit stealth bomber, and the Navy opted to extend its Hornet to the F/A-18E and F/A-18F Super Hornet. The Marine Corps voted not to take the Super Hornet in favor of waiting for the F-35B STOVL replacement for the AV-8B. The Corps also decided to stretch out its dwindling fleet of aging EA-6B Prowlers and not take advantage of the EA-18G Growler variant of the Hornet. Plans are to fly the EA-6Bs until 2015, with no relief in sight as of this writing.

[Opposite] An AH-1Z fires rockets on a test range. The Cobra has come a long way since its introduction in Vietnam. The slim, almost racer-like silhouette has grown into a hefty, power-enhanced weapons hauler.

[Top Right] This view of a UH-1Y of HMLAT-303 shows the splayed exhausts, part of the redesign to protect the helicopter from SAMs. The Huey's four-bladed main rotor is also shown. (LCpl. Christopher O'Quin)

[Bottom Right] The crew of a new UH-1Y prepares to take off from USS *Boxer* (LHD-4) during a training exercise before the ship deploys in January 2009. (Lt. [jg] Jared A. Burgamy)

The Marine Corps' greatest development program involved its complete revision and upgrade of its fleet of stalwart helicopters. The Cobra and Huey were redesigned and strengthened, while the CH-53 received the same attention. As 2008 transitioned to 2009 the CH-46 fleet was still very much in action, but as the revolutionary MV-22B Osprey continued to replace the Sea Knight, that aircraft will eventually pass from the scene, leaving behind a stellar record of performance and accomplishment.

The AH-1Z Viper takes advantage of new digital technology and is meant to keep the team concept with the equally improved UH-1Y. Indeed, the two helicopters share an 84 percent commonality of parts. The "Zulu" certainly looks like earlier Cobras; its most distinctive change is its four-blade main rotor and tail rotor. Its redesigned stub wings will carry increased ordnance, and, with its new weapons delivery systems, the Viper will undoubtedly retain its predecessor's enviable place as the premier attack helicopter in the world. Plans originally called for 180 AH-1Ws to be remanufactured as AH-1Zs.

The UH-1Y, which had been given the name Venom, was introduced to the fleet in January 2007 and quickly went to HMLAT-303 at Camp Pendleton. Original plans called for the Venom to replace 100 UH-1Ns. Both new helicopters provide a common cockpit upgrade to maintain a large degree of commonality for better maintainability and supportability. The Venom will give the Marine Corps increased capabilities in command and control as well as assault support in day and night and in adverse weather.

As the H-1 Upgrade Program began, inspection of existing UH-1Ns revealed an unexpected amount of corrosion as well as other prohibitive issues with the thirty-year-old airframes. The Marines decided to shift the program to manufacturing *new* aircraft, which would have the benefit of allowing the Marine Corps to retain its UH-1Ns in service when they are most needed in Iraq and Afghanistan and not subject them to a lengthy remanufacturing process. This decision, coupled with an increase in H-1 numbers to accommodate the Marine Corps' "Growth in Force" initiative, has increased the total number of upgraded aircraft to 123 UH-1Ys and 226 AH-1Zs by 2016.

At the time of writing, the Viper's initial operational date is expected to be 2011, while the UH-1Y received its initial operational clearance designation in August 2008. The new Huey deployed in January 2009 with HMM-163 (REIN) and the 13th MEU aboard USS *Boxer* (LHD-4).

The last of the quartet of Marine Corps helicopters of the Vietnam–post-Vietnam period to receive major redesign and upgrade is the big Sikorsky CH-53 Sea Stallion. While three squadrons of MAG-24, 1st MAW, at Kaneohe Bay, Hawaii, still fly the CH-53D at the time of writing, it is the tri-engine Echo that has served "in every clime and place" for the last three decades. (Now considered a medium-lift helicopter, the Delta is expected to carry on until 2013, when it will be replaced by the Osprey.)

The Corps' heavy-lift capability received a major shot in the arm with the arrival of the CH-53A in January 1967, when HMH-463 took the first aircraft to Vietnam. Indeed, it was these early CH-53s that brought the TRAP (Tactical Recovery of Aircraft and Personnel) concept to its modern status. Earlier efforts to retrieve damaged aircraft by helicopter had seen some success with the CH-37 Mojave, but the "Deuce" was limited in power and lift capability and it remained for the H-53 to truly make TRAP its own.

HMH-463 recovered more than four hundred downed aircraft during its year-long deployment, an incredible achievement. When the CH-53E was under design, great attention was given to enhancing its TRAP capability. Part of the specs was the stipulation that the Echo had to fly fifty miles, pick up another CH-53E, and fly those fifty miles back. Although TRAP is not a specific Marine Corps mission and is rarely used in combat, it has become an additional assignment for the Marines. The rescue of USAF Capt. Scott O'Grady in Bosnia in 1995 was a TRAP success flown by Marine Corps helicopters. (One might consider the daring Israeli heist of an Egyptian SA-2 radar site in December 1969, using CH-53As, as a highly modified TRAP mission.)[2]

With the CH-53E now showing its age, the Corps has begun evaluating and redesigning the veteran helicopter and come up with the CH-53K. The Kilo will be able to lift 27,000 pounds even in high altitudes and high temperatures such as those in Afghanistan, which hindered the CH-46 in OEF. Col. Paul Croisetiere, the H-53 Program Manager in 2006 wrote, "The CH-53D and CH-53E will see service lives approaching 50 years, and it is very reasonable to expect the CH-53K to see a service life well in excess of that. [With an IOC of 2015], the CH-53K will see service well past 2060, or a century of H-53 service in the Marine Corps."[3] With enlarged external sponsons that will increase the internal fuel load, the CH-53K's range will double that of the CH-53E. The Kilo's engines will be certainly increase in power, perhaps using the same power plants that equip the MV-22 Osprey.

In addition to the new family of combat helicopters, and after a lengthy selection process, the Marine Corps chose a new presidential aircraft for HMX-1 at MCAS Quantico. The aging H-3s had reached the end of their service life, after a 34-year career as the presidential helicopter, and the Agusta Westland VH-71 was selected in 2007 as the new "Marine One." Twenty-eight VH-71s were ordered, with five in the first batch to be followed by the remaining 23. The aircraft would have undergone a period of retrofit and refinement with HX-21, at NAS Patuxent River in southern Maryland before it entered service.

However, in early March 2009, concerns developed about the new helicopter's burgeoning price, which had nearly doubled. Newly-installed President Barack Obama did not help matters when he appeared to disparage the overall concept of a presidential helicopter during an impromptu news conference on February 23, 2009. His off-the-cuff comments generated a flurry of activity. Ironically, the question that started it all came from his recent election rival, Arizona Senator John McCain, himself well known as a Naval Aviator and Vietnam prisoner of war. Rumors flew that the VH-71 program was being cancelled and that the remaining 11 VH-3Ds would continue to fly in their occasional role as "Marine One."

The rumors proved true and the VH-71 was officially cancelled in early June 2009, with new plans for a replacement aircraft program being placed under consideration.

Maybe the Last New Fighter

By the time this edition appears in late 2009, the Marine Corps' two primary tactical jets—the AV-8B Harrier and the F/A-18 Hornet—will have been in service for nearly forty and twenty-five years, respectively. Quite a long period of frontline service, especially when the time includes considerable combat in very harsh conditions at sea and ashore. Although it is not unusual in the post–Korean War period for military aircraft to enjoy long careers, technology and changing financial pictures create a constantly changing list of requirements and necessities.

The Harrier, in particular, has perhaps seen its best days. Indeed, Britain's Royal Navy retired its pioneering Sea Harrier in 2006 for money concerns and changes in force projection philosophies. The British will continue to fly

RAF GR Harriers, while their senior service will await the introduction of the F-35 around 2012.

Although the AV-8 will continue to fly for other nations—Spain, India, Thailand, and Italy—the U.S. Marine Corps has already designated the STOVL successor, namely the Lockheed-Martin F-35B Lightning II. The name was chosen to commemorate that the United States and Great Britain—one of the primary future foreign operators of the aircraft—both flew planes named Lightning. The Lockheed P-38 escort fighter was flown primarily by U.S. Army squadrons in Europe and the Pacific, but it was also flown in very small numbers by the RAF during trial operations over Europe. And one of Britain's most important interceptors during the Cold War was the twin-jet English Electric Lightning.

Born out of a conference in the mid-1990s that established requirements for the next generation of American tactical fighter, originally called the Joint Strike Fighter (JSF), the new aircraft quickly became the subject of individual programs as required by the specific service. The Air Force's needs were, of course, different from those of the Navy, which needed to make the aircraft carrier capable. The Marines, seeking a Harrier replacement, placed the greatest pressure to make the new aircraft able to launch and recover vertically and operate close to the front, thus making the Marine Corps' JSF potentially the most advanced and ambitious model of the entire JSF program. Folding into the design the ability for supersonic flight and stealth configuration, the JSF soon became a very involved project.

The F-35A made its first flight on December 8, 2006. This model will replace many aircraft now in service, including the F-16, the A-10, and, as mentioned, the AV-8B and F/A-18A, B, C, and D. The first F-35B rolled off the Lockheed assembly line in December 2007 and made its first flight on June 11, 2008. The F-35B incorporates a turbo-fan engine, a two-stage, counter-rotating shaft-driven lift fan and a swiveling exhaust nozzle to vector thrust downward. Plans for the first F-35B squadron call for VMFAT-501, the training squadron, to stand up in 2010.

Writing in the 2008 *MCAA Journal*, Lt. Gen. George Trautman, Deputy Commandant for Air, commented, "The Joint Strike Fighter will join the Osprey in revolutionizing aviation warfighting concepts and our contributions to the joint force. The JSF's unmatched fusion of fifth generation sensors, robust communication and network interoperability, and kinetic and non-kinetic attack options, blended with an advanced low observable airframe and new survivability features, will completely change Marine tactical aviation."

Yet there is concern about just how much the F-35B will be able to contribute with its single-seat layout. The aging EA-6B fleet has no successor to what has become a vital Marine mission. And the Hornet and the Harrier will be on the verge of retirement as the JSF enters the fleet. There is talk of a two-seat ECM version of the F-35B. As it stands now, the electronic countermeasures mission is just too much for one pilot, but the Marines have decided to forego the oncoming F-18G Growler, the designated replacement for the Navy's Prowlers.

With the eventual retirement of the F/A-18D, there will also be the continuing need for a FAC(A) replacement. FAC(A) duties have become the sole domain of the two-seat Hornet, especially with the retirement of the Navy's F-14 Tomcat in 2006. Thus, another question of burden falls on the JSF. Adding another cockpit to the already encumbered F-35B, with all its lift systems and components, makes such a redesign really unrealistic. Should the Marines consider buying several of the Navy's F-35C carrier version, adding that second cockpit? It's a question that will no doubt see a lot of discussion.[4]

At this writing, one has to wonder, with the growing infusion of UAVs and their derivatives if the period of the manned aircraft is approaching its end or at least a decisive fork. Could the F-35 series be the last major American manned strike/light-attack fighter? Only time will tell.

Notes on the Reserves

The Marine Corps' Reserve aviation component has certainly received a workout in the last decade, as well as a restructuring. Squadrons have mobilized to answer the call for service in Iraq and Afghanistan and have

[Opposite] An F-35B prototype in landing configuration with landing gear down and upper and lower lift-fan doors and dorsal auxiliary-inlet doors (mid-fuselage) open. (Photo courtesy Lockheed Martin)

demonstrated their unique ability to leave their civilian lives and occupations to become Marines at the tip of the spear. However, financial and logistical matters being what they are in the early twenty-first century, many of these squadrons no sooner returned from their last deployment than to be served with schedules for decommissioning or retreating to cadre status. Decomissioning is death, while cadre means that there is a chance for resuscitation in the near or far future.

VMFA-321, the first military squadron to offer a combat air patrol umbrella to Washington, D.C., immediately after 9/11, was the first to go, decommissioning in September 2004. Two of the Reserve VMFAs—134 and 142—went into cadre status in the summers of 2007 and 2008, respectively. The possibility exists for these two squadrons to become Reserve F-35 squadrons several years down the road. Thus, of the four Reserve VMFAs, only the Cowboys of VMFA-112 still fly at NAS JRB Fort Worth.

Helicopter squadrons were not immune. With plans to consolidate all the reserve CH-53Es into one unit, HMH-772 at NAS Willow Grove, Pennsylvania, the veteran CH-53E squadron HMH-769 decommissioned in August 2008, followed by one half of the Reserve Cobra contingent, HMLA-775 in September 2008. MAG-42 decommissioned in July 2008 and MAG-46 will follow a year later.

Yet, with all the "death and destruction," there is long-term hope for the Corps' trusty reservists. The UH-1Y and even the MV-22 are slated to enter 4th Wing inventories by the middle of the second decade of the new century, followed by KC-130Js and even UAVs. New squadrons and redesignated and reequipped old units will stand up to build a strong and capable aviation reserve.

A New Museum and a Last Word

If the reader, who is obviously interested in the Marine Corps either from personal experience or on an outside level, has not seen the new National Museum of the Marine Corps at Quantico, I want to end this new edition with a strong suggestion that he or she visit this splendid new display as soon as possible. A fine, focused homage to the Corps and all it represents, the museum has something for everyone, and in particular, several fine aviation exhibits from the beginning to the present day. Aircraft of all periods hang overhead, positioned in flight, or perhaps on the ground as they might be when they were operational. Displays of various scenes such as the layout of Chu Lai, complete with A-4 SATS field in 1966, or the view from the aft end of an actual CH-46 at Khe Sanh in 1968, plus honor boards and galleries all depict the Marine Corps' rich, still-evolving aviation history. The museum is easy to get to and is free and open to the public. You're also likely to find yourself mixing with new immaculately dressed Marines on a break from their studies on the base. Most military services have a dedicated museum to tell their particular story, but this newest is certainly one of the best I have seen.

The possibility of a new museum was raised in 1979, and finally, on November 10, 2006, the Marine Corps' 231st birthday, the doors were opened in a magnificent ceremony that featured remarks by President

George W. Bush and the presentation of a posthumous Medal of Honor to the family of Cpl. Jason L. Dunham for his heroism in OIF. There have been and are a few other museums across the United States devoted to Marine Corps subjects, all excellent in their own individual right. However, this truly wonderful all-encompassing structure and all that it includes is worth a dedicated trip to the Washington, D.C., area.

A description of the new museum is a fitting way to end—for now—this history of Marine Corps aviation and all that it represents. To negotiate all that lies before us, we need to continue to build on this stellar history and to maintain a strong military force, perhaps smaller, leaner, and decidedly more intelligent, but we need it, nonetheless. And we definitely need a Marine Corps and its dedicated air arm.

Appendix A
First 100 Marine Corps Aviators

Number	Name	Date of Designation	Naval Aviator Number
1	Alfred Austell Cunningham	17 Sep 1915	5
2	Bernard Lewis Smith	1 Jul 1914	6
3	William Maitland McIlvain	10 Mar 1915	12
4	Francis Thomas Evans	9 Mar 1916	26
5	Roy Stanley Geiger	9 Jun 1917	49
6	David Lukens Shoemaker Brewster	5 Jul 1917	55
7	Edmund Gillette Chamberlain	9 Oct 1917	96 ½ & 768
8	Russell Alger Presley	9 Nov 1917	100 ¾ & 769
9	Doyle Bradford	5 Nov 1917	111 ½
10	Clifford Lawrence Webster	5 Nov 1917	112 ½
11	Arthur Houston Wright	6 Dec 1917	148 & 803
12	Herman Alexander Peterson	2 Nov 1917	163 ½
13	George McCully Laughlin III	12 Dec 1917	165 & 790
14	Charles Burton Ames	21 Dec 1917	193
15	John Howard Weaver	21 Jan 1918	251 & 794
16	Alvin Lochinvar Prichard	21 Jan 1918	279
17	George Conan Willman	22 Jan 1918	299 & 795
18	Herbert Dalzell Elvidge	12 Mar 1918	424
19	Hazen Curtis Pratt	8 Mar 1918	426
20	Sidney "E" Clark	8 Mar 1918	442 & 800
21	Frederick Commodore Schley	8 Mar 1918	443 & 801
22	Charles Alfred Needham	14 Mar 1918	444
23	John Bartow Bates	25 Mar 1918	449
24	Ralph Talbot	10 Apr 1918	456
25	Thomas Carrington Comstock	26 Mar 1918	473 & 789
26	Francis Osborne Clarkson	28 Mar 1918	474 & 788
27	Guy Mowrey Williamson	25 Mar 1918	477
28	Grover Cleveland Alder	25 Mar 1918	479
29	Edward Kenealy	23 Mar 1918	480
30	Donald Newell Whiting	1 Apr 1918	503
31	Howard Albert Strong	2 Apr 1918	505
32	John Parke McMurran	1 Apr 1918	508 & 791

Number	Name	Date of Designation	Naval Aviator Number
33	James Kendrick Noble	1 Apr 1918	510 & 792
34	Vincent Case Young	1 Apr 1918	519
35	Province Law Pogue	19 Jun 1918	522 & 782
36	Duncan Hugh Cameron	26 Mar 1918	527 & 787
37	George Fred Donovan	26 Mar 1918	532 & 798
38	William Herbert Derbyshire	28 Feb 1918	533 & 770
39	Frederick Brock Davy	28 Feb 1918	534 & 771
40	Douglas Bennett Roben	14 Mar 1918	535 & 774
41	Arthur Hallett Page Jr.	14 Mar 1918	536 & 775
42	Gove Compton	14 Mar 1918	537 & 773
43	Thomas James Butler	10 Apr 1918	541 & 786
44	Thomas Rodney Shearer	4 Apr 1918	559
45	Ford Ovid Rogers	14 Apr 1918	560
46	Homer Carter Bennett	11 Apr 1918	562 & 797
47	John Edmond Powell	4 Apr 1918	563
48	William Morrison Barr	8 Apr 1918	567 & 799
49	Harry Eldridge Stovall	11 Apr 1918	568
50	Harvey Byrd Mims	4 Dec 1917	576
51	Winfield Scott Shannon	17 Apr 1918	583
52	Everett Robert Brewer	17 Apr 1918	585
53	John George Estill Kipp	17 Apr 1918	586
54	Frederick Louis Kolb	17 Apr 1918	587
55	George Franklin Kremm	17 Apr 1918	588
56	Jesse Arthur Nelson	17 Apr 1918	589
57	Herman Judson Jesse	17 Apr 1918	590
58	William Webster Head	17 Apr 1918	591
59	Gustav Henry Kaemmerling	17 Apr 1918	592
60	Jesse Floyd Dunlap	17 Apr 1918	593
61	Trevor George Williams	17 Apr 1918	594
62	Clyde Noble Bates	17 Apr 1918	595
63	Melville Edward Ingalls Sullivan	17 Apr 1918	596
64	Francis Patrick Mulcahy	17 Apr 1918	597
65	Benjamin Louis Harper	17 Apr 1918	598
66	Walter Harold Batts	17 Apr 1918	599
67	Henry Teasdale Young	17 Apr 1918	600
68	Karl Schmolsmire Day	17 Apr 1918	601
69	Fred Sevier Robillard	17 Apr 1918	602
70	Melchior Borner Trelfall	17 Apr 1918	603
71	Harold Cornell Major	17 Apr 1918	604
72	Robert Sidney Lytle	17 Apr 1918	605
73	Thomas Caldwell Turner	14 Mar 1918	772
74	Kenneth Brown Collings	26 Mar 1918	776
75	Donald Buford Cowles	4 Apr 1918	777
76	Maco Stewart Jr.	4 Apr 1918	778
77	Henry Sidney Ehret Jr.	6 Apr 1918	779
78	Raymond Joseph Kirwan	8 Apr 1918	780
79	Frank Nelms Jr.	19 Jun 1918	781
80	Harvey Chester Norman	23 May 1918	783

Number	Name	Date of Designation	Naval Aviator Number
81	Delmar Leighton	23 May 1918	784
82	John Thomas Brecton	11 Apr 1918	785
83	William Wheelwright Torrey	22 Mar 1918	793
84	Joseph White Austin	23 Mar 1918	796
85	Bunn Gradon Barnwell	28 May 1918	804
86	Walter Josephs Willoughby	19 Jun 1918	805
87	Chester Julius Peters	19 Jun 1918	806
88	Roswell Emory Davis	19 Jun 1918	807
89	Horace Wilbur Leeper	25 Jun 1918	808
90	Byron Brazil Freeland	25 Jun 1918	809
91	Robert James Paisley	19 Jun 1918	810
92	Charles Thomas Holloway II	1 Jul 1918	811
93	Frank Henry Fleer	2 Jul 1918	812
94	Maurice Kingsley Heartfield	2 Jul 1918	813
95	Robert James Archibald	8 Jul 1918	814
96	Arthur Judson Sherman	8 Jul 1918	815
97	Philip William Blood	8 Jul 1918	816
98	Albert Aloysius Kuhlen	28 Jun 1918	817
99	Earl Francis War	30 Jun 1918	818
100	August Koerbling	1 Jul 1918	819

Note: Aviators with two designation numbers generally transferred from the Navy to the Marine Corps, receiving a second number from the Marines. The lower number is used to establish precedence. Numbers with fractions resulted from several aviators being given the same designation number. Also, dates of designation should not be confused with dates of precedence, which are reflected by naval aviator numbers and are often much earlier than designation dates.

Appendix B
Directors, Deputy Chiefs of Staff, and Deputy Commandants for Marine Corps Aviation

Maj. Alfred A. Cunningham	17 Nov 1919–12 Dec 1920
Lt. Col. Thomas C. Turner	13 Dec 1920–2 Mar 1925
Maj. Edward H. Brainard	3 Mar 1925–9 May 1929
Col. Thomas C. Turner	10 May 1929–28 Oct 1931
Maj. Roy S. Geiger	6 Nov 1931–29 May 1935
Col. Ross E. Rowell	30 May 1935–10 Mar 1939
Brig. Gen. Ralph J. Mitchell	11 Mar 1939–29 Mar 1943
Maj. Gen. Roy S. Geiger	13 May 1943–15 Oct 1943
Brig. Gen. Louis E. Woods	15 Oct 1943–17 Jul 1944
Maj. Gen. Field Harris	18 Jul 1944–24 Feb 1948
Maj. Gen. William J. Wallace	24 Feb 1948–1 Sep 1950
Brig. Gen. Clayton C. Jerome	1 Sep 1950–15 Apr 1952
Lt. Gen. William O. Brice	1 Apr 1952–31 Jul 1955
Lt. Gen. Christian F. Schilt	1 Aug 1955–31 Mar 1957
Lt. Gen. Verne J. McCaul	1 Apr 1957–2 Dec 1957
Maj. Gen. Samuel S. Jack	14 Jan 1958–20 Feb 1958
Maj. Gen. John C. Munn	21 Feb 1958–14 Dec 1959
Maj. Gen. Arthur F. Binney	15 Dec 1959–10 Sep 1961
Col. Keith B. McCutcheon	11 Sep 1961–17 Feb 1962
Col. Marion E. Carl	18 Feb 1962–4 Jul 1962
Brig. Gen. Norman J. Anderson	5 Jul 1962–20 Oct 1963
Maj. Gen. Louis B. Robertshaw	21 Oct 1963–15 Jun 1966
Maj. Gen. Keith B. McCutcheon	15 Jun 1966–18 Feb 1970
Maj. Gen. Homer S. Hill	19 Feb 1970–24 Aug 1972
Maj. Gen. Edward S. Fris	25 Aug 1972–27 Aug 1974
Brig. Gen. Philip D. Shutler	28 Aug 1974–Jan 1975
Maj. Gen. Victor A. Armstrong	Jan 1975–21 Aug 1975
Lt. Gen. Thomas H. Miller Jr.	22 Aug 1975–29 Jun 1979
Lt. Gen. William J. White	30 Jun 1979–30 Jun 1982
Lt. Gen. William H. Fitch	1 Jul 1982–31 Aug 1984
Lt. Gen. Keith A. Smith	1 Sep 1984–29 Apr 1988
Lt. Gen. Charles H. Pitman	30 Apr 1988–16 Aug 1990
Lt. Gen. Duane A. Wills	17 Aug 1990–30 Jun 1993
Lt. Gen. Richard A. Hearney	1 Jul 1993–15 Jul 1994

Lt. Gen. Harold W. Blot	16 Jul 1994–21 Jul 1996
Lt. Gen. Terrence R. Dake	22 Jul 1996–17 Aug 1998
	(later promoted to general as ACMC)
Lt. Gen. Frederick McCorkle	8 Aug 1998–2 Aug 2001
Lt. Gen. William L. Nyland	3 Aug 2001–2 Oct 2002
	(later promoted to general as ACMC)
Lt. Gen. Michael A. Hough	3 Oct 2002–2 Nov 2005
Lt. Gen. John G. Castellaw	3 Nov 2005–4 Jul 2007
Lt. Gen. George J. Trautman III	5 Jul 2007–

Note: On April 1, 1936, the title of the senior aviator attached to Headquarters, Marine Corps, changed from Officer in Charge, Aviation, to Director of Aviation, and on April 25, 1962, became Deputy Chief of Staff (Air). The title changed yet again in 1998 to Deputy Commandant for Aviation.

Acronyms

ACE	air combat element
ACF	Air Combat Fighter
ACM	air combat maneuvering
AMAD	aircraft mounted accessory drive
APU	auxiliary power unit
ARG	advanced research group
ARVN	Army of the Republic of Vietnam
ATARS	Advanced Tactical Aerial Reconnaissance System
ATF	amphibious task force
ATO	air tasking order
BAI	battlefield air interdiction
BARCAP	barrier contact air patrol
BCP	border control point
BDA	bomb damage assessment
BuAer	Bureau of Aeronautics
CAG	Commander, Air Group
CAP	combat air patrol
CAS	close air support
CASEVAC	casualty evacuation
CFACC	combined force air component commander
CNO	Chief of Naval Operations
COIN	counterinsurgency
ComAirNorSols	Commander, Air, Northern Solomons
ComAirSols	Commander, Aircraft, Solomons
CSAR	combat search and rescue
CVS	antisubmarine carrier
CVW	carrier attack wing
DASC	Direct Air Support Center
DFC	Distinguished Flying Cross
DI	drill instructor
DMZ	demilitarized zone
ECM	electronic countermeasures
ECMO	electronic countermeasures officer
ELINT	electronic intelligence

EOD	explosive ordnance detail
EW	electronic warfare
FAC	forward air controller
FARP	forward arming and refueling point
FEAF	Far East Air Force
FLIR	forward-looking infrared radar
FMF	Fleet Marine Force
FOB	forward operating base
GCA	ground control approach
GCI	ground control intercept
HAC	helicopter aircraft commander
HMLA	helicopter Marine light-attack squadron
H&MS	headquarters and maintenance squadron
IFR	instrument flight rules
I MAC	I Marine Amphibious Corps
I MHG	I Marine Expeditionary Force Headquarters Group
IP	initial point
IR	infrared
ICS	intercom system
JDAMs	Joint Direct Attack Munitions
JSF	Joint Strike Fighter
JSOWs	Joint Stand-Off Weapons
KTO	Kuwait Theater of Operations
LAAM	light anti-aircraft missile
LAPES	Low Altitude Parachute Extraction System
LFASCUs	Landing Force Air Support Control Units
LSD	laser designator
LZ	landing zone
MAF	Marine Amphibious Force
MAG	Marine Aircraft Group
MAGSDAGUPAN	Marine Aircraft Groups, Dagupan
MAGSZAM	Marine Aircraft Groups, Zamboanga
MAGTF	Marine Air-Ground Task Force
MALS	Marine Aviation Logistics Squadron
MARHUKS	Marine hunter/killers
MAW	Marine Aircraft Wing
MEB	Marine Expeditionary Brigade
MEU	Marine Expeditionary Unit
MOPP	Mission Oriented Protective Posture
MTDS	Marine Tactical Data System
MUV	Marine Unit Vietnam
NAF	Naval Air Facility
NAG	Northern Arabian Gulf
NAP	Naval Aviation Pilot
NBC	nuclear, biological, chemical
NFO	naval flight officer
NVA	North Vietnamese Army
NVGs	night-vision goggles
OEF	Operation Enduring Freedom
OIF	Operation Iraqi Freedom

ONW	Operation Northern Watch
OSW	Operation Southern Watch
POL	petroleum, oil, and lubricants
POW	prisoner of war
RIO	radar intercept officer
RSO	radar systems officer
RPG	rocket propelled grenade
SAM	surface-to-air missile
SAR	search-and-rescue
SAS	Special Air Service
SATS	Short Airfield for Tactical Support
SCAR	strike coordination and reconnaissance
SEAD	suppression of enemy air defenses
SOC	special operations capable
TAC	tactical air controller
TacAir	tactical aviation
TACC	Tactical Air Control Center
TADC	Tactical Air Direction Center
TAF	Tactical Air Force
TAOC	Tactical Air Operations Center
TBFDS	Tactical Bulk Fuel Dispensing System
TFBD	tactical bulk refueling system
TRAP	Tactical Recovery of Aircraft and Personnel
UAS	unmanned aircraft system
UAV	unmanned aerial vehicle
VC	Viet Cong
VIFFing	vectoring in forward flight
V/STOL	vertical/short takeoff landing
WSO	weapons system officer

Notes

CHAPTER 1: THE BEGINNING, 1912–1918

1. The installation in 1999 of a commemorative plaque at Marblehead, Massachusetts, renewed the occasional question of what the correct date is to celebrate the birth of Marine Corps aviation. The marker notes that Cunningham took off on August 1, 1912—the first takeoff by a Marine—but the official birthday remains as noted, May 22, 1912, the date he reported for training duty at Annapolis. However, having been immediately sent off on expeditionary duty, he returned to find the Annapolis aircraft in disrepair. He got orders to report to Marblehead, where he eventually made his first flight, albeit with an instructor, as recorded. He soloed on August 20. Thus, Marblehead enjoys the honor of perhaps—depending on interpretation—being the birthplace, if not having the corresponding birth date of Marine Corps aviation. I highly recommend a pilgrimage to the old town and the lovingly maintained park with the picturesque little site unique to all members, past and present, of Marine Corps aviation.

2. Major A. A. Cunningham, quoted in Lt. Col. Edward C. Johnson, USMC, *Marine Corps Aviation: The Early Years 1912–1940*, History and Museum Division Headquarters, USMC, 1977.

3. Ibid, 25.

CHAPTER 2: BETWEEN WARS, 1919–1941

1. Major A. A. Cunningham, quoted in Lt. Col. Edward C. Johnson, USMC, *Marine Corps Aviation: The Early Years 1912–1940*, History and Museum Division Headquarters, USMC, 1977, 27.

2. Ibid, 31.

CHAPTER 3: WORLD WAR II: ON THE DEFENSIVE

1. Unpublished contemporary article by Bill Wolf, Reference Branch, Marine Corps History Division, Quantico, VA, 2007.

2. Maj. Gen. Marion E. Carl, USMC, with Barrett Tillman, *Pushing the Envelope: The Career of Fighter Ace and Test Pilot Marion Carl*, Annapolis, MD: Naval Institute Press, 1994.

3. Dr. Frank J. Olynyk. USMC *Credits for the Destruction of Enemy Aircraft in Air-to-Air Combat, World War 2*. Aurora, OH: Privately Published, October 1981.

CHAPTER 4: CACTUS IN THE PACIFIC: GUADALCANAL

1. Jiro Horikoshi, *Eagles of Mitsubishi: The Story of the Zero Fighter*, Seattle, WA: University of Washington Press, 1981.

2. Maj. Gen. Marion E. Carl, USMC with Barrett Tillman, *Pushing the Envelope: The Career of Fighter Ace and Test Pilot Marion Carl,* Annapolis, MD: Naval Institute Press, 1994.

3. Ibid.

4. T. G. Miller Jr., *The Cactus Air Force,* New York: Bantam Books, 1981.

5. *Naval Aviation News,* May 1982.

6. Quoted in Robert Sherrod, *History of Marine Corps Aviation in World War II,* San Rafael, CA: Presidio Press, 1980.

7. Brig. Gen. Samuel B. Griffith II. *The Battle for Guadalcanal,* Baltimore: Nautical & Aviation Publishing Company of America, 1979.

CHAPTER 5: ISLAND HOPPING

1. Gregory Boyington, *Baa Baa Black Sheep,* New York: Putnam's, 1958.

2. John M. Foster, *Hell in the Heavens,* Washington, DC: Zenger Publishing, 1961.

3. Ibid.

4. Author interview with Lt. Col. John F. Bolt, April 11, 1995, Orlando, Florida.

5. Foster, *Hell in the Heavens.*

6. *The Wartime Journals of Charles A. Lindbergh,* New York: Harcourt Brace Jovanovich, 1970.

CHAPTER 6: CARRYING THE WAR TO JAPAN

1. Maj. Charles W. Boggs Jr., USMC, *Marine Aviation in the Philippines,* Washington, DC: U.S. Government Printing Office, 1951.

2. Ibid.

3. Ibid.

4. *History of the Second World War,* Marshall Cavendish Promotions Ltd., 1974. This highly detailed account was a monthly subscription issued as a magazine addressing specific events, battles, personalities, and causes.

5. Robert Sherrod, *History of Marine Corps Aviation in World War II,* San Rafael, CA: Presidio Press, 1980.

6. Brig. Gen. E. H. Simmons, USMC (Ret.), *The United States Marines 1775–1975,* New York: Viking Press, 1974.

7. Allan R. Millett, *Semper Fidelis: The History of the United States Marine Corps,* New York: MacMillan, 1980.

CHAPTER 7: POST-WAR ACTIVITIES

1. Lt. Col. Eugene W. Rawlis, USMC, *Marines and Helicopters 1946–1962,* History and Museums Division, Headquarters, USMC, 1976.

CHAPTER 8: ANOTHER WAR IN ASIA: KOREA

1. Maj. Daniel C. Georgia, USMC (Ret.), *Marine Composite Squadron—A History of the Early Days,* unpublished manuscript.

2. Ibid.

CHAPTER 9: KOREAN STALEMATE

1. *Naval Aviation News,* November 1952.

2. G. G. O'Rourke, with E. T. Wooldridge, *Night Fighters over Korea,* Annapolis: Naval Institute Press, 1998.

3. *Leatherneck,* October 1953.

4. Letter to the author, 2001, quoted in Maj. Gen. John P. Condon, USMC (Ret.), with Cmdr. Peter B. Mersky, USNR (Ret.), *Corsairs to Panthers: U.S. Marine Aviation in Korea,* Washington, DC: Korean War Commemorative Series Monograph, U.S. Marine Corps Historical Center, 2002.

5. Brig. Gen. E. H. Simmons, USMC (Ret.), *The United States Marines 1775–1975,* New York: Viking Press, 1974.

6. *The American Weekly,* August 23, 1953.

7. Ibid.

8. Author interview with Lt. Col. John F. Bolt, April 11, 1995, Orlando, Florida.

9. Author interview with Jerry Coleman, 2000.

10. Jerry Coleman with Richard Goldstein, *An American Journey: My Life on the Field, In the Air, and On the Air,* Chicago: Triumph Books, 2008.

11. Ibid.

12. Data obtained from Volume V of the excellent operational history, *U.S. Marine Operations in Korea, 1950–1953,* Washington, DC: Historical Division, Headquarters, U.S. Marine Corps, 1972.

CHAPTER 10: POST–KOREAN WAR DEVELOPMENTS

1. Jerry O'Rourke, "The Douglas Navy F4D Ford," *Journal of the American Aviation Historical Society,* Summer 1979.

2. Ibid.

3. Author interview, 1983.

CHAPTER 11: VIETNAM: THE EARLY STAGES

1. Details of this account and other VMCJ stories can be found on a very interesting Web site devoted to VMCJ operations and history, www.mcara.us/home.html. The site is maintained by retired Marine Col. H. Wayne Whitten.

2. www.mcara.us/home.html.

3. Gen. John R. Dailey, USMC (Ret.), interview with the author, Washington, DC, March 6, 2007.

4. Details courtesy of Col. H. Wayne Whitten, USMC (Ret.).

5. "Marine Corps Skyhawks," in *Replica in Scale,* by Fred Roos, 3, no. 1, Fall 1974.

6. Author interview with Gen. John R. Dailey, USMC (Ret.), Washington, DC, March 6, 2007.

7. *Marine Corps Gazette,* May 1969.

8. Gen. William Momyer, USAF (Ret), *Airpower in Three Wars,* Washington, DC: Government Printing Office, 1978.

CHAPTER 12: THE COMMUNIST WAITING GAME PAYS OFF

1. Istvan Toperczer, *MiG-21 Units of the Vietnam War,* Osprey Publications, 2001.

CHAPTER 13: POST-VIETNAM FUTURE

1. Russell Murray II, "The AV-8B—Rising Vertically through the Air, Invulnerable to Runaway Cuts," a treatise on the AV-8B, 1978.

CHAPTER 15: TAKING THE MEASURE OF SADDAM

1. Interview by Lt. Col. Brendan Greeley, USMC (Ret.), "Marine Air: There When Needed, with Lt. Gen. Royal N. Moore," U.S. Naval Institute *Proceedings,* November 1991.

2. Ibid.

CHAPTER 16: DESERT STORM

1. Letter to author, November 1996.

2. Ibid.

3. Brig. Gen. E. H. Simmons, USMC (Ret.), "Getting Marines to the Gulf," U.S. Naval Institute *Proceedings,* May 1991.

4. Author phone interview, 1996.

5. Letter to author, November 1996.

6. "The 1st Marine Division in the Attack, an Interview with Major General J. M. Myatt, USMC," U.S. Naval Institute *Proceedings,* November 1991.

7. LCpl. Bryan Lieske, "Survivor," *Marines,* March 1997.

8. Ibid.

9. Ibid.

10. Author interview with Col. John P. Oppenhuizen, June 26, 1991, Norfolk, VA.

CHAPTER 18: FIGHTING IN THE NEW WORLD OF TERRORISM

1. Col. Richard D. Mullen (USMCR), e-mail to author, August 9, 2008.

2. Maj. Michael V. Franzak, USMC, "Nightmares in Afghanistan," *Naval Aviation News,* May–June 2003.

3. Cdr. Paul Mackley, "TacAir Integration: Where the Rubber Meets the Road," *Naval Aviation News,* May–June 2005.

4. Chris Amos, "Integration at an End?" *Navy Times,* August 18, 2008.

CHAPTER 19: PERSIAN GULF WAR II: TAKING SADDAM, *AGAIN!*

1. Rebecca Grant, "Marine Air in the Mainstream," *Air Force Magazine,* June 2004.

2. Ibid.

3. Gen. Michael W. Hagee, USMC, interview with Dr. Fred H. Allison, November 29, 2005, Arlington, VA. Transcript, USMC History Division, Quantico, VA.

4. Maj. Gen. James F. Amos, USMC, interview with Col. James J. Coulter and Lt. Col. Michael Visconage, May 16, 2003, Arlington, VA. Transcript, USMC History Division, Quantico, VA.

5. Tony Holmes, *U.S. Marine Corps and RAAF Hornet Units of Operation Iraqi Freedom,* UK and New York: Osprey Publications, 2006.

6. Ibid.

7. *The Yellow Sheet, Summer 2006, Quarterly of the Marine Corps Aviation Association,* interview by Dr. Fred H. Allison for the USMC Oral History Program of the History Division, Marine Corps University.

CHAPTER 20: CONTINUING THE WAR THAT WAS FINISHED

1. Maj. Fred H. Allison, USMCR (Ret.), "Close Air Support: A Core Contributor to Successful Integrated Operations in Fallujah," *Marine Corps Gazette,* October 2008.

2. E-mail to the author from Col. Rick Mullen, USMCR, August 21, 2008.

3. Ibid.

4. Ruchnoy Pulemyot Kalashnikova, basically a Russian-manufactured hand-held 7.62-mm machine gun.

5. "A Letter Home from Indonesia," *Naval Aviation News,* March–April 2005.

6. Maj. John S. Payne, USMC, interview by Lt. Col. John Way, February 5, 2005, for the Marine Corps History Division, Quantico, VA. Quoted in Allison, "Close Air Support."

7. Ibid.

8. An illustration of the high level of experience in Reserve squadrons is the attainment of 5,000 hours in the Hornet alone by Lt. Col. Harry G. Constant, then the CO of VMFA-134 in May 2006. This number represents time in a single aircraft, not a total in his log books. Many aviators seldom reach this high number in a twenty-year career, let alone in a single type. A Navy pilot had previously reached the number in Hornets, thus making Lieutenant Colonel Constant the first Marine aviator with that amount of Hornet time.

9. Alfred M. Biddlecomb, ed., "*Enterprise* and Iwo Jima Complete Afghanistan Ops," *Naval Aviation News,* January–February 2007.

10. Bradley Klapper, "Helicopter-plane Osprey faring well in Iraq," Associated Press, October 20, 2008.

11. Capt. Jonathan H. Brandt, "The VMM-263 Thunder Chickens Make Aviation History," *The Yellow Sheet,* Spring 2008 Quarterly.

12. Maj. Owen M. Coulman, "HMLA-773 Red Dogs in Iraq: The Saga Continues . . ." *The Yellow Sheet,* Spring 2008 Quarterly.

13. LCpl. Laura A. Mapes, USMC, *Desert Warrior* staff, "VMA-311 Returns from a Different Iraq," *Desert Warrior,* the base newspaper for MCAS Yuma, October 16, 2008.

14. Ibid.

CHAPTER 21: DEALING WITH THE PRESENT, PLANNING FOR THE FUTURE

1. Col. Robert Rice, "Marine UAVs: The Small Planes with the Bigger Missions," *The MCAA Journal,* 2004.

2. Thanks to Col. Rick Mullen, USMCR, for a brief overview of the TRAP mission in an e-mail, August 21, 2008.

3. "Marine Corps Heavy Lift Helicopters: Long History, Rich Legacy," *The MCAA Journal,* 2006.

4. See Capt. Walter Suarez, "JSF, the Need for a Two-seat Variant," *Marine Corps Gazette,* October 2008.

Recommended Reading

For those who would like to read more about a specific area of Marine aviation or a specific squadron or aircraft, I would suggest the following books and sources. In general:

Allan R. Millett. *Semper Fidelis: The History of the United States Marine Corps.* New York: MacMillan, 1980.

Brig. Gen. E. H. Simmons, USMC (Ret.). *The United States Marines 1775–1975.* New York: Viking, 1974. A third edition was published in 1998 by the Naval Institute Press.

The Marine Corps Association has published a massive volume providing a daily chronology of Marine Corps history reaching to 2003 and the beginning of Operation Iraqi Freedom (OIF) and Operation Enduring Freedom (OEF), accompanied by photos and artwork.

Merrill L. Bartlett and Jack Sweetman. *Leathernecks: An Illustrated History of the United States Marine Corps.* Annapolis: U.S. Naval Institute, 2008. This is a less hefty treatment of the 230-year history of the Corps, with a few references to aviation events.

Norman Polmar. *Aircraft Carriers: A Graphic History of Carrier Aviation and Its Influence on World Events.* Garden City, NY: Doubleday, 1969. A greatly updated two-volume set was published in 2006 by Potomac Books, Dulles, VA.

Robert Sherrod. *History of Marine Corps Aviation in World War II.* San Rafael, CA: Presidio Press, 1980 edition.

Brig. Gen. Samuel B. Griffith II. *The Battle for Guadalcanal.* Baltimore: Nautical & Aviation Publishing Company of America, 1979.

T. G. Miller Jr. *The Cactus Air Force.* New York: Bantam Books, 1981.

Gregory Boyington. *Baa Baa Black Sheep.* New York: Putnam's, 1958. Also available in a paperback edition from Bantam.

Two pictorial books are also worth reading, although one is out of print: William T. Larkins. *U.S. Marine Corps Aircraft 1914–1959.* Concord, CA: Aviation History Publications, 1959, and Thomas E. Doll. *Flying Leathernecks in World War II.* Fallbrook, CA: Aero Publishers Inc., 1971.

The History and Museums Division of the Headquarters, Marine

Corps, in Quantico, Virginia, is responsible for an excellent and ambitious writing program. To date, it has published several useful volumes on Marine operations in Vietnam, as well as several squadron histories, including VMA-223, VMA-311, VMFA-115, VMFA-312, VMFA-232, HMM-161, and VMO-6. There is also a volume on the period 1912–40, entitled *Marine Corps Aviation: the Early Years*. Expansive and highly detailed series of monographs on World War II and Korea include dedicated volumes on aviation subjects. A series on the Persian Gulf War of 1991 and the War on Terror/Operation Iraqi Freedom and Operation Enduring Freedom will also include volumes on Marine Corps air operations. All of these Marine-produced and -sponsored works are nominally priced and should be read by anyone interested in the subject.

For specific aircraft, I recommend the following works:

Bruce Robertson, ed. *United States Navy and Marine Corps Fighters 1918–1962*. UK: Harleyford Publications Ltd., 1962.

Barrett Tillman. *Corsair: The F4U in World War II and Korea*. Annapolis: U.S. Naval Institute, 1979.

Barrett Tillman. *The Dauntless Divebomber in World War II*. Annapolis: U.S. Naval Institute, 1976.

Barrett Tillman. *Hellcat*. Annapolis: U.S. Naval Institute, 1979.

Jess C. Barrow. *Marine Fighting Squadron Nine (VF-9M)*. Blue Ridge Summit, PA: TAB Books, 1981.

Michael O'Leary. *United States Naval Fighters of World War II in Action*. UK: Blandford Press, Ltd., 1980.

Barrett Tillman. *MiG Master: The Story of the F-8 Crusader*. Baltimore: Nautical & Aviation Publishing Company of America, 1980.

Barrett Tillman. *The Wildcat in World War II*. Baltimore: Nautical & Aviation Publishing Company of America, 1983.

Peter Mersky. *U.S. Navy and Marine Corps F-8 Crusader Units in the Vietnam War*. New York: Osprey Publications, 1998.

Peter Mersky. *U.S. Navy and Marine Corps RF-8 Crusader Units in Vietnam and Cuba*. New York: Osprey Publications, 1998.

Peter Mersky. *U.S. Navy and Marine Corps A-4 Skyhawk Units in the Vietnam War*. New York: Osprey Publications, 2007.

Certain periodicals are also worthwhile sources of material on military aviation in general. Two of those dealing specifically with Navy and Marine aviation are *Naval Aviation News,* the U.S. government's oldest military publication, and *The Hook,* a quarterly journal from the Tailhook Association of California, a well-produced publication dealing primarily with carrier aviation.

The highly respected U.S. Naval Institute's *Proceedings* and *Naval History* also carry articles dealing with aviation, both current and historical.

Several books on the 1991 Gulf War give good overviews of the conflict, as well as of the various equipment and organizations that fought it. One of the best written of these overviews is Michael R. Gordon and Gen. Bernard E. Trainer. *The Generals' War: The Inside Story of the Conflict in the Gulf*. Boston: Little, Brown, 1995. *Gulf Air War Debrief*. UK: Aerospace Publishing, 1992, remains one of the best surveys of aircraft, weapons, and squadrons during the war. It is replete with color photos and drawings and with personal experiences of coalition aircrewmen.

Every month seems to produce a new book on OIF and OEF, often with sections dealing with aviation. With the uncertainty of how long these operations will continue, the production of such books is open-ended. Memoirs and a few modern histories abound. The British publisher Osprey has produced a series of short (usually ninety-six pages), well-illustrated, and relatively inexpensive paperbound books on a wide variety of related subjects, including specific aircraft, aces, squadrons, and conflicts. Highly recommended and readily available from major booksellers and catalogs. American and British publishers, as well as several European and Asian houses, have also produced their fair share of normally satisfactory books dealing with the same wide variety of topics. I would go so far as to say that not only have events increased with incredible frequency over the last decade since the last edition was published, but so has the broad-spectrum coverage of all related subjects. It's a reader's market limited only by one's wallet.

Index

Aero Scouts, Osprey specialized missions in Iraq, 361–2
Amen, William T.: U.S. Navy pilot with first jet kill, 143
Anaconda, Operation: early OEF action, 323–4
Andre, John W.: made ace in Korea, 146

Baker, Doyle, Vietnam MiG killer with USAF, 243–4
Badoeng Strait (CVE-116), 120, 132
Bataan (LHD-5) in OEF, 322
Barnett, George
    Marine Aeronautic Company, 7, 8
Bauer, Harold W.: Medal of Honor at Guadalcanal, 54, 62, 63
Belcher, B.T., Jr., 27
Bell AH-1 Hueycobra
    AH-1G arrives in Vietnam, 235–6
    AH-1T in Grenada, 1983, 269, 271
    AH-1W in OIF, 336–7
    AH-1Z Viper, 369–70
    UH-1Y Venom, 370
Bell V-22 Osprey, 279–80, 307, 314–5; first deployments, 358–62
Berryman, Michael C., AV-8 pilot and POW in Desert Storm, 299
Bennington (CV-20), 101, 104–5
Block Island (CVE-106), 106, 108
Boeing aircraft 1920s, 1930s
    F4B, 34
    O2B (DH-4), 17
Boeing-Vertol CH-46 Sea Knight, 216–7; problems, 223–4; in OIF, 332–3, 357
Bon Homme Richard (CVA-31), 191
Bonhomme Richard (LHD-6) in OEF, 324, 349
Bolt, John F., with the Black Sheep, 78
    ace in Korea, 149–50, 159
Bosnia, 309–14
    Aviano Air Base, first Marine aircraft, 1993, 310–1
    O'Grady rescue, 311–2
    Operation Deliberate Force, 312
Boyington, Gregory R., "Pappy,"
    Medal of Honor, 74–8;
    death, 276

Brewster F2A Buffalo, 47–9
Bunker Hill (CV-17), 101, 104–5

Cactus Air Force, 57
Carl, Marion E.,
    at Midway, 50
    at Guadalcanal, 58
    CO, VMF-122, 112–3
    Vietnam, 199–200, 218–9
Cessna O-1 Birddog TAC, 231
Chance Vought F-8 Crusader, 173–7
    in Vietnam, 214–6
(The) Choisin Breakout, 126–9
Chesarek, William D., Jr., receives British DFC in OIF, 357–8
Clapp, Archie J., Shufly CO, 184, 188
Clausen, Raymond M., Medal of Honor, Vietnam, 224–5
Cleeland, David, shot down in Korea, 142
Cleveland (LPD-7), with MARHUKs, 243
Coleman Gerald F., New York Yankees baseball team second baseman
    in Korea, 159–61
Condon, John P.,
    planning Yamamoto intercept mission, 70
    CO, VMF-311, 114
    in Korea, 142
    in Vietnam, 184, 188
Conley, Robert F., CO VMF(M)-513,
    MiG kill, 148
    in Vietnam, 198
Consolidated OY-1, 103, 122–3
Cram, Jack R., at Guadalcanal, 60–3
    CO, VMB-612, 88–9
Cunningham, Alfred A., 1–11, 14,
    post World War I, 15–16
Curtiss aircraft
    A-1/2, 2
    C-3, 4, 5
    F6C, 23
    F8C-5, 34
    N-9, 6,7,8
    R4C-1, 32–3
    R5C Commando, 108–9
    R-6, 8
    SBC-3, 38–9
    SB2C Helldiver, 91–2
    SOC-3 Seagull, 36–7

Dailey, John, 196
DeBlanc, Jeff, Medal of Honor at Guadalcanal, 69
De Havilland DH-4, 8, 9,12
De Havilland DH-9, 11, 12
Deliberate Force, Operation, air campaign in the Balkans, 312–3
DeLong, Phillip C., early aerial kills in Korea, 144–5
Denver (LPD-9), with MARHUKS, 243
Desert Fox, Operation, 329

Donovan, Joseph P., CH-46 pilot with two Navy Crosses in Vietnam, 238
Douglas AD Skyraider, 137–42
Douglas A4D Skyhawk, 172–3
    in Vietnam, 206–9, 210, 260–1
    leaves service, 288
Douglas F3D Skyknight, 114, 147–9
    aerial kills in Korea
    EF-10B in Vietnam, 194–8
Douglas F4D Skyray, 170–2
Douglas R2D-1, 39
Douglas SBD Dauntless, 40

Easter Invasion (Vietnam), 1972, 239–41
Elrod, Henry T., 42–4
Enduring Freedom, Operation (OEF), 321
    first strikes, 322
Enlisted aviators, 31
    in Korea, 153–6
Evans, Francis T., 5, 6, 9

Fairchild R4Q, 127
First Provisional Marine Brigade (Korea), 120
Fleming, Richard E., Medal of Honor dive-bomber pilot at Midway, 52
Folmar, Jesse G., MiG killer in an F4U (Korea), 142–3
Fontana, Paul, VMF-112 CO at Guadalcanal, 66
    CO VMF-311, 114
Foss, Joseph J., 60, 66
    stopped at airline gate with his Medal of Honor, 320–1
Foster, John M., 77
Franklin (CV-13), 103

Galer, Robert, CO VMF-224,
    Medal of Honor at Guadalcanal, 59–60
    in Korea, 142
Geiger, Roy S.,
    at Guadalcanal, 57, 66
    CG III Amphibious Corps, 105, 109, 116
Gilbert Islands (CVE-107), 106, 108
Glenn, John H.,
    in Korea, 150–2;
    Project Bullet, 174–5
Great Lakes BG-1, 36–7
Grenada, 1983, 269–73
Grumman aircraft in the Marine Corps, 34
    A-6A/EA-6A Intruder in Vietnam, 213–4, Desert Storm, 283, EA-6B Prowler,
        Desert Storm, 283–4, 289–90, 307–8; integration with USAF, 326–7;
        OIF, 335
    F3F-2, 35
    F4F Wildcat, 36
    F7F Tigercat, 125, 129, with VMF(N)-513, 131
    F9F Panther, 129
    TF-9J Cougar in Vietnam, 209–10
    J2F Duck, 39, 40

Hanson, Robert, Medal of Honor Corsair pilot, 78–80
Helicopter carriers (LPHs), 182
Henderson, Lofton, at Midway, 52
Howard, Tim, AH-1T pilot in Grenada, 1983, received Silver Star and DFC, 271

Inchon, 124–6
Iraqi Freedom, Operation (OIF), 330

Katrina, Hurricane, killer Gulf Coast storm, 2004, 350
Kearsarge (LHD-3), role in O'Grady rescue in the Balkans, 311, 356
Khe Sanh, 225–9
Kunz, Charles, at Midway, 48–9
Kurth, Michael M., CO HMLA-369, received Navy Cross in Desert Storm, 298

Lam Son 719, invasion of Laos, 1971, 239
Larkins, Claude E., CG 1st MAW in China, 111
Lasseter, Lee, Vietnam MiG killer, 1972, 245
Lebanon, 1983, 267–9
Lefaivre, Ed, sets records with the F4D Skyray, 170
Libya, 1986, 272–4
Lindbergh, Charles A., 81–3
Linebacker, Operation, 248
Lockheed aircraft
        C-130, 179; Khe Sanh, 225–7, 318; OEF, 322–3
        PV-1 Ventura night fighters, 83
        TO-1, 112–3
Lockheed-Martin F-35B Lightning II, STOVL fighter, 371–3
Long Island (CVE-1), at Guadalcanal, 54
Ludden, Charles H., air wing commander, 1965, 239
Lytle, Robert L., 11–2

Magill, Charles, Desert Storm MiG killer, 293–4
Mangrum, Richard, at Guadalcanal, 54
Marine Aeronautic Company, 7, 8
McCutcheon, Keith B., 95;
        in Vietnam, 219;
        Harrier supporter, 256
McDonnell/McDonnell-Douglas/Boeing aircraft
        AV-8 Harrier, 256–60; Desert Storm, 292, 298–301, 307;
                in OEF, 323, 356–7; in OIF, 338–9
        FD-1/FH-1 Phantom, 112
        F2H-2P Banshee, 154
        F4H/F-4 Phantom II, 177–9; arrives in Vietnam, 193;
                RF-4B in Vietnam, 210–3; leaves service, 275–6; RF-4B/VMFP-3, 286
        F/A-18 Hornet, 265–7; Desert Storm, 284; Bosnia at Aviano, 310–1;
                in OIF, 335; OEF, 353–6
McIlvain, William M., 4, 5, 8
Midway (CVA-41), fall of Saigon, 250
MiG-15, 146–7, 151–2
Miller, Thomas H.,
        in Korea, 159;
        record flights in F4H, 178–9;
        goes to UK to see Harrier, 256, 257

Mitsubishi A6M Zero, 56–7
Mulcahy, Francis P., 12;
    at Guadalcanal, 69;
    CG 10th Army Tactical Air Force, 106, 109
Murray, Russ, opposed Harrier for USMC, 256;
    endorses F/A-18, 265

Nassau (LHA-4), Desert Storm, 291, 298
Naval Aviation Pilots (NAPs) in Korea, 153–6
Niagra, Operation, at Khe Sanh, 230–1
Night fighters, 83–5
    Hellcats and VMF(N)-541, 90; VMF(N)-533, 91
North American aircraft
    FJ Fury, 168–9
    OV-10 Bronco, 233; Desert Storm, 292–3, 307
    PBJ Mitchel, 88–9
Northern Bombing Group, World War I, 9

O'Grady, Scott, USAF F-16 pilot rescued by USMC in Bosnia, 311–2

Pitcairn Autogyro, 28
Pless, Stephen W., Medal of Honor flight in Vietnam, 224
PO-2 communist nuisance aircraft in Korea, 131, 149
Power, Tyrone, 108–9
Prisoners of War (POWs) in Korea, 162, 164
Project Bullet, Glenn's supersonic dash across the U.S., 174–5
Provide Comfort, Operation, 303–4
Putnam, Paul A., CO VMF-211 at Midway, 41

Reserves in Korea, 159–60;
    post-Korea, 251–5;
        late 20th century, 315–6,
    OIF, 337–8,
    Reserve helicopters in OEF, 342–8,
    VMFA-142 in OIF, first USMCR VMF mobilized since Korea, 355–6;
        decommissioning of reserve squadrons, 374
Robinson, Robert G., Medal of Honor, 1918, 13
Royal Air Force (RAF), 11
Rowell, Ross, in Nicaragua, 27–9, 32, 86–7

Sailer, Joe., Jr., 69
Samuel B. Roberts (FFG-58), struck mine, 276
Sanborn, Russell A.C., AV-8 pilot and POW in Desert Storm, 299
Sanderson, Lawson, 21, 2
SATS, at Chu Lai, Vietnam, 199
Schilt, Christian F.,
    Medal of Honor, 1928, 28–9,
    in Korea, 131,
    death, 276
Seagle, Jeb, AH-1T pilot in Grenada, received posthumous Navy Cross, 271
Sellers, Thomas M., last Marine aerial kill in Korea, 151
Shepherd Board, 116
Shufly, Operation, first operations in Vietnam, 183–9
Sicily (CVE-118), 121, 132

Sikorsky aircraft
   CH-37, 202–5
   CH-53 Sea Stallon, 217–8, in OEF, 342–5, CH-53K, 371
   HO3S, 116
   HRS-1 in Korea, 134–7
   JRS-1, 35
   RS-1, 32
   VH-3D presidential helicopter, new helo cancelled, 371
Smith, Bernard L., 2, 4
Smith, John L., CO VMF-223,
   Medal of Honor at Guadalcanal, 54, 55, 58–9;
   in Korea, 161
Somalia, Operation Eastern Exit, 295–6;
   return 1992, 308
Squadrons:
   HMH-769, 316, 342
   HMH-772, 350
   HMLA-167, 276
   HLMA-269, 297–8
   HMLA-367, 294–5
   HMLA-773, 316, 338, 345–8
   HMLA-775, 316, 338, 342, 348–9
   HMM-161, 229
   HMM-362, 184
   HMM-774, 295–7
   HMX-1, 116, 368
   HMR-161, 134–7
   VF-1M, 21
   VF-2M, 21
   VF-9M, 22, 23, 24, 25
   VMA-121, 137–8
   VMA-225, 200
   VMA-251, 137–8
   VMA-331
   VMA-513, 325
   VMA(AW)-242, 222
   VMA(AW)-224, 241–2
   VMA(AW)-533, 222, 245–6
   VMAQ-2, 289, 293
   VMAQ-4, 352
   VMB-612, 88, 110
   VMB-611, 97
   VMC-1, 137–8
   VMCJ-1, 191, 195, 213
   VMF-1, 25
   VMF-115, 94, 98, 170, 172, 246
   VMF-121, 60
   VMF-124, 72, 101
   VMF-211, 41–2
   VMF-212, 63, 128
   VMF-213, 74, 101
   VMF-221, 50
   VMF-223, 96

VMF-235, 169
VMF-311, 129, 132–3, 208, 247
VMF-312, 126, 128, 145, 169
VMF-313, 94
VMF-323, 120, 142
VMA-115, 333
VMFA-142, 355–6, 374
VMFA-212, 326
VMFA-251, 322
VMFA-312, 329
VMFA-321, 321, 374
VMFA-333, 245
VMFA(AW)-121, 301–2
VMFA(AW)-224, 310–1
VMF(AW)-232, 216
VMF(AW)-235, 216
VMF(AW)-314, 179
VMF(N)-513, 126, 129–30
VMF(N)-531, 83
VMF(N)-532, 84–5
VMF(N)-542, 125, 130, 133–4, 231
VMFP-3, 296–8
VMGR-252, 323
VMGR-452, 352
VMJ-1, 154
VMM-162, 359
VMM-263, 359
VMM-266, 359
VMO-4/5, 102
VMO-6, 122, 169, 237
VMR-952, 108
VMS-3, 39
VMSB-142, 68
VMSB-231, 41
VMSB-241, 47, 96
VMSB-341, 97
VMU-1, 364
VMU-2, 364
VMU-3, 366
Standard, E-1 fighter, 9
Stark (FFG-31), struck by Iraqi missile, 275
Super Gaggle at Khe Sanh, 227
Swett, James E., Medal of Honor at Guadalcanal, 74

Tactical Air Direction Center (TADC), Vietnam, 201
Talbot, Ralph, Medal of Honor, 1918, 13
Thomas-Morse MB-3 scout, 17–18
Todd, James, R., NAP in Korea, 155–6
Towers, John H., 1, 3
Tripoli (LPH-10) in Somalia 1992, 308
Truex, Lowell "Red," NAP in Korea, 155
Turner, Thomas C., 15–17; death in Haiti, 31

Unmanned Aerial Vehicles (UAVs), 318, 328, 363–7

Valley Forge (CV-45), in Korea, 119
Vought aircraft
    AU-1 (Corsair) in Korea, 142
    F4U Corsair, 71, 121,
    O2U, 28–9
    SU-2, 35
    SB2U Vindicator, 37, 38, 39–40, 47
    VE-7, 27

Walsh, Ken, Medal of Honor Corsair pilot, 73–4
Wasp (LHD-1) in OEF, 323
Wildfang, Henry, C-130 NAP at Khe Sanh, 226
Williams, T.S. "Ted," 157–8
Wright B-1/2, 2
Women aviators, 308, 367–8

About the Author

PETER B. MERSKY graduated from the Rhode Island School of Design in 1967 and was commissioned through the Navy's Aviation Officer Candidate School in 1968. He served in various assignments on active duty and in the Naval Reserve, retiring as a commander in 1992. He worked as a government illustrator in the Washington, D.C., area and then as the assistant editor and then editor of *Approach*, the Navy and Marine Corps aviation safety magazine. He has written more than a dozen books and a hundred magazine articles and has reviewed nearly six hundred books in his regular column for *Naval Aviation News* and other periodicals.